SEVEN SEAS ENTERTAINMENT PRESENTS

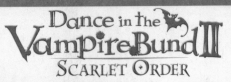

Dance in the Vampire Bund II
Scarlet Order

story & art by NOZOMU TAMAKI VOLUME 3

TRANSLATION
Adrienne Beck

ADAPTATION
Janet Houck

LETTERING
Roland Amago

LAYOUT
Bambi Eloriaga-Amago

COVER DESIGN
Nicky Lim

PROOFREADER
Shanti Whitesides
Lee Otter

ASSISTANT EDITOR
Lissa Pattillo

MANAGING EDITOR
Adam Arnold

PUBLISHER
Jason DeAngelis

Edited by MEDIA FACTORY.
First published in Japan in 2014 by KADOKAWA CORPORATION, Tokyo.
English translation rights reserved by Seven Seas Entertainment, LLC.
under the license from KADOKAWA CORPORATION, Tokyo.

ISBN: 978-1-626922-02-0
Printed in Canada
First Printing: October 2015
10 9 8 7 6 5 4 3 2 1

READING DIRECTIONS

This book reads from ***right to left***, Japanese style. If this is your first time reading manga, you start reading from the top right panel on each page and take it from there. If you get lost, just follow the numbered diagram here. It may seem backwards at first, but you'll get the hang of it! Have fun!!

1
2
3
4
5
6
7
8
9

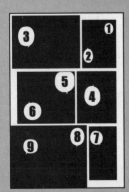

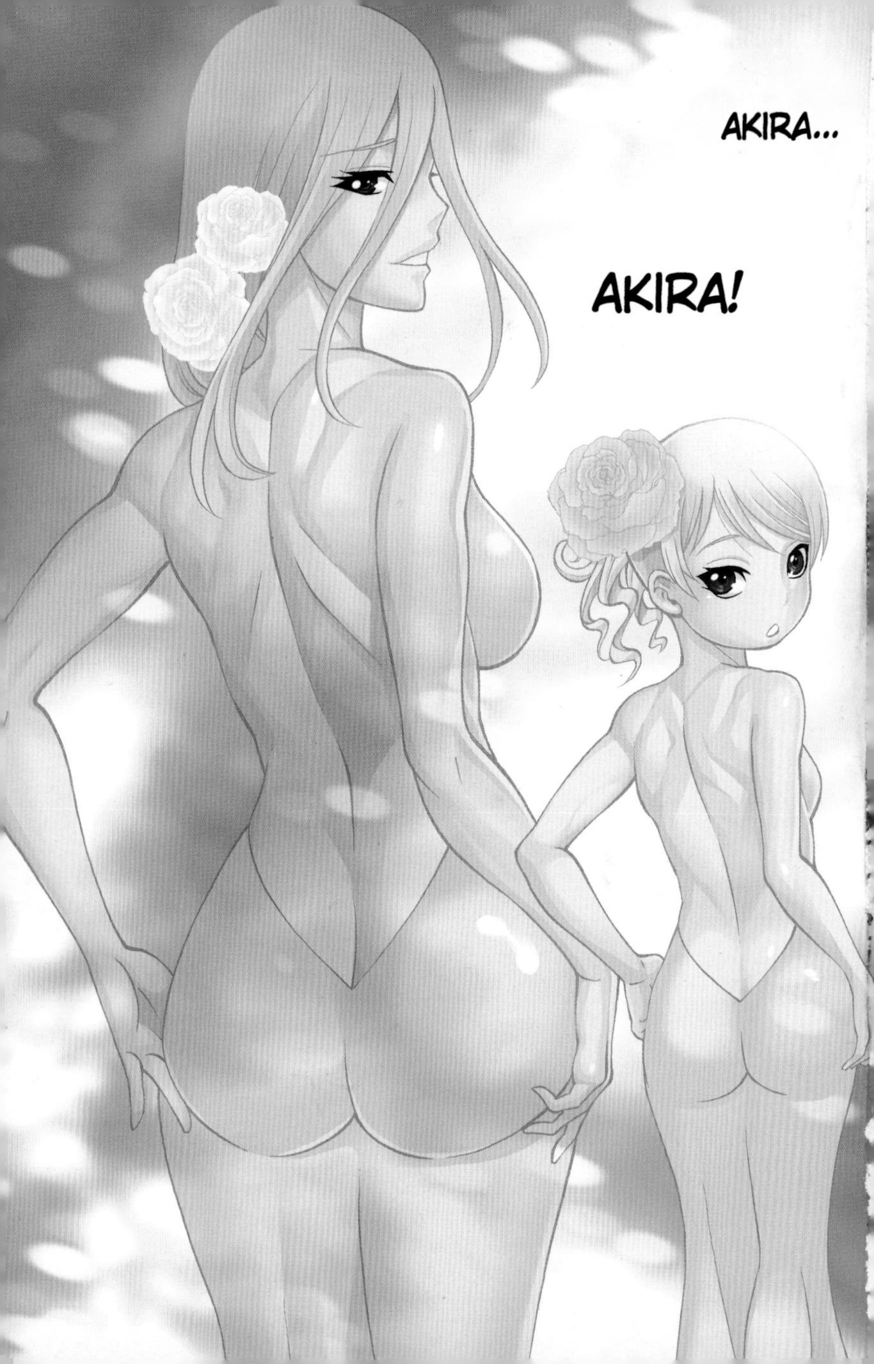
AKIRA...
AKIRA!

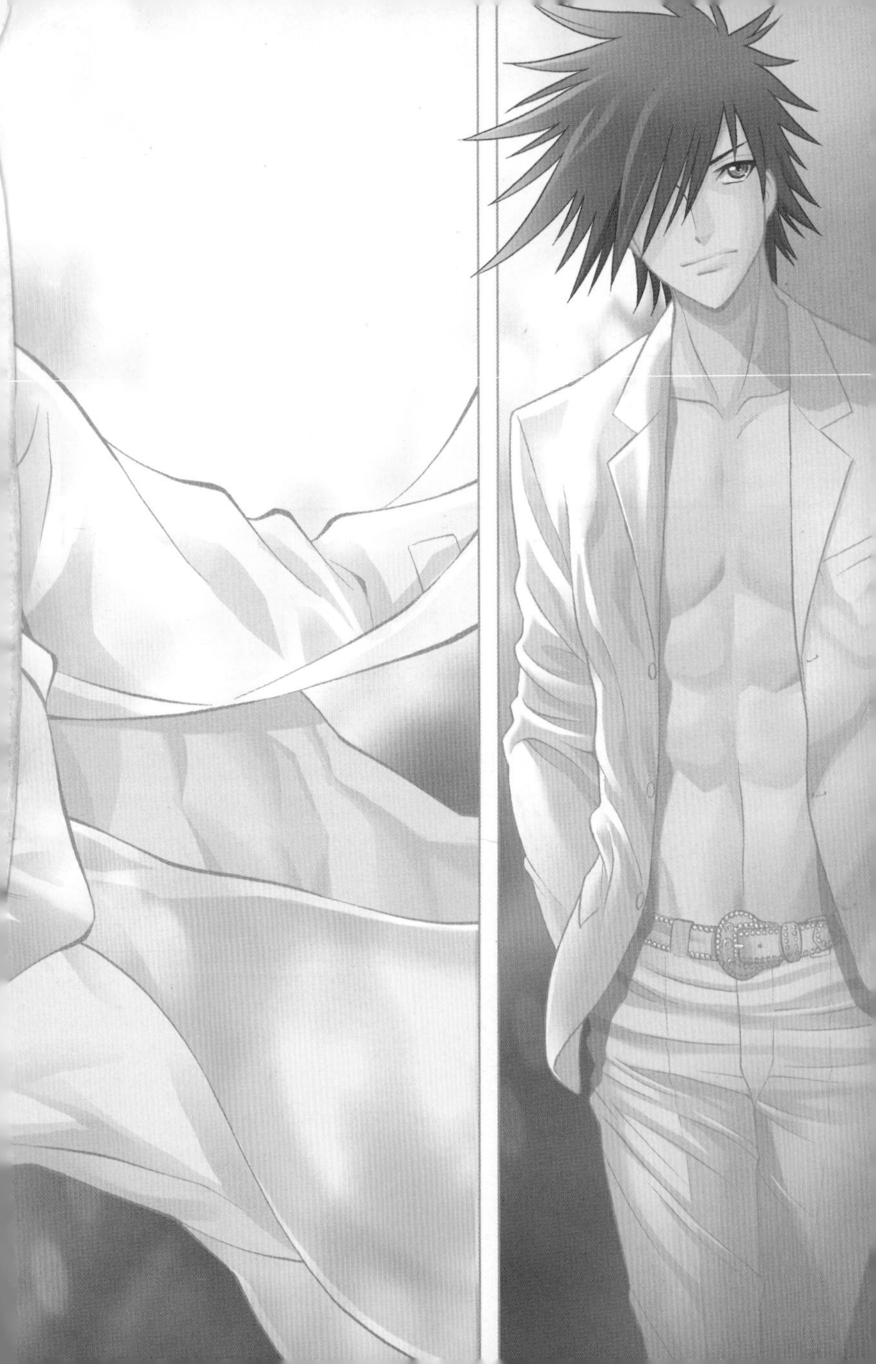

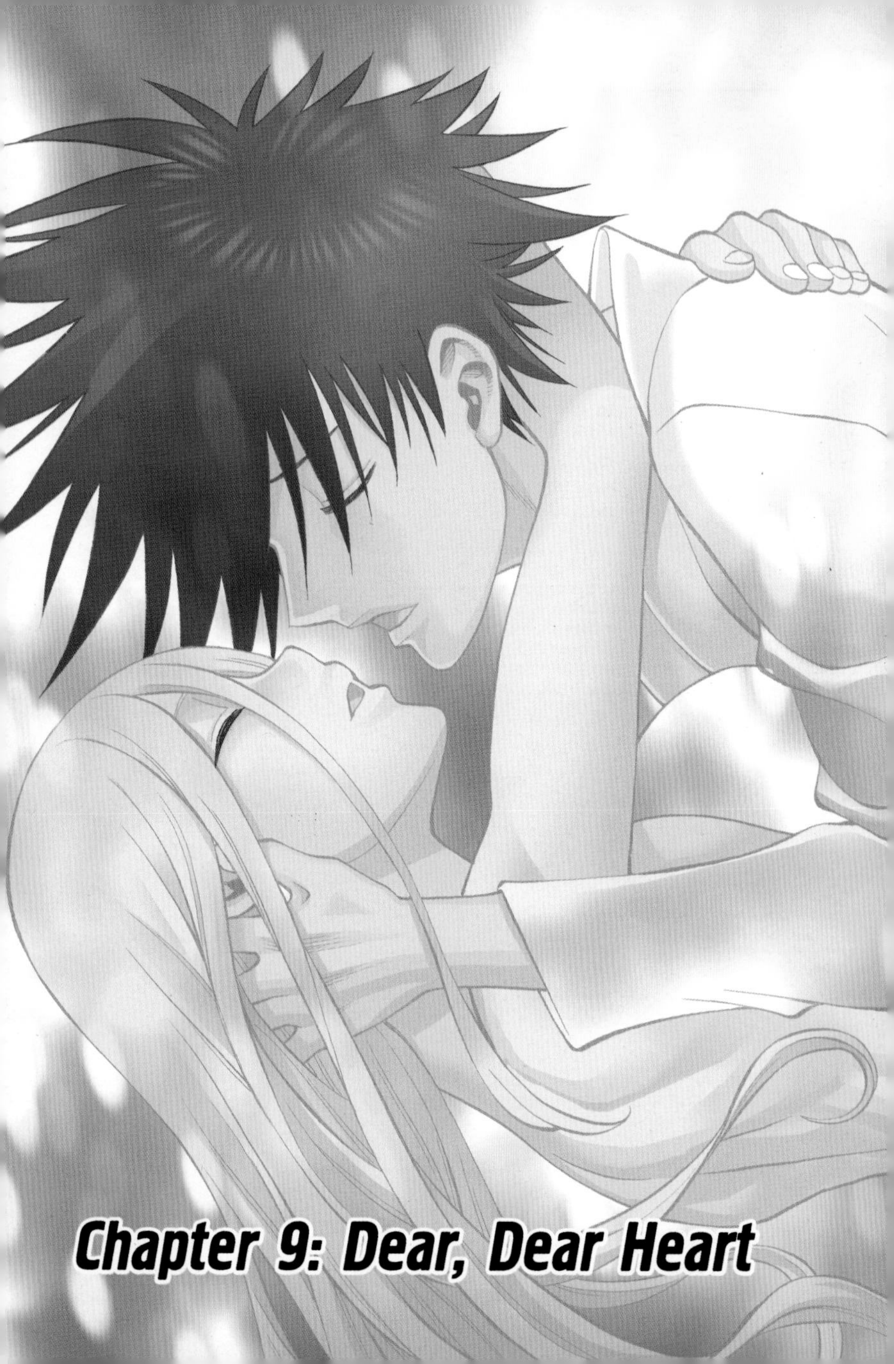

Chapter 9: Dear, Dear Heart

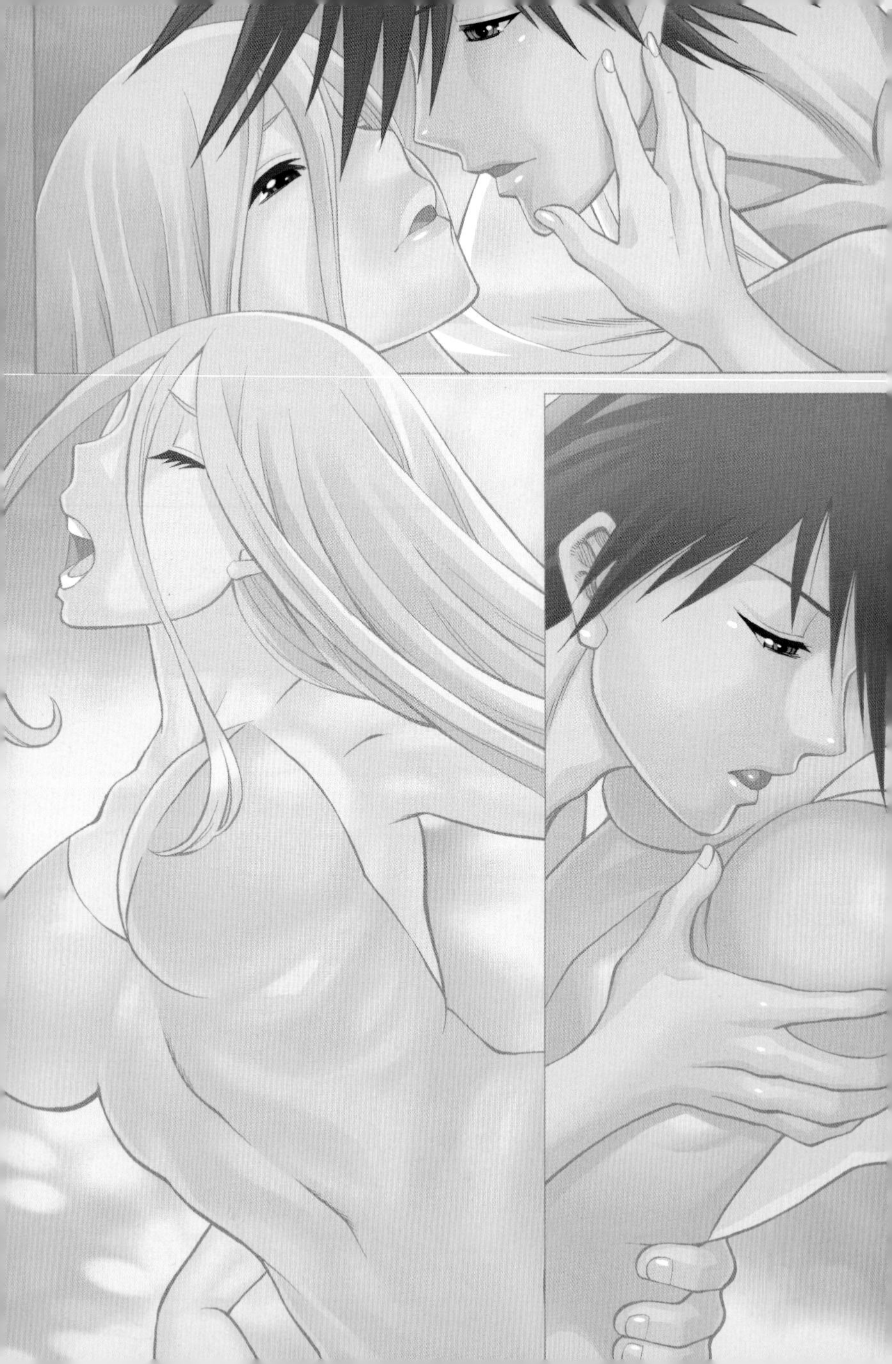

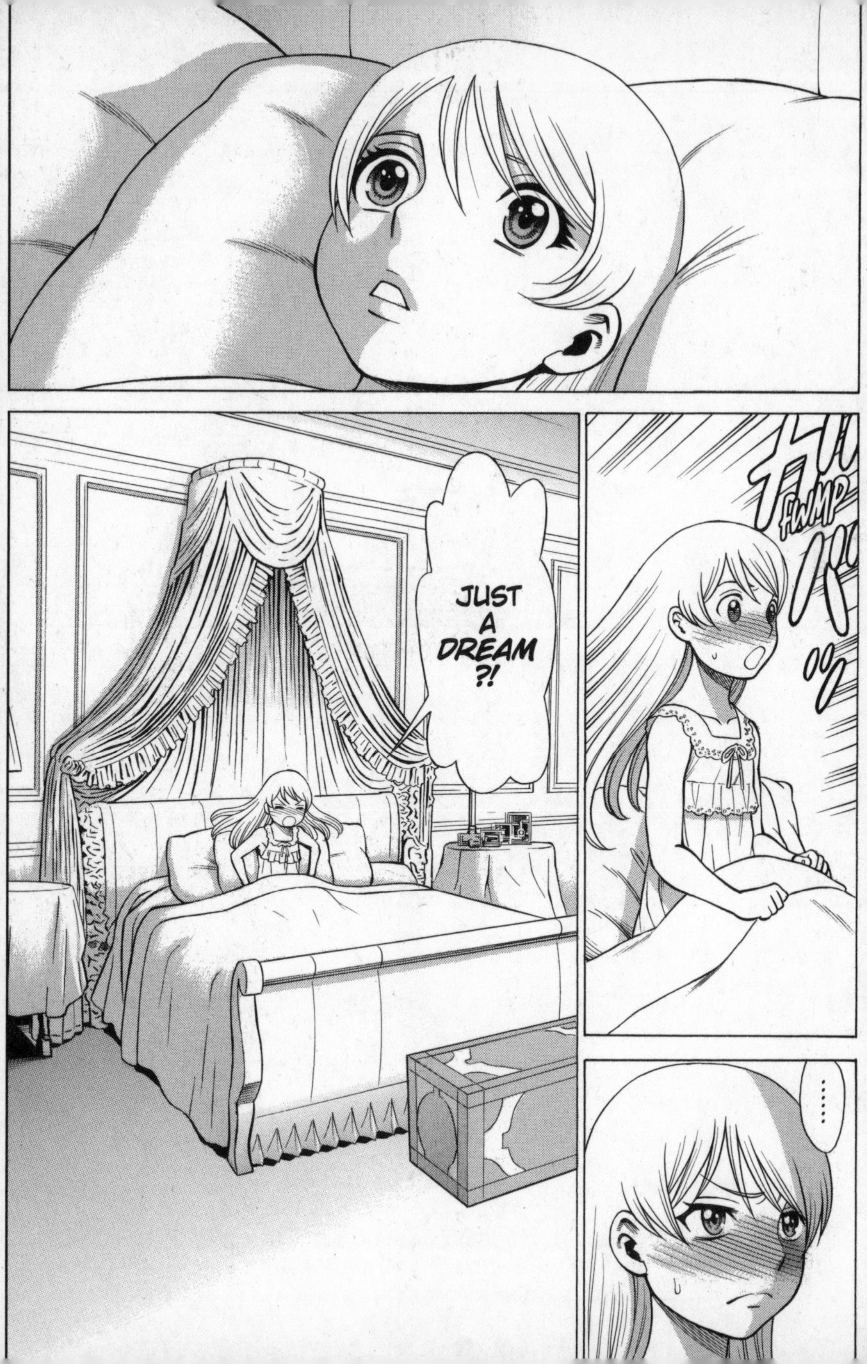
FWMP
JUST A DREAM ?!
......

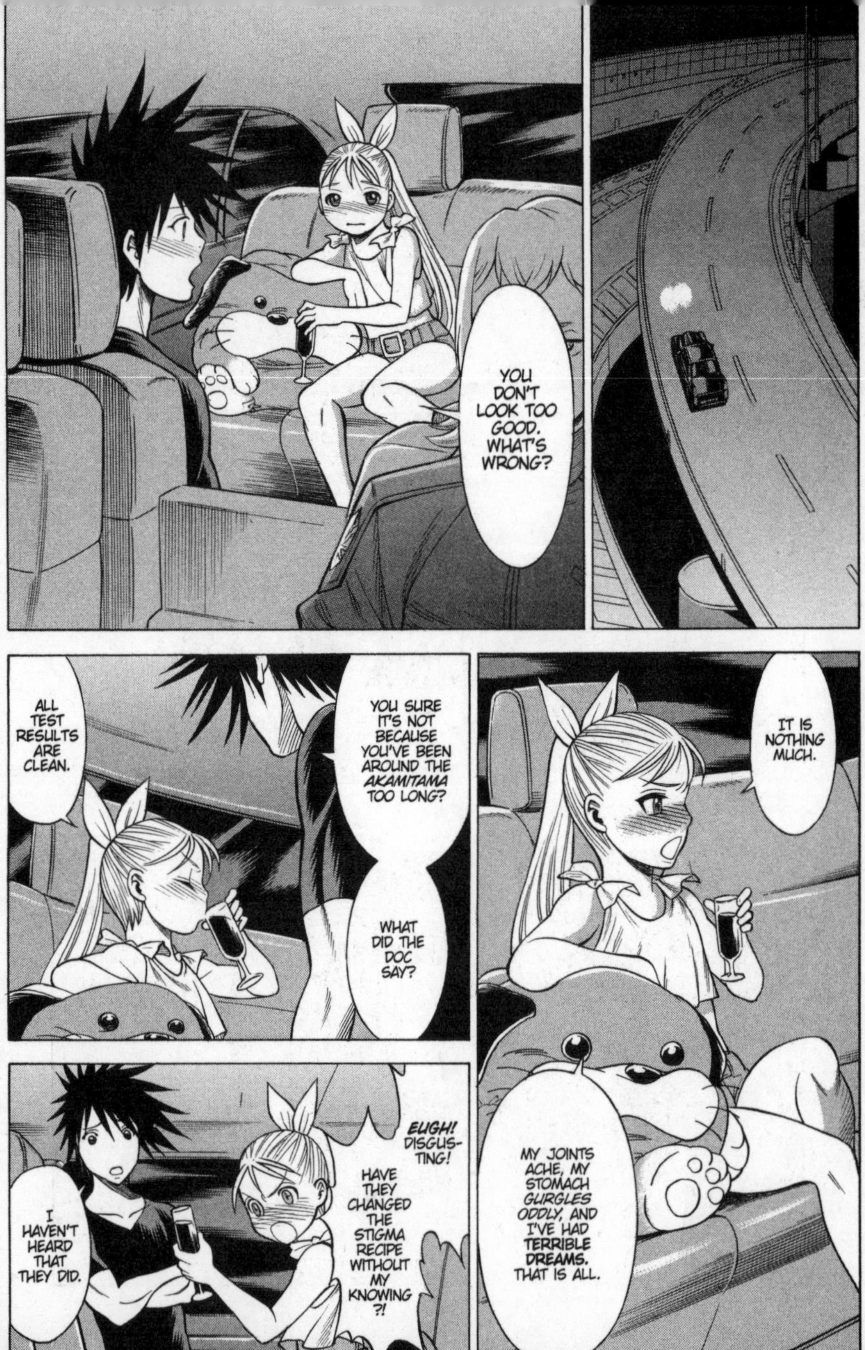
YOU DON'T LOOK TOO GOOD. WHAT'S WRONG?
IT IS NOTHING MUCH.
MY JOINTS ACHE, MY STOMACH *GURGLES ODDLY*, AND I'VE HAD **TERRIBLE DREAMS.** THAT IS ALL.
YOU SURE IT'S NOT BECAUSE YOU'VE BEEN AROUND THE *AKAMITAMA* TOO LONG?
WHAT DID THE DOC SAY?
ALL TEST RESULTS ARE CLEAN.
EUGH! DISGUSTING!
HAVE THEY CHANGED THE STIGMA RECIPE WITHOUT MY KNOWING?!
I HAVEN'T HEARD THAT THEY DID.

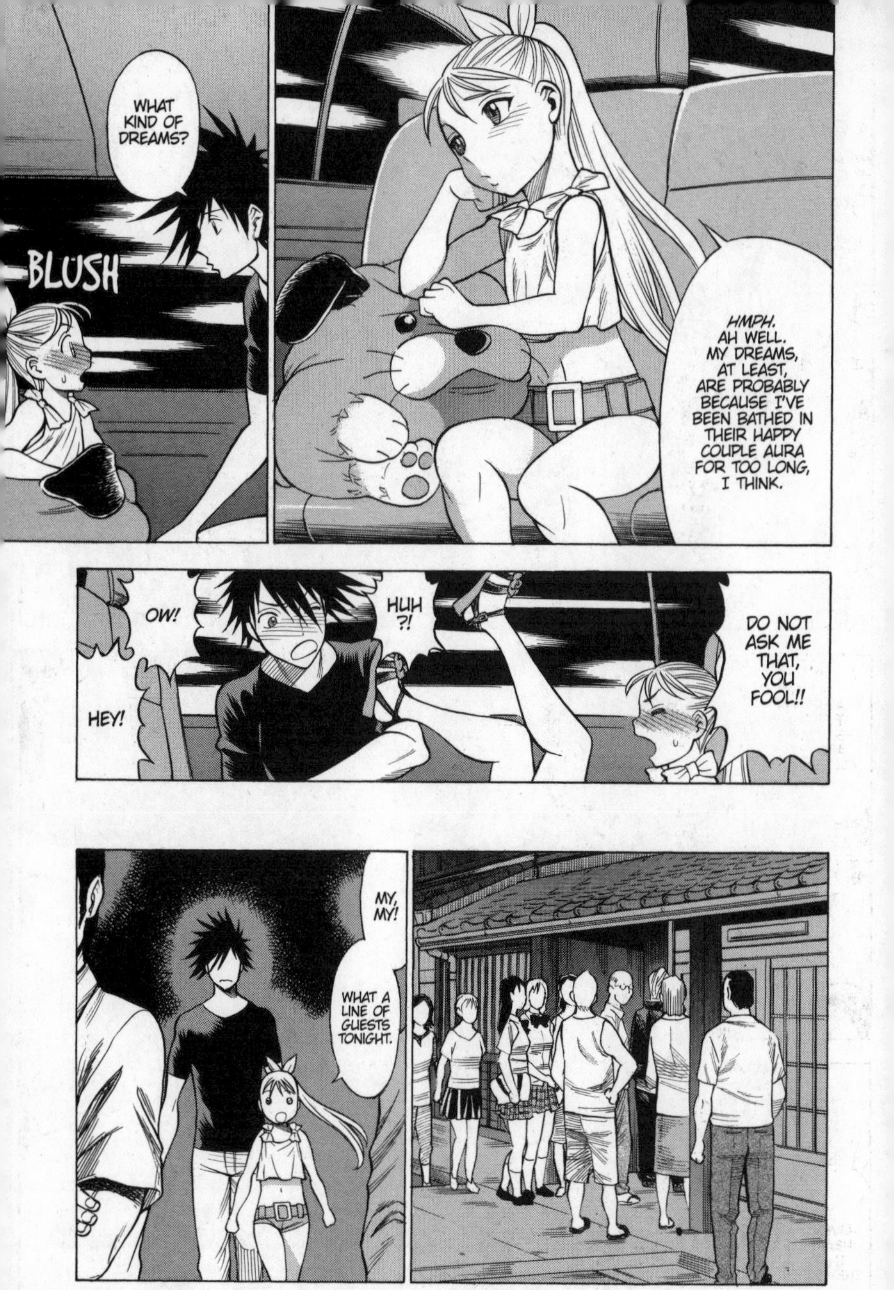
HMPH. AH WELL. MY DREAMS, AT LEAST, ARE PROBABLY BECAUSE I'VE BEEN BATHED IN THEIR HAPPY COUPLE AURA FOR TOO LONG, I THINK.
WHAT KIND OF DREAMS?
BLUSH
DO NOT ASK ME THAT, YOU FOOL!!
HUH ?!
OW!
HEY!
MY, MY!
WHAT A LINE OF GUESTS TONIGHT.

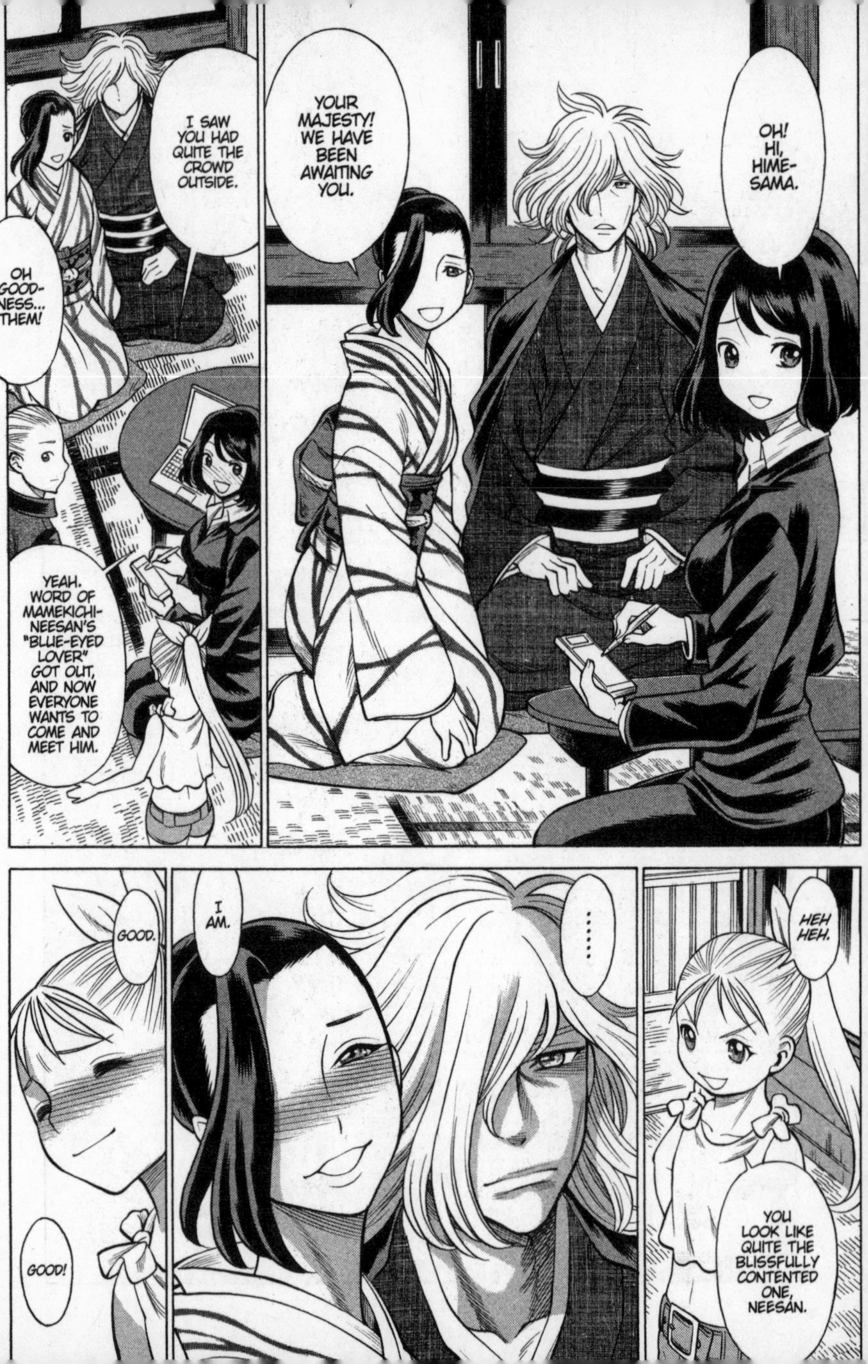
OH! HI, HIME-SAMA.
YOUR MAJESTY! WE HAVE BEEN AWAITING YOU.
I SAW YOU HAD QUITE THE CROWD OUTSIDE.
OH GOODNESS... THEM!
YEAH. WORD OF MAMEKICHI-NEESAN'S "BLUE-EYED LOVER" GOT OUT, AND NOW EVERYONE WANTS TO COME AND MEET HIM.
HEH HEH.
YOU LOOK LIKE QUITE THE BLISSFULLY CONTENTED ONE, NEESAN.
......
I AM.
GOOD.
GOOD!

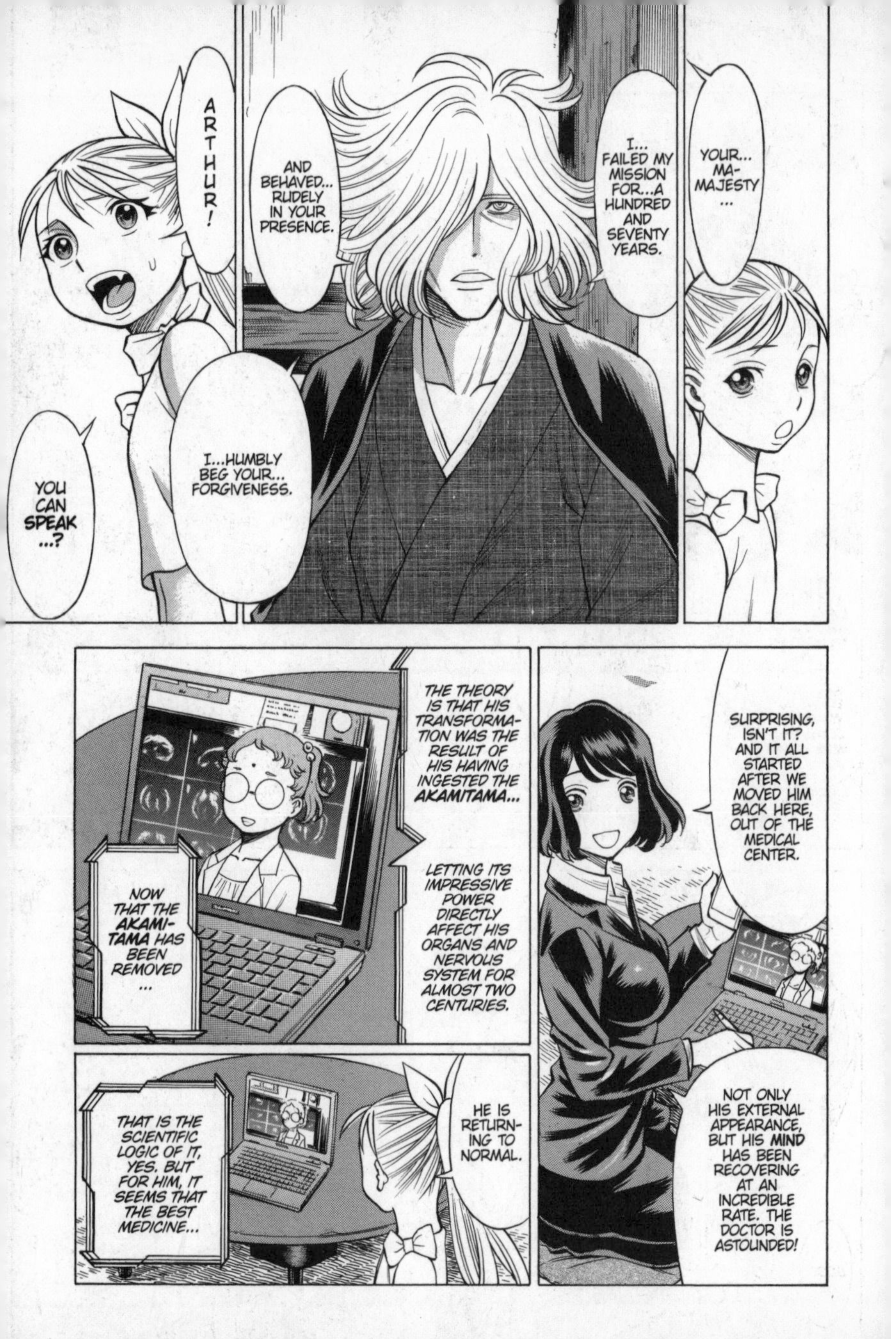
YOUR... MA-MAJESTY ...
I... FAILED MY MISSION FOR...A HUNDRED AND SEVENTY YEARS.
AND BEHAVED... RUDELY IN YOUR PRESENCE.
I...HUMBLY BEG YOUR... FORGIVENESS.
ARTHUR!
YOU CAN SPEAK ...?
SURPRISING, ISN'T IT? AND IT ALL STARTED AFTER WE MOVED HIM BACK HERE, OUT OF THE MEDICAL CENTER.
NOT ONLY HIS EXTERNAL APPEARANCE, BUT HIS MIND HAS BEEN RECOVERING AT AN INCREDIBLE RATE. THE DOCTOR IS ASTOUNDED!
THE THEORY IS THAT HIS TRANSFORMATION WAS THE RESULT OF HIS HAVING INGESTED THE AKAMITAMA...
LETTING ITS IMPRESSIVE POWER DIRECTLY AFFECT HIS ORGANS AND NERVOUS SYSTEM FOR ALMOST TWO CENTURIES.
NOW THAT THE AKAMITAMA HAS BEEN REMOVED ...
HE IS RETURNING TO NORMAL.
THAT IS THE SCIENTIFIC LOGIC OF IT, YES. BUT FOR HIM, IT SEEMS THAT THE BEST MEDICINE...

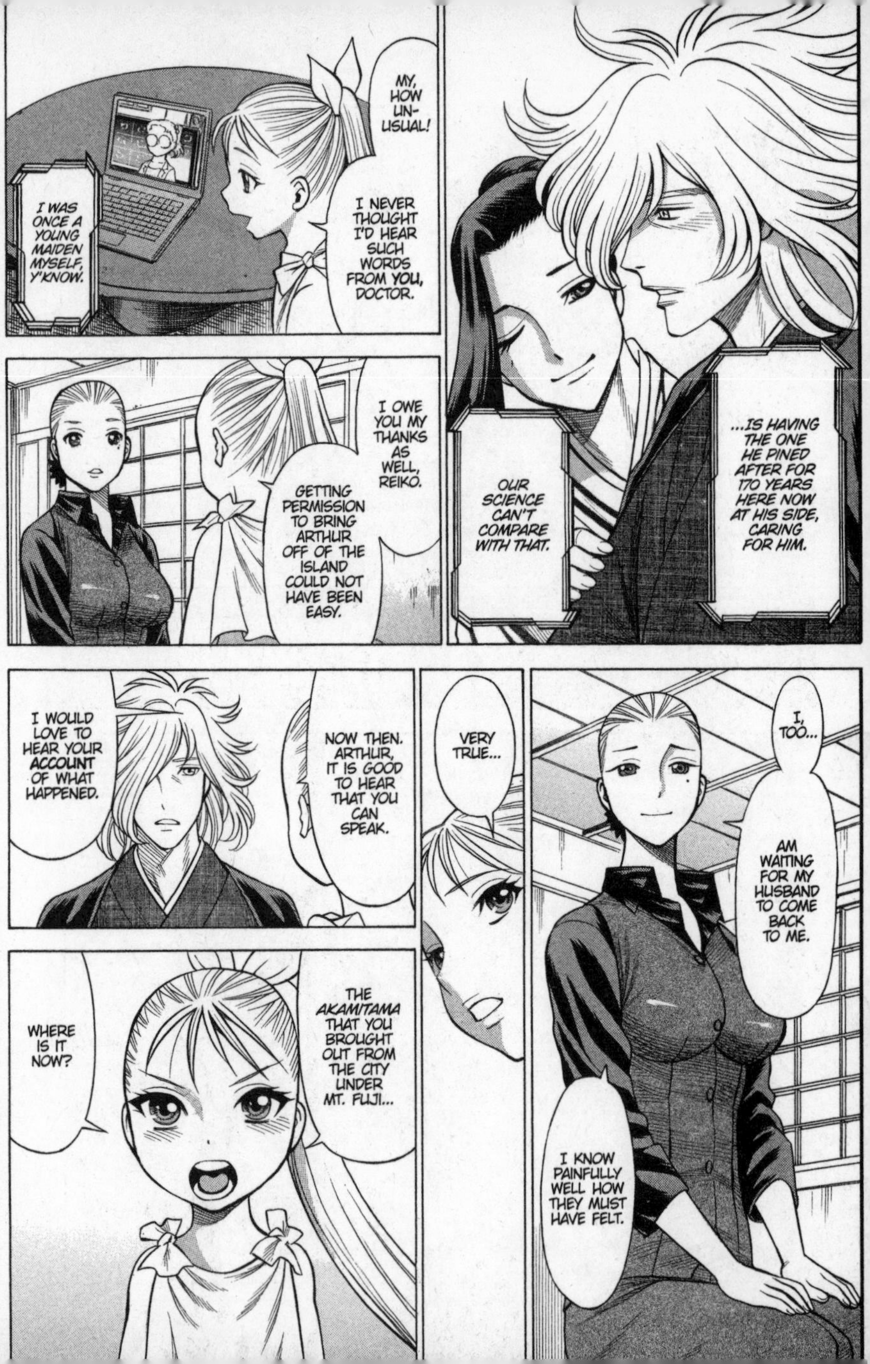
...IS HAVING THE ONE HE PINED AFTER FOR 170 YEARS HERE NOW AT HIS SIDE, CARING FOR HIM.
OUR SCIENCE CAN'T COMPARE WITH THAT.
MY, HOW UN-USUAL!
I NEVER THOUGHT I'D HEAR SUCH WORDS FROM YOU, DOCTOR.
I WAS ONCE A YOUNG MAIDEN MYSELF, Y'KNOW.
I OWE YOU MY THANKS AS WELL, REIKO.
GETTING PERMISSION TO BRING ARTHUR OFF OF THE ISLAND COULD NOT HAVE BEEN EASY.
I, TOO...
AM WAITING FOR MY HUSBAND TO COME BACK TO ME.
I KNOW PAINFULLY WELL HOW THEY MUST HAVE FELT.
VERY TRUE...
NOW THEN. ARTHUR, IT IS GOOD TO HEAR THAT YOU CAN SPEAK.
I WOULD LOVE TO HEAR YOUR ACCOUNT OF WHAT HAPPENED.
THE AKAMITAMA THAT YOU BROUGHT OUT FROM THE CITY UNDER MT. FUJI...
WHERE IS IT NOW?

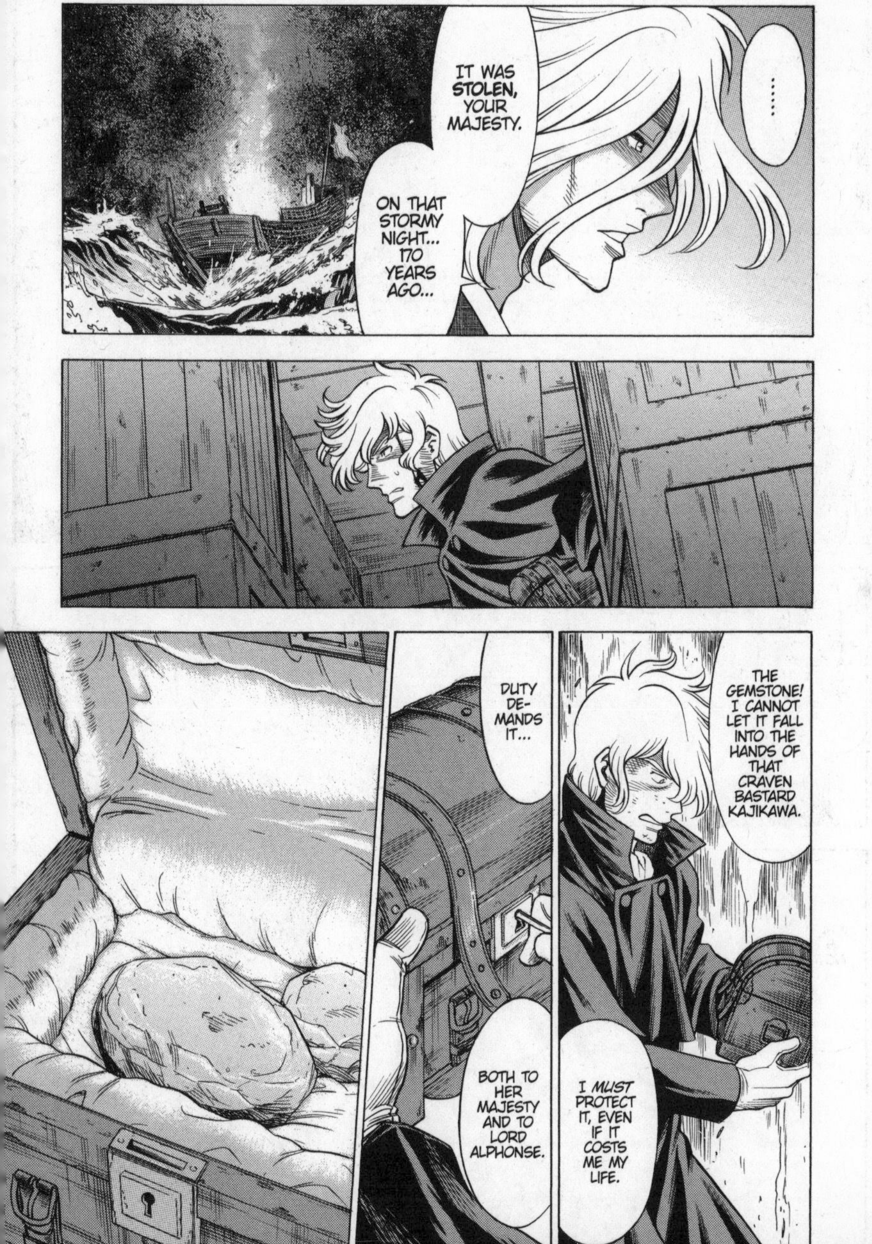
......
IT WAS STOLEN, YOUR MAJESTY.
ON THAT STORMY NIGHT... 170 YEARS AGO...
THE GEMSTONE! I CANNOT LET IT FALL INTO THE HANDS OF THAT CRAVEN BASTARD KAJIKAWA.
I MUST PROTECT IT, EVEN IF IT COSTS ME MY LIFE.
DUTY DE-MANDS IT...
BOTH TO HER MAJESTY AND TO LORD ALPHONSE.

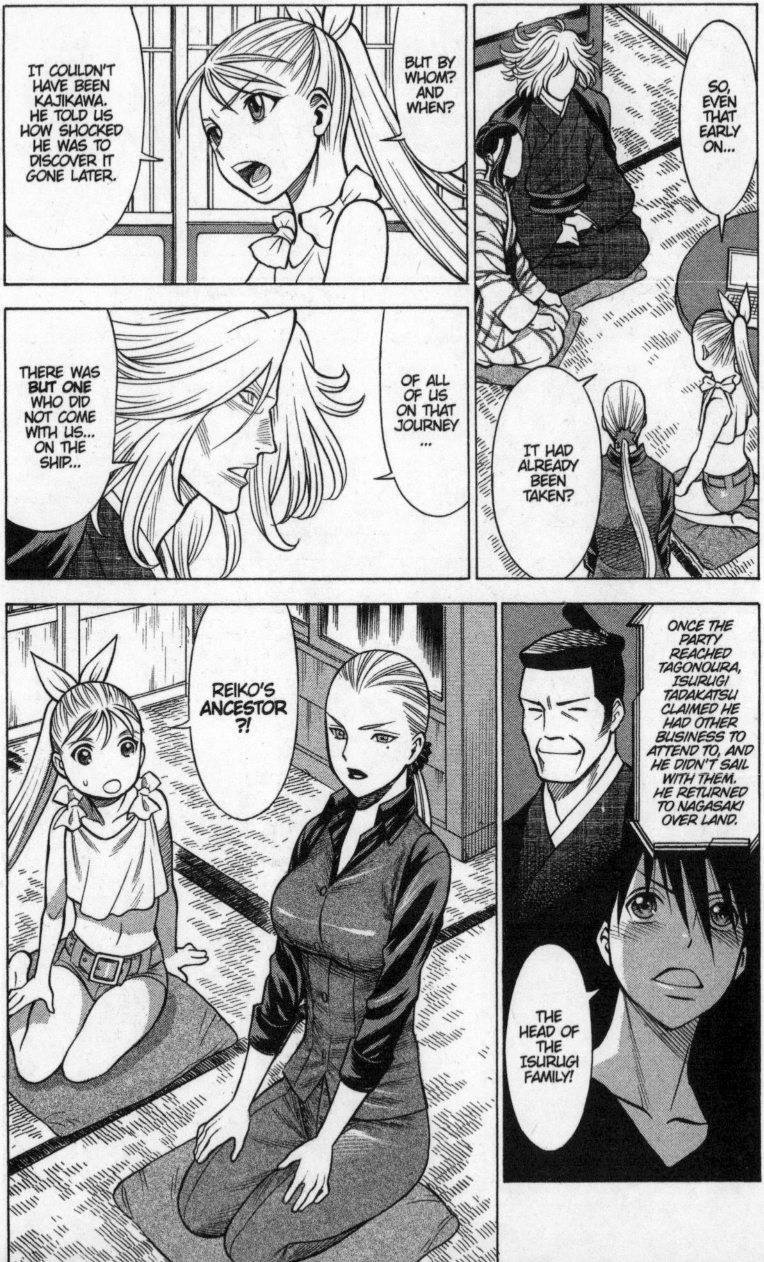
SO, EVEN THAT EARLY ON...
IT HAD ALREADY BEEN TAKEN?
BUT BY WHOM? AND WHEN?
IT COULDN'T HAVE BEEN KAJIKAWA. HE TOLD US HOW SHOCKED HE WAS TO DISCOVER IT GONE LATER.
OF ALL OF US ON THAT JOURNEY...
THERE WAS BUT ONE WHO DID NOT COME WITH US... ON THE SHIP...
ONCE THE PARTY REACHED TAGONOURA, ISURUGI TADAKATSU CLAIMED HE HAD OTHER BUSINESS TO ATTEND TO, AND HE DIDN'T SAIL WITH THEM. HE RETURNED TO NAGASAKI OVER LAND.
THE HEAD OF THE ISURUGI FAMILY!
REIKO'S ANCESTOR?!

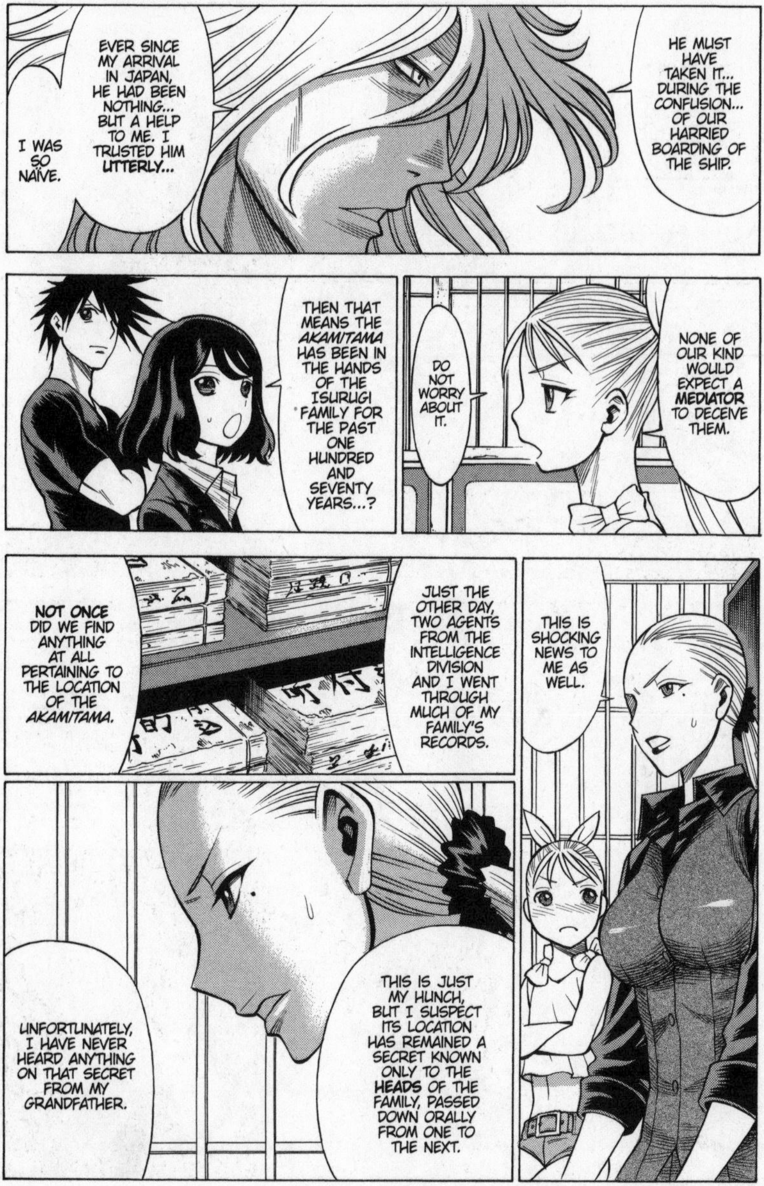
HE MUST HAVE TAKEN IT... DURING THE CONFUSION... OF OUR HARRIED BOARDING OF THE SHIP.
EVER SINCE MY ARRIVAL IN JAPAN, HE HAD BEEN NOTHING... BUT A HELP TO ME. I TRUSTED HIM **UTTERLY...**
I WAS SO NAÏVE.
NONE OF OUR KIND WOULD EXPECT A **MEDIATOR** TO DECEIVE THEM.
DO NOT WORRY ABOUT IT.
THEN THAT MEANS THE *AKAMITAMA* HAS BEEN IN THE HANDS OF THE ISURUGI FAMILY FOR THE PAST ONE HUNDRED AND SEVENTY YEARS...?
THIS IS SHOCKING NEWS TO ME AS WELL.
JUST THE OTHER DAY, TWO AGENTS FROM THE INTELLIGENCE DIVISION AND I WENT THROUGH MUCH OF MY FAMILY'S RECORDS.
NOT ONCE DID WE FIND ANYTHING AT ALL PERTAINING TO THE LOCATION OF THE *AKAMITAMA*.
THIS IS JUST MY HUNCH, BUT I SUSPECT ITS LOCATION HAS REMAINED A SECRET KNOWN ONLY TO THE **HEADS** OF THE FAMILY, PASSED DOWN ORALLY FROM ONE TO THE NEXT.
UNFORTUNATELY, I HAVE NEVER HEARD ANYTHING ON THAT SECRET FROM MY GRANDFATHER.

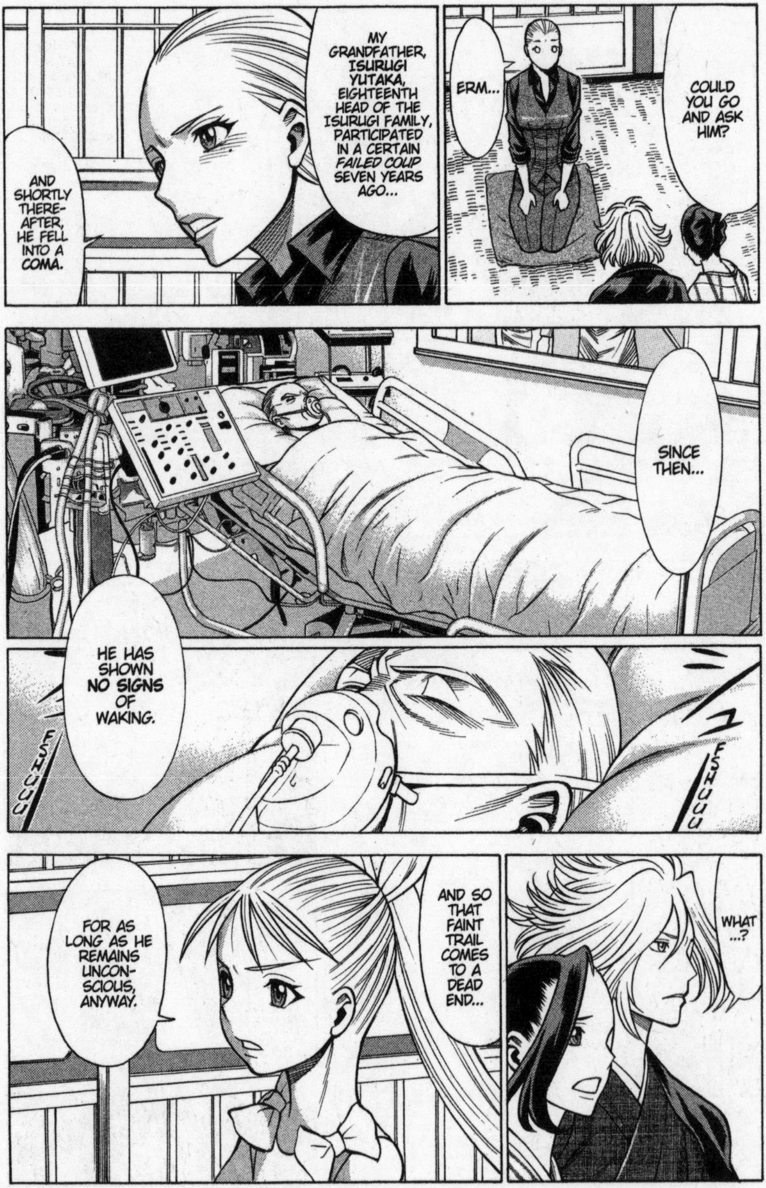
COULD YOU GO AND ASK HIM?
ERM...
MY GRANDFATHER, ISURUGI YUTAKA, EIGHTEENTH HEAD OF THE ISURUGI FAMILY, PARTICIPATED IN A CERTAIN *FAILED COUP* SEVEN YEARS AGO...
AND SHORTLY THERE-AFTER, HE FELL INTO A COMA.
SINCE THEN...
FSHUUU
HE HAS SHOWN **NO SIGNS** OF WAKING.
FSHUUU
WHAT ...?
AND SO THAT FAINT TRAIL COMES TO A DEAD END...
FOR AS LONG AS HE REMAINS UNCON-SCIOUS, ANYWAY.

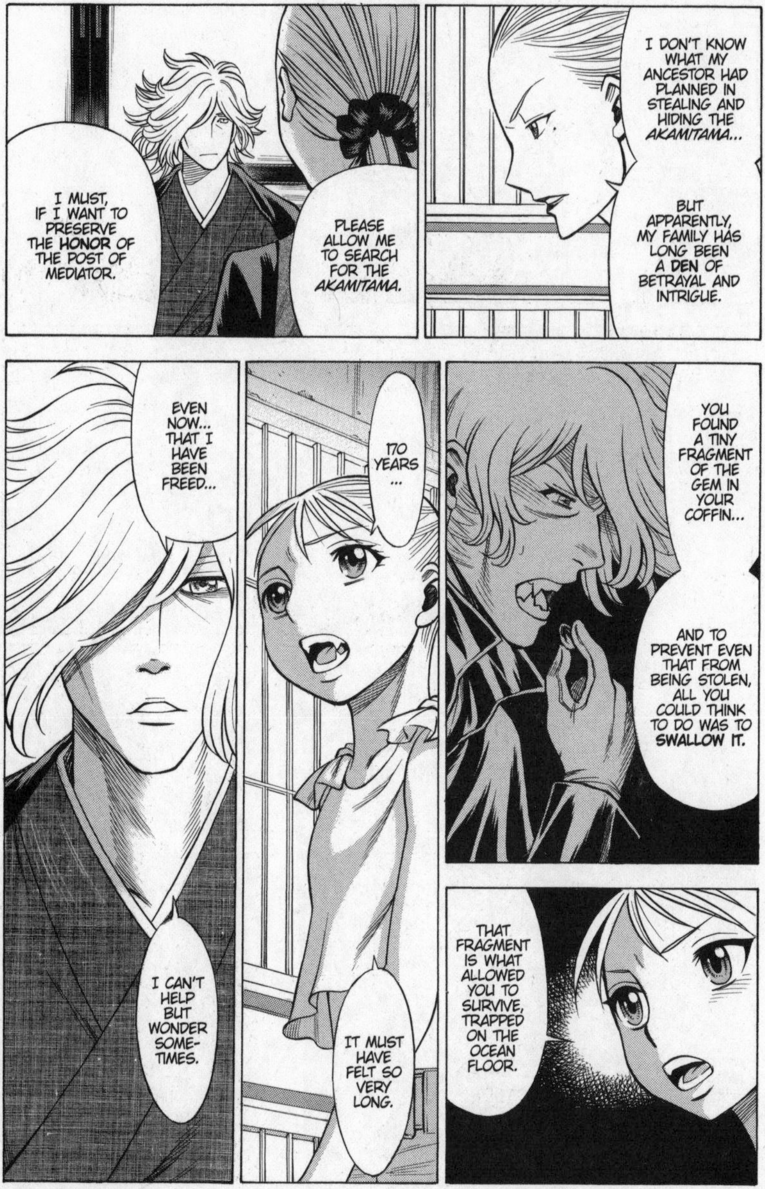
I DON'T KNOW WHAT MY ANCESTOR HAD PLANNED IN STEALING AND HIDING THE *AKAMITAMA*...
BUT APPARENTLY, MY FAMILY HAS LONG BEEN A **DEN** OF BETRAYAL AND INTRIGUE.
PLEASE ALLOW ME TO SEARCH FOR THE *AKAMITAMA*.
I MUST, IF I WANT TO PRESERVE THE **HONOR** OF THE POST OF MEDIATOR.
YOU FOUND A TINY FRAGMENT OF THE GEM IN YOUR COFFIN...
AND TO PREVENT EVEN THAT FROM BEING STOLEN, ALL YOU COULD THINK TO DO WAS TO **SWALLOW IT.**
THAT FRAGMENT IS WHAT ALLOWED YOU TO SURVIVE, TRAPPED ON THE OCEAN FLOOR.
170 YEARS ...
IT MUST HAVE FELT SO VERY LONG.
EVEN NOW... THAT I HAVE BEEN FREED...
I CAN'T HELP BUT WONDER SOME-TIMES.

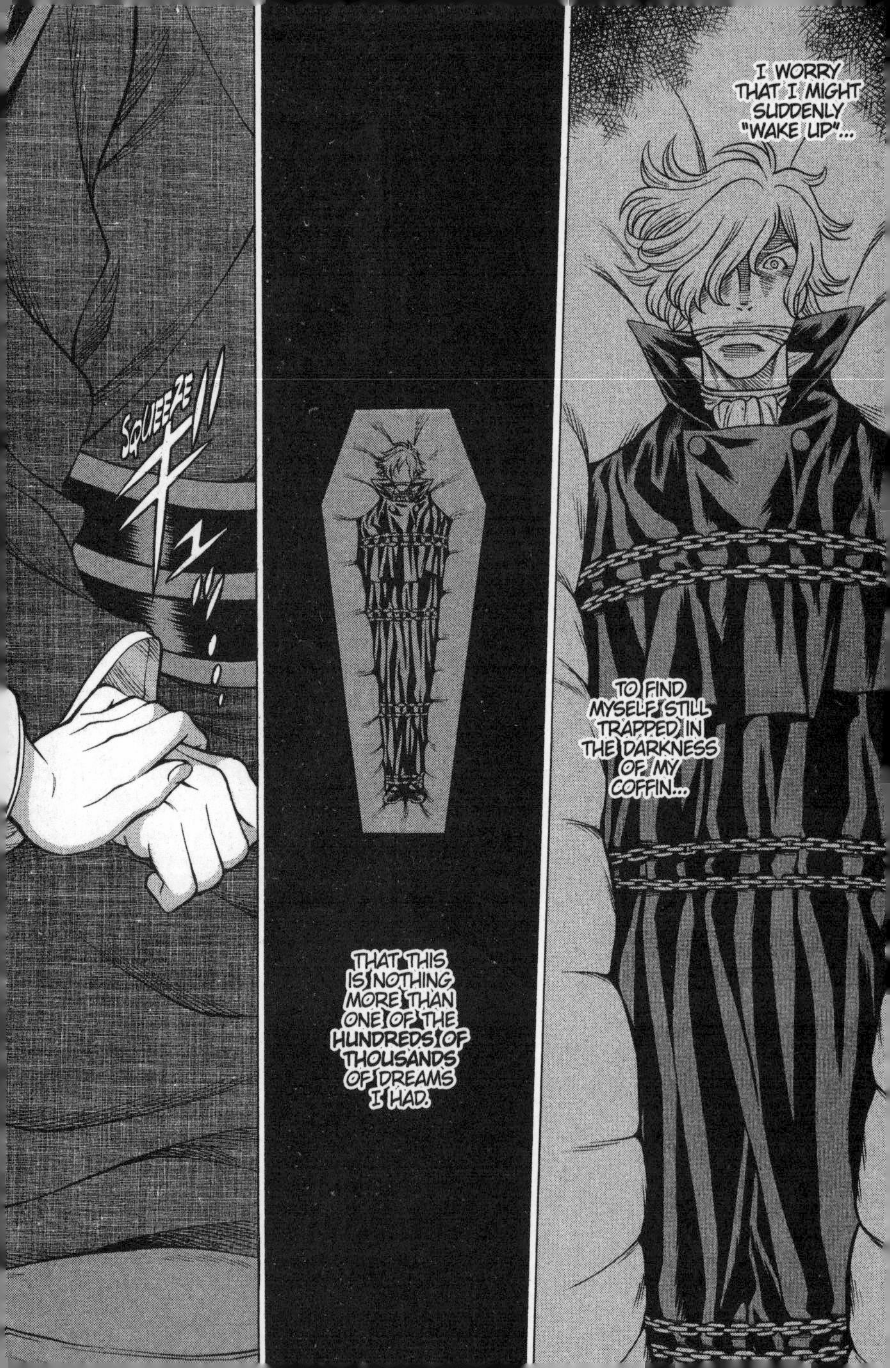
I WORRY THAT I MIGHT SUDDENLY "WAKE UP"...
TO FIND MYSELF STILL TRAPPED IN THE DARKNESS OF MY COFFIN...
THAT THIS IS NOTHING MORE THAN ONE OF THE HUNDREDS OF THOUSANDS OF DREAMS I HAD.
SQUEEEZE!!

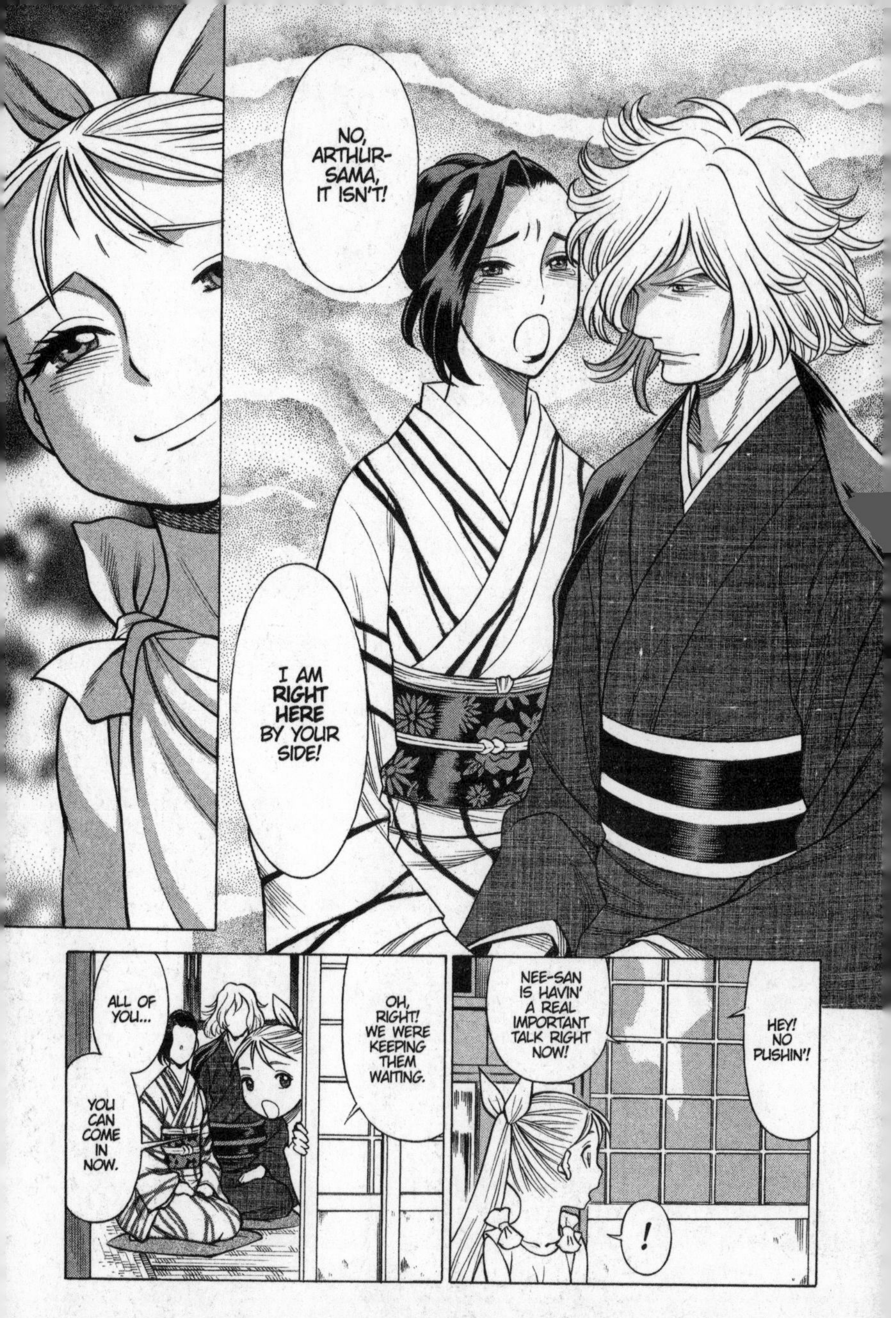
NO, ARTHUR-SAMA, IT ISN'T!
I AM RIGHT HERE BY YOUR SIDE!
HEY! NO PUSHIN'!
NEE-SAN IS HAVIN' A REAL IMPORTANT TALK RIGHT NOW!
!
OH, RIGHT! WE WERE KEEPING THEM WAITING.
ALL OF YOU...
YOU CAN COME IN NOW.

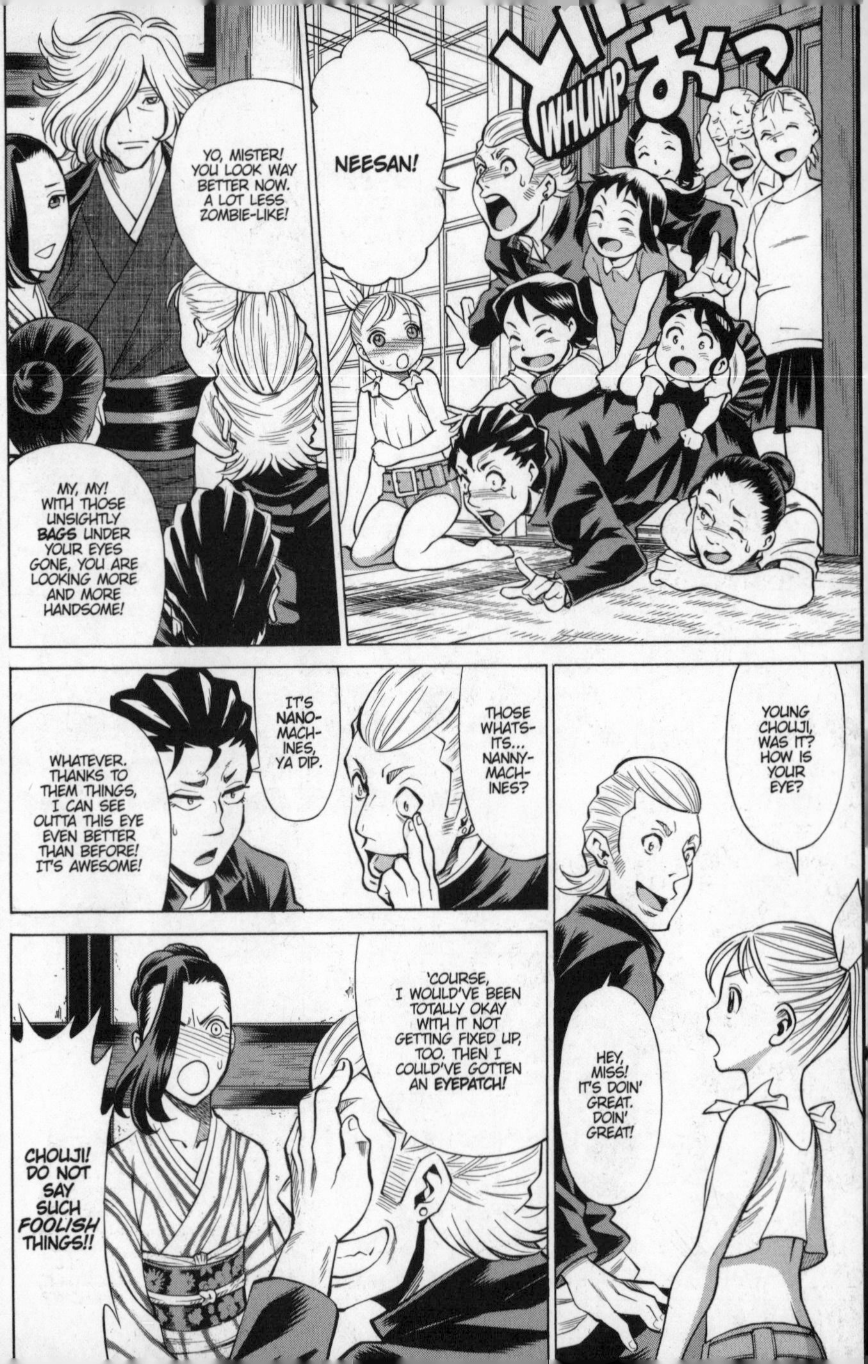

どおっ
WHUMP
NEESAN!
YO, MISTER! YOU LOOK WAY BETTER NOW. A LOT LESS ZOMBIE-LIKE!
MY, MY! WITH THOSE UNSIGHTLY BAGS UNDER YOUR EYES GONE, YOU ARE LOOKING MORE AND MORE HANDSOME!
YOUNG CHOUJI, WAS IT? HOW IS YOUR EYE?
HEY, MISS! IT'S DOIN' GREAT. DOIN' GREAT!
THOSE WHATS-ITS... NANNY-MACHINES?
IT'S NANO-MACHINES, YA DIP.
WHATEVER. THANKS TO THEM THINGS, I CAN SEE OUTTA THIS EYE EVEN BETTER THAN BEFORE! IT'S AWESOME!
'COURSE, I WOULD'VE BEEN TOTALLY OKAY WITH IT NOT GETTING FIXED UP, TOO. THEN I COULD'VE GOTTEN AN EYEPATCH!
CHOUJI! DO NOT SAY SUCH FOOLISH THINGS!!

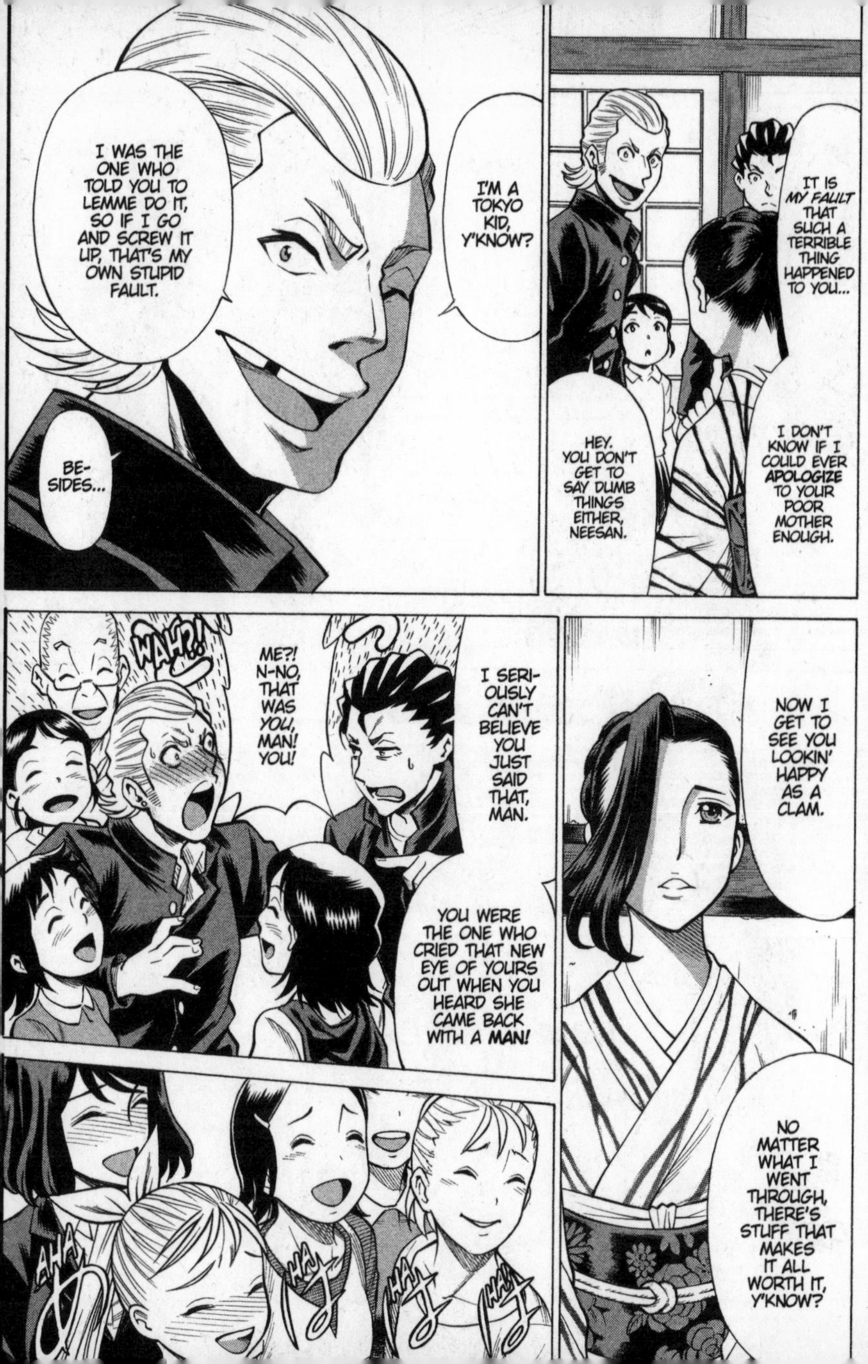
IT IS *MY FAULT* THAT SUCH A TERRIBLE THING HAPPENED TO YOU...
I DON'T KNOW IF I COULD EVER APOLOGIZE TO YOUR POOR MOTHER ENOUGH.
HEY. YOU DON'T GET TO SAY DUMB THINGS EITHER, NEESAN.
I'M A TOKYO KID, Y'KNOW?
I WAS THE ONE WHO TOLD YOU TO LEMME DO IT, SO IF I GO AND SCREW IT UP, THAT'S MY OWN STUPID FAULT.
BE-SIDES...
NOW I GET TO SEE YOU LOOKIN' HAPPY AS A CLAM.
NO MATTER WHAT I WENT THROUGH, THERE'S STUFF THAT MAKES IT ALL WORTH IT, Y'KNOW?
I SERI-OUSLY CAN'T BELIEVE YOU JUST SAID THAT, MAN.
ME?! N-NO, THAT WAS *YOU*, MAN! YOU!
WAH?!
YOU WERE THE ONE WHO CRIED THAT NEW EYE OF YOURS OUT WHEN YOU HEARD SHE CAME BACK WITH A **MAN**!
HA
HA
HA
AHA

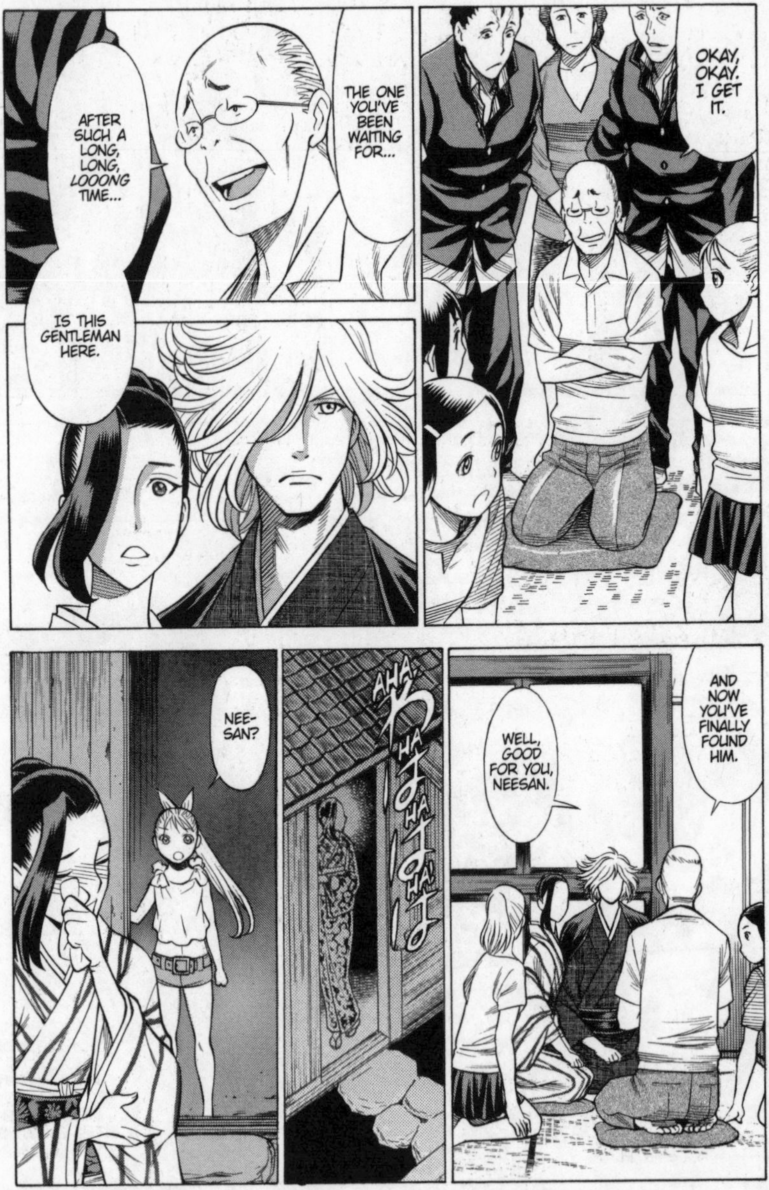
OKAY, OKAY. I GET IT.
THE ONE YOU'VE BEEN WAITING FOR...
AFTER SUCH A LONG, LONG, LOOONG TIME...
IS THIS GENTLEMAN HERE.
AND NOW YOU'VE FINALLY FOUND HIM.
WELL, GOOD FOR YOU, NEESAN.
AHA HA HA HA
NEE-SAN?

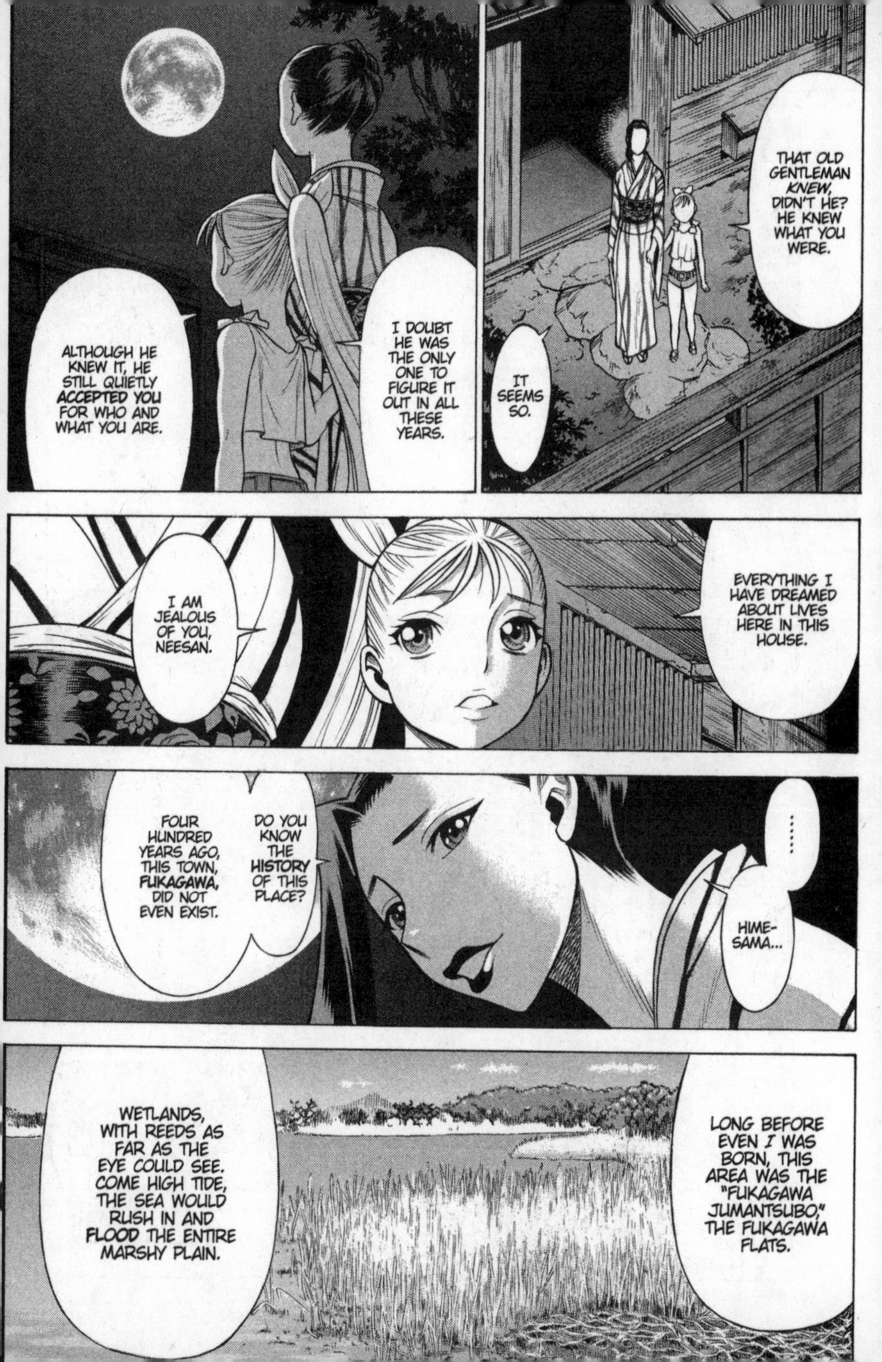
THAT OLD GENTLEMAN KNEW, DIDN'T HE? HE KNEW WHAT YOU WERE.
IT SEEMS SO.
I DOUBT HE WAS THE ONLY ONE TO FIGURE IT OUT IN ALL THESE YEARS.
ALTHOUGH HE KNEW IT, HE STILL QUIETLY ACCEPTED YOU FOR WHO AND WHAT YOU ARE.
EVERYTHING I HAVE DREAMED ABOUT LIVES HERE IN THIS HOUSE.
I AM JEALOUS OF YOU, NEESAN.
......
HIME-SAMA...
DO YOU KNOW THE HISTORY OF THIS PLACE?
FOUR HUNDRED YEARS AGO, THIS TOWN, FUKAGAWA, DID NOT EVEN EXIST.
LONG BEFORE EVEN I WAS BORN, THIS AREA WAS THE "FUKAGAWA JUMANTSUBO," THE FUKAGAWA FLATS.
WETLANDS, WITH REEDS AS FAR AS THE EYE COULD SEE. COME HIGH TIDE, THE SEA WOULD RUSH IN AND FLOOD THE ENTIRE MARSHY PLAIN.

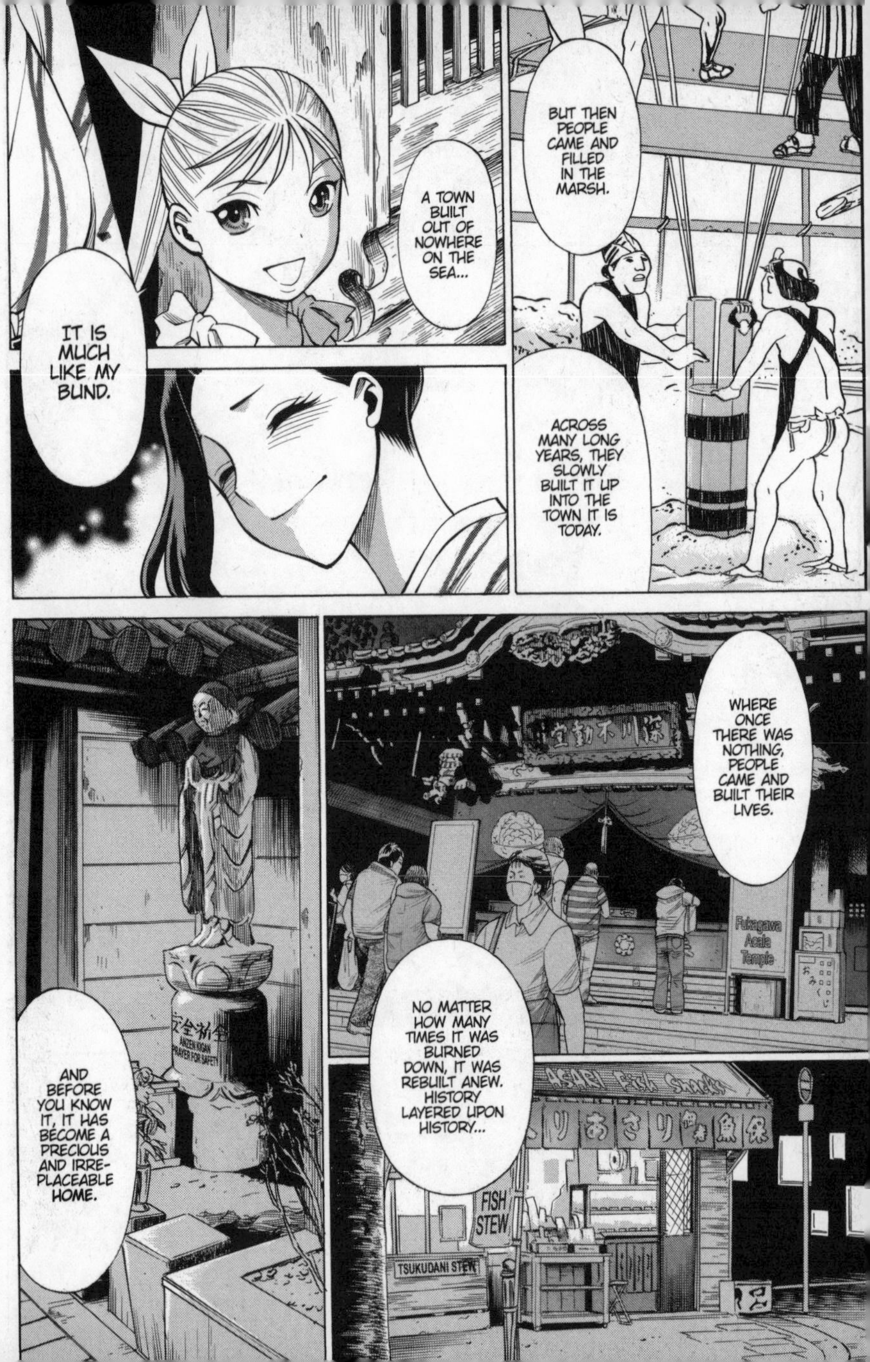
BUT THEN PEOPLE CAME AND FILLED IN THE MARSH.
ACROSS MANY LONG YEARS, THEY SLOWLY BUILT IT UP INTO THE TOWN IT IS TODAY.
A TOWN BUILT OUT OF NOWHERE ON THE SEA...
IT IS MUCH LIKE MY BLIND.
深川不動堂
WHERE ONCE THERE WAS NOTHING, PEOPLE CAME AND BUILT THEIR LIVES.
Fukagawa Acala Temple
NO MATTER HOW MANY TIMES IT WAS BURNED DOWN, IT WAS REBUILT ANEW. HISTORY LAYERED UPON HISTORY...
ASARI Fish Snacks
FISH STEW
TSUKUDANI STEW
安全祈願
ANZEN KIGAN
PRAYER FOR SAFETY
AND BEFORE YOU KNOW IT, IT HAS BECOME A PRECIOUS AND IRRE-PLACEABLE HOME.

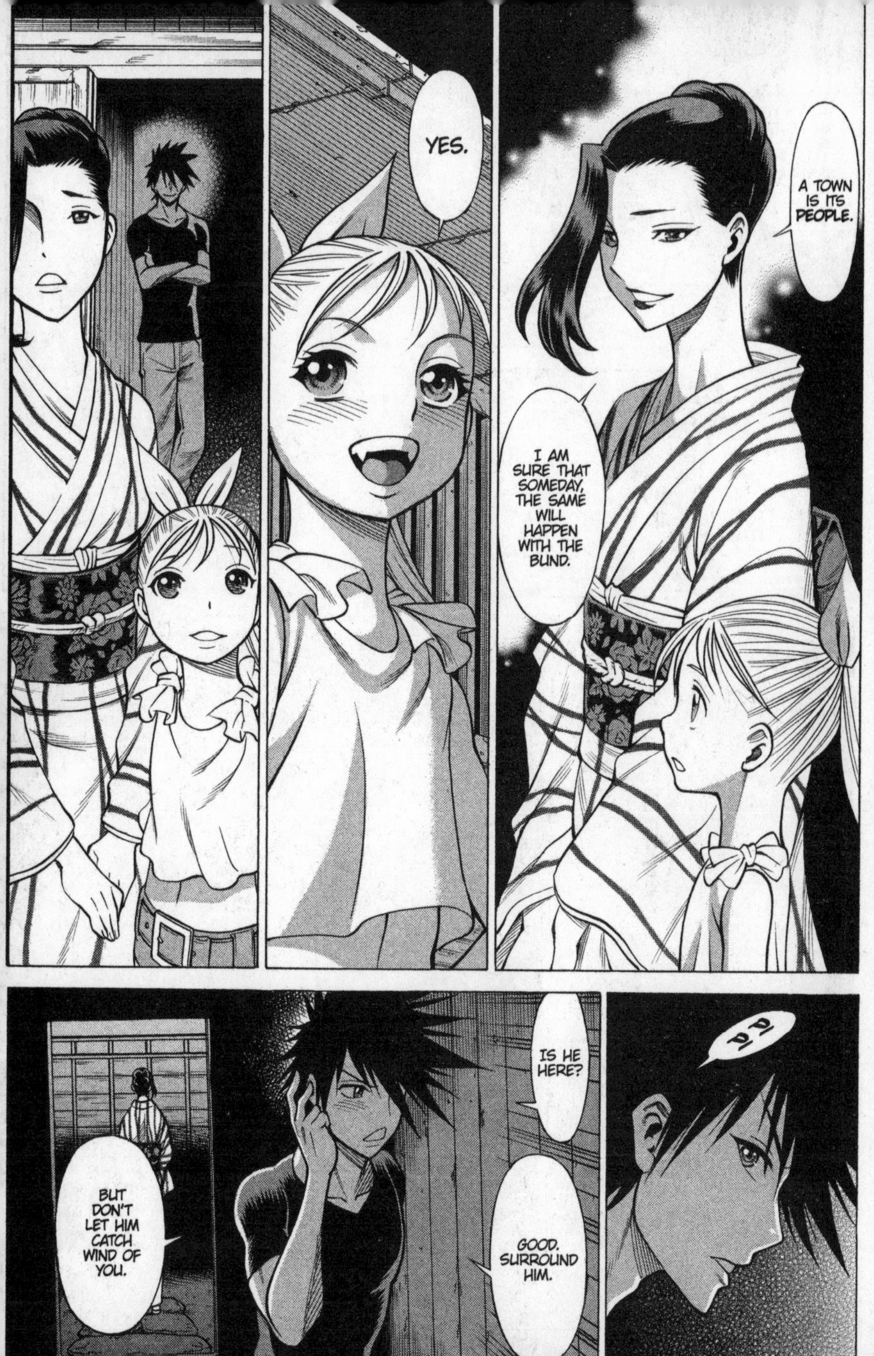

A TOWN IS ITS PEOPLE.
I AM SURE THAT SOMEDAY, THE SAME WILL HAPPEN WITH THE BUND.
YES.
PI PI
IS HE HERE?
GOOD. SURROUND HIM.
BUT DON'T LET HIM CATCH WIND OF YOU.

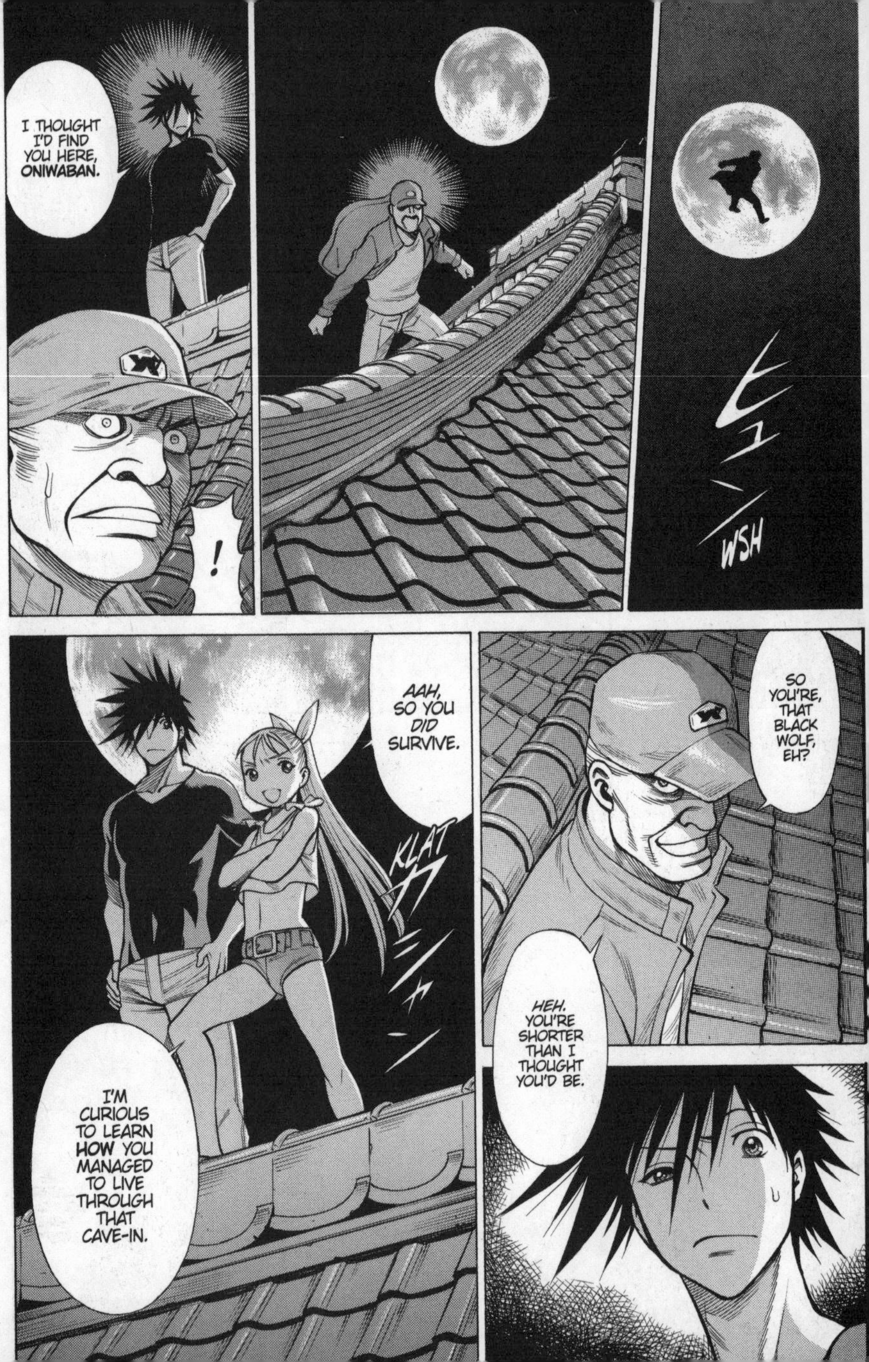
WSH
I THOUGHT I'D FIND YOU HERE, ONIWABAN.
!
SO YOU'RE, THAT BLACK WOLF, EH?
HEH. YOU'RE SHORTER THAN I THOUGHT YOU'D BE.
AAH, SO YOU DID SURVIVE.
KLAT
I'M CURIOUS TO LEARN HOW YOU MANAGED TO LIVE THROUGH THAT CAVE-IN.

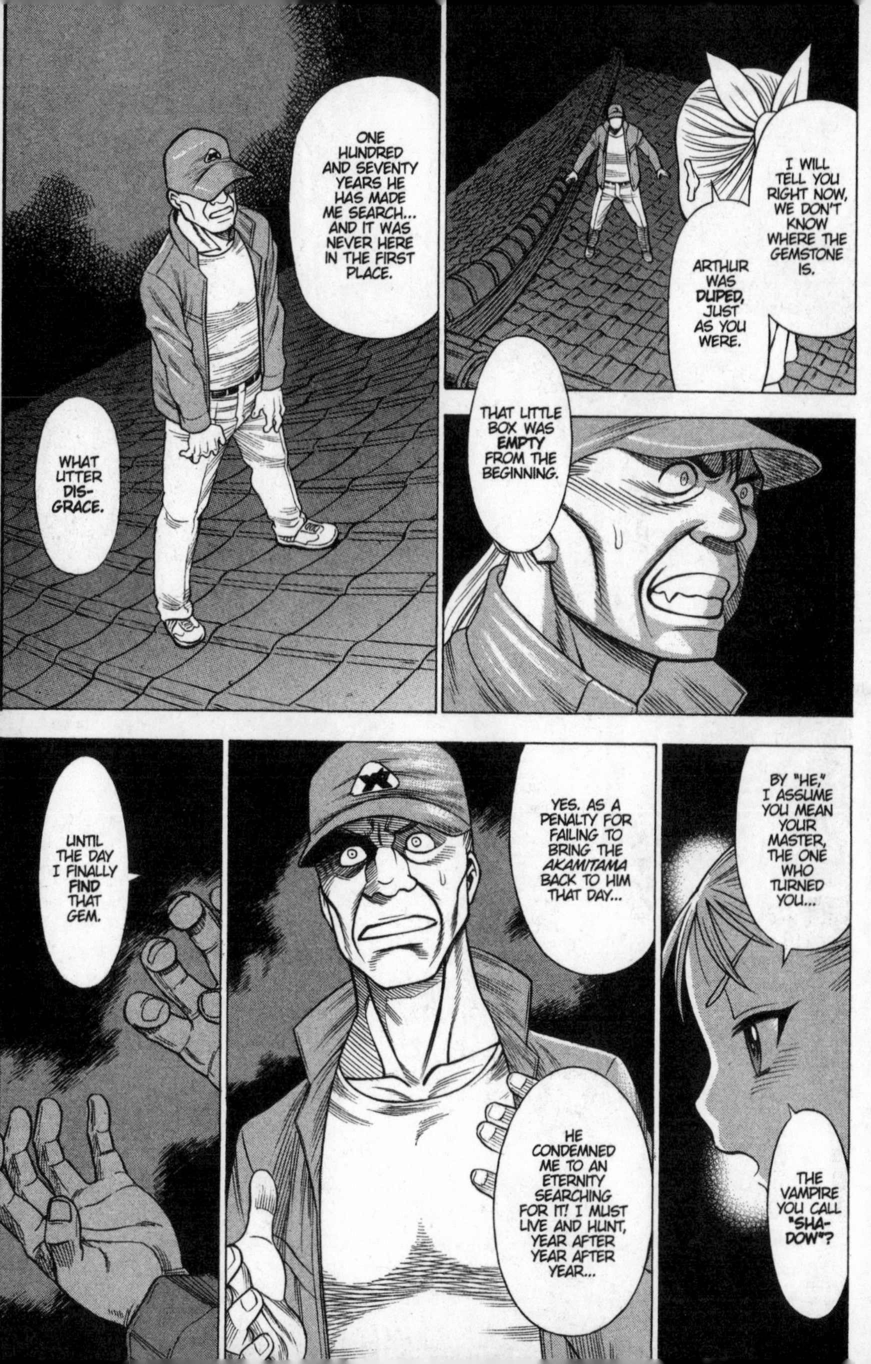
I WILL TELL YOU RIGHT NOW, WE DON'T KNOW WHERE THE GEMSTONE IS.
ARTHUR WAS **DUPED**, JUST AS YOU WERE.
THAT LITTLE BOX WAS **EMPTY** FROM THE BEGINNING.
ONE HUNDRED AND SEVENTY YEARS HE HAS MADE ME SEARCH... AND IT WAS NEVER HERE IN THE FIRST PLACE.
WHAT UTTER DISGRACE.
BY "HE," I ASSUME YOU MEAN YOUR MASTER, THE ONE WHO TURNED YOU...
THE VAMPIRE YOU CALL "SHADOW"?
YES. AS A PENALTY FOR FAILING TO BRING THE *AKAMITAMA* BACK TO HIM THAT DAY...
HE CONDEMNED ME TO AN ETERNITY SEARCHING FOR IT! I MUST LIVE AND HUNT, YEAR AFTER YEAR AFTER YEAR...
UNTIL THE DAY I FINALLY FIND THAT GEM.

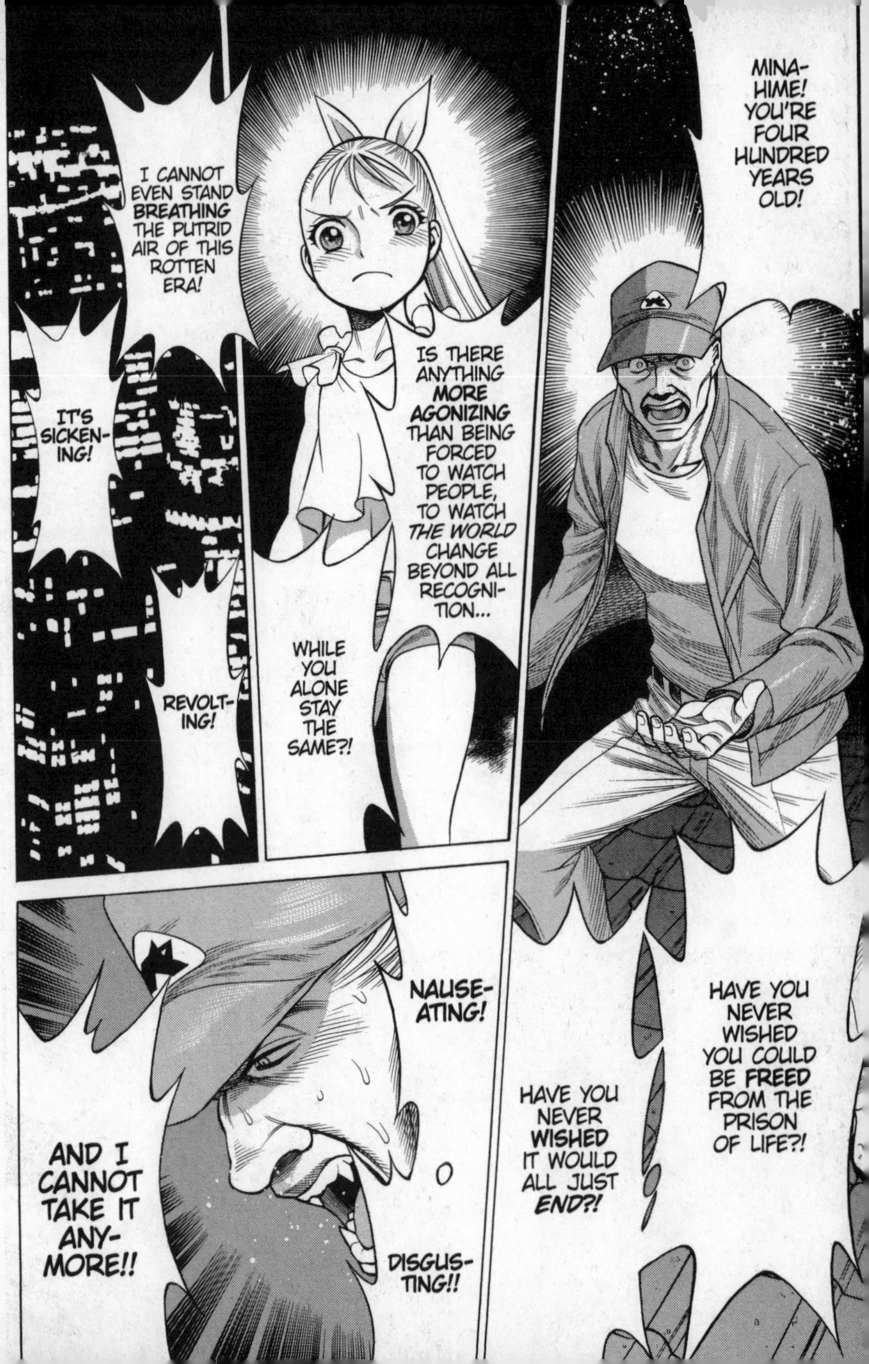
MINA-HIME! YOU'RE FOUR HUNDRED YEARS OLD!
IS THERE ANYTHING MORE AGONIZING THAN BEING FORCED TO WATCH PEOPLE, TO WATCH THE WORLD CHANGE BEYOND ALL RECOGNITION...
WHILE YOU ALONE STAY THE SAME?!
I CANNOT EVEN STAND BREATHING THE PUTRID AIR OF THIS ROTTEN ERA!
IT'S SICKENING!
REVOLTING!
HAVE YOU NEVER WISHED YOU COULD BE FREED FROM THE PRISON OF LIFE?!
HAVE YOU NEVER WISHED IT WOULD ALL JUST END?!
NAUSEATING!
AND I CANNOT TAKE IT ANYMORE!!
DISGUSTING!!

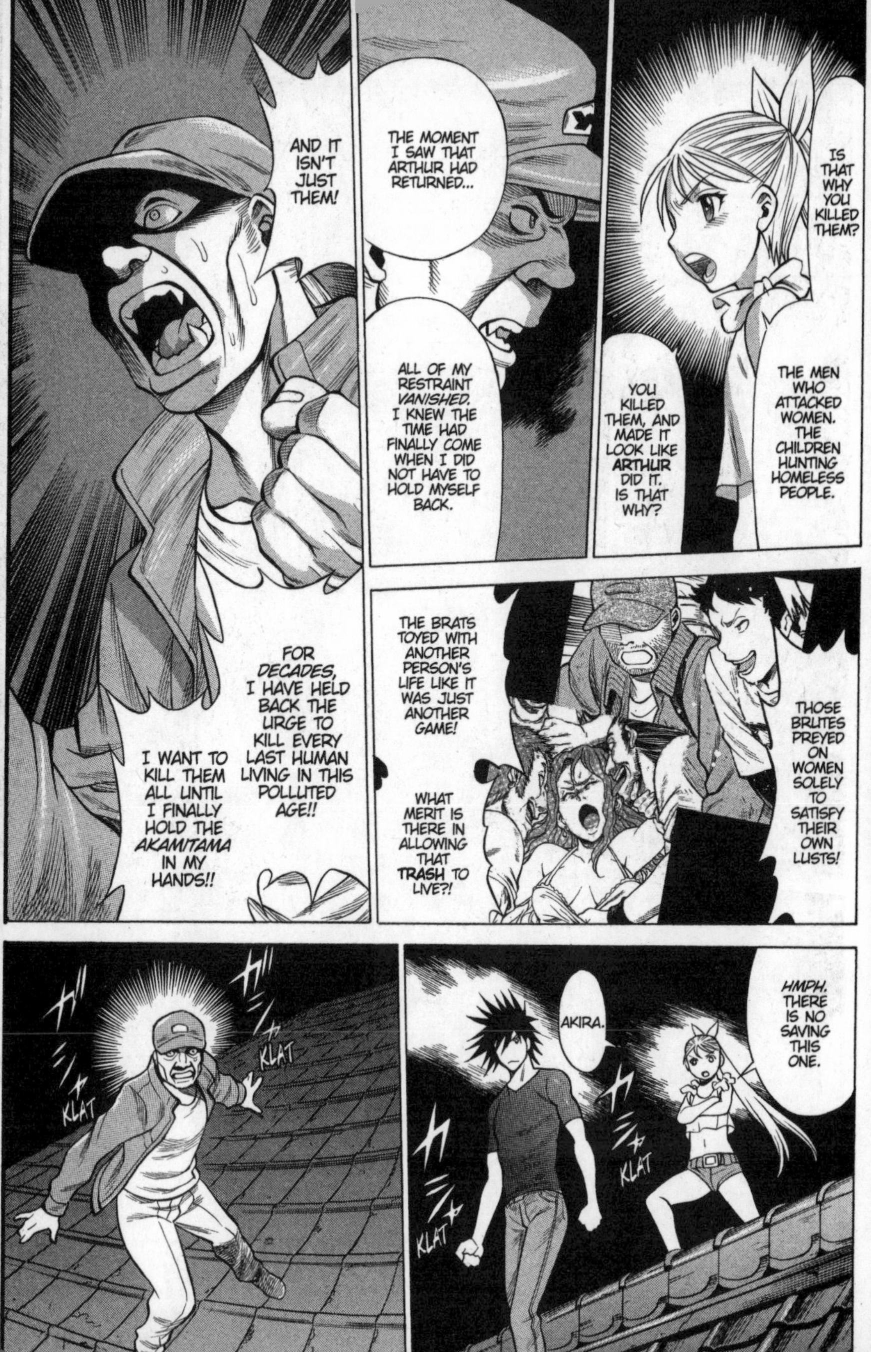
IS THAT WHY YOU KILLED THEM?
THE MEN WHO ATTACKED WOMEN. THE CHILDREN HUNTING HOMELESS PEOPLE.
YOU KILLED THEM, AND MADE IT LOOK LIKE ARTHUR DID IT. IS THAT WHY?
THE MOMENT I SAW THAT ARTHUR HAD RETURNED...
ALL OF MY RESTRAINT VANISHED. I KNEW THE TIME HAD FINALLY COME WHEN I DID NOT HAVE TO HOLD MYSELF BACK.
THOSE BRUTES PREYED ON WOMEN SOLELY TO SATISFY THEIR OWN LUSTS!
THE BRATS TOYED WITH ANOTHER PERSON'S LIFE LIKE IT WAS JUST ANOTHER GAME!
WHAT MERIT IS THERE IN ALLOWING THAT TRASH TO LIVE?!
AND IT ISN'T JUST THEM!
FOR DECADES, I HAVE HELD BACK THE URGE TO KILL EVERY LAST HUMAN LIVING IN THIS POLLUTED AGE!!
I WANT TO KILL THEM ALL UNTIL I FINALLY HOLD THE AKAMITAMA IN MY HANDS!!
HMPH. THERE IS NO SAVING THIS ONE.
AKIRA.
KLAT
KLAT
KLAT
KLAT

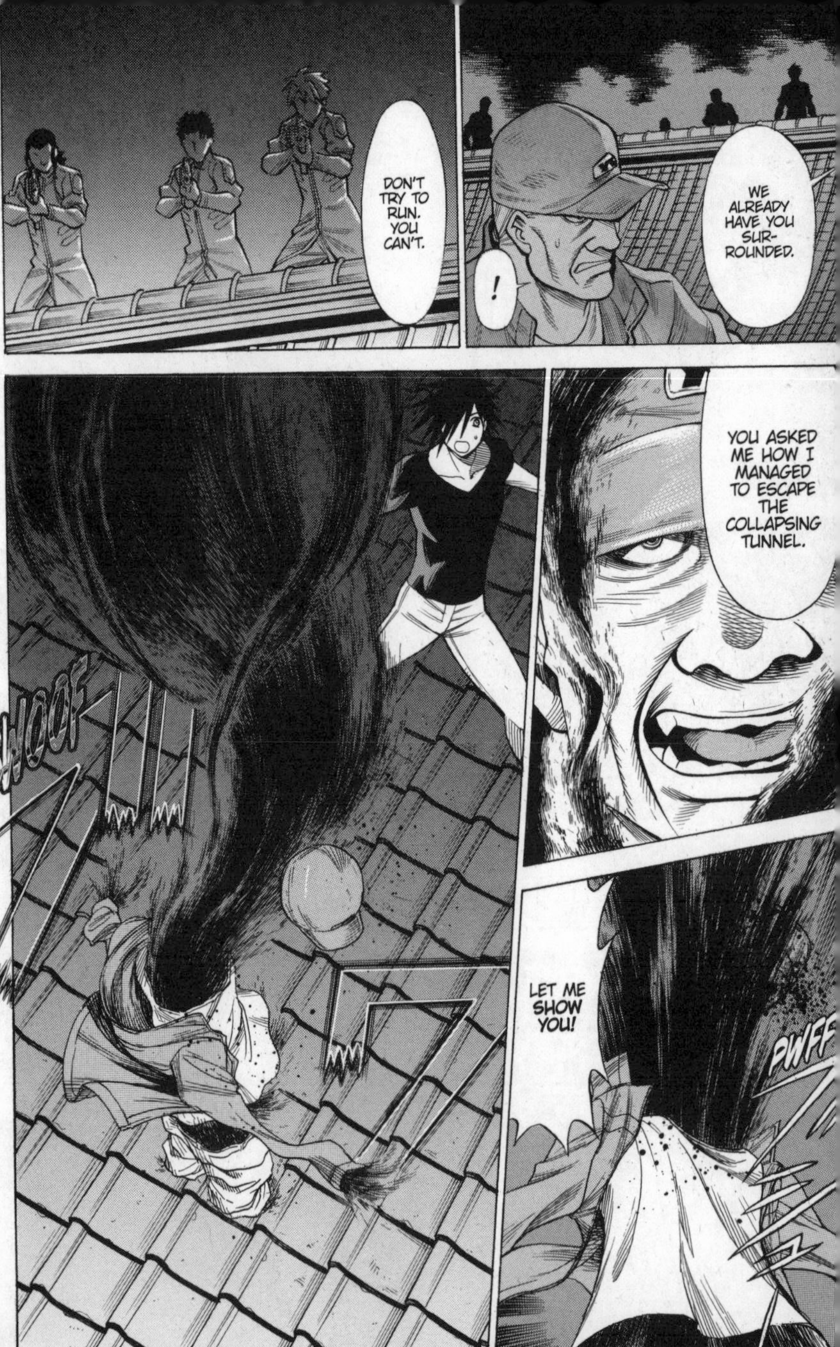
WE ALREADY HAVE YOU SUR-ROUNDED.
!
DON'T TRY TO RUN. YOU CAN'T.
YOU ASKED ME HOW I MANAGED TO ESCAPE THE COLLAPSING TUNNEL.
LET ME SHOW YOU!
PWFF
BWOOF

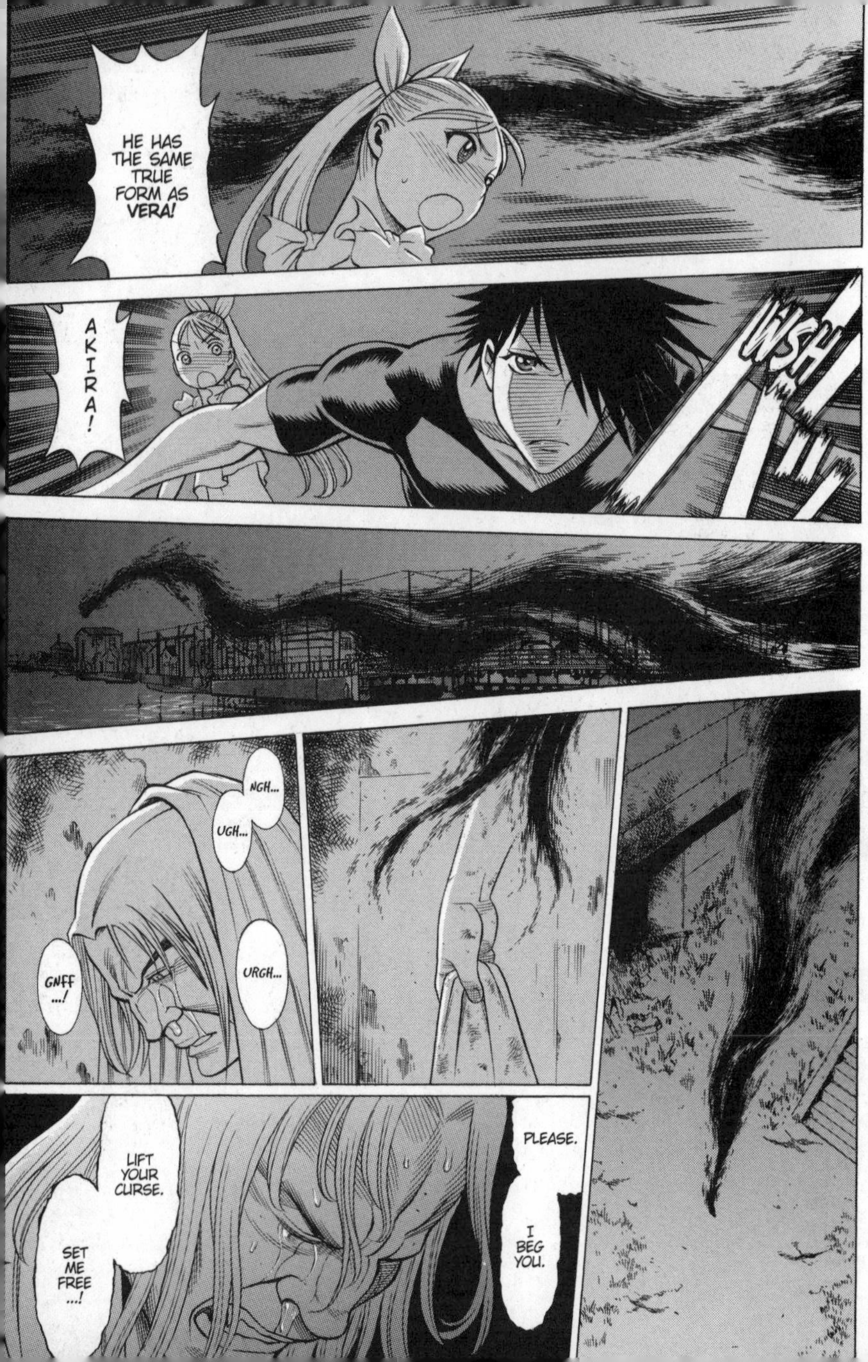
HE HAS THE SAME TRUE FORM AS VERA!
WSH
AKIRA!
NGH...
UGH...
URGH...
GNFF ...!
PLEASE.
I BEG YOU.
LIFT YOUR CURSE.
SET ME FREE ...!

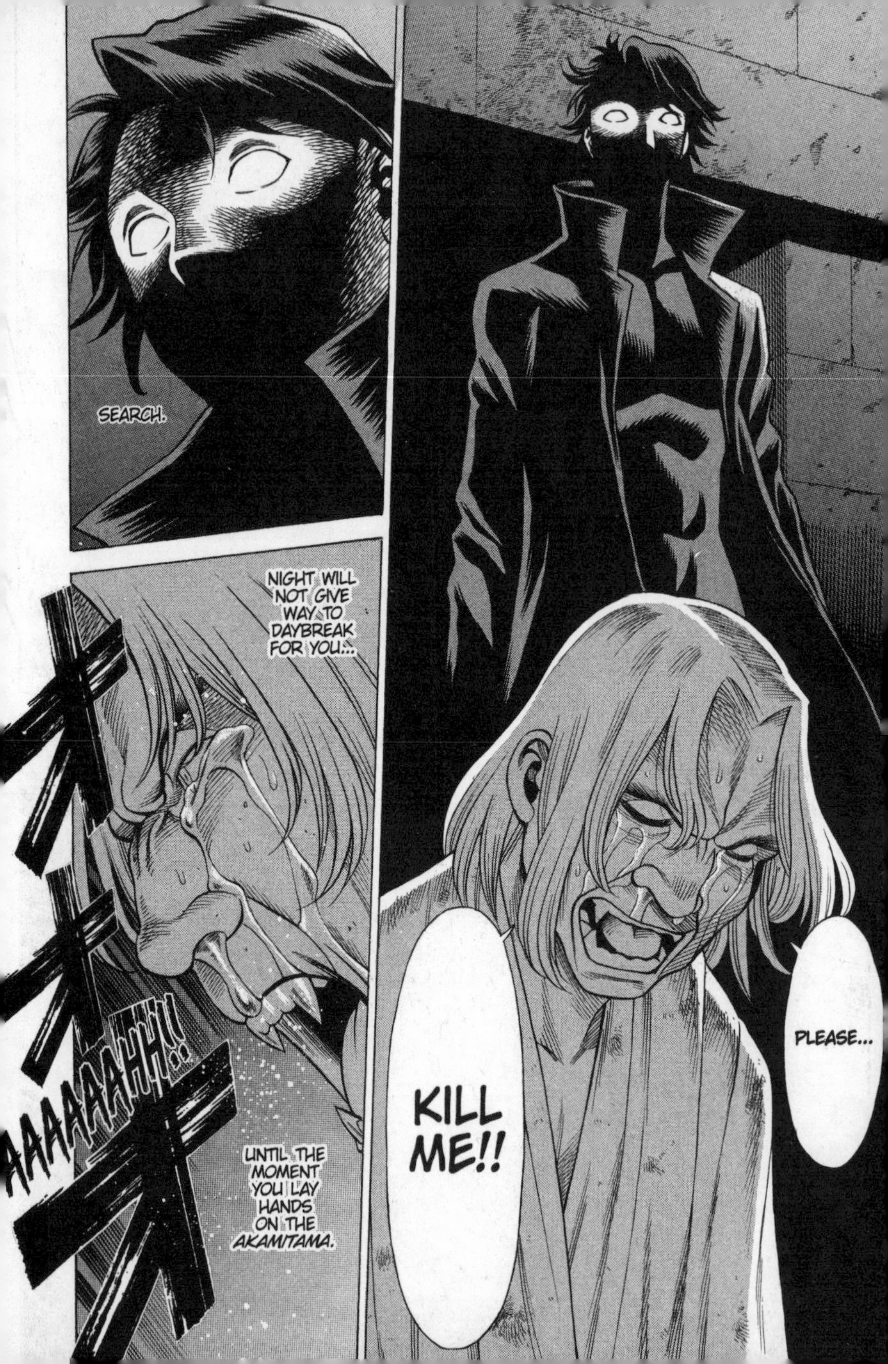
PLEASE...
KILL ME!!
SEARCH.
NIGHT WILL NOT GIVE WAY TO DAYBREAK FOR YOU...
AAAAAAHH!!
UNTIL THE MOMENT YOU LAY HANDS ON THE AKAMITAMA.

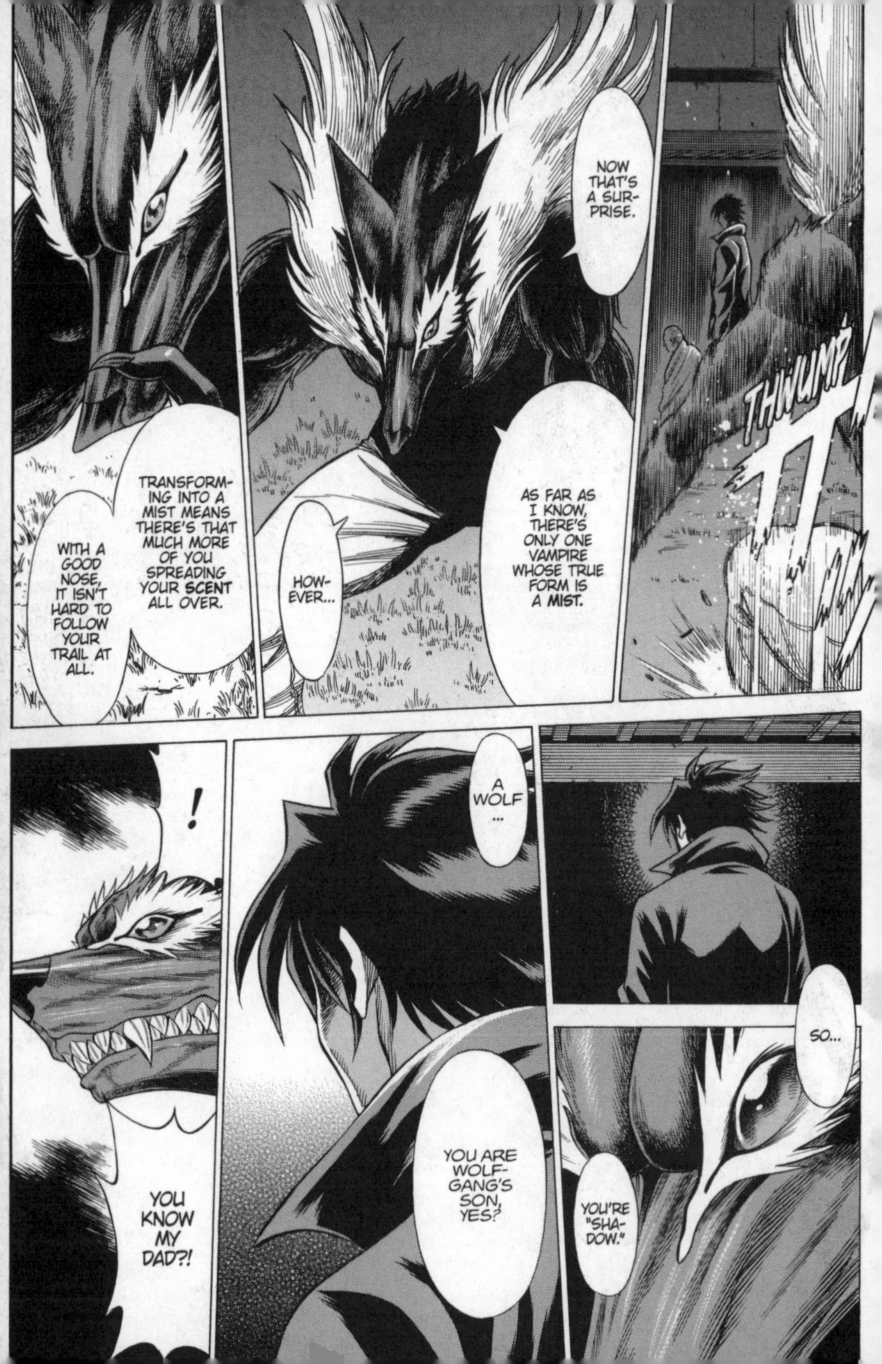
THWUMP
NOW THAT'S A SURPRISE.
AS FAR AS I KNOW, THERE'S ONLY ONE VAMPIRE WHOSE TRUE FORM IS A **MIST.**
HOWEVER...
TRANSFORMING INTO A MIST MEANS THERE'S THAT MUCH MORE OF YOU SPREADING YOUR **SCENT** ALL OVER.
WITH A GOOD NOSE, IT ISN'T HARD TO FOLLOW YOUR TRAIL AT ALL.
SO...
YOU'RE "SHADOW."
A WOLF...
YOU ARE WOLFGANG'S SON, YES?
!
YOU KNOW MY DAD?!

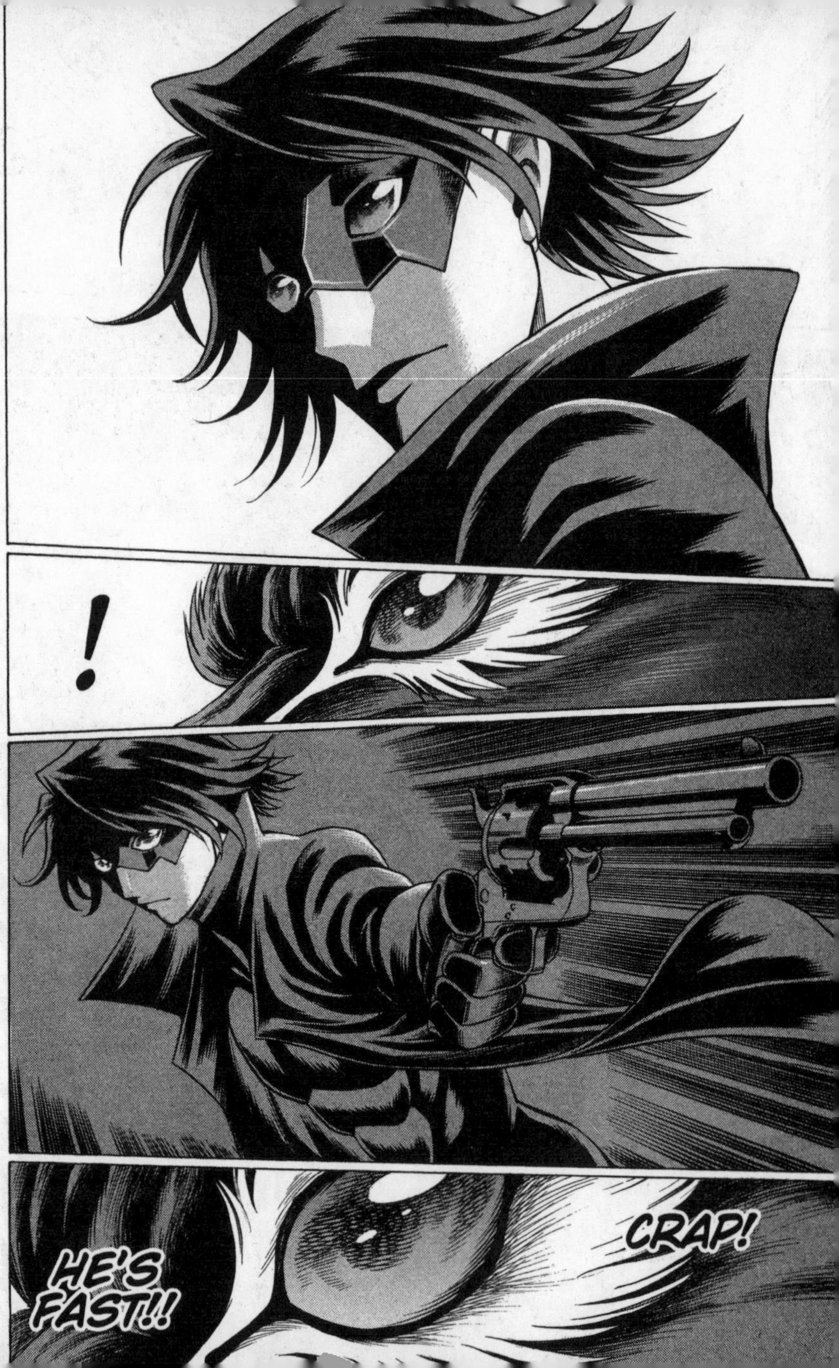
!
CRAP!
HE'S FAST!!

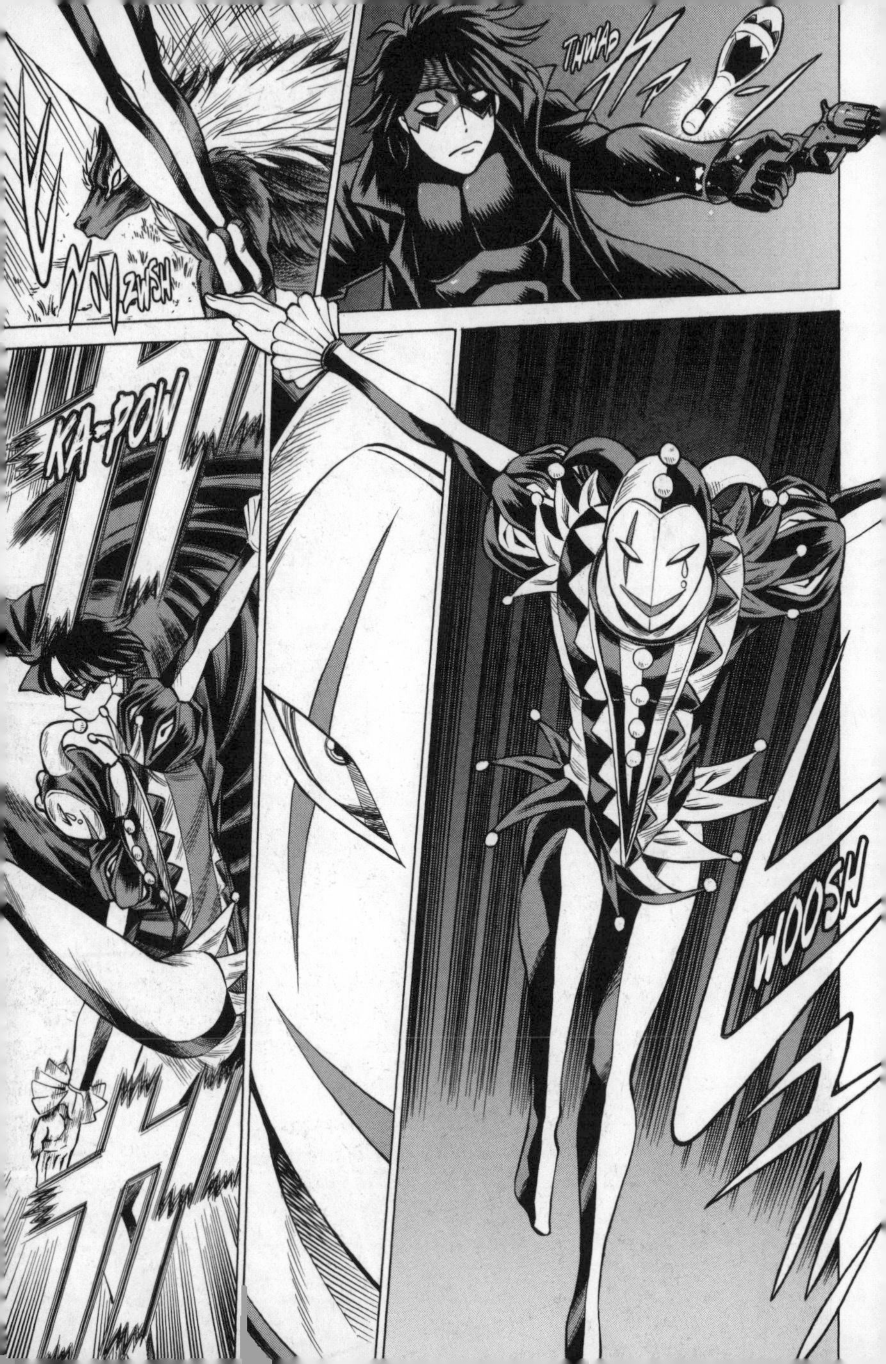
THWAP
ZWSH
WOOSH
KA-POW

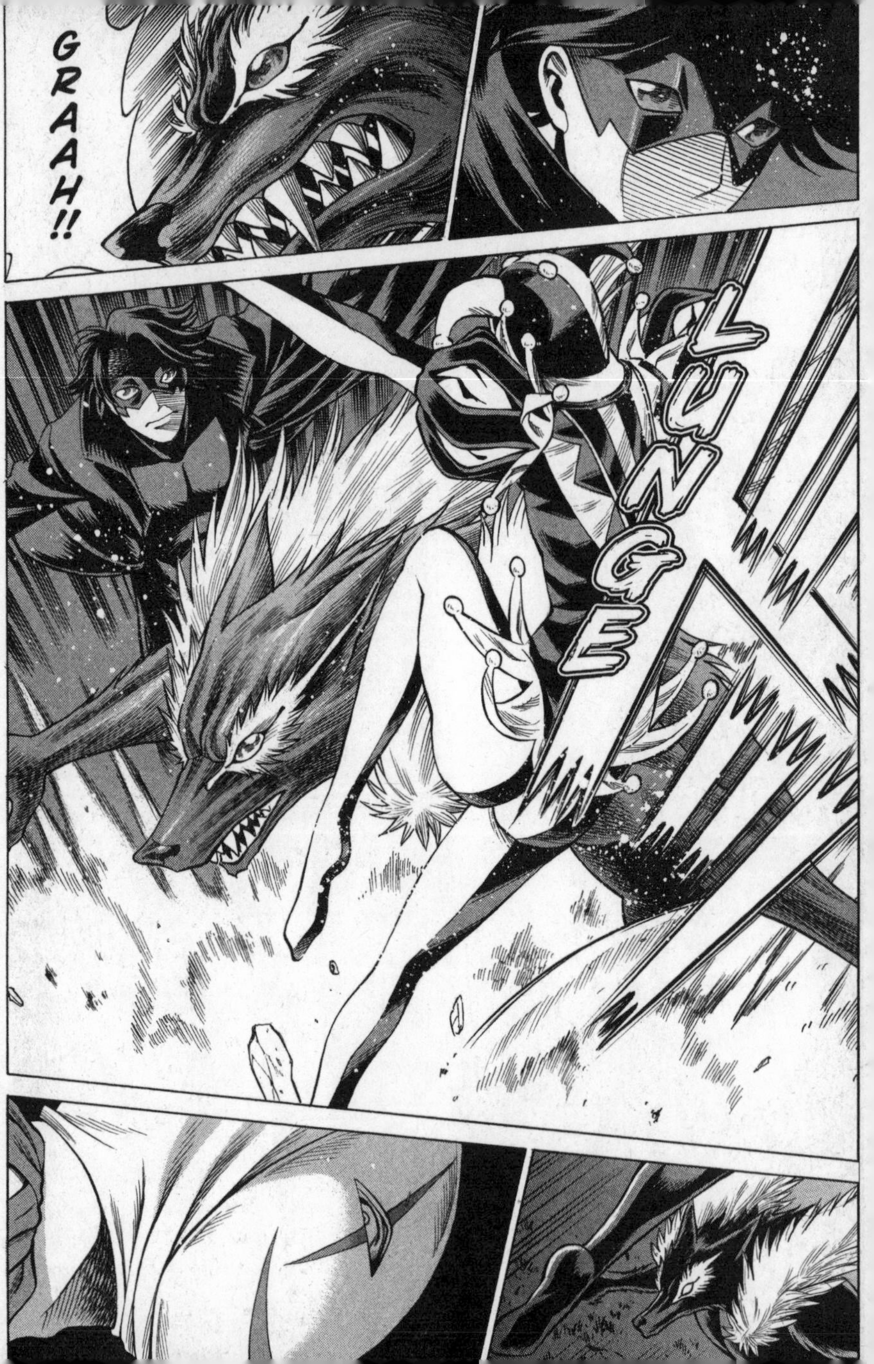
GRAAAH!!
LUNGE

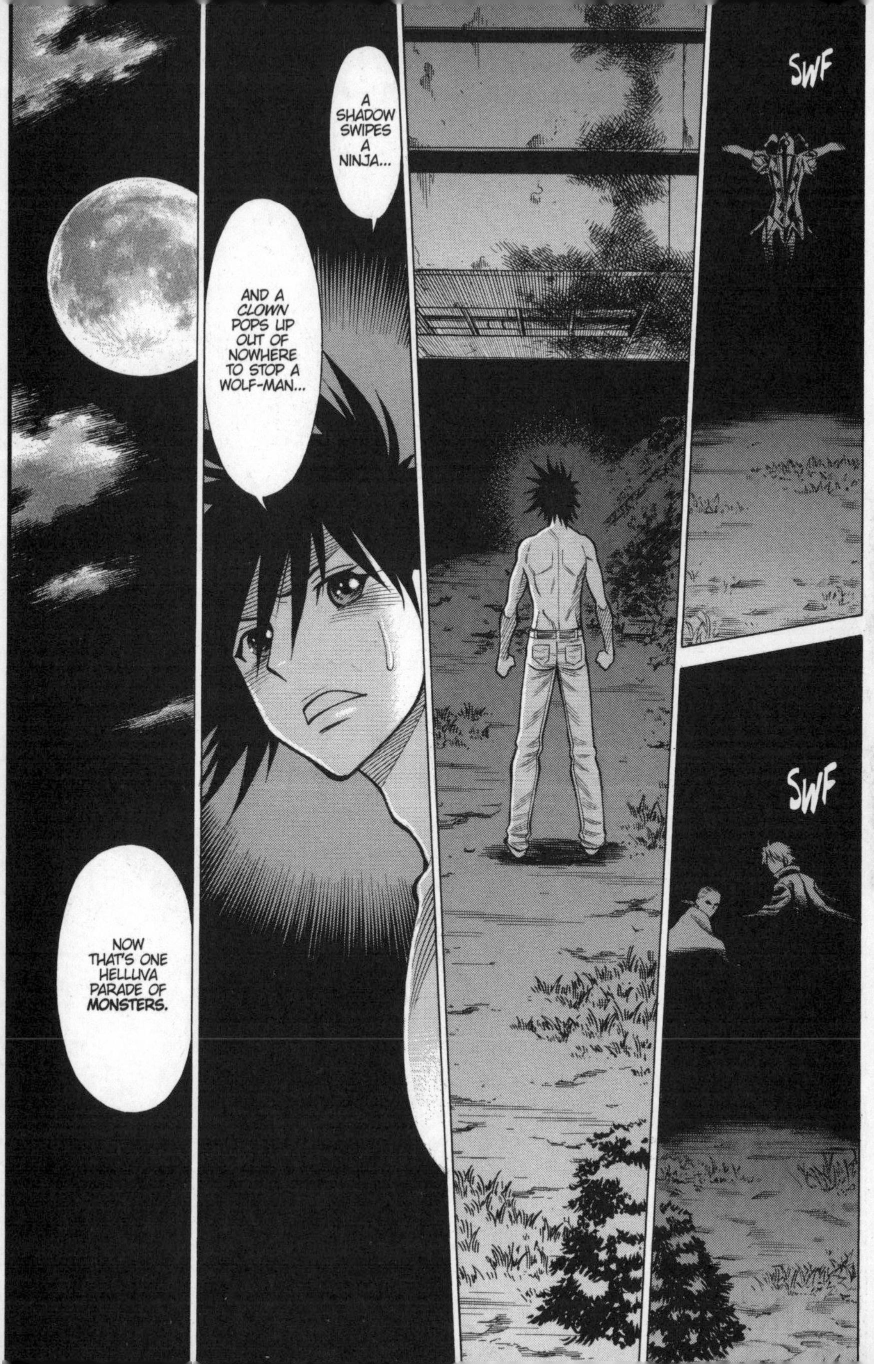
SWF
SWF
A SHADOW SWIPES A NINJA...
AND A CLOWN POPS UP OUT OF NOWHERE TO STOP A WOLF-MAN...
NOW THAT'S ONE HELLUVA PARADE OF MONSTERS.

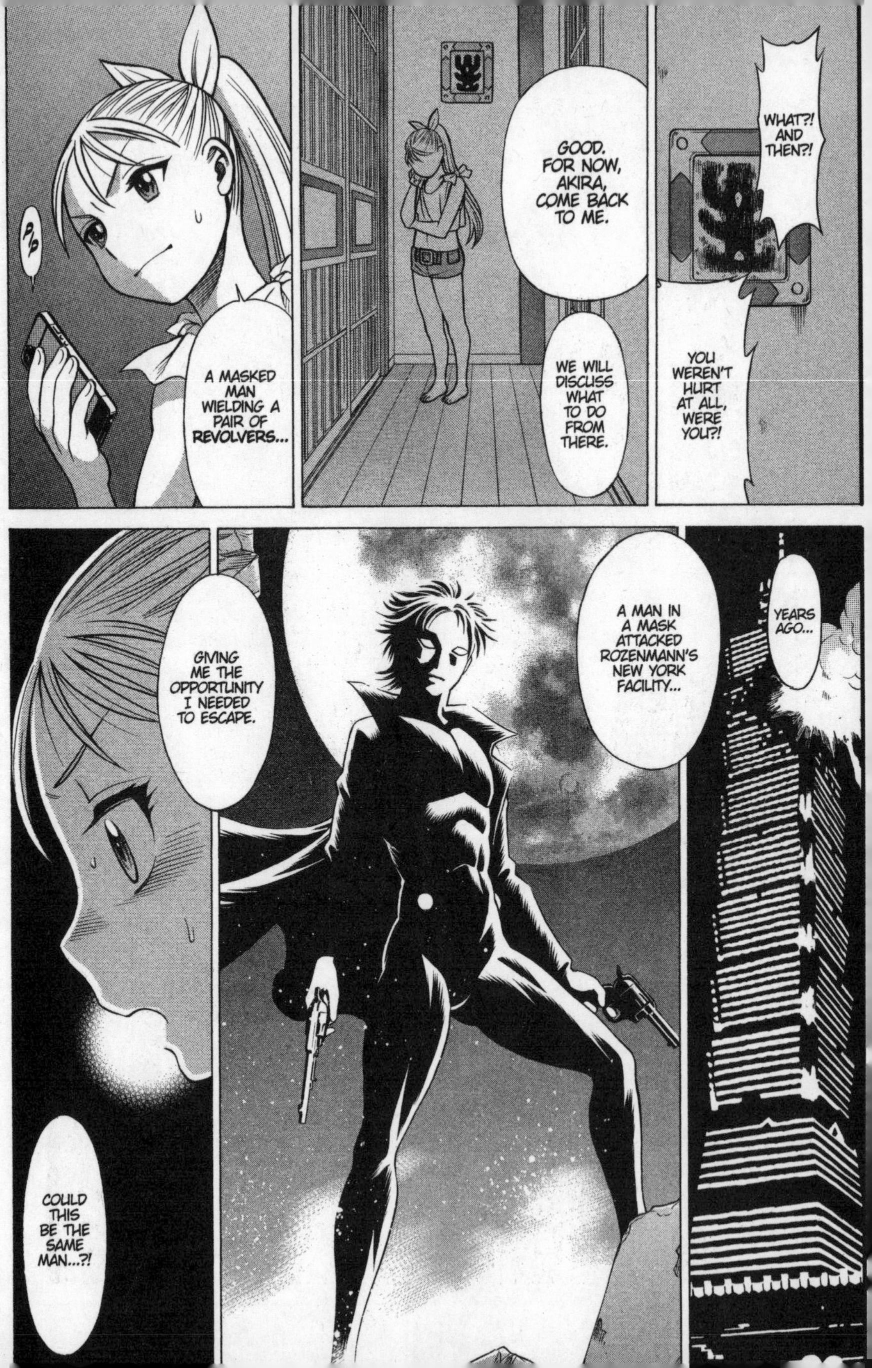
WHAT?! AND THEN?!
YOU WEREN'T HURT AT ALL, WERE YOU?!
GOOD. FOR NOW, AKIRA, COME BACK TO ME.
WE WILL DISCUSS WHAT TO DO FROM THERE.
PIP
A MASKED MAN WIELDING A PAIR OF REVOLVERS...
YEARS AGO...
A MAN IN A MASK ATTACKED ROZENMANN'S NEW YORK FACILITY...
GIVING ME THE OPPORTUNITY I NEEDED TO ESCAPE.
COULD THIS BE THE SAME MAN...?!

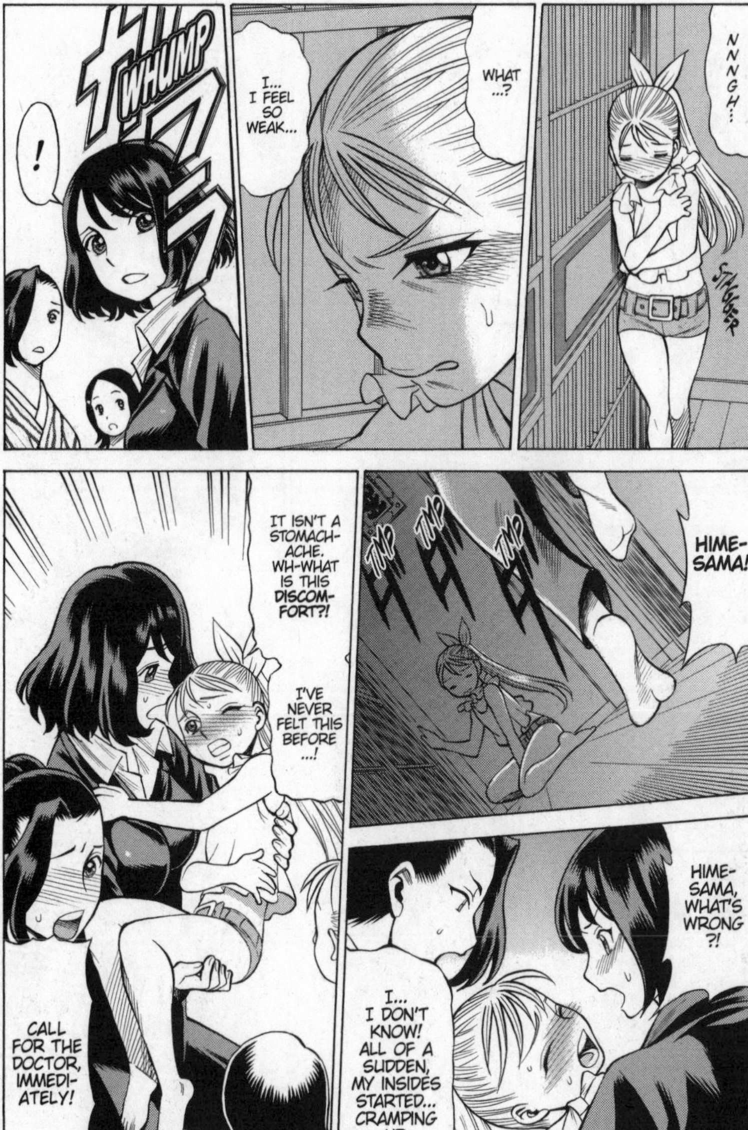
NNNGH...
STAGGER
WHAT ...?
I... I FEEL SO WEAK...
WHUMP
!
HIME-SAMA!
TMP TMP TMP
HIME-SAMA, WHAT'S WRONG?!
I... I DON'T KNOW! ALL OF A SUDDEN, MY INSIDES STARTED... CRAMPING UP.
IT ISN'T A STOMACHACHE. WH-WHAT IS THIS DISCOMFORT?!
I'VE NEVER FELT THIS BEFORE ...!
CALL FOR THE DOCTOR, IMMEDIATELY!

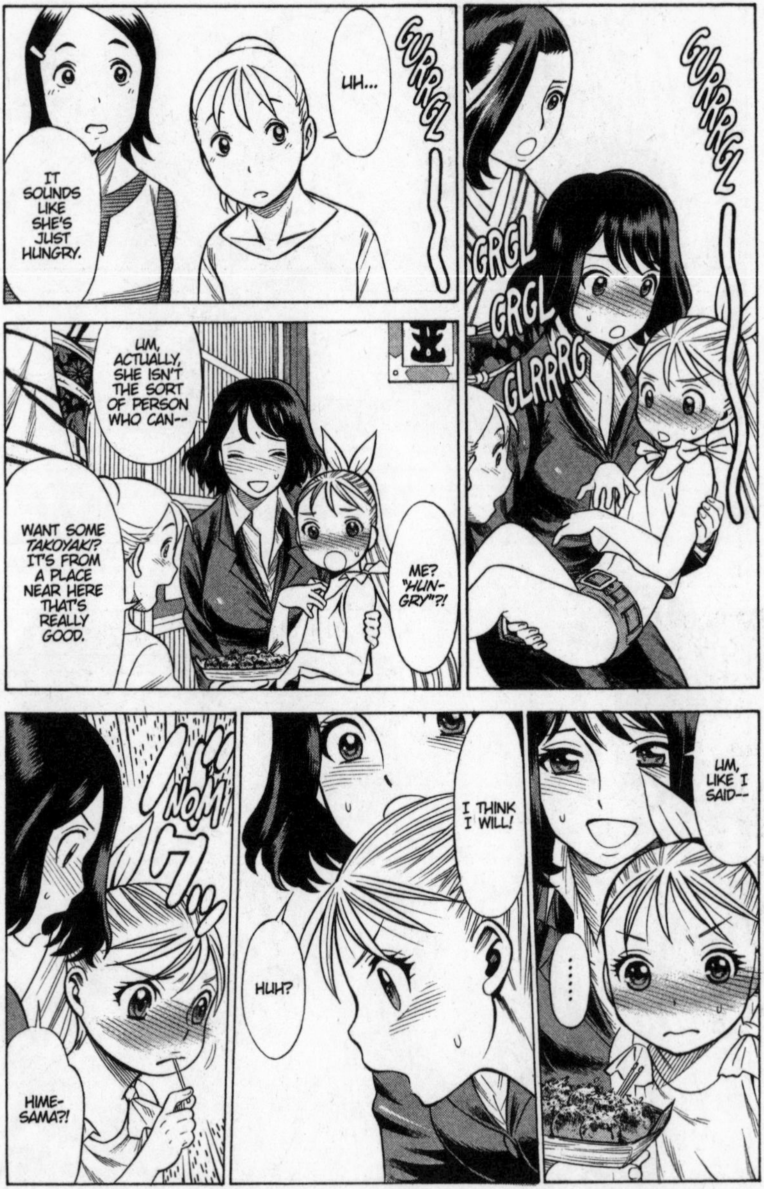
GURRRGL
GRGL
GRGL
GLRRRG
GURRGL
UH...
IT SOUNDS LIKE SHE'S JUST HUNGRY.
ME? "HUN-GRY"?!
UM, ACTUALLY, SHE ISN'T THE SORT OF PERSON WHO CAN--
WANT SOME *TAKOYAKI*? IT'S FROM A PLACE NEAR HERE THAT'S REALLY GOOD.
UM, LIKE I SAID--
......
I THINK I WILL!
HUH?
NOM...
HIME-SAMA?!

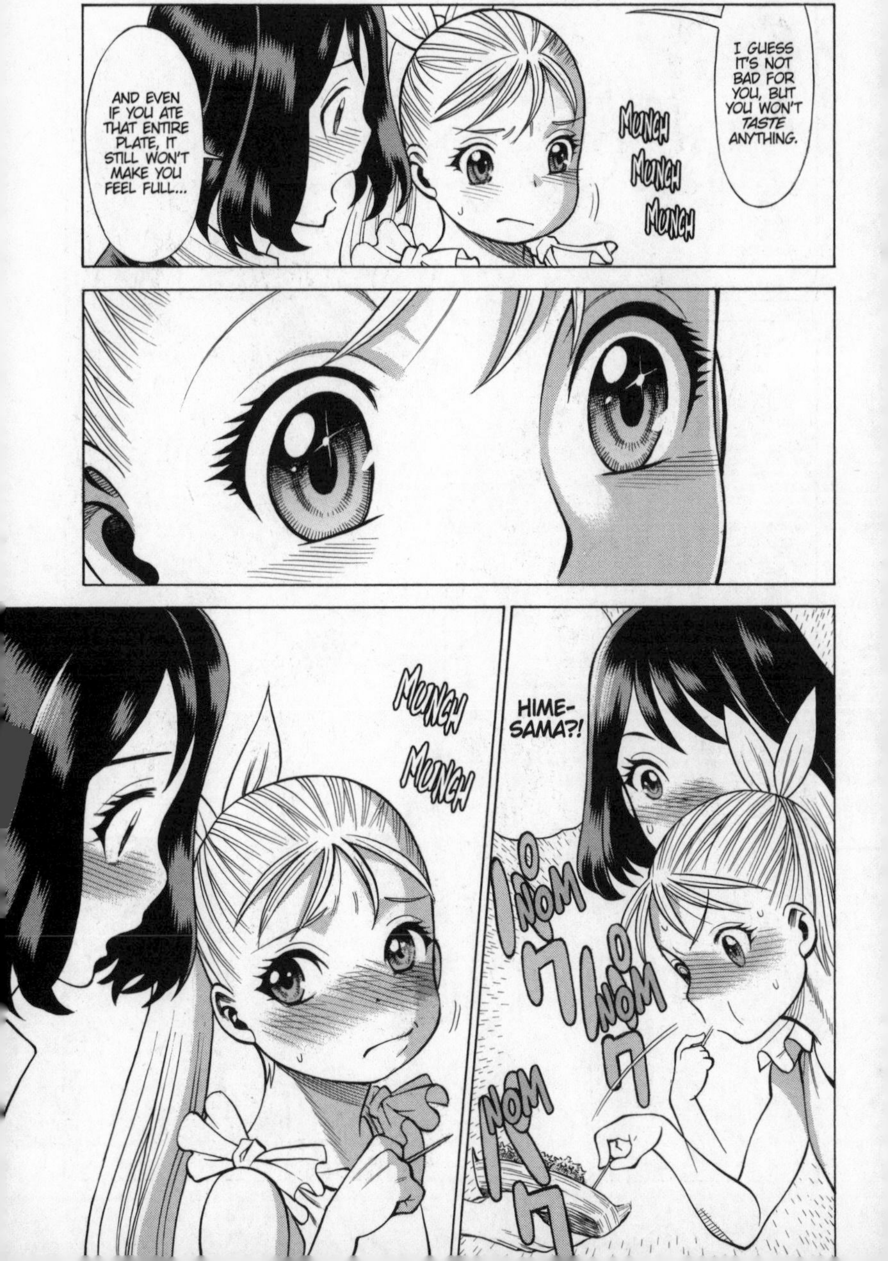
I GUESS IT'S NOT BAD FOR YOU, BUT YOU WON'T *TASTE* ANYTHING.
MUNCH MUNCH MUNCH
AND EVEN IF YOU ATE THAT ENTIRE PLATE, IT STILL WON'T MAKE YOU FEEL FULL...
HIME-SAMA?!
NOM NOM NOM
MUNCH MUNCH

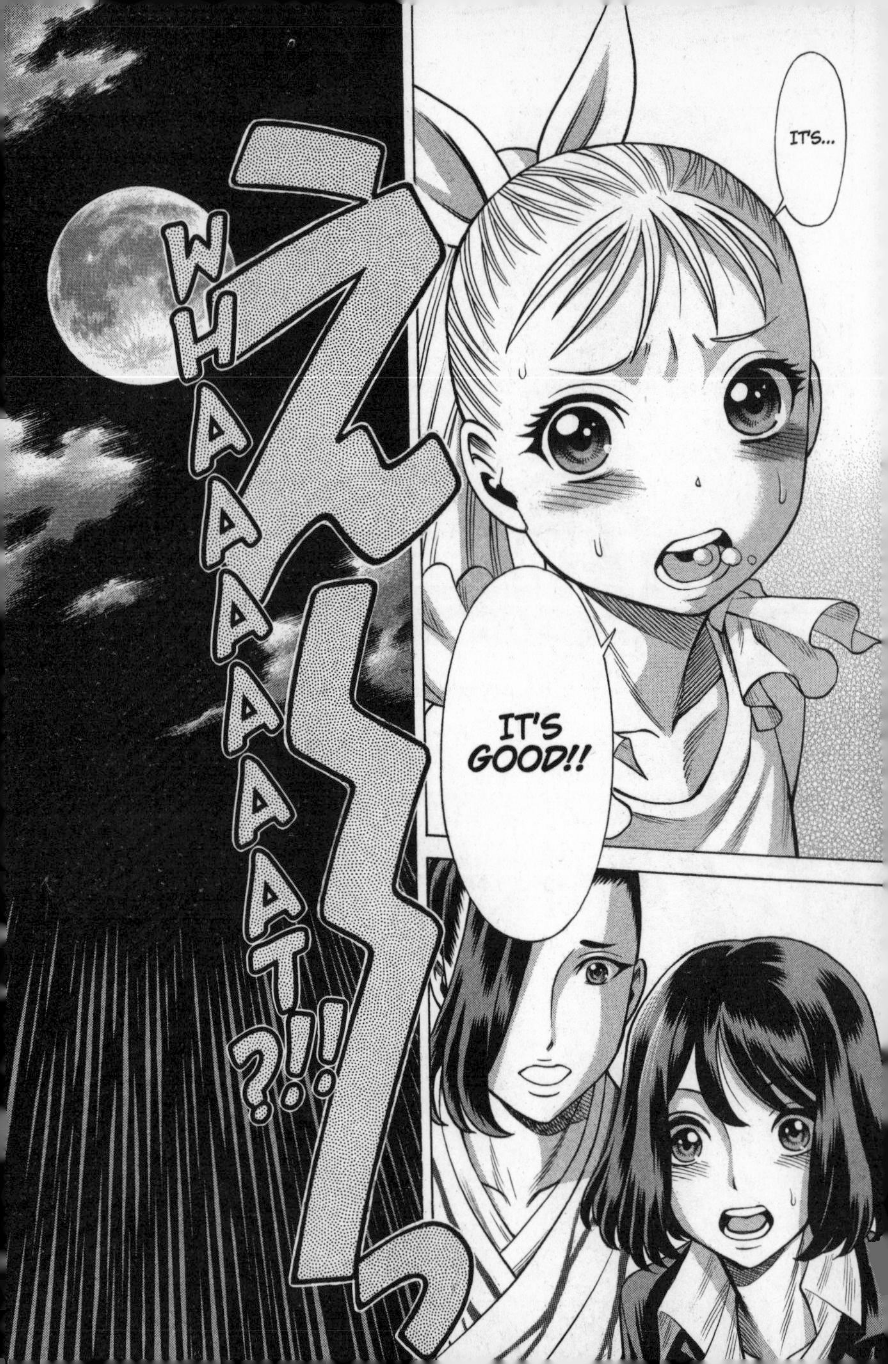
IT'S...
IT'S GOOD!!
WHAAAAAAT?!!

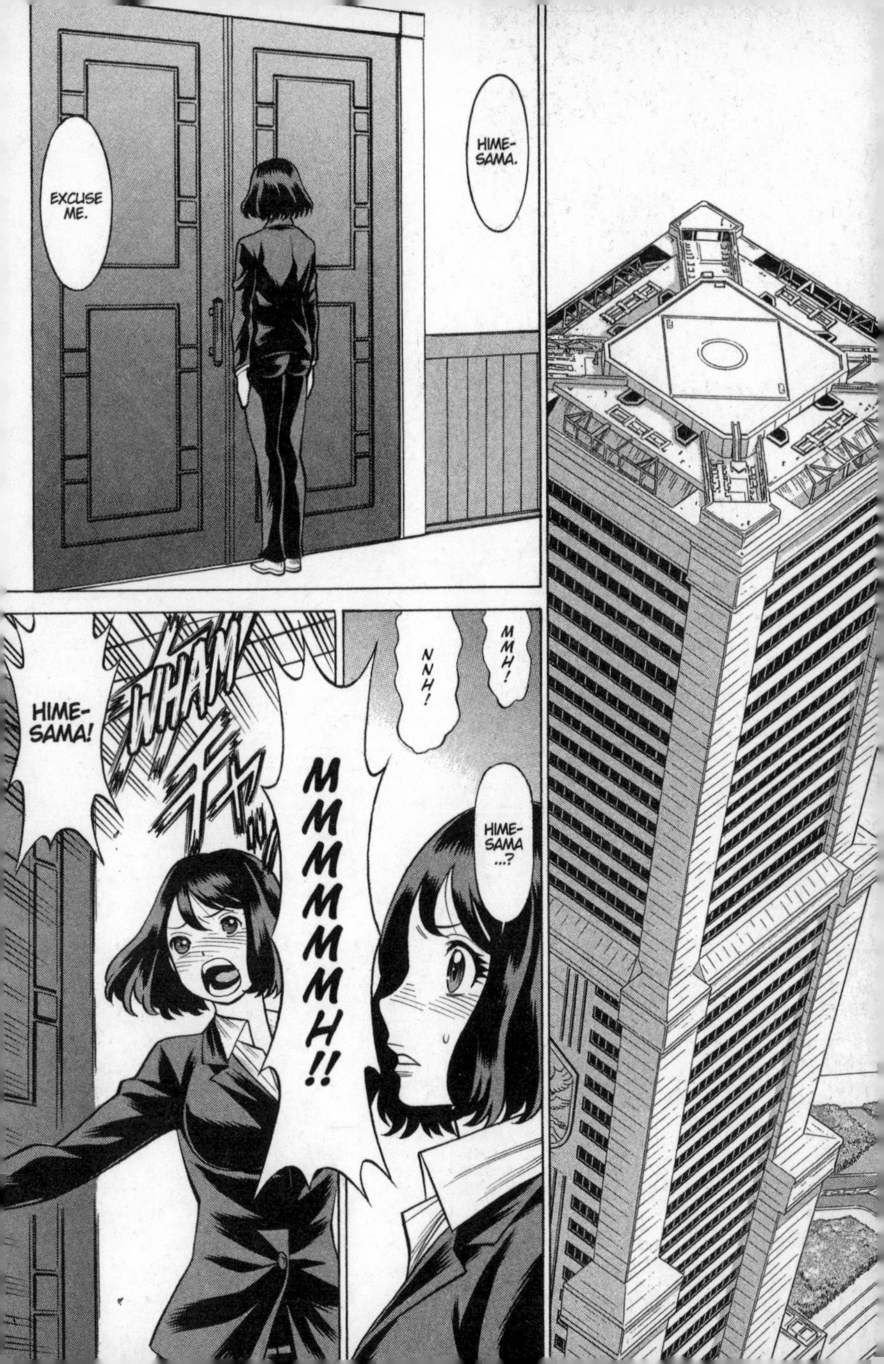
HIME-SAMA.
EXCUSE ME.
MMH!
NNH!
HIME-SAMA...?
MMMMMMMH!!
WHAM
HIME-SAMA!

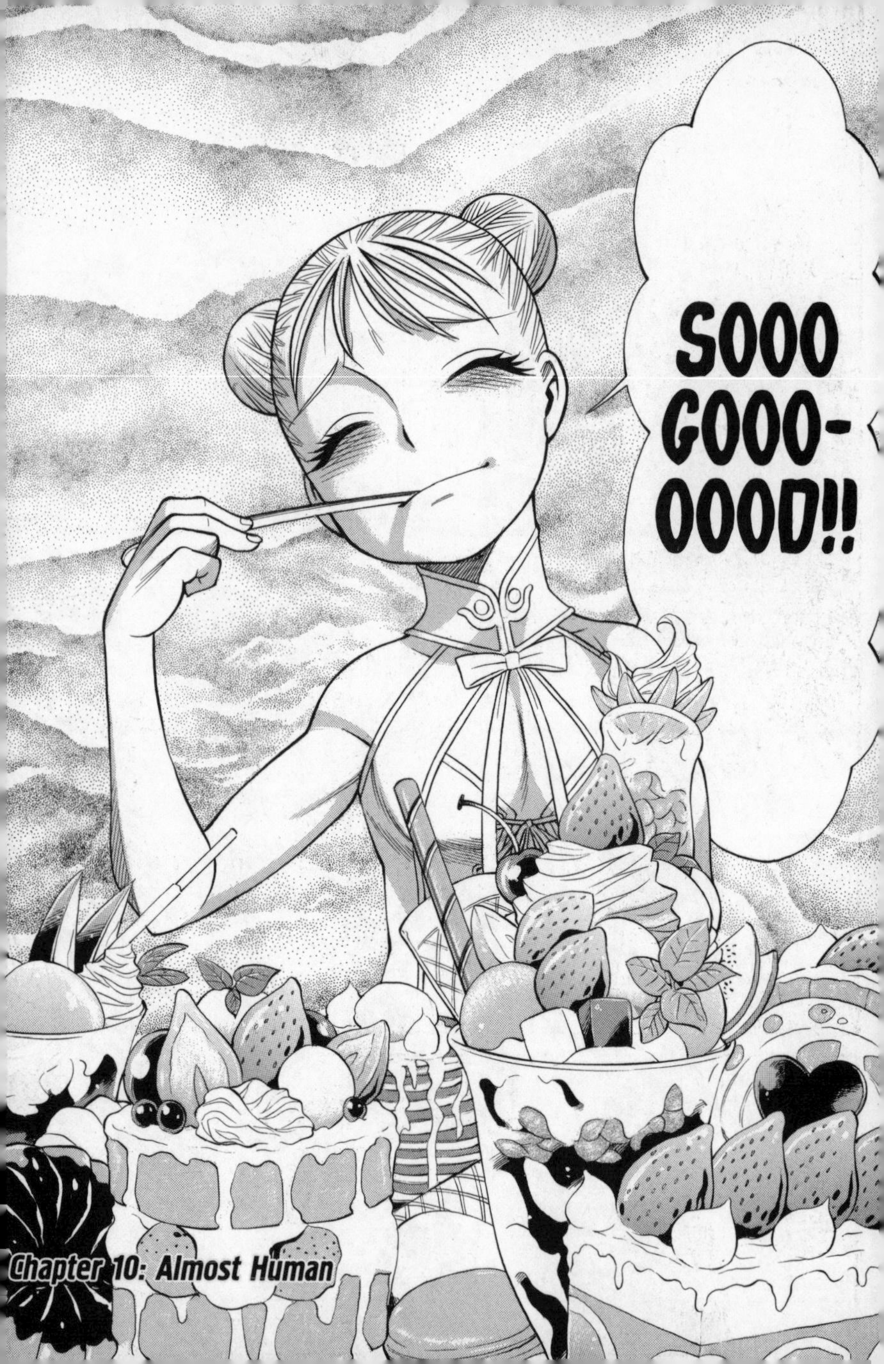
SOOO GOOO-OOOD!!
Chapter 10: Almost Human

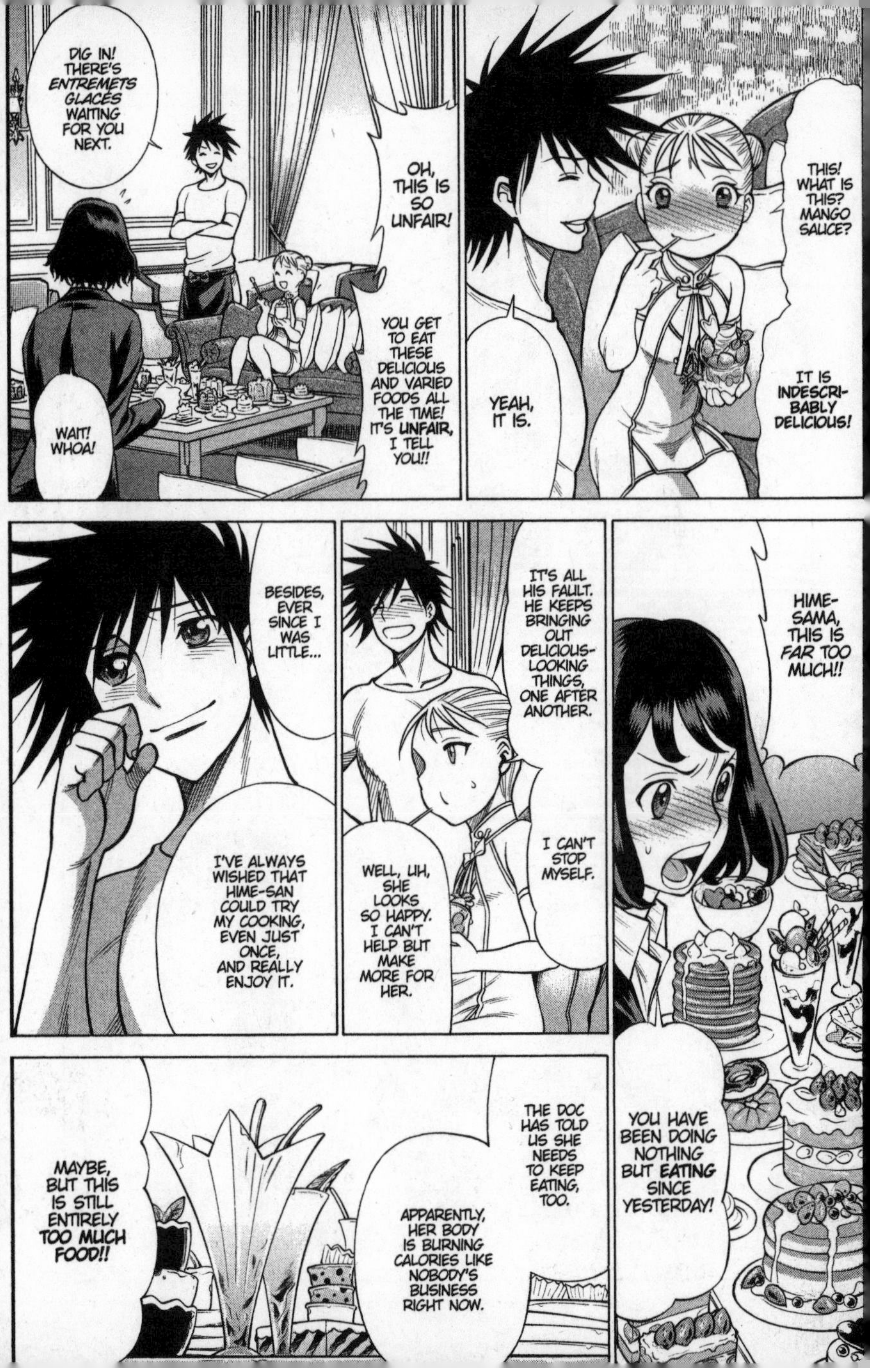
THIS! WHAT IS THIS? MANGO SAUCE?
IT IS INDESCRIBABLY DELICIOUS!
YEAH, IT IS.
OH, THIS IS SO UNFAIR!
YOU GET TO EAT THESE DELICIOUS AND VARIED FOODS ALL THE TIME! IT'S UNFAIR, I TELL YOU!!
DIG IN! THERE'S ENTREMETS GLACÉS WAITING FOR YOU NEXT.
WAIT! WHOA!
HIME-SAMA, THIS IS FAR TOO MUCH!!
YOU HAVE BEEN DOING NOTHING BUT EATING SINCE YESTERDAY!
IT'S ALL HIS FAULT. HE KEEPS BRINGING OUT DELICIOUS-LOOKING THINGS, ONE AFTER ANOTHER.
I CAN'T STOP MYSELF.
WELL, UH, SHE LOOKS SO HAPPY. I CAN'T HELP BUT MAKE MORE FOR HER.
BESIDES, EVER SINCE I WAS LITTLE...
I'VE ALWAYS WISHED THAT HIME-SAN COULD TRY MY COOKING, EVEN JUST ONCE, AND REALLY ENJOY IT.
THE DOC HAS TOLD US SHE NEEDS TO KEEP EATING, TOO.
APPARENTLY, HER BODY IS BURNING CALORIES LIKE NOBODY'S BUSINESS RIGHT NOW.
MAYBE, BUT THIS IS STILL ENTIRELY TOO MUCH FOOD!!

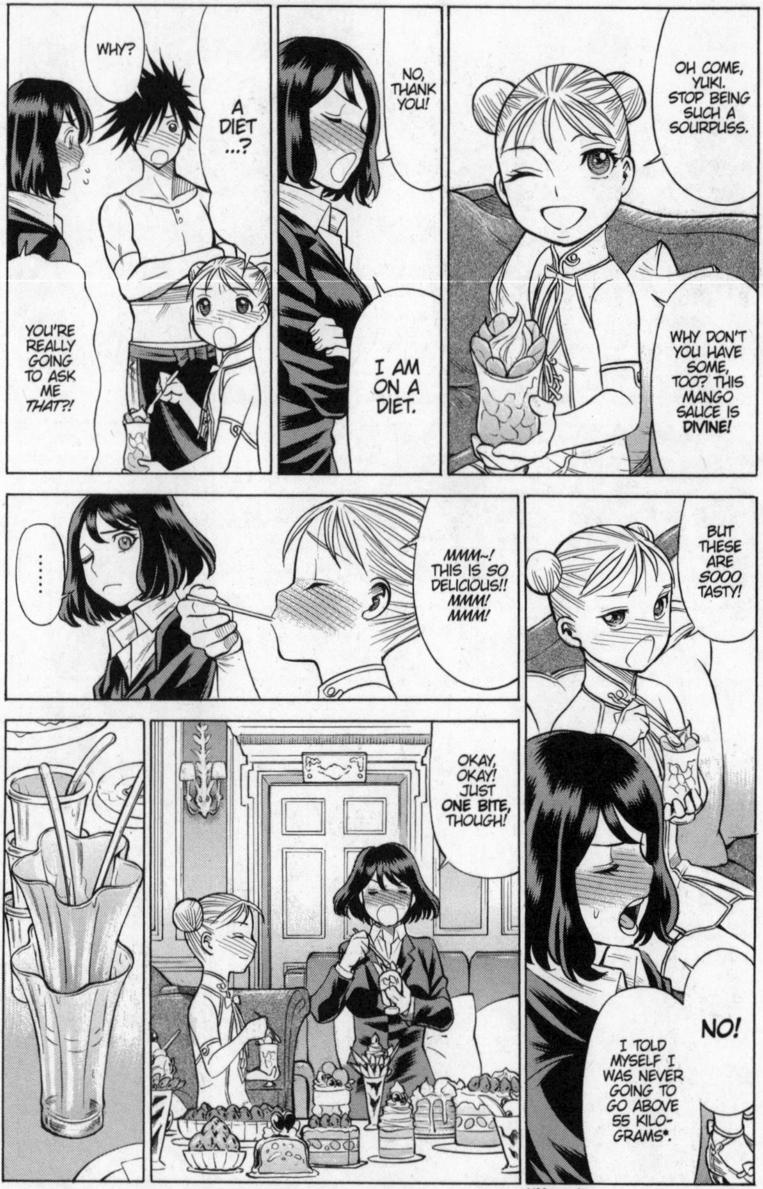
OH COME, YUKI. STOP BEING SUCH A SOURPUSS.
WHY DON'T YOU HAVE SOME, TOO? THIS MANGO SAUCE IS DIVINE!
NO, THANK YOU!
I AM ON A DIET.
WHY?
A DIET ...?
YOU'RE REALLY GOING TO ASK ME THAT?!
BUT THESE ARE SOOO TASTY!
NO!
I TOLD MYSELF I WAS NEVER GOING TO GO ABOVE 55 KILO-GRAMS*.
MMM~! THIS IS SO DELICIOUS!! MMM! MMM!
......
OKAY, OKAY! JUST ONE BITE, THOUGH!

*120 pounds.

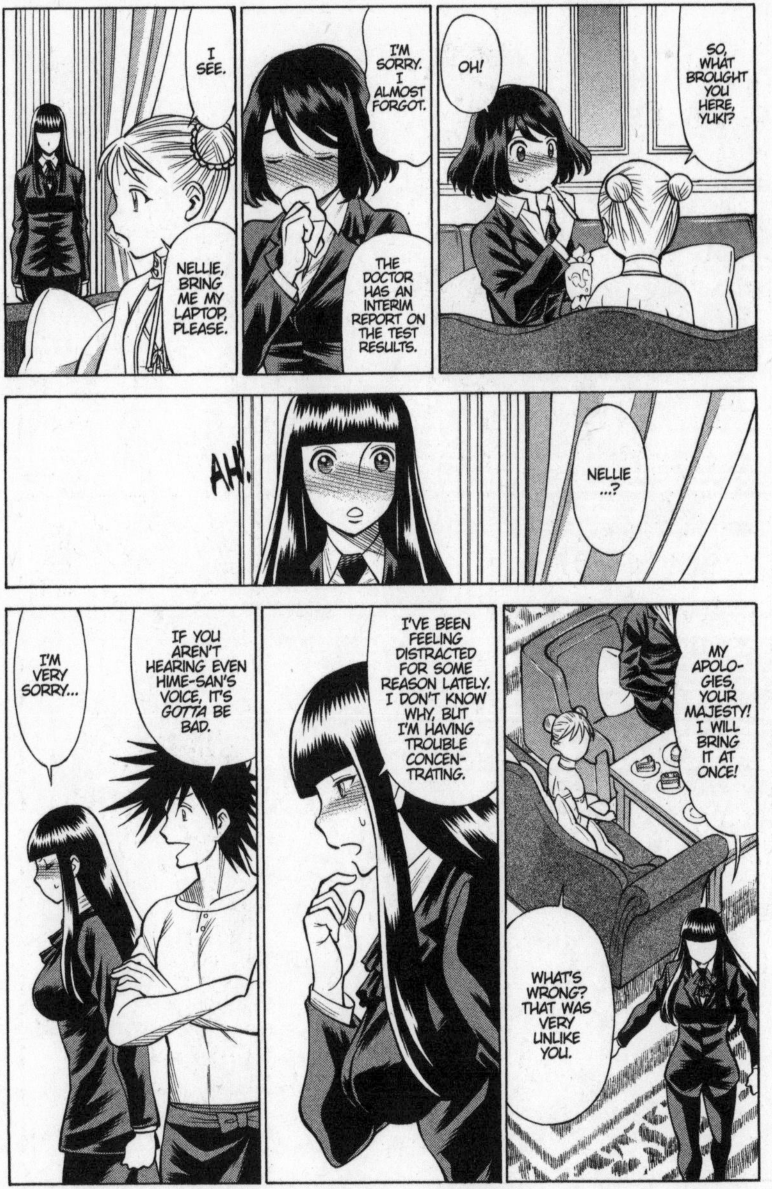
SO, WHAT BROUGHT YOU HERE, YUKI?
OH!
I'M SORRY. I ALMOST FORGOT.
THE DOCTOR HAS AN INTERIM REPORT ON THE TEST RESULTS.
I SEE.
NELLIE, BRING ME MY LAPTOP, PLEASE.
NELLIE ...?
AH!
MY APOLOGIES, YOUR MAJESTY! I WILL BRING IT AT ONCE!
WHAT'S WRONG? THAT WAS VERY UNLIKE YOU.
I'VE BEEN FEELING DISTRACTED FOR SOME REASON LATELY. I DON'T KNOW WHY, BUT I'M HAVING TROUBLE CONCEN-TRATING.
IF YOU AREN'T HEARING EVEN HIME-SAN'S VOICE, IT'S *GOTTA* BE BAD.
I'M VERY SORRY...

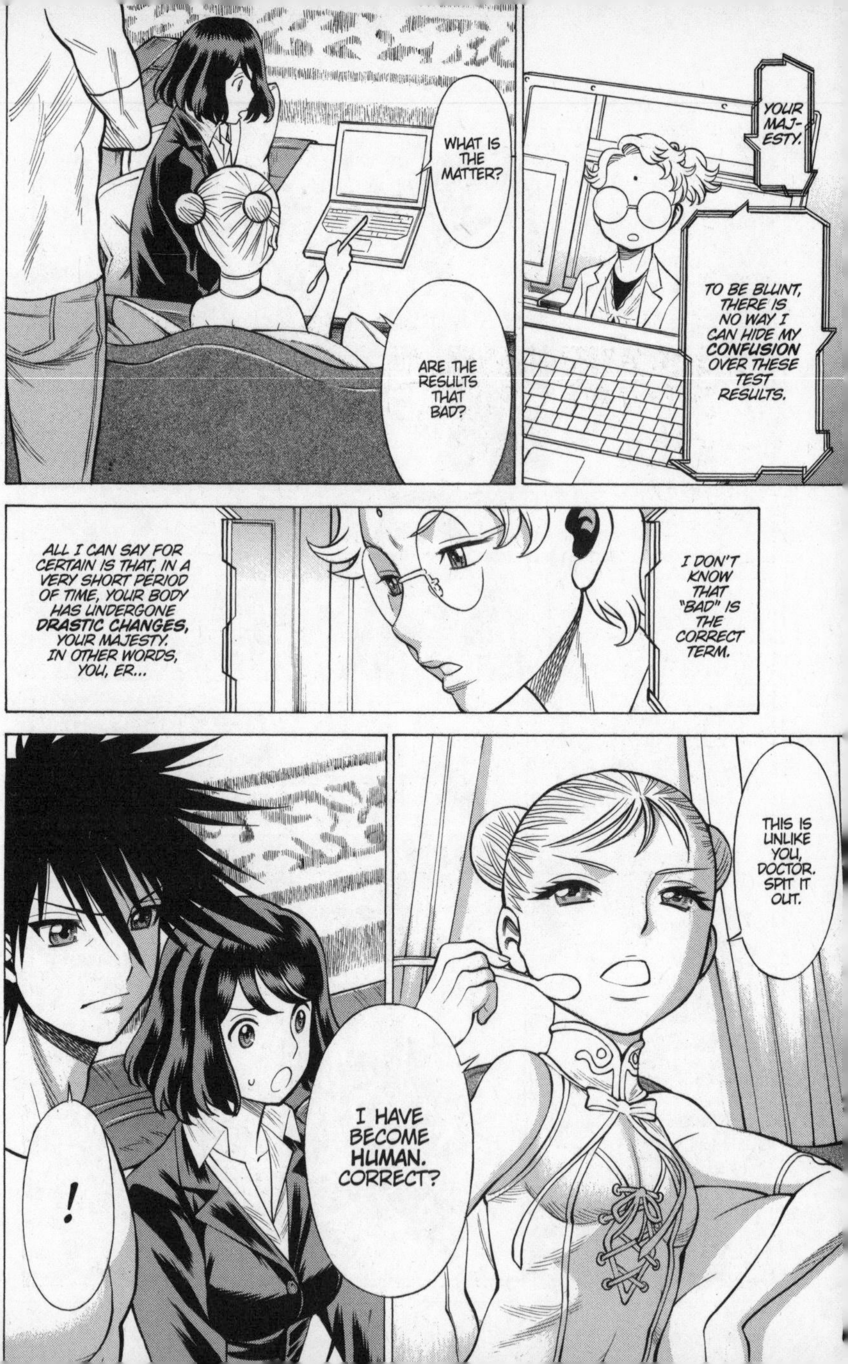

YOUR MAJ-ESTY.
TO BE BLUNT, THERE IS NO WAY I CAN HIDE MY CONFUSION OVER THESE TEST RESULTS.
WHAT IS THE MATTER?
ARE THE RESULTS THAT BAD?
I DON'T KNOW THAT "BAD" IS THE CORRECT TERM.
ALL I CAN SAY FOR CERTAIN IS THAT, IN A VERY SHORT PERIOD OF TIME, YOUR BODY HAS UNDERGONE DRASTIC CHANGES, YOUR MAJESTY. IN OTHER WORDS, YOU, ER...
THIS IS UNLIKE YOU, DOCTOR. SPIT IT OUT.
I HAVE BECOME HUMAN. CORRECT?
!

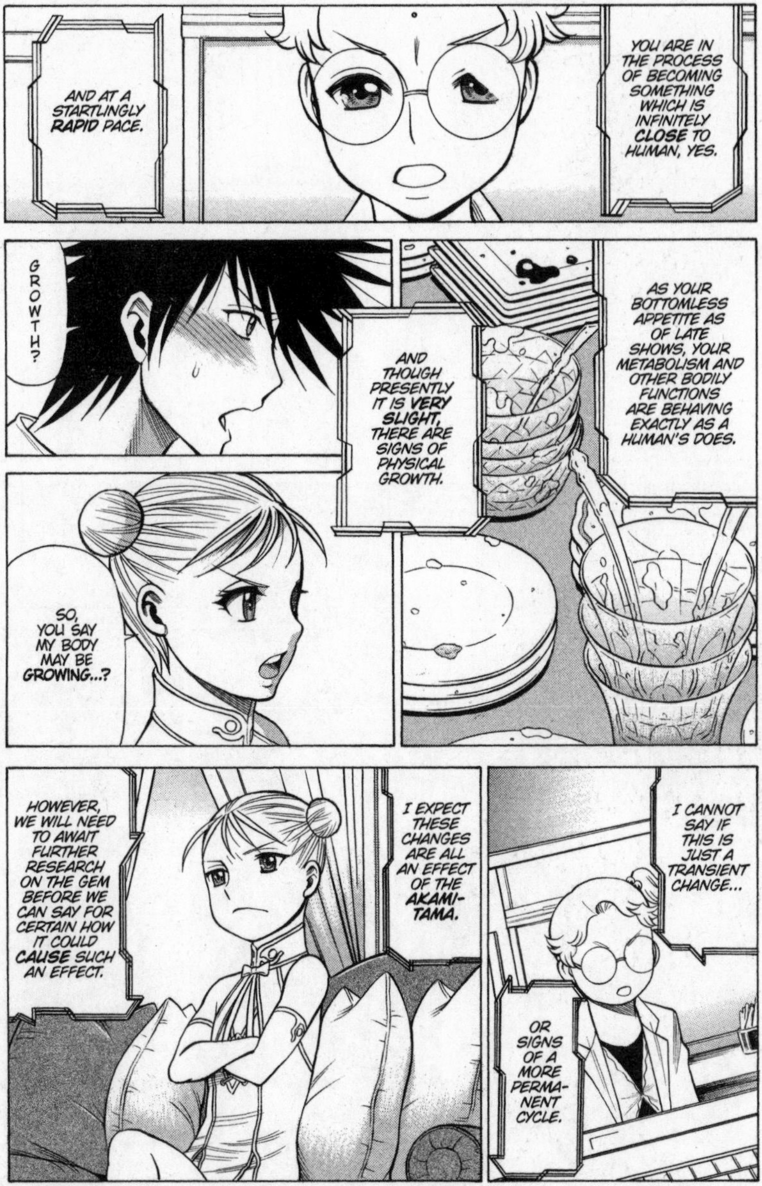

YOU ARE IN THE PROCESS OF BECOMING SOMETHING WHICH IS INFINITELY CLOSE TO HUMAN, YES.
AND AT A STARTLINGLY RAPID PACE.
AS YOUR BOTTOMLESS APPETITE AS OF LATE SHOWS, YOUR METABOLISM AND OTHER BODILY FUNCTIONS ARE BEHAVING EXACTLY AS A HUMAN'S DOES.
AND THOUGH PRESENTLY IT IS VERY SLIGHT, THERE ARE SIGNS OF PHYSICAL GROWTH.
GROWTH?
SO, YOU SAY MY BODY MAY BE GROWING...?
I CANNOT SAY IF THIS IS JUST A TRANSIENT CHANGE...
OR SIGNS OF A MORE PERMANENT CYCLE.
I EXPECT THESE CHANGES ARE ALL AN EFFECT OF THE AKAMITAMA.
HOWEVER, WE WILL NEED TO AWAIT FURTHER RESEARCH ON THE GEM BEFORE WE CAN SAY FOR CERTAIN HOW IT COULD CAUSE SUCH AN EFFECT.

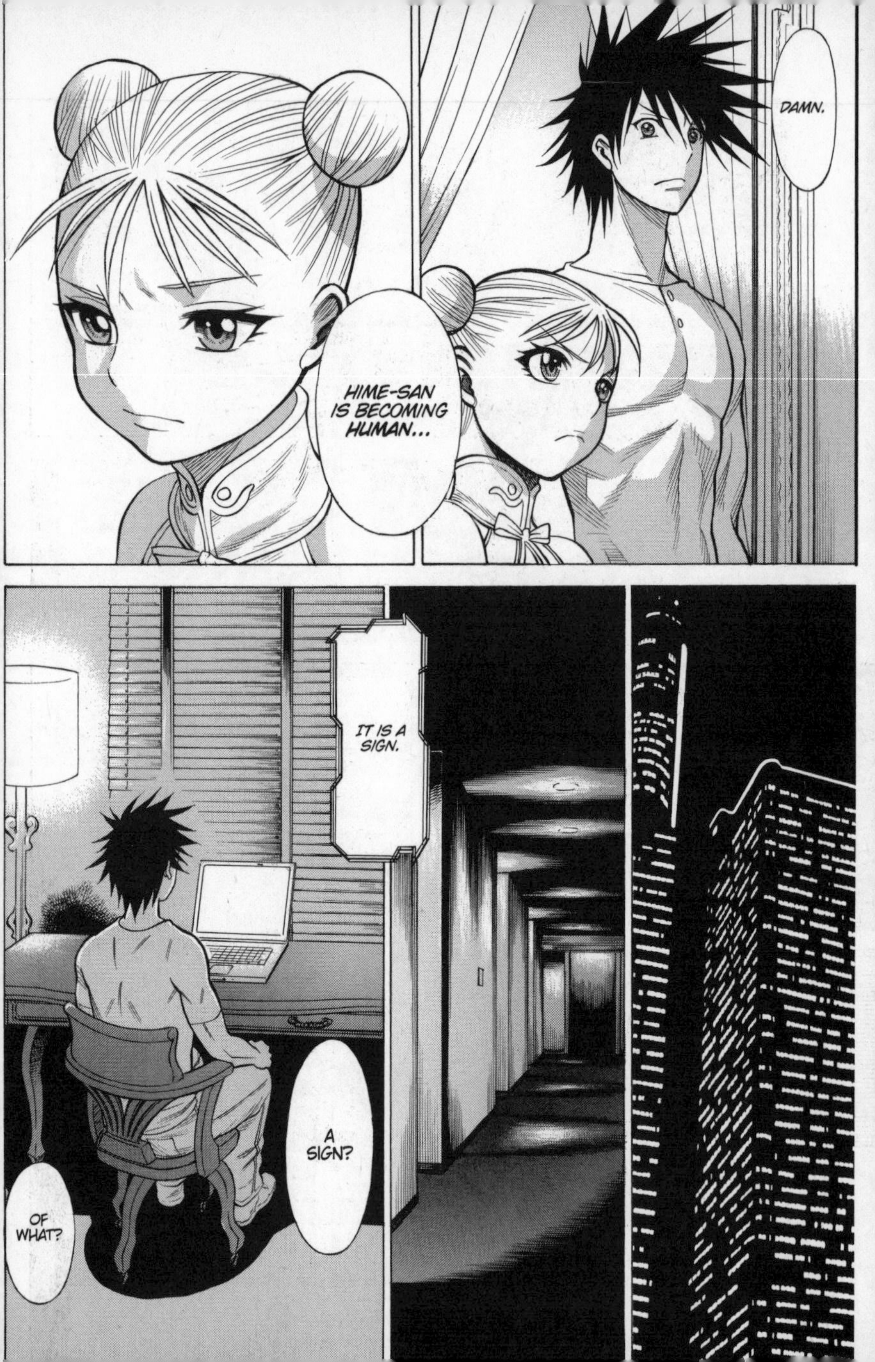
DAMN.
HIME-SAN IS BECOMING HUMAN...
IT IS A SIGN.
A SIGN?
OF WHAT?

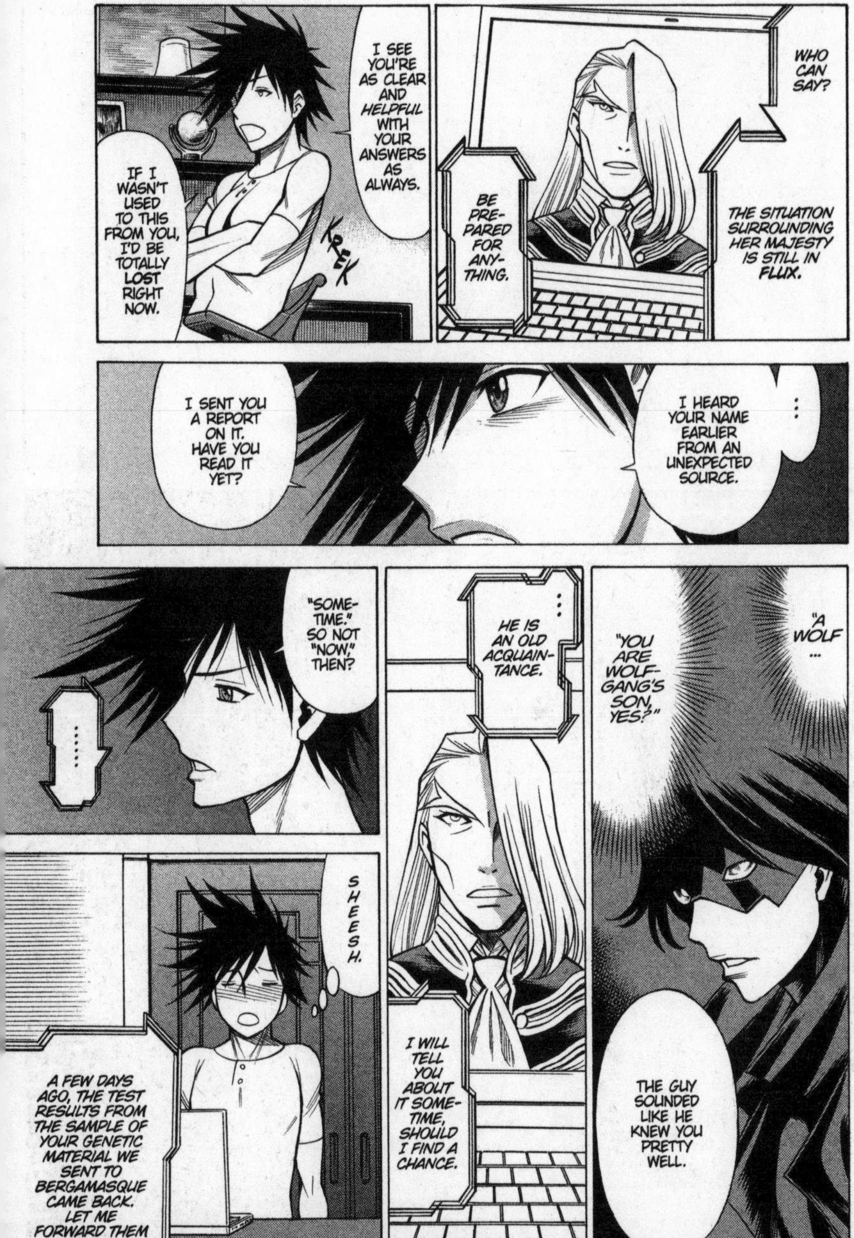
WHO CAN SAY?
THE SITUATION SURROUNDING HER MAJESTY IS STILL IN FLUX.
BE PRE-PARED FOR ANY-THING.
I SEE YOU'RE AS CLEAR AND HELPFUL WITH YOUR ANSWERS AS ALWAYS.
KREEK
IF I WASN'T USED TO THIS FROM YOU, I'D BE TOTALLY LOST RIGHT NOW.
...
I HEARD YOUR NAME EARLIER FROM AN UNEXPECTED SOURCE.
I SENT YOU A REPORT ON IT. HAVE YOU READ IT YET?
"A WOLF ...
"YOU ARE WOLF-GANG'S SON, YES?"
THE GUY SOUNDED LIKE HE KNEW YOU PRETTY WELL.
...
HE IS AN OLD ACQUAIN-TANCE.
I WILL TELL YOU ABOUT IT SOME-TIME, SHOULD I FIND A CHANCE.
"SOME-TIME." SO NOT "NOW," THEN?
......
SHEESH.
A FEW DAYS AGO, THE TEST RESULTS FROM THE SAMPLE OF YOUR GENETIC MATERIAL WE SENT TO BERGAMASQUE CAME BACK. LET ME FORWARD THEM TO YOU.

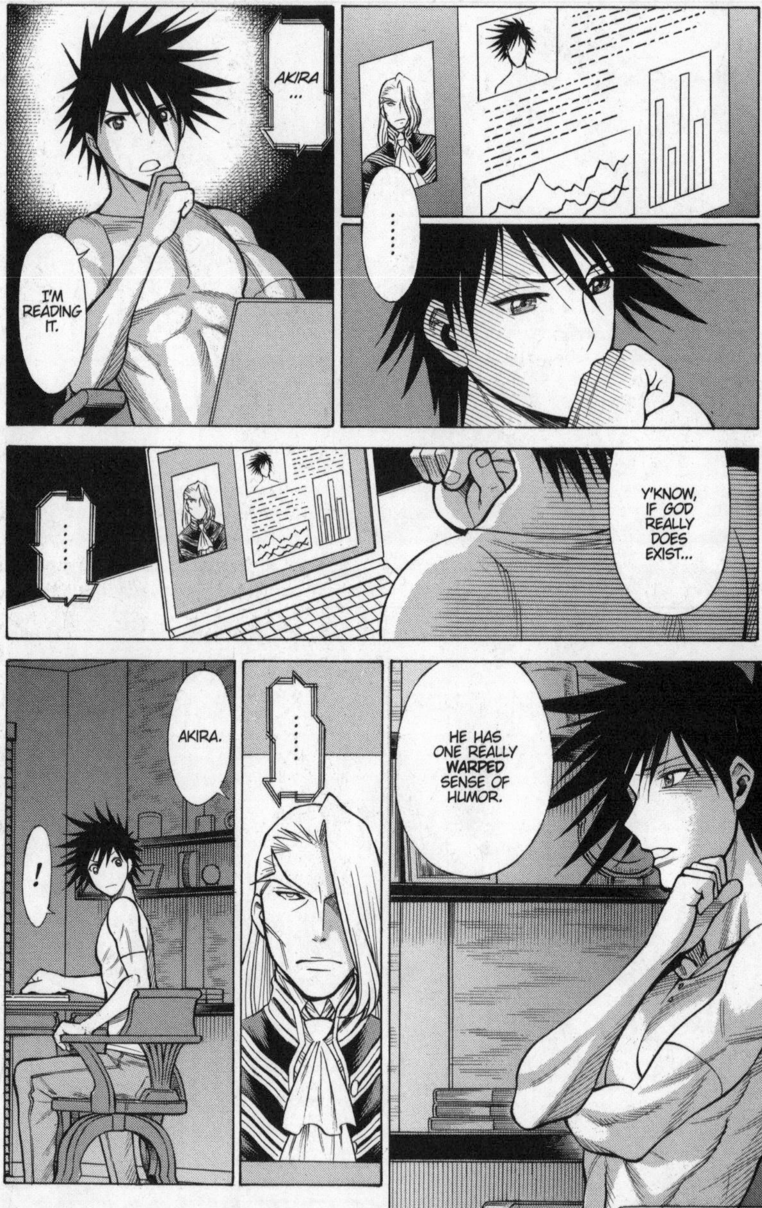
......
AKIRA ...
I'M READING IT.
Y'KNOW, IF GOD REALLY DOES EXIST...
......
HE HAS ONE REALLY **WARPED** SENSE OF HUMOR.
......
AKIRA.
!

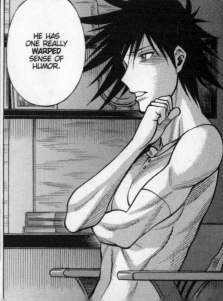

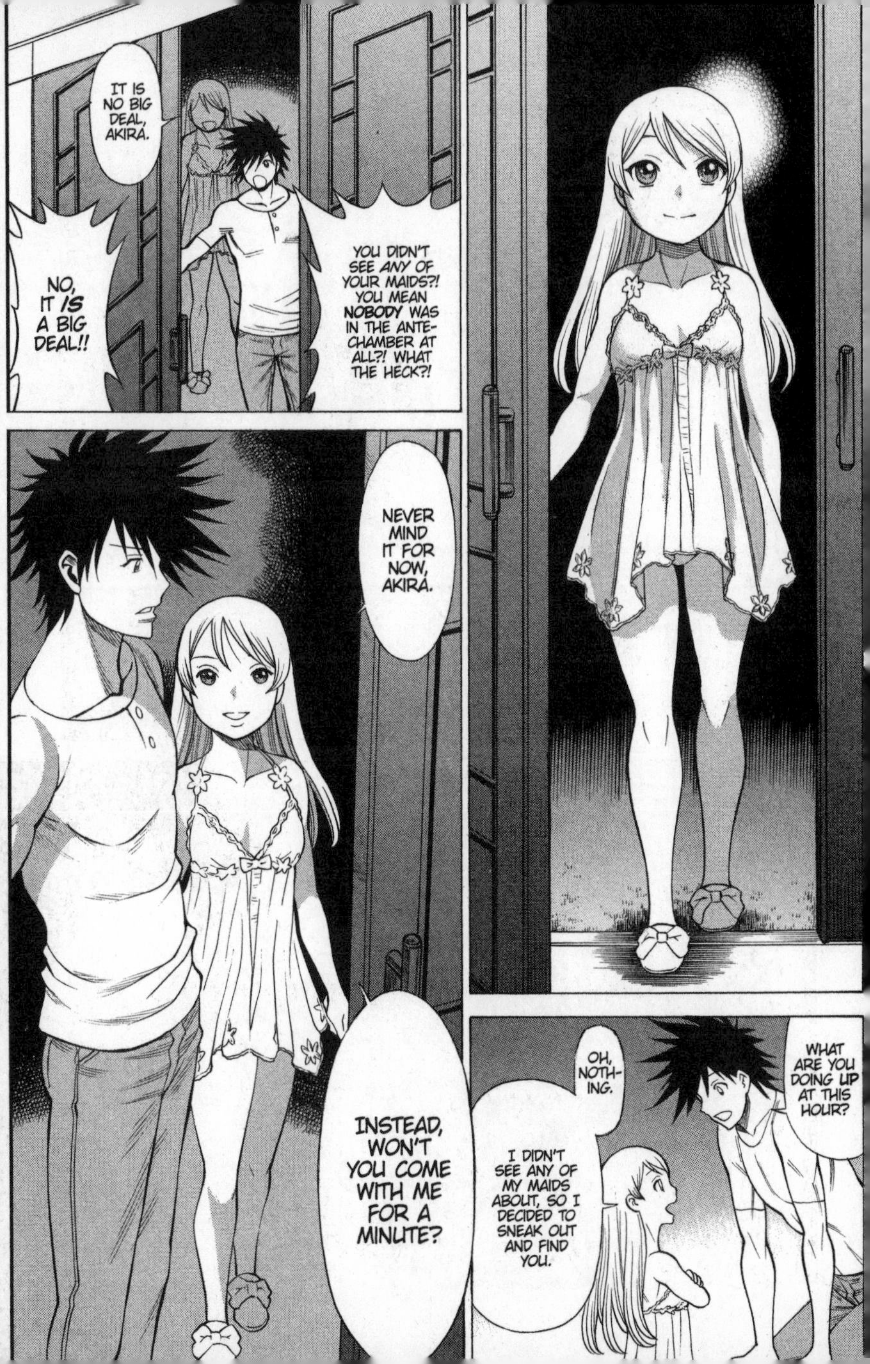
WHAT ARE YOU DOING UP AT THIS HOUR?
OH, NOTHING.
I DIDN'T SEE ANY OF MY MAIDS ABOUT, SO I DECIDED TO SNEAK OUT AND FIND YOU.
YOU DIDN'T SEE *ANY* OF YOUR MAIDS?! YOU MEAN **NOBODY** WAS IN THE ANTE-CHAMBER AT ALL?! WHAT THE HECK?!
IT IS NO BIG DEAL, AKIRA.
NO, IT ***IS*** A BIG DEAL!!
NEVER MIND IT FOR NOW, AKIRA.
INSTEAD, WON'T YOU COME WITH ME FOR A MINUTE?

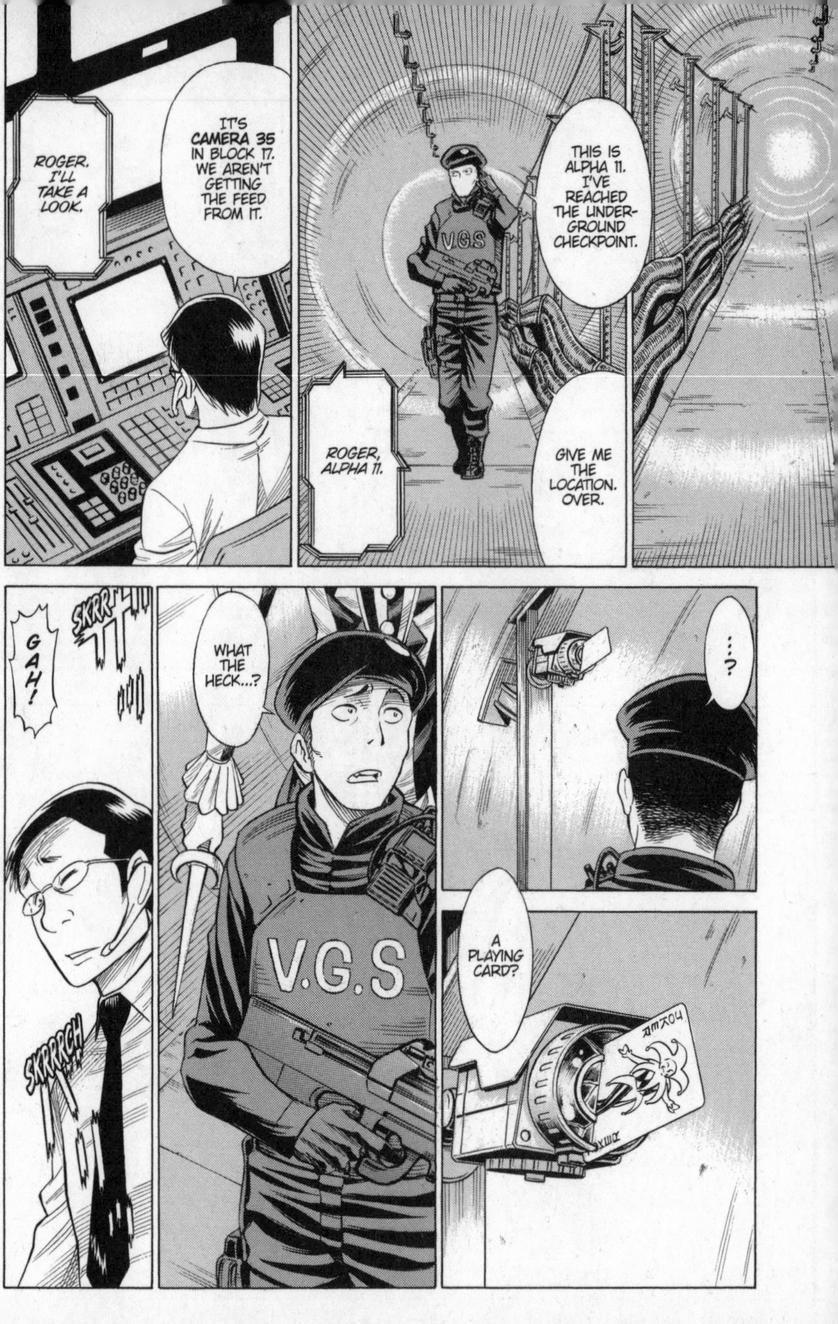
THIS IS ALPHA 11. I'VE REACHED THE UNDERGROUND CHECKPOINT.
GIVE ME THE LOCATION. OVER.
ROGER, ALPHA 11.
IT'S CAMERA 35 IN BLOCK 17. WE AREN'T GETTING THE FEED FROM IT.
ROGER. I'LL TAKE A LOOK.
...?
A PLAYING CARD?
WHAT THE HECK...?
SKRR
GAH!
SKRRRCH

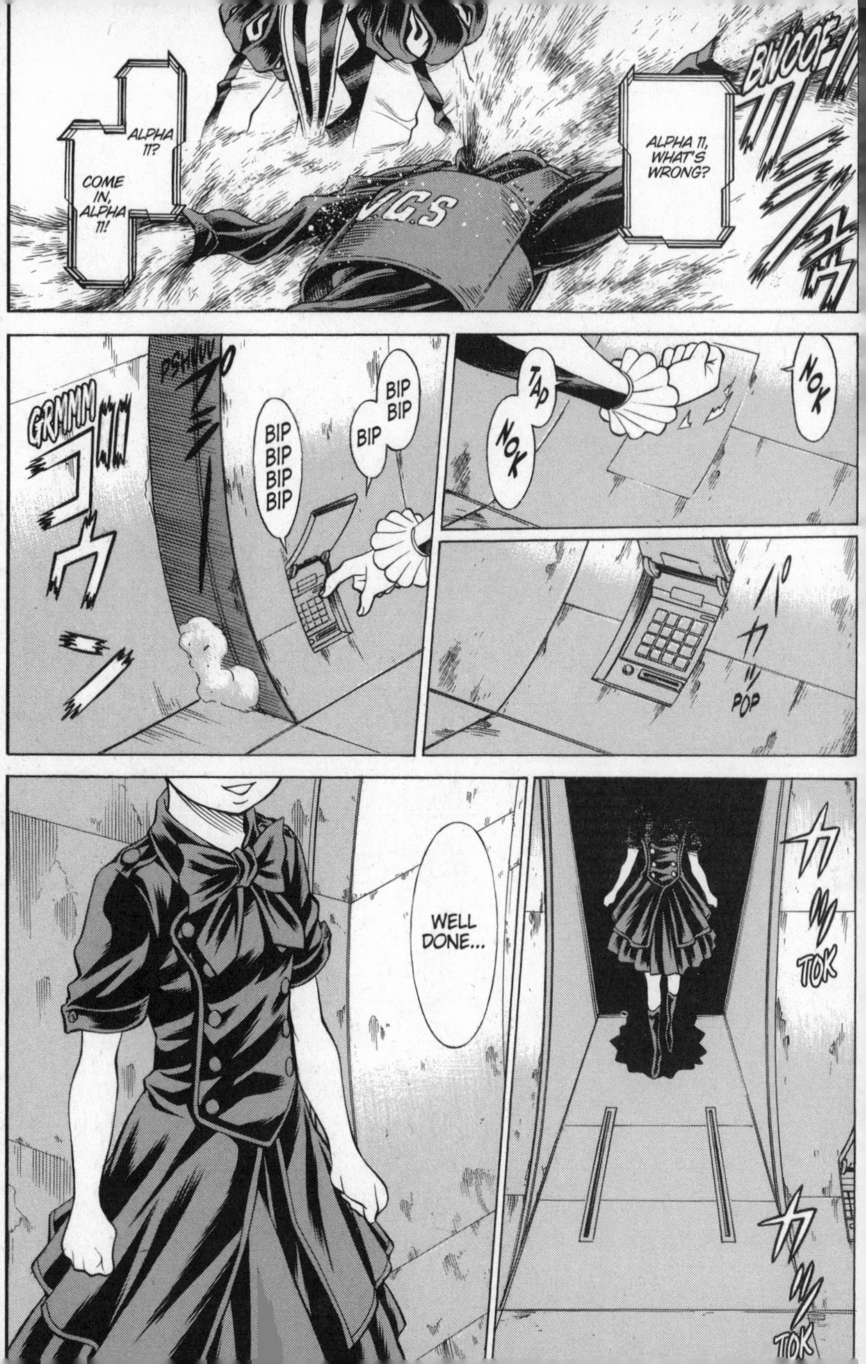
BWOOF!!
ALPHA 11, WHAT'S WRONG?
ALPHA 11?
COME IN, ALPHA 11!
NOK
TAP
NOK
POP
BIP BIP BIP
BIP BIP BIP BIP
PSHUUU
GRMMM
TOK
TOK
WELL DONE...

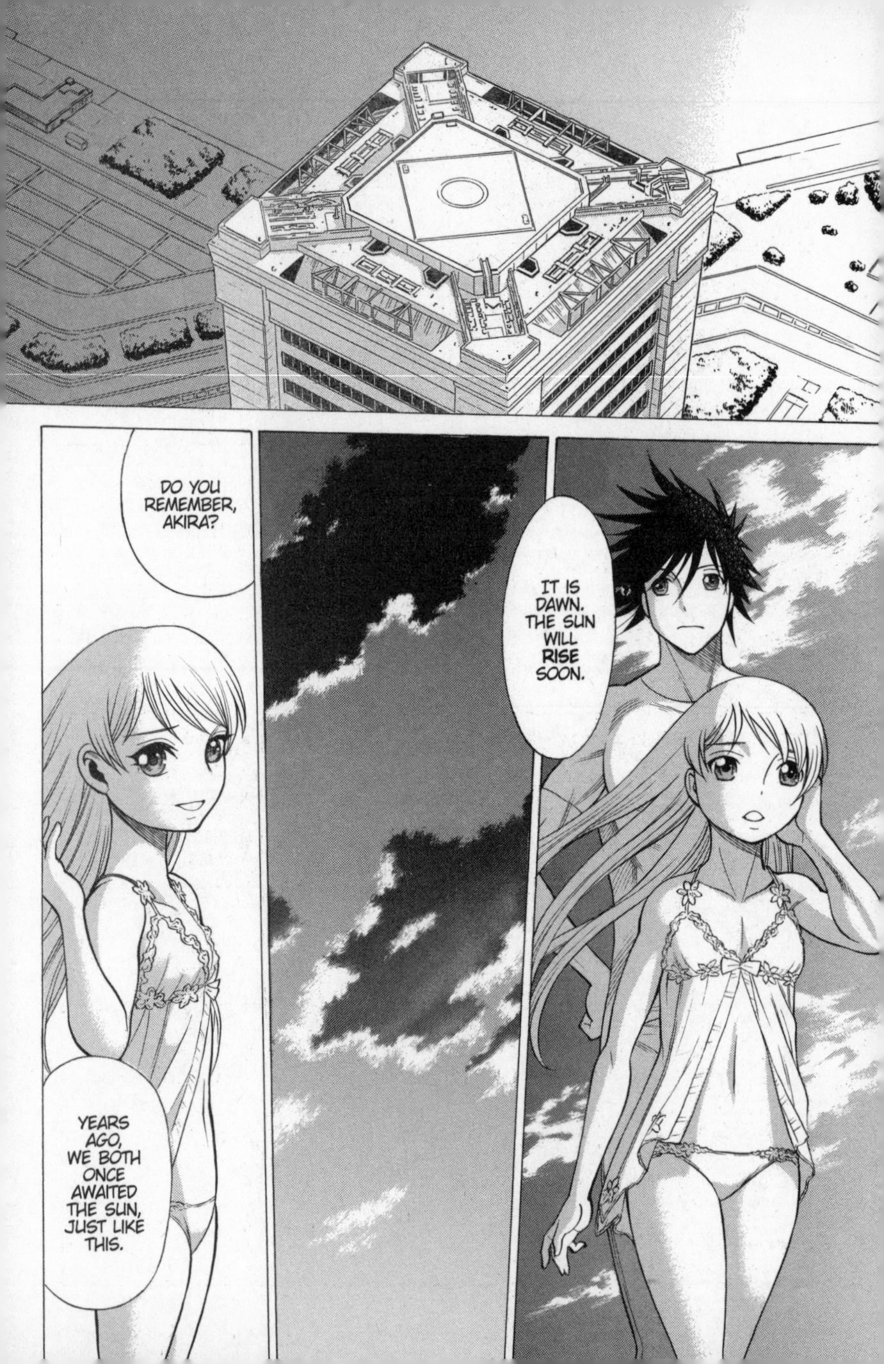
IT IS DAWN. THE SUN WILL RISE SOON.
DO YOU REMEMBER, AKIRA?
YEARS AGO, WE BOTH ONCE AWAITED THE SUN, JUST LIKE THIS.

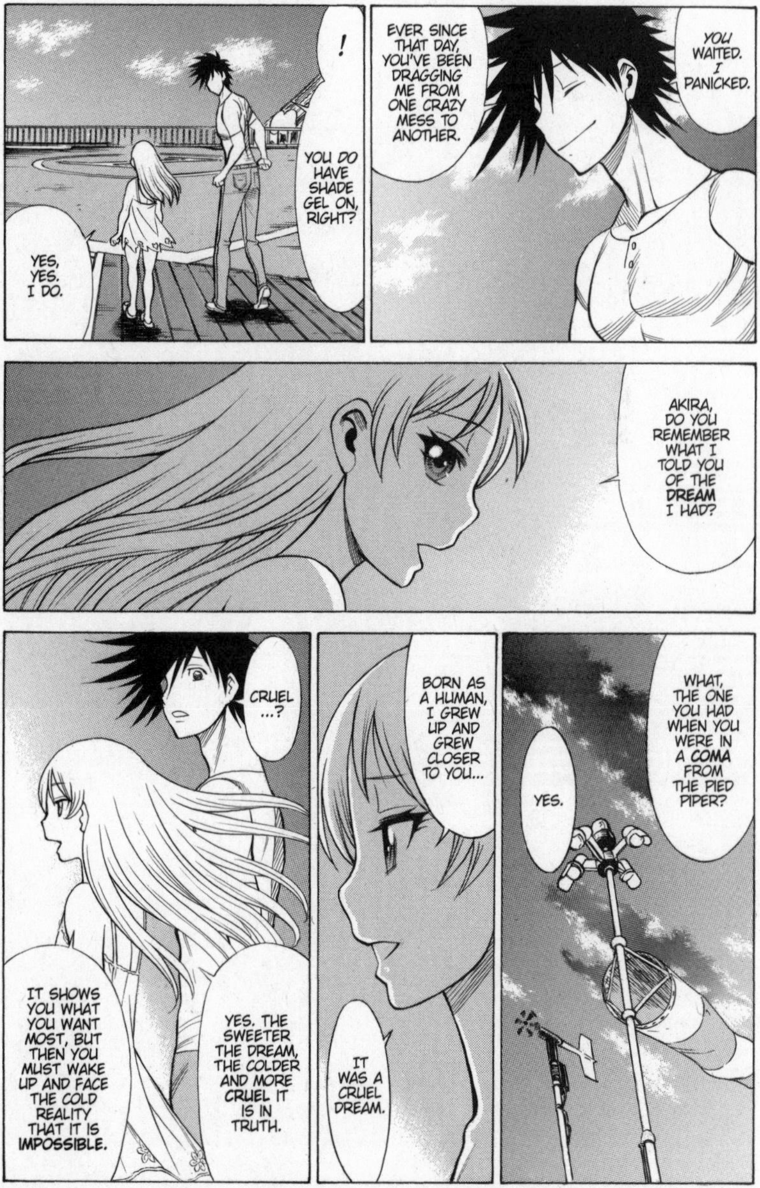
YOU WAITED. I PANICKED.
EVER SINCE THAT DAY, YOU'VE BEEN DRAGGING ME FROM ONE CRAZY MESS TO ANOTHER.
!
YOU DO HAVE SHADE GEL ON, RIGHT?
YES, YES. I DO.
AKIRA, DO YOU REMEMBER WHAT I TOLD YOU OF THE DREAM I HAD?
WHAT, THE ONE YOU HAD WHEN YOU WERE IN A COMA FROM THE PIED PIPER?
YES.
BORN AS A HUMAN, I GREW UP AND GREW CLOSER TO YOU...
IT WAS A CRUEL DREAM.
CRUEL ...?
YES. THE SWEETER THE DREAM, THE COLDER AND MORE CRUEL IT IS IN TRUTH.
IT SHOWS YOU WHAT YOU WANT MOST, BUT THEN YOU MUST WAKE UP AND FACE THE COLD REALITY THAT IT IS IMPOSSIBLE.

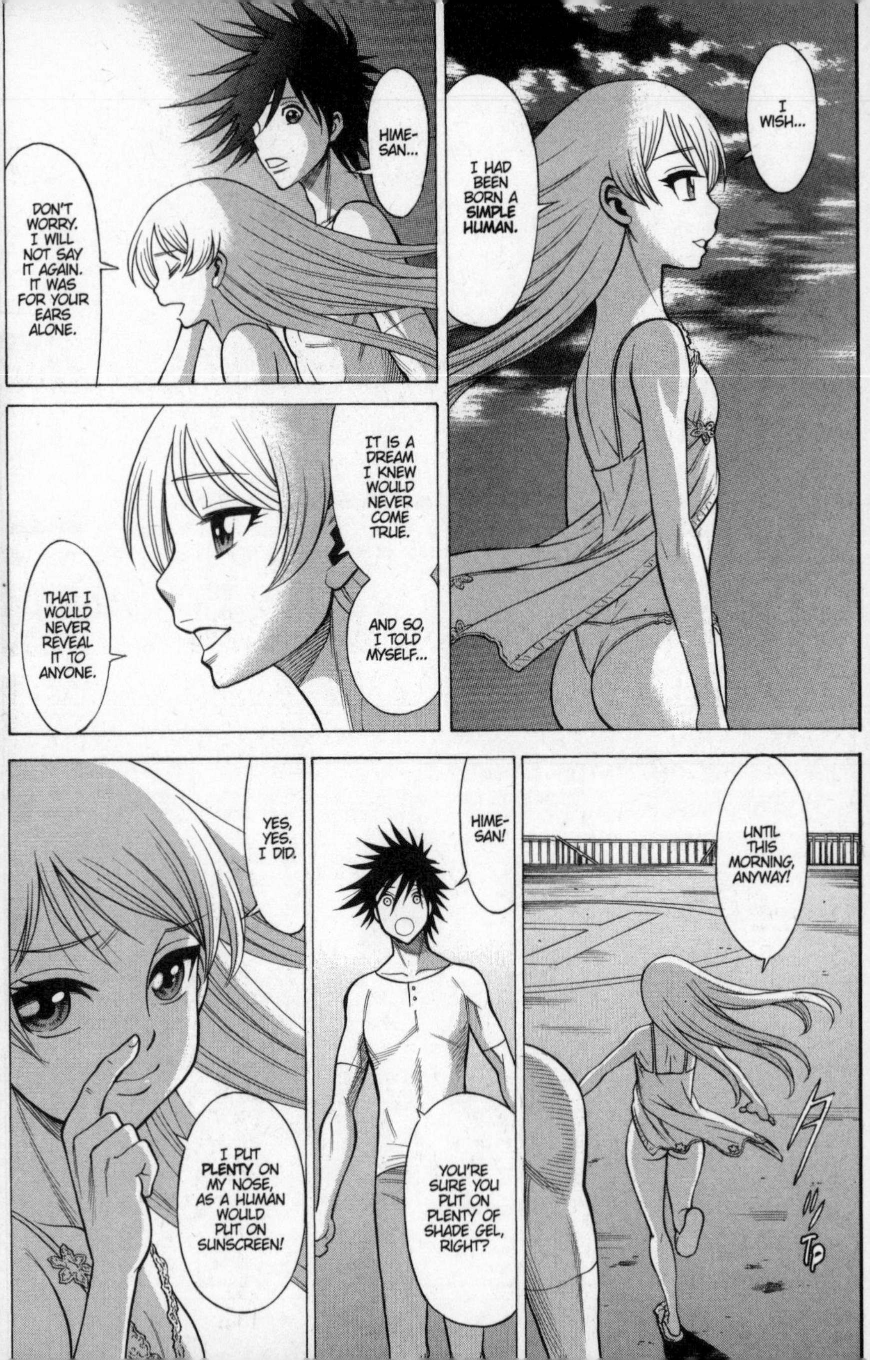
I WISH...
I HAD BEEN BORN A **SIMPLE HUMAN.**
HIME-SAN...
DON'T WORRY. I WILL NOT SAY IT AGAIN. IT WAS FOR YOUR EARS ALONE.
IT IS A DREAM I KNEW WOULD NEVER COME TRUE.
AND SO, I TOLD MYSELF...
THAT I WOULD NEVER REVEAL IT TO ANYONE.
UNTIL THIS MORNING, ANYWAY!
TP
HIME-SAN!
YOU'RE SURE YOU PUT ON PLENTY OF SHADE GEL, RIGHT?
YES, YES. I DID.
I PUT **PLENTY** ON MY NOSE, AS A HUMAN WOULD PUT ON SUNSCREEN!

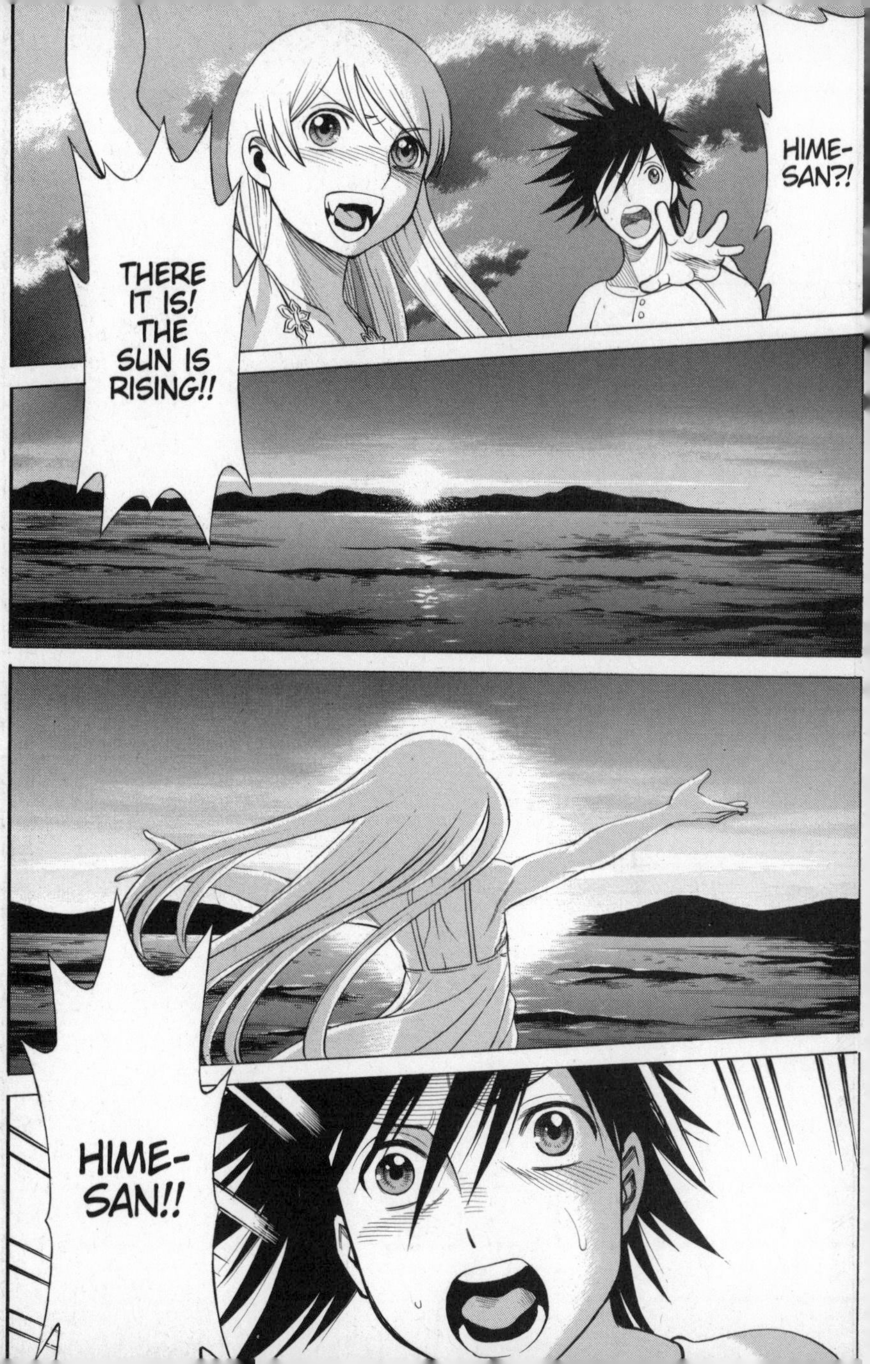
HIME-SAN?!
THERE IT IS! THE SUN IS RISING!!
HIME-SAN!!

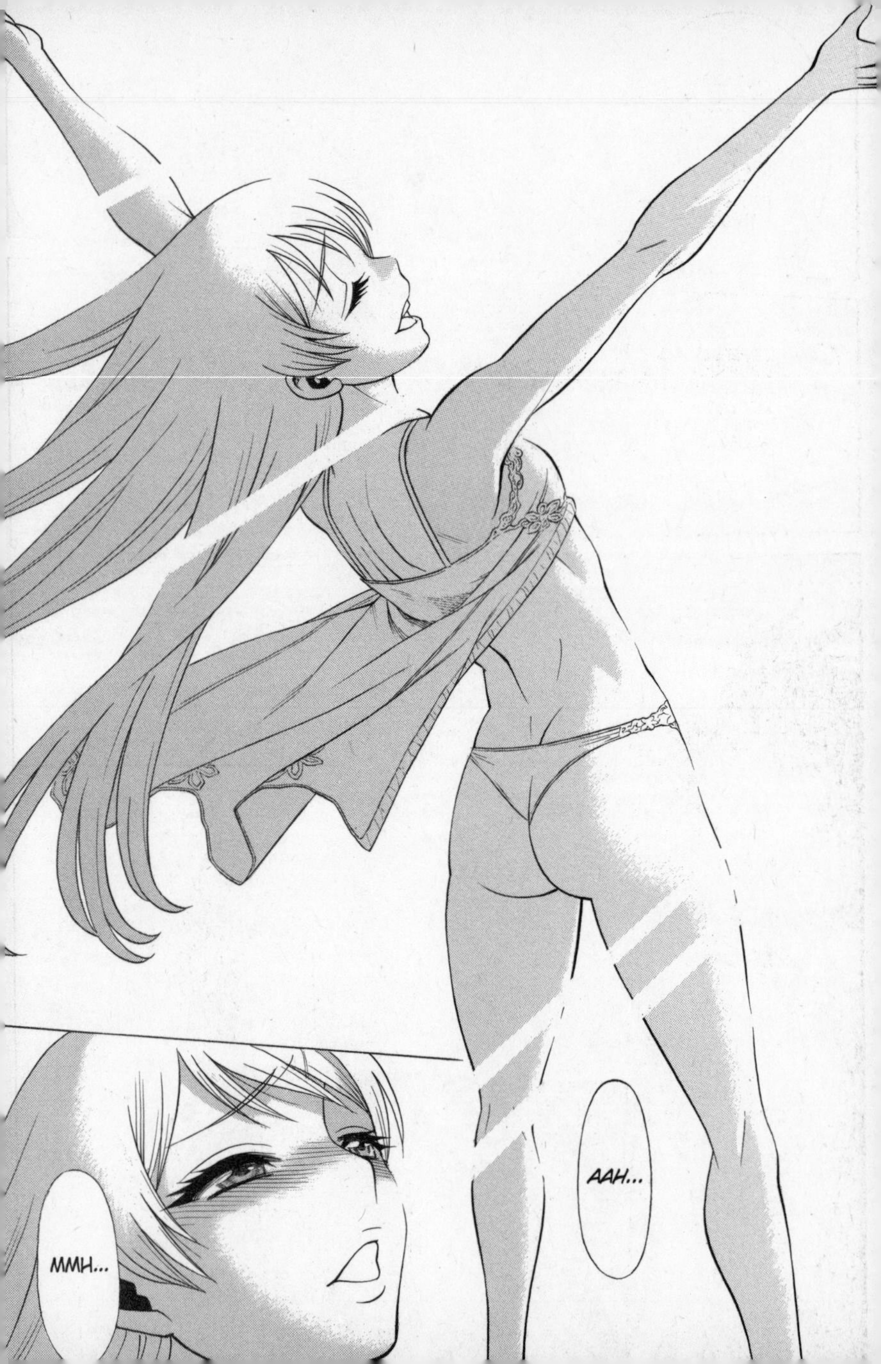
AAH...
MMH...

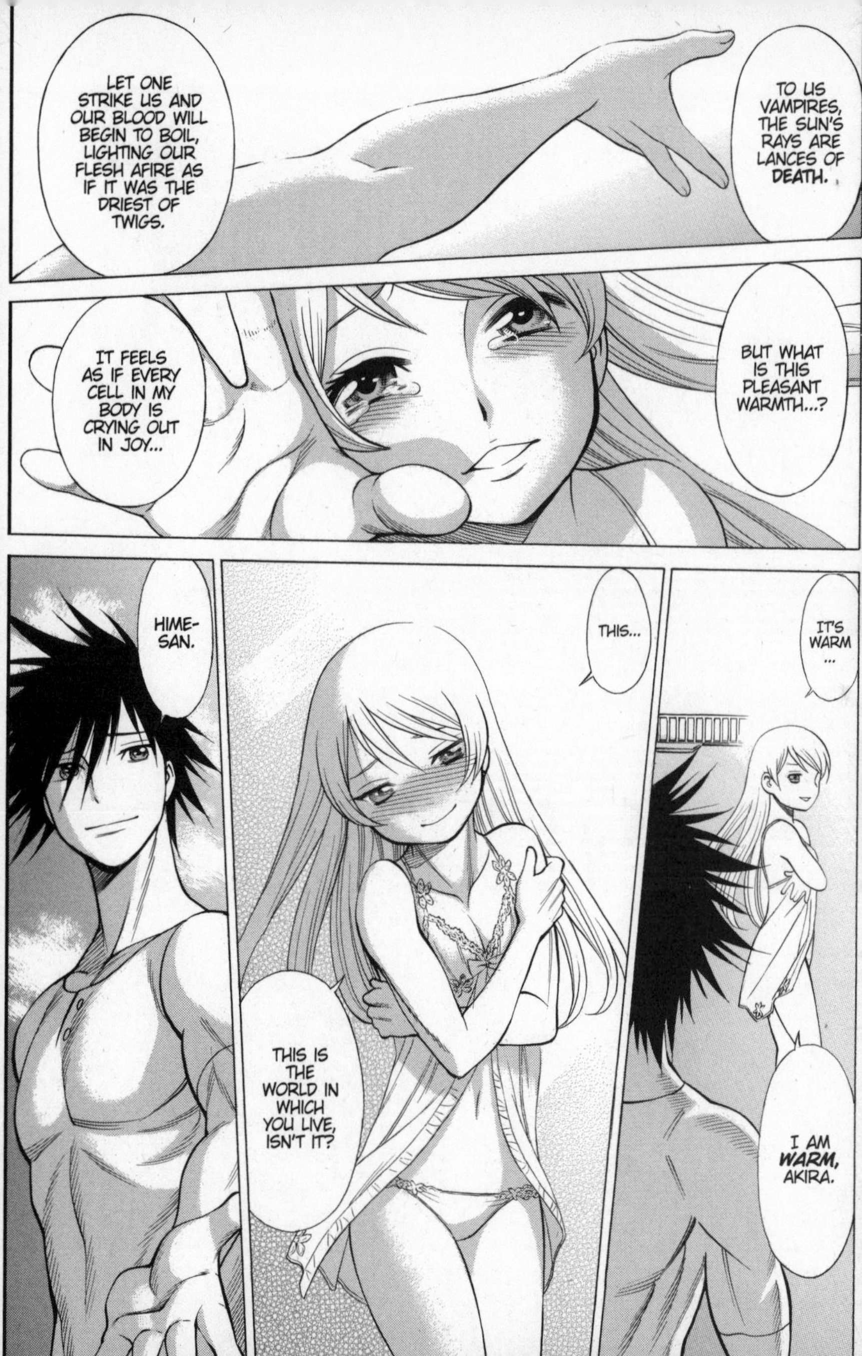
TO US VAMPIRES, THE SUN'S RAYS ARE LANCES OF DEATH.
LET ONE STRIKE US AND OUR BLOOD WILL BEGIN TO BOIL, LIGHTING OUR FLESH AFIRE AS IF IT WAS THE DRIEST OF TWIGS.
BUT WHAT IS THIS PLEASANT WARMTH...?
IT FEELS AS IF EVERY CELL IN MY BODY IS CRYING OUT IN JOY...
IT'S WARM ...
I AM WARM, AKIRA.
THIS...
THIS IS THE WORLD IN WHICH YOU LIVE, ISN'T IT?
HIME-SAN.

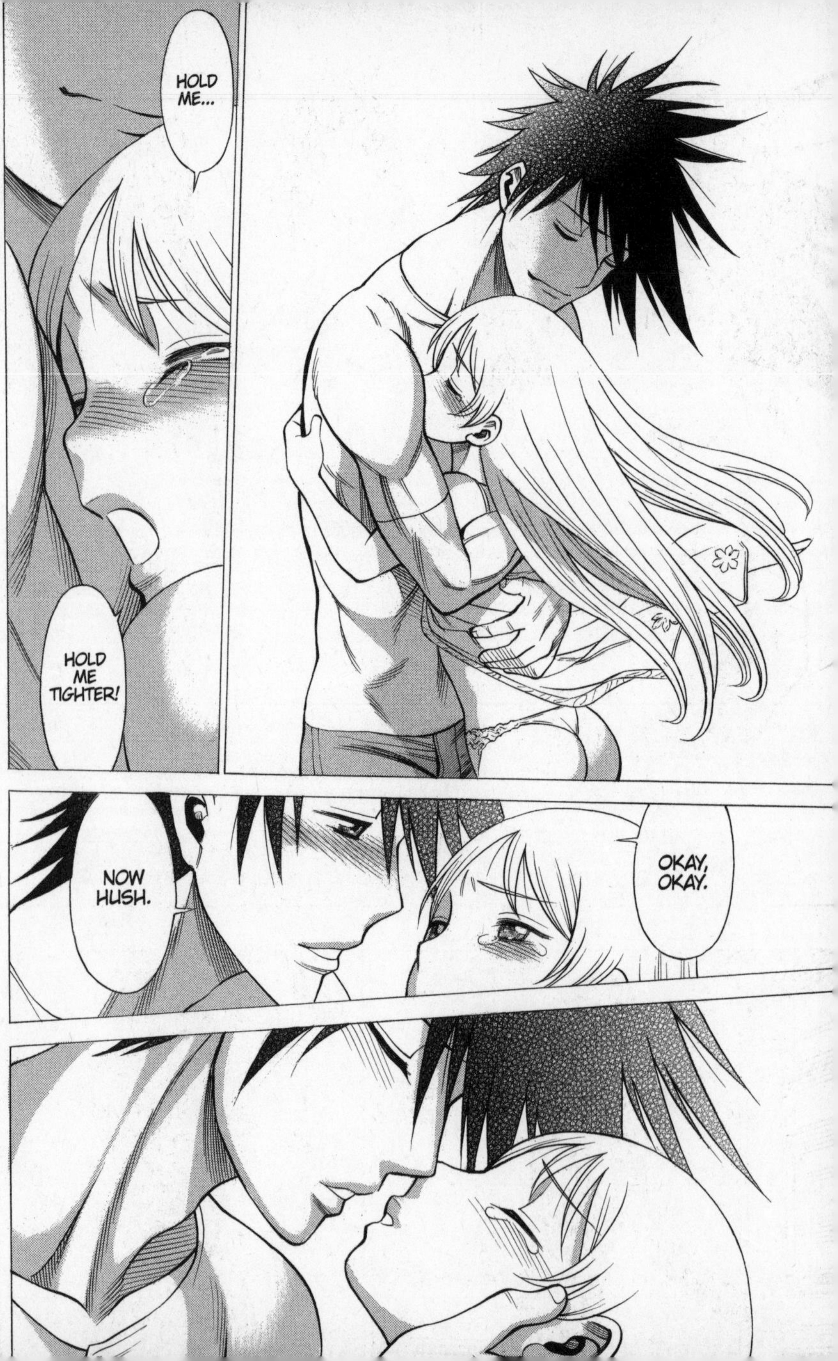
HOLD ME...
HOLD ME TIGHTER!
OKAY, OKAY.
NOW HUSH.

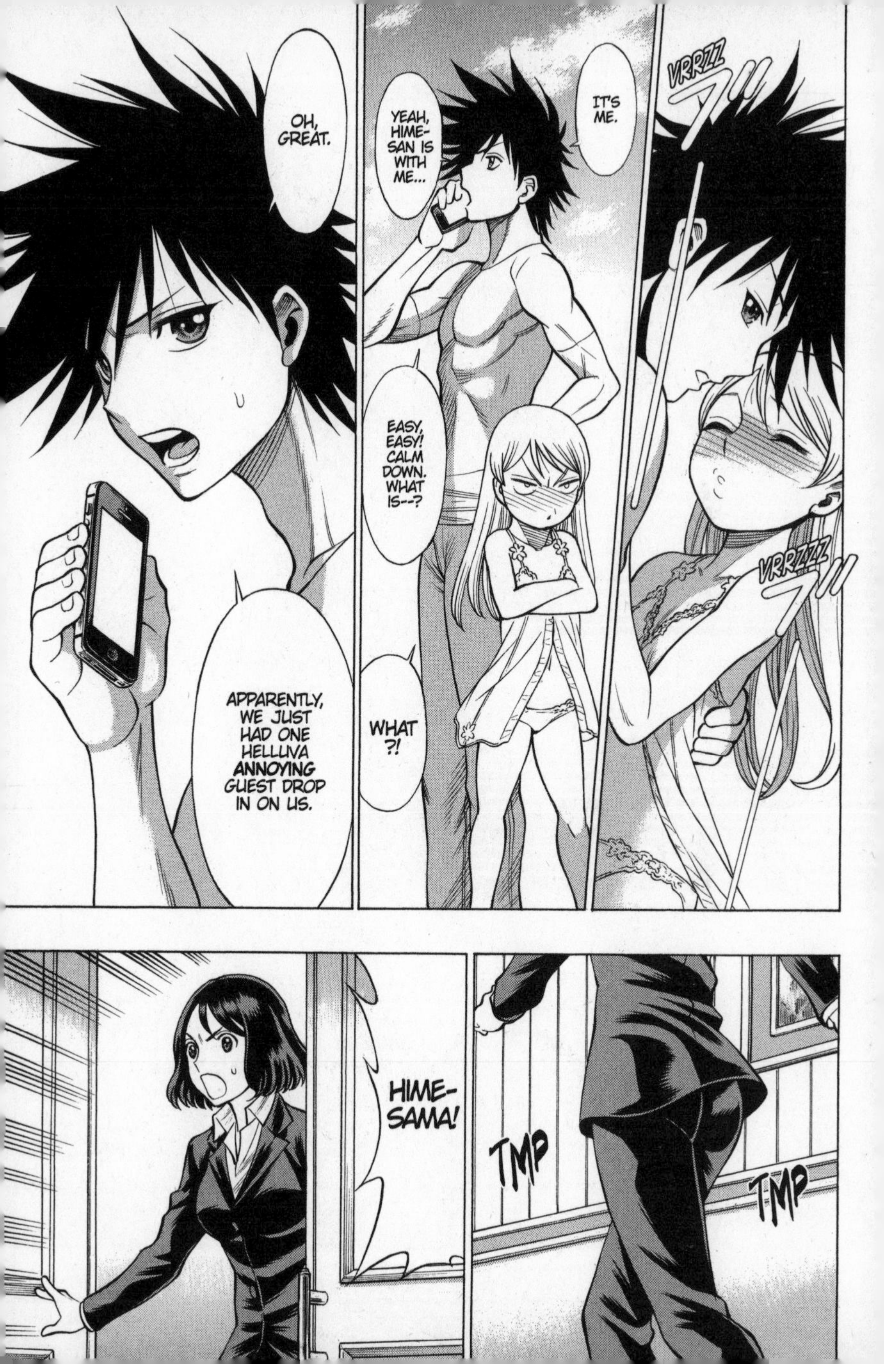
VRRZZ
VRRZZZ
IT'S ME.
YEAH, HIME-SAN IS WITH ME...
EASY, EASY! CALM DOWN. WHAT IS--?
WHAT ?!
OH, GREAT.
APPARENTLY, WE JUST HAD ONE HELLUVA ANNOYING GUEST DROP IN ON US.
TMP
TMP
HIME-SAMA!

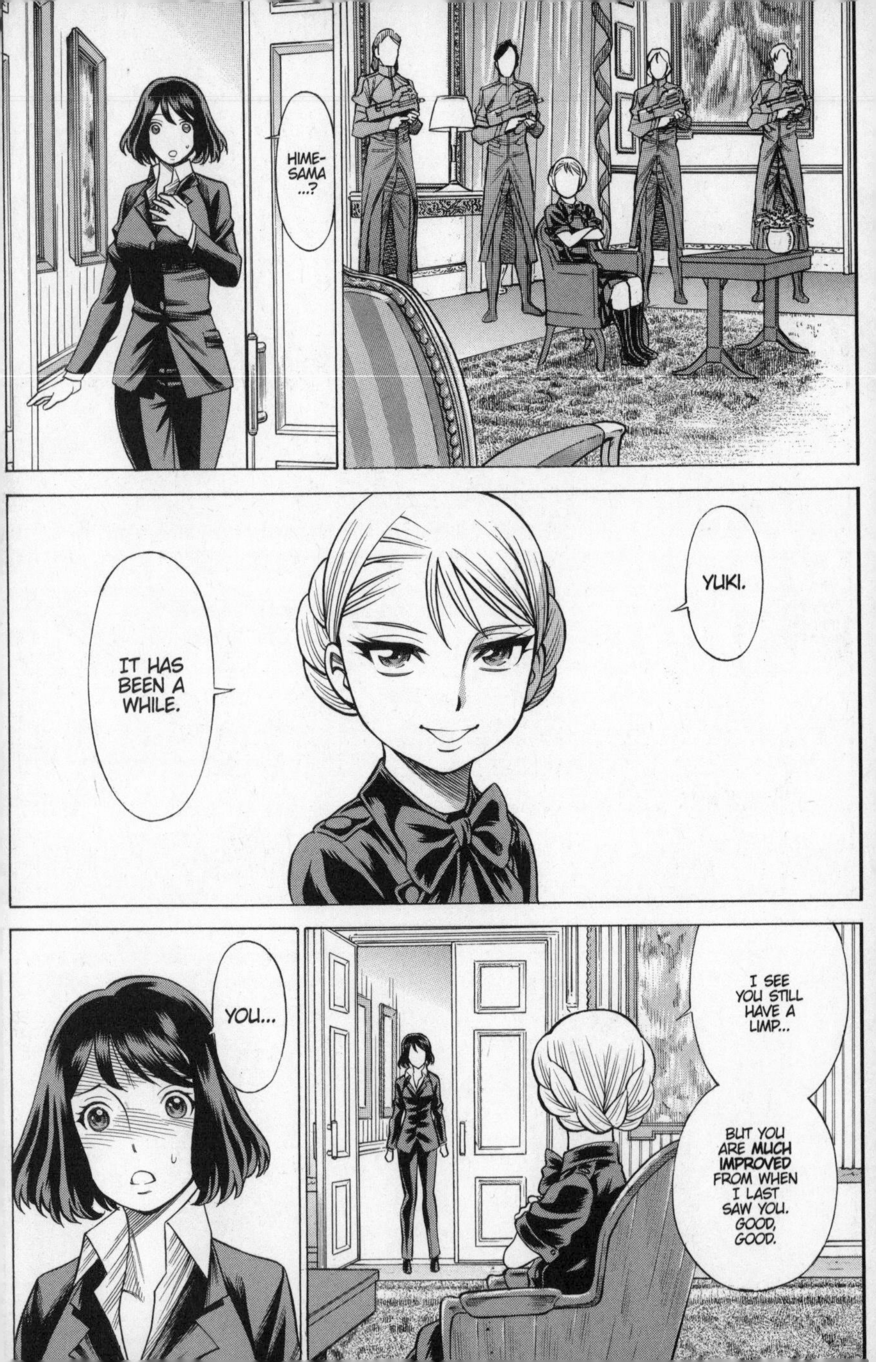
HIME-SAMA...?
YUKI.
IT HAS BEEN A WHILE.
I SEE YOU STILL HAVE A LIMP...
BUT YOU ARE MUCH IMPROVED FROM WHEN I LAST SAW YOU. GOOD, GOOD.
YOU...

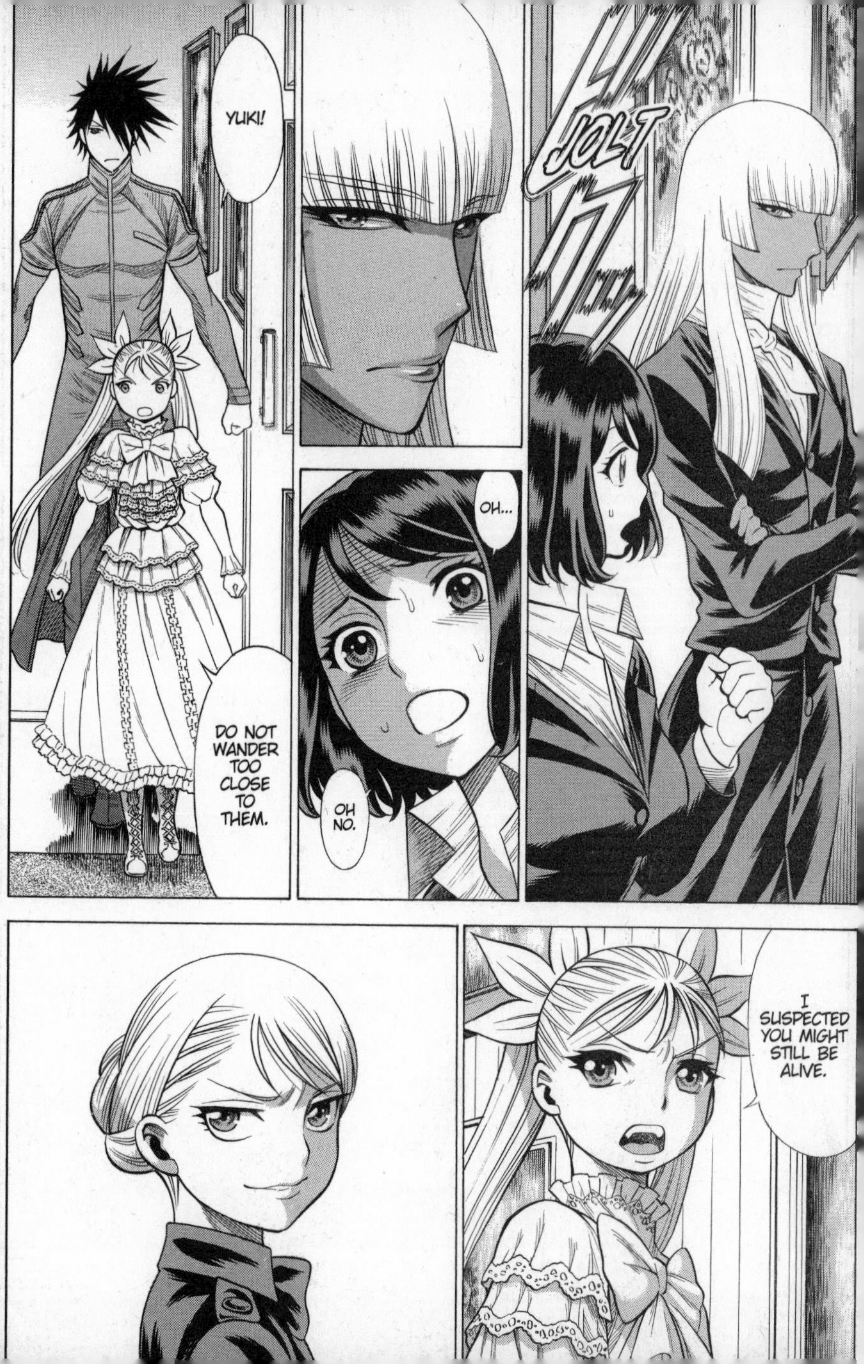
JOLT
OH...
OH NO.
YUKI!
DO NOT WANDER TOO CLOSE TO THEM.
I SUSPECTED YOU MIGHT STILL BE ALIVE.

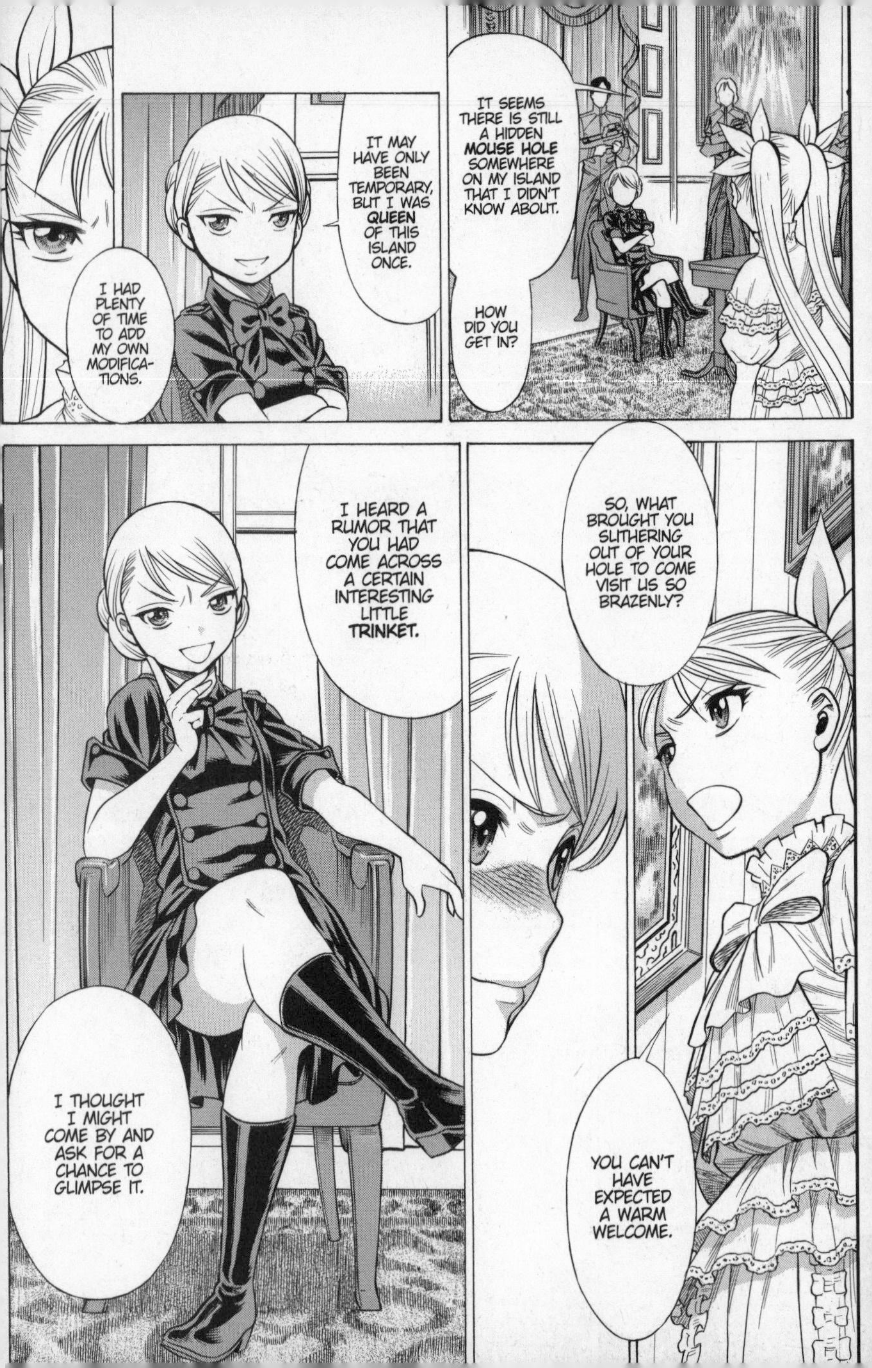
IT SEEMS THERE IS STILL A HIDDEN **MOUSE HOLE** SOMEWHERE ON MY ISLAND THAT I DIDN'T KNOW ABOUT.
HOW DID YOU GET IN?
IT MAY HAVE ONLY BEEN TEMPORARY, BUT I WAS **QUEEN** OF THIS ISLAND ONCE.
I HAD PLENTY OF TIME TO ADD MY OWN MODIFICA-TIONS.
SO, WHAT BROUGHT YOU SLITHERING OUT OF YOUR HOLE TO COME VISIT US SO BRAZENLY?
YOU CAN'T HAVE EXPECTED A WARM WELCOME.
I HEARD A RUMOR THAT YOU HAD COME ACROSS A CERTAIN INTERESTING LITTLE **TRINKET.**
I THOUGHT I MIGHT COME BY AND ASK FOR A CHANCE TO GLIMPSE IT.

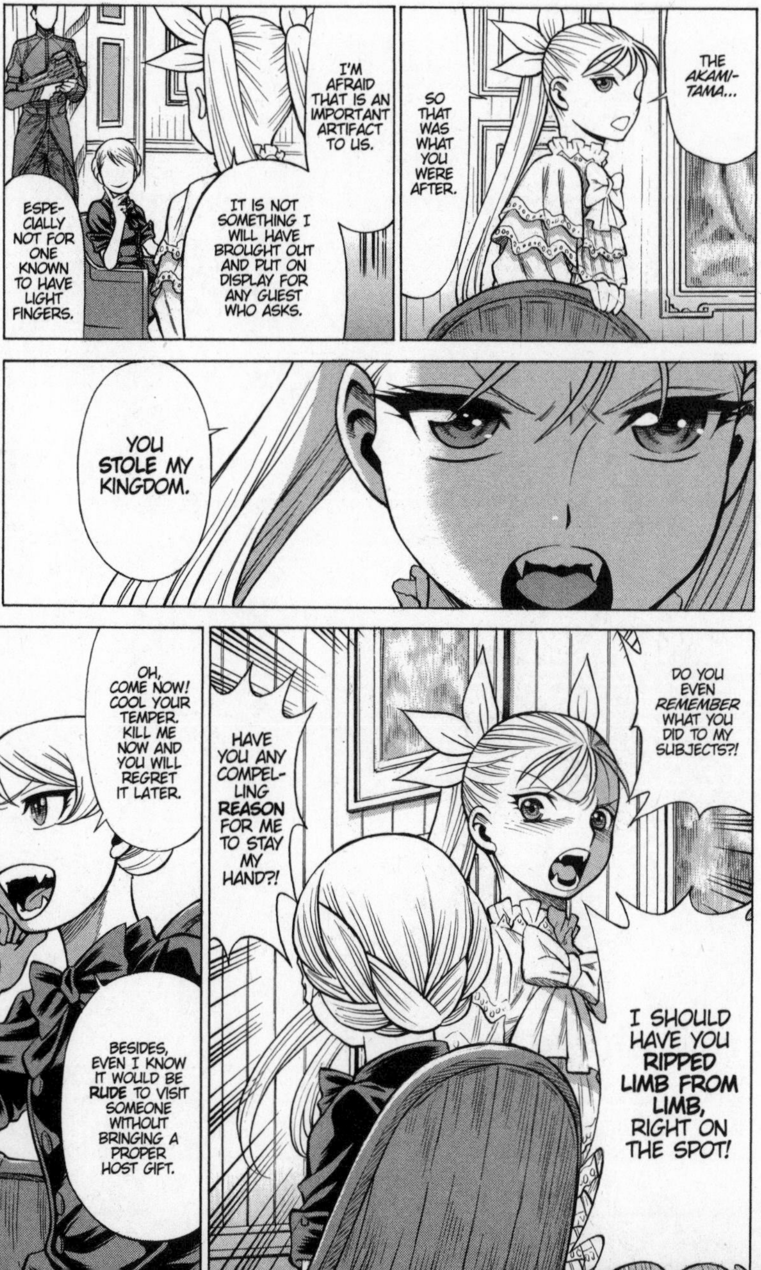
THE *AKAMITAMA*...
SO THAT WAS WHAT YOU WERE AFTER.
I'M AFRAID THAT IS AN IMPORTANT ARTIFACT TO US.
IT IS NOT SOMETHING I WILL HAVE BROUGHT OUT AND PUT ON DISPLAY FOR ANY GUEST WHO ASKS.
ESPECIALLY NOT FOR ONE KNOWN TO HAVE LIGHT FINGERS.
YOU **STOLE** MY **KINGDOM.**
DO YOU EVEN *REMEMBER* WHAT YOU DID TO MY SUBJECTS?!
HAVE YOU ANY COMPELLING **REASON** FOR ME TO STAY MY HAND?!
I SHOULD HAVE YOU **RIPPED LIMB FROM LIMB,** RIGHT ON THE SPOT!
OH, COME NOW! COOL YOUR TEMPER. KILL ME NOW AND YOU WILL REGRET IT LATER.
BESIDES, EVEN I KNOW IT WOULD BE **RUDE** TO VISIT SOMEONE WITHOUT BRINGING A PROPER HOST GIFT.

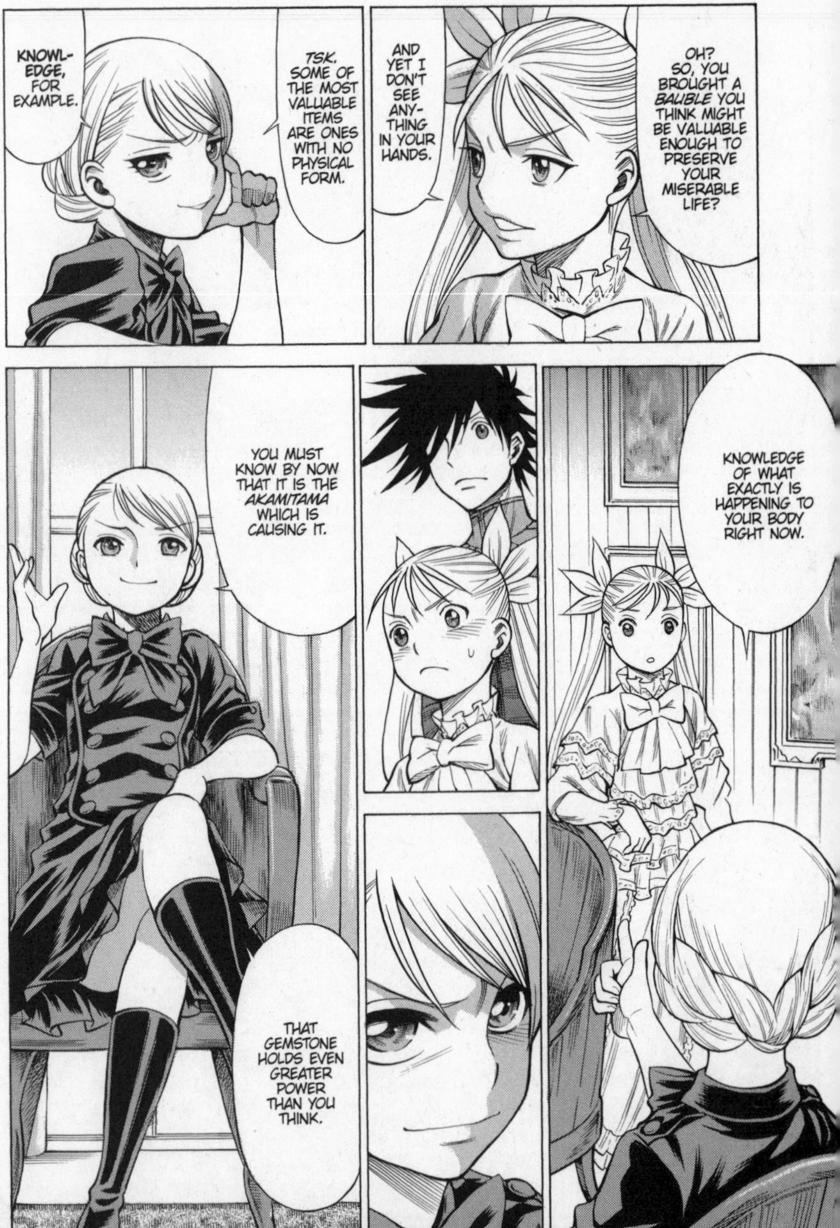
OH? SO, YOU BROUGHT A *BAUBLE* YOU THINK MIGHT BE VALUABLE ENOUGH TO PRESERVE YOUR MISERABLE LIFE?
AND YET I DON'T SEE ANYTHING IN YOUR HANDS.
TSK. SOME OF THE MOST VALUABLE ITEMS ARE ONES WITH NO PHYSICAL FORM.
KNOWL-EDGE, FOR EXAMPLE.
KNOWLEDGE OF WHAT EXACTLY IS HAPPENING TO YOUR BODY RIGHT NOW.
THAT GEMSTONE HOLDS EVEN GREATER POWER THAN YOU THINK.
YOU MUST KNOW BY NOW THAT IT IS THE *AKAMITAMA* WHICH IS CAUSING IT.

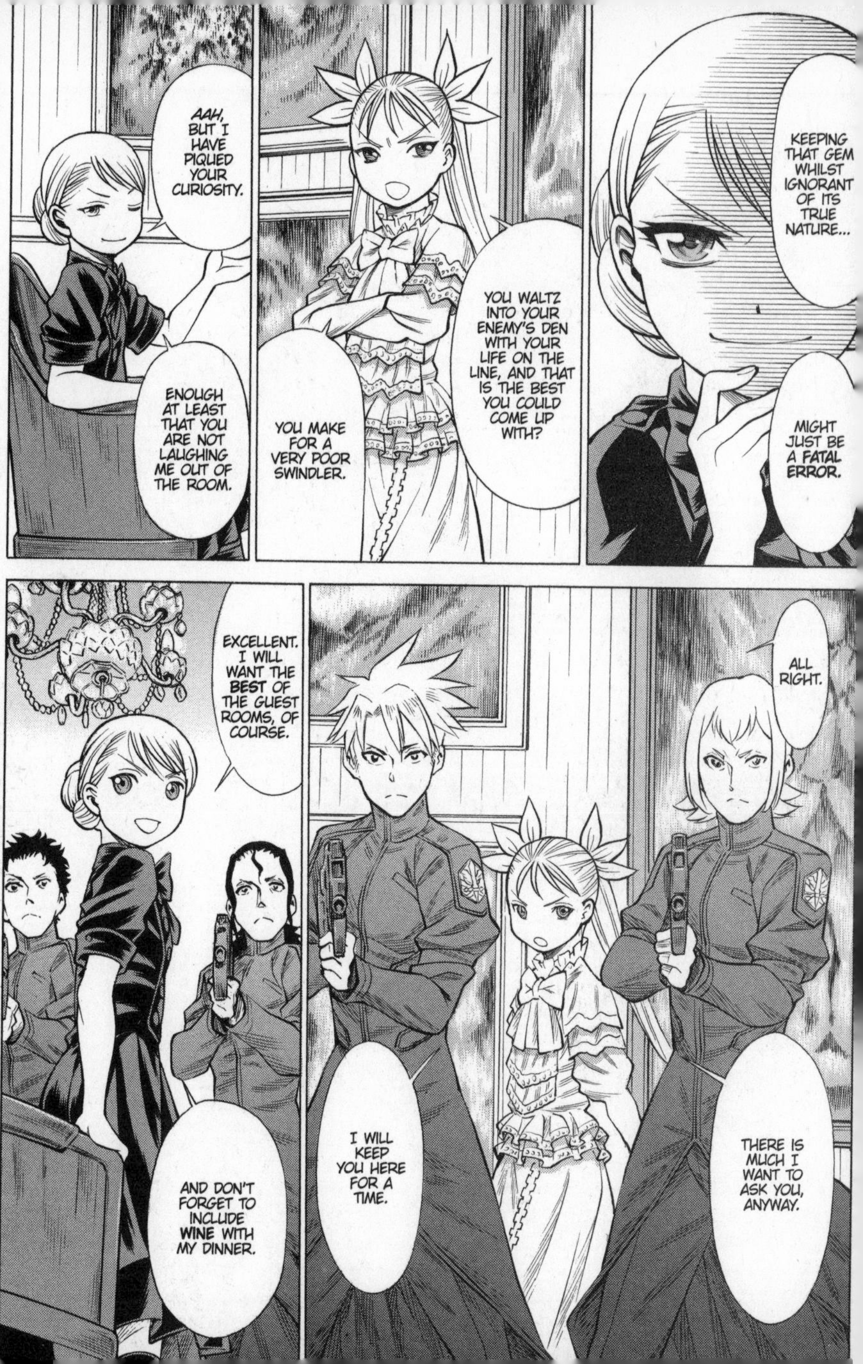
KEEPING THAT GEM WHILST IGNORANT OF ITS TRUE NATURE...
MIGHT JUST BE A **FATAL ERROR.**
YOU WALTZ INTO YOUR ENEMY'S DEN WITH YOUR LIFE ON THE LINE, AND THAT IS THE BEST YOU COULD COME UP WITH?
YOU MAKE FOR A VERY POOR SWINDLER.
AAH, BUT I HAVE PIQUED YOUR CURIOSITY.
ENOUGH AT LEAST THAT YOU ARE NOT LAUGHING ME OUT OF THE ROOM.
ALL RIGHT.
THERE IS MUCH I WANT TO ASK YOU, ANYWAY.
I WILL KEEP YOU HERE FOR A TIME.
EXCELLENT. I WILL WANT THE **BEST** OF THE GUEST ROOMS, OF COURSE.
AND DON'T FORGET TO INCLUDE **WINE** WITH MY DINNER.

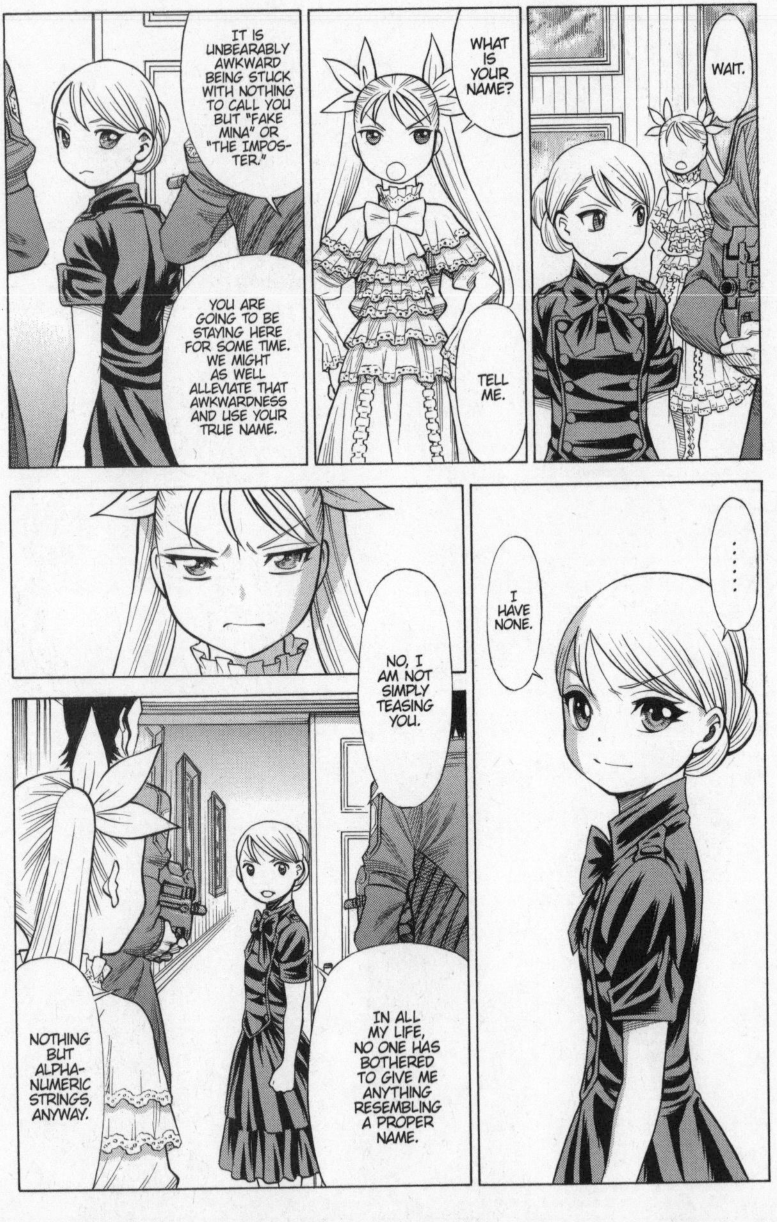
WAIT.
WHAT IS YOUR NAME?
TELL ME.
IT IS UNBEARABLY AWKWARD BEING STUCK WITH NOTHING TO CALL YOU BUT "FAKE MINA" OR "THE IMPOSTER."
YOU ARE GOING TO BE STAYING HERE FOR SOME TIME. WE MIGHT AS WELL ALLEVIATE THAT AWKWARDNESS AND USE YOUR TRUE NAME.
......
I HAVE NONE.
NO, I AM NOT SIMPLY TEASING YOU.
IN ALL MY LIFE, NO ONE HAS BOTHERED TO GIVE ME ANYTHING RESEMBLING A PROPER NAME.
NOTHING BUT ALPHA-NUMERIC STRINGS, ANYWAY.

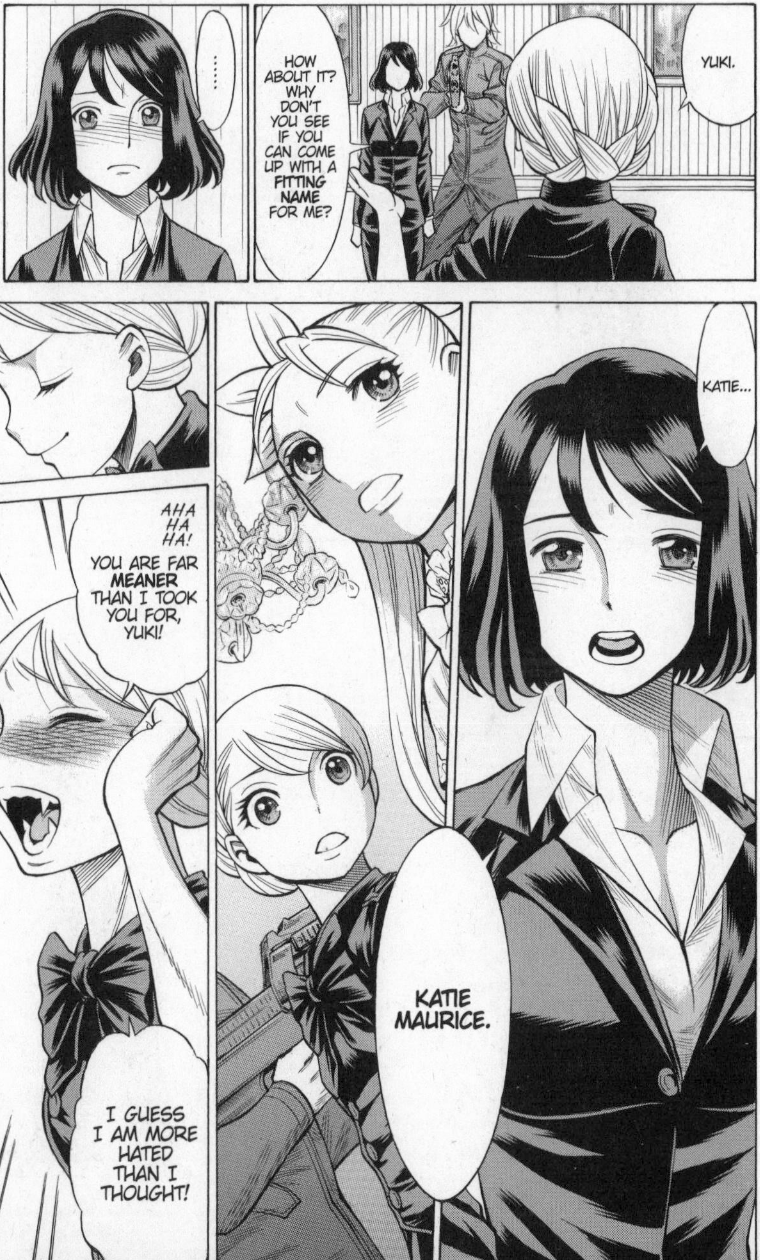
YUKI.
HOW ABOUT IT? WHY DON'T YOU SEE IF YOU CAN COME UP WITH A FITTING NAME FOR ME?
......
KATIE...
KATIE MAURICE.
HEH.
AHA HA HA! YOU ARE FAR MEANER THAN I TOOK YOU FOR, YUKI!
I GUESS I AM MORE HATED THAN I THOUGHT!

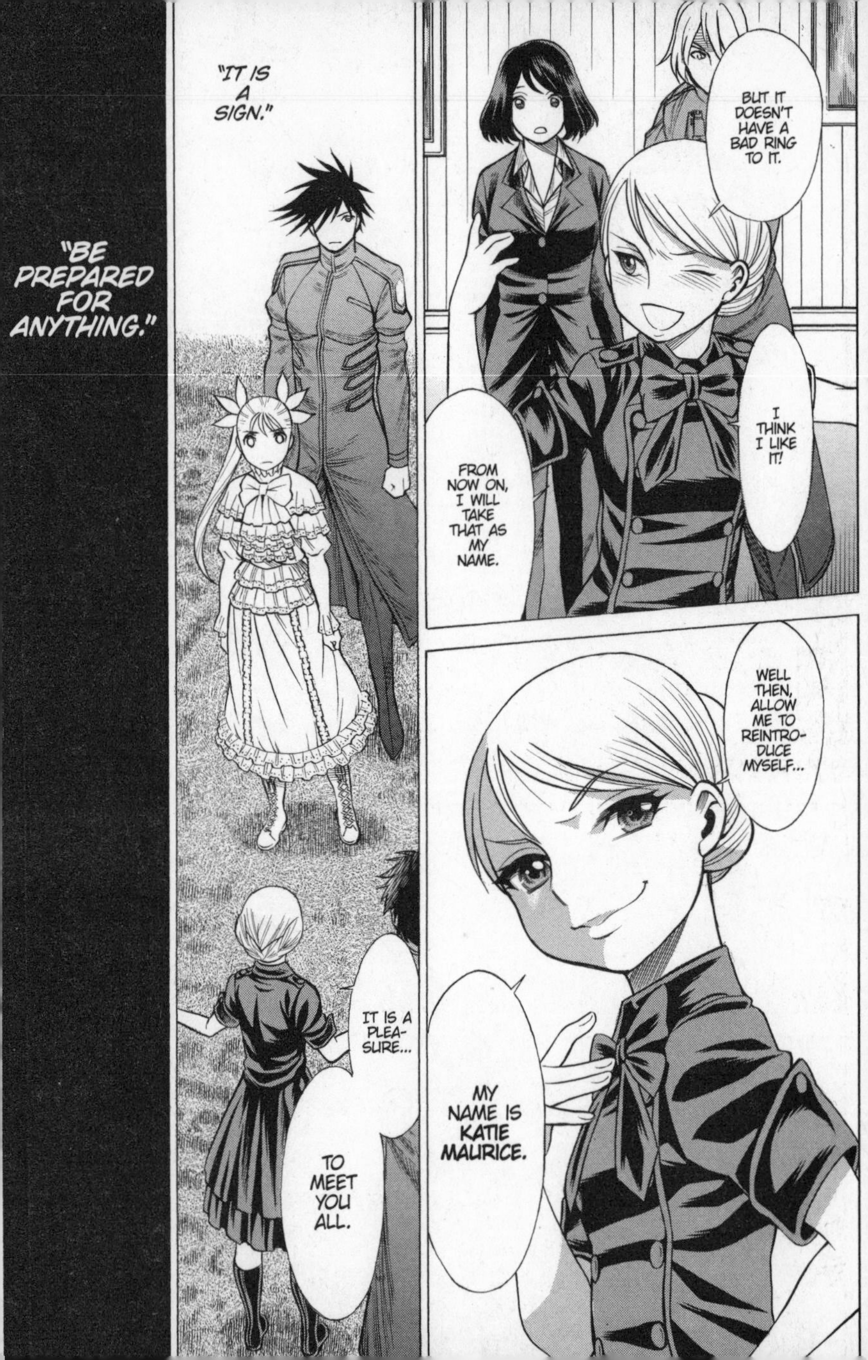
BUT IT DOESN'T HAVE A BAD RING TO IT.
I THINK I LIKE IT!
FROM NOW ON, I WILL TAKE THAT AS MY NAME.
WELL THEN, ALLOW ME TO REINTRODUCE MYSELF...
MY NAME IS KATIE MAURICE.
"IT IS A SIGN."
IT IS A PLEASURE...
TO MEET YOU ALL.
"BE PREPARED FOR ANYTHING."

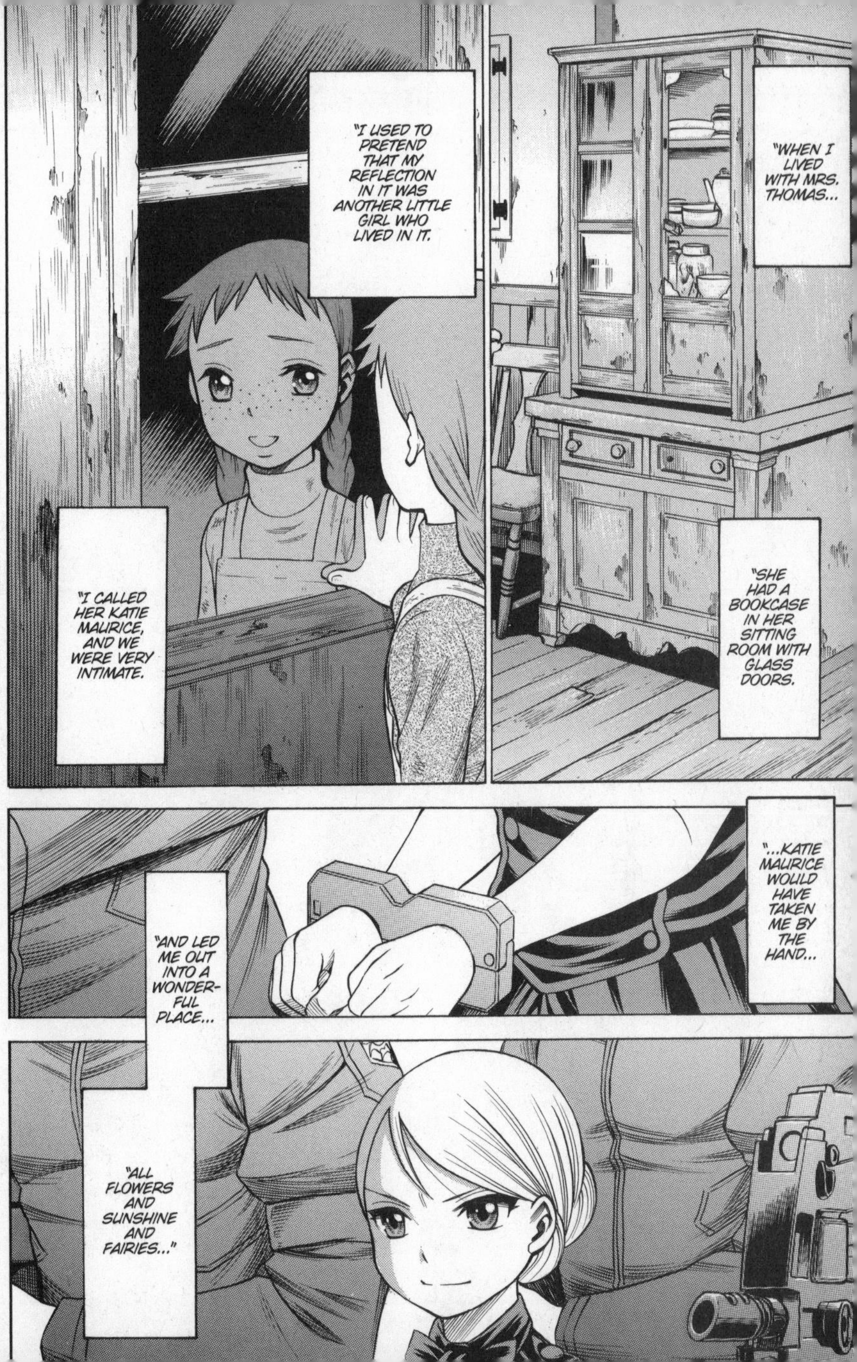
"WHEN I LIVED WITH MRS. THOMAS...
"SHE HAD A BOOKCASE IN HER SITTING ROOM WITH GLASS DOORS.
"I USED TO PRETEND THAT MY REFLECTION IN IT WAS ANOTHER LITTLE GIRL WHO LIVED IN IT.
"I CALLED HER KATIE MAURICE, AND WE WERE VERY INTIMATE.
"...KATIE MAURICE WOULD HAVE TAKEN ME BY THE HAND...
"AND LED ME OUT INTO A WONDER-FUL PLACE...
"ALL FLOWERS AND SUNSHINE AND FAIRIES..."

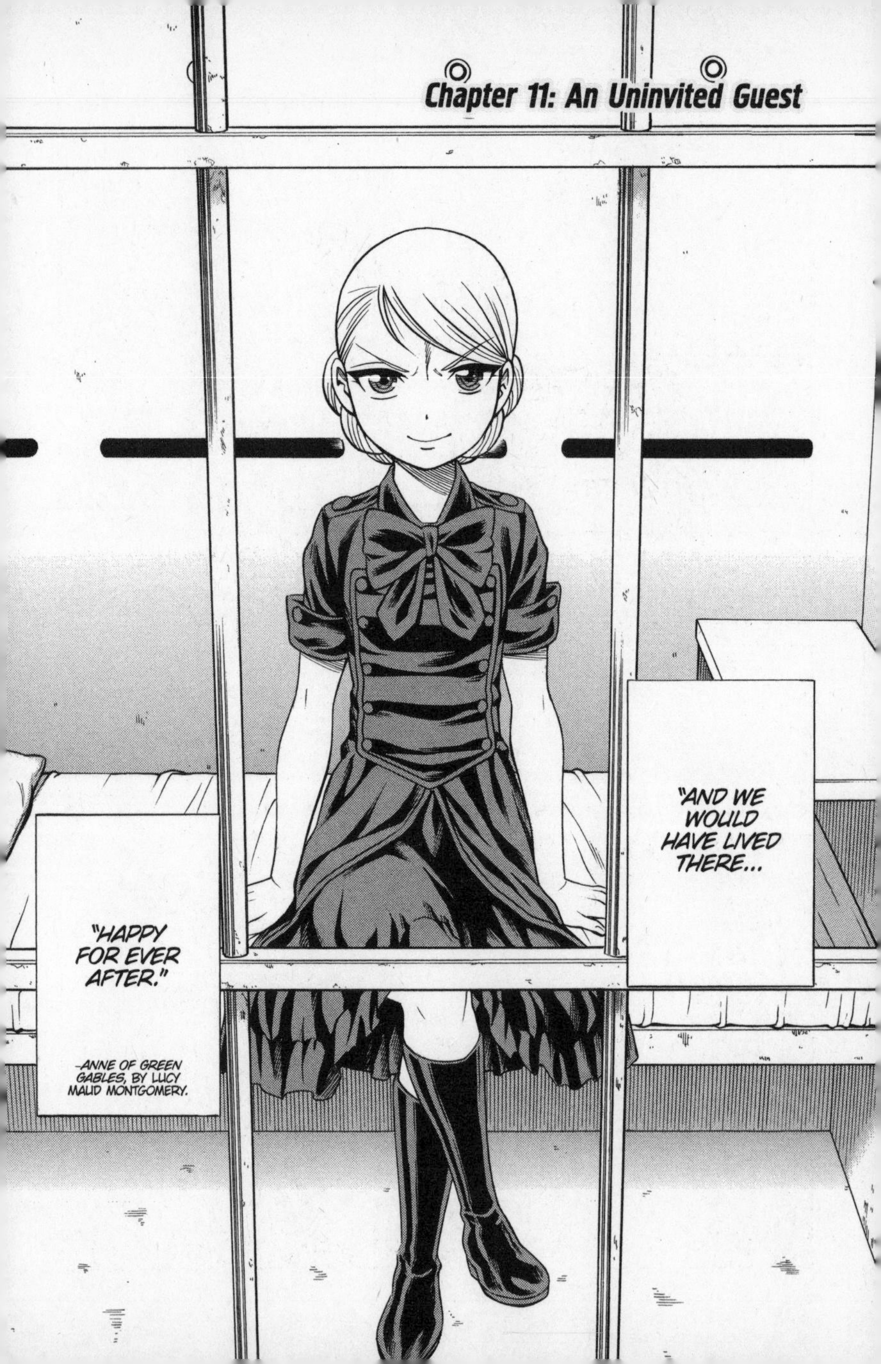
Chapter 11: An Uninvited Guest
"AND WE WOULD HAVE LIVED THERE...
"HAPPY FOR EVER AFTER."
-ANNE OF GREEN GABLES, BY LUCY MAUD MONTGOMERY.

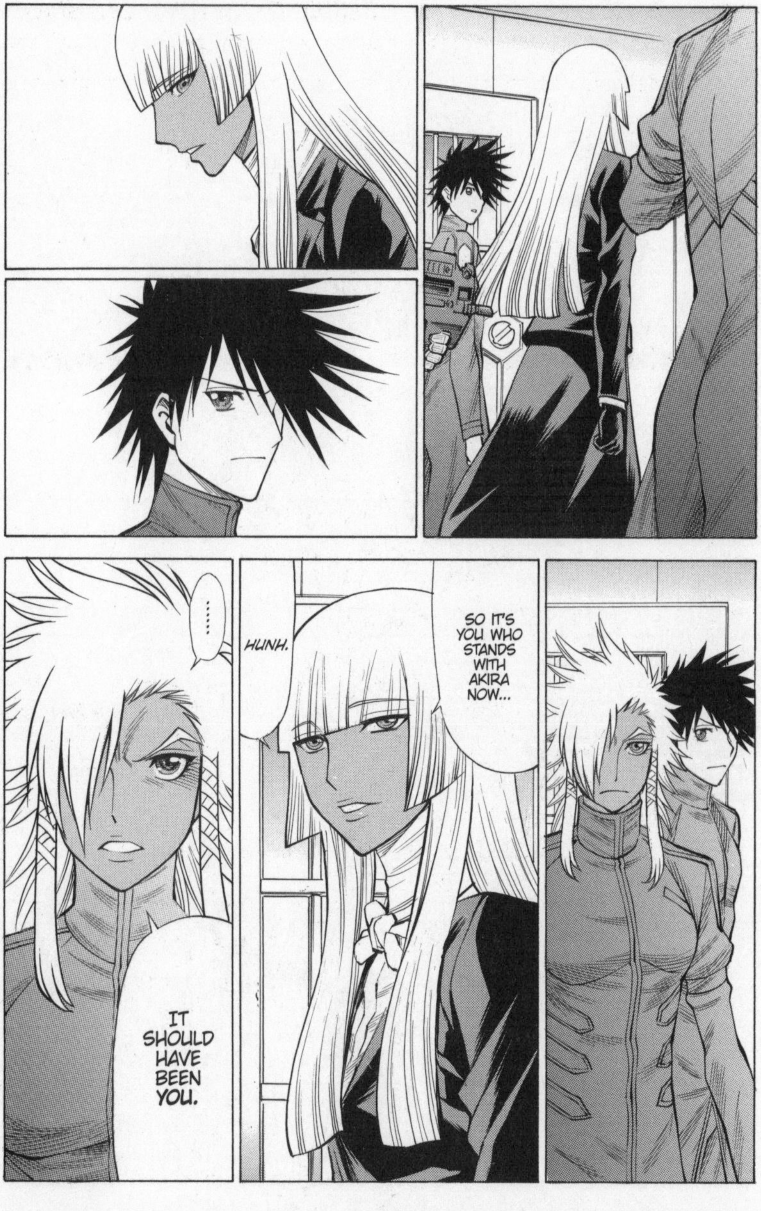
SO IT'S YOU WHO STANDS WITH AKIRA NOW...
HUNH.
......
IT SHOULD HAVE BEEN YOU.

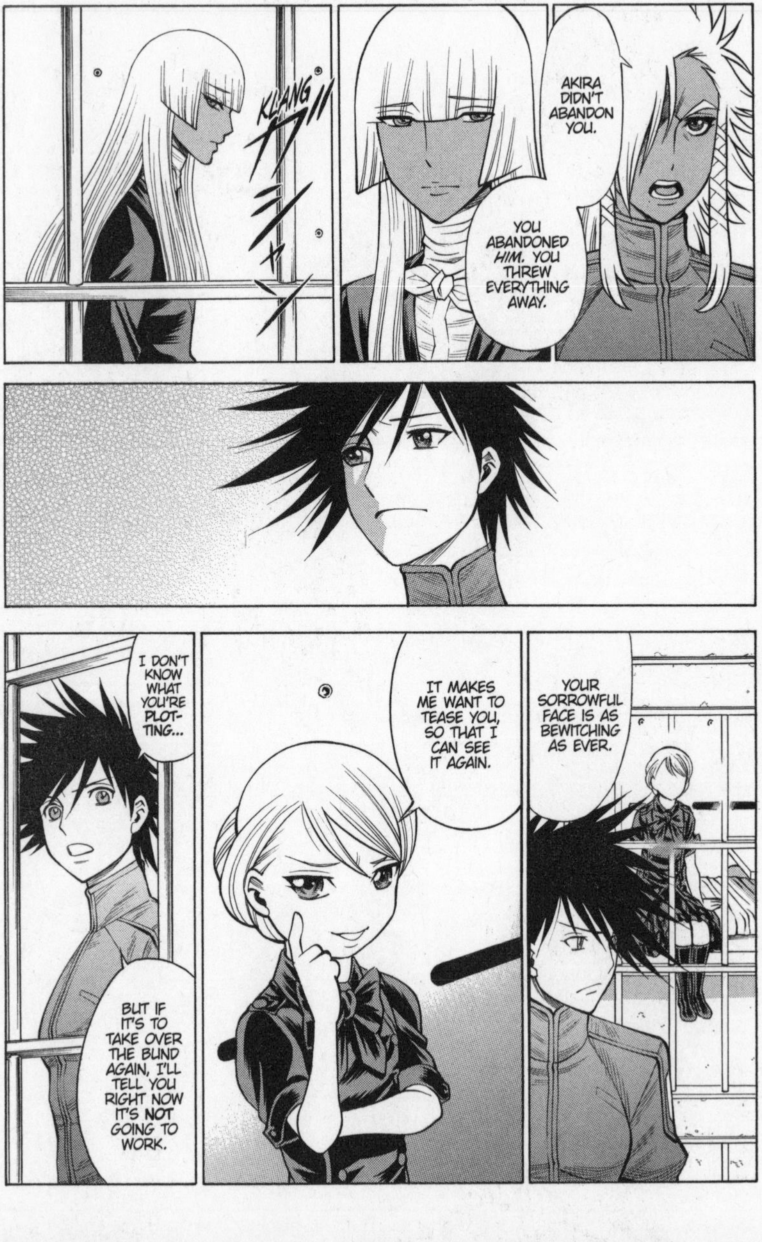
AKIRA DIDN'T ABANDON YOU.
YOU ABANDONED *HIM*. YOU THREW EVERYTHING AWAY.
KLANG
YOUR SORROWFUL FACE IS AS BEWITCHING AS EVER.
IT MAKES ME WANT TO TEASE YOU, SO THAT I CAN SEE IT AGAIN.
I DON'T KNOW WHAT YOU'RE PLOT-TING...
BUT IF IT'S TO TAKE OVER THE BUND AGAIN, I'LL TELL YOU RIGHT NOW IT'S **NOT** GOING TO WORK.

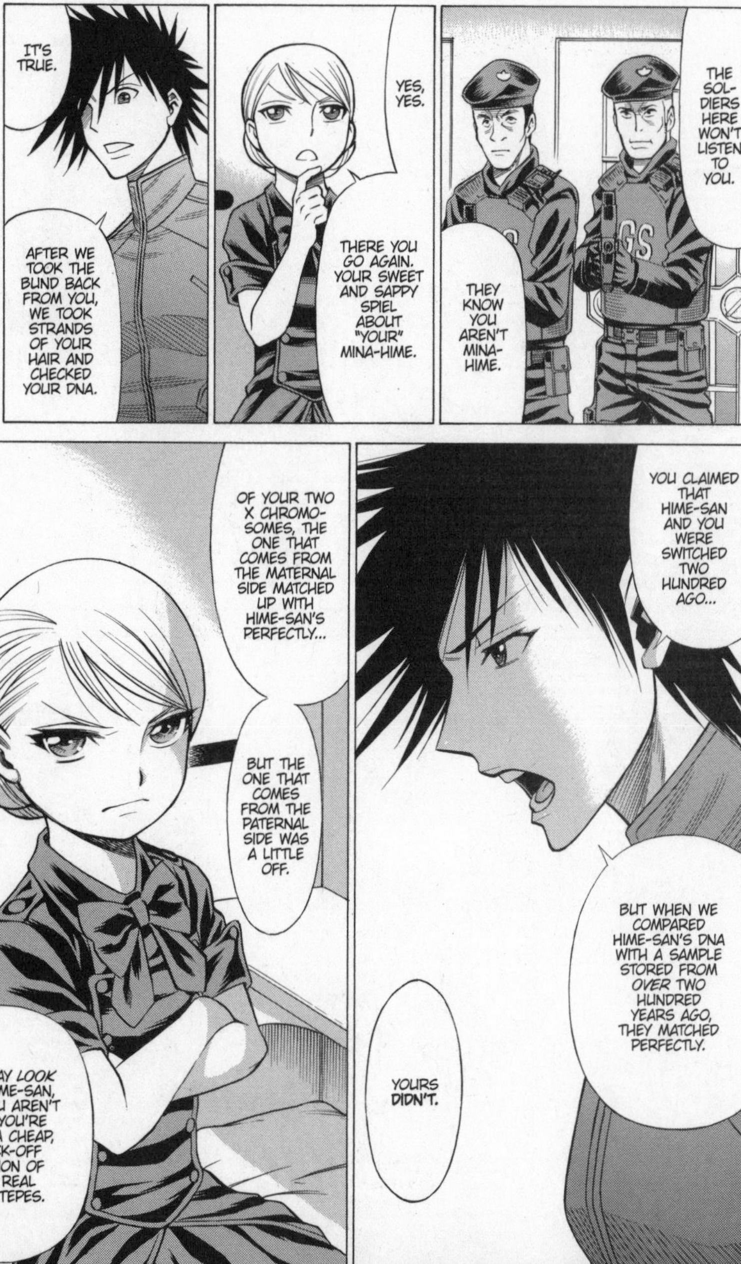
THE SOL-DIERS HERE WON'T LISTEN TO YOU.
THEY KNOW YOU AREN'T MINA-HIME.
YES, YES.
THERE YOU GO AGAIN. YOUR SWEET AND SAPPY SPIEL ABOUT "YOUR" MINA-HIME.
IT'S TRUE.
AFTER WE TOOK THE BUND BACK FROM YOU, WE TOOK STRANDS OF YOUR HAIR AND CHECKED YOUR DNA.
YOU CLAIMED THAT HIME-SAN AND YOU WERE SWITCHED TWO HUNDRED AGO...
BUT WHEN WE COMPARED HIME-SAN'S DNA WITH A SAMPLE STORED FROM *OVER* TWO HUNDRED YEARS AGO, THEY MATCHED PERFECTLY.
YOURS DIDN'T.
OF YOUR TWO X CHROMO-SOMES, THE ONE THAT COMES FROM THE MATERNAL SIDE MATCHED UP WITH HIME-SAN'S PERFECTLY...
BUT THE ONE THAT COMES FROM THE PATERNAL SIDE WAS A LITTLE OFF.
YOU MAY *LOOK* LIKE HIME-SAN, BUT YOU AREN'T HER. YOU'RE JUST A CHEAP, KNOCK-OFF VERSION OF THE REAL MINA TEPES.

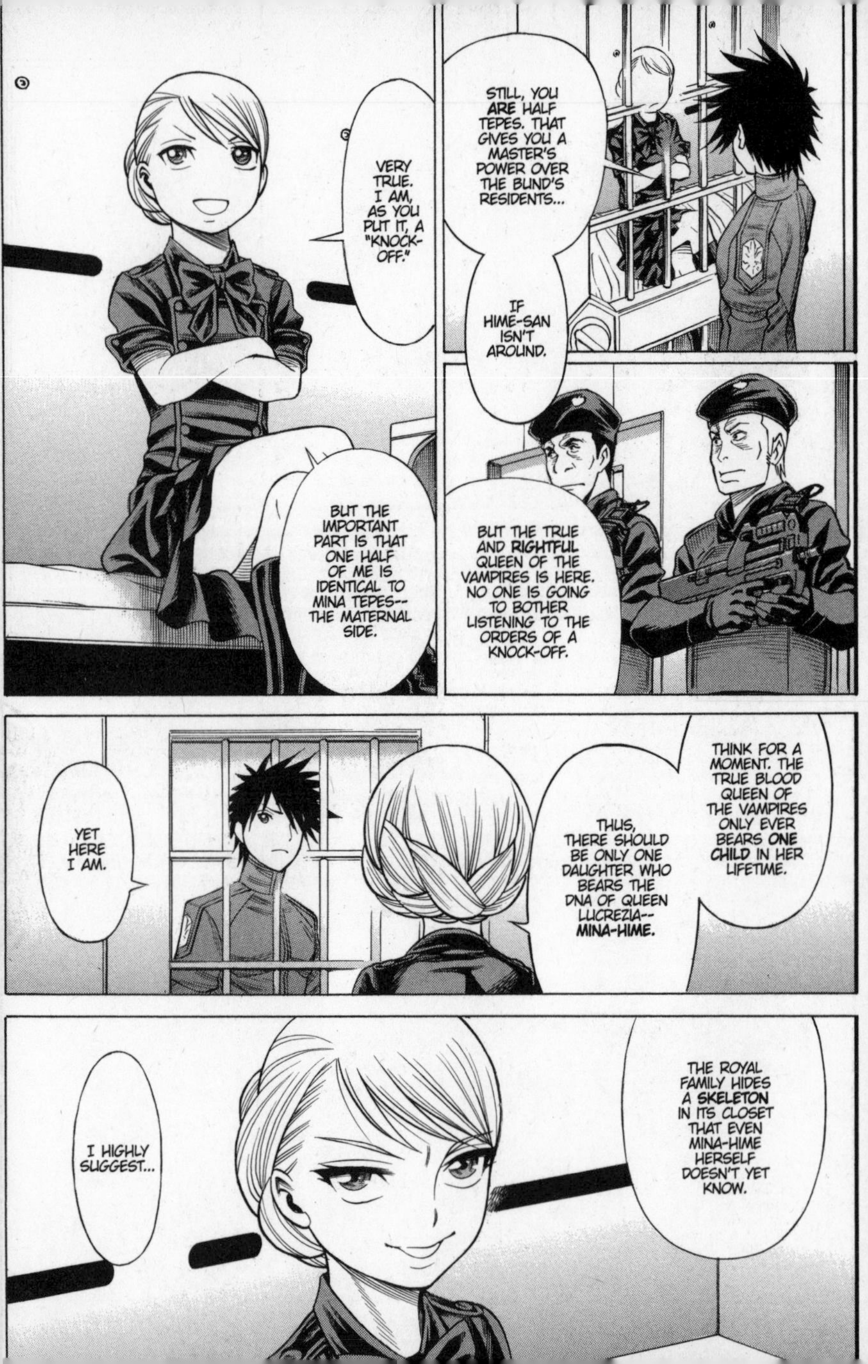
STILL, YOU ARE HALF TEPES. THAT GIVES YOU A MASTER'S POWER OVER THE BUND'S RESIDENTS...
IF HIME-SAN ISN'T AROUND.
BUT THE TRUE AND RIGHTFUL QUEEN OF THE VAMPIRES IS HERE. NO ONE IS GOING TO BOTHER LISTENING TO THE ORDERS OF A KNOCK-OFF.
VERY TRUE. I AM, AS YOU PUT IT, A "KNOCK-OFF."
BUT THE IMPORTANT PART IS THAT ONE HALF OF ME IS IDENTICAL TO MINA TEPES-- THE MATERNAL SIDE.
THINK FOR A MOMENT. THE TRUE BLOOD QUEEN OF THE VAMPIRES ONLY EVER BEARS ONE CHILD IN HER LIFETIME.
THUS, THERE SHOULD BE ONLY ONE DAUGHTER WHO BEARS THE DNA OF QUEEN LUCREZIA-- MINA-HIME.
YET HERE I AM.
THE ROYAL FAMILY HIDES A SKELETON IN ITS CLOSET THAT EVEN MINA-HIME HERSELF DOESN'T YET KNOW.
I HIGHLY SUGGEST...

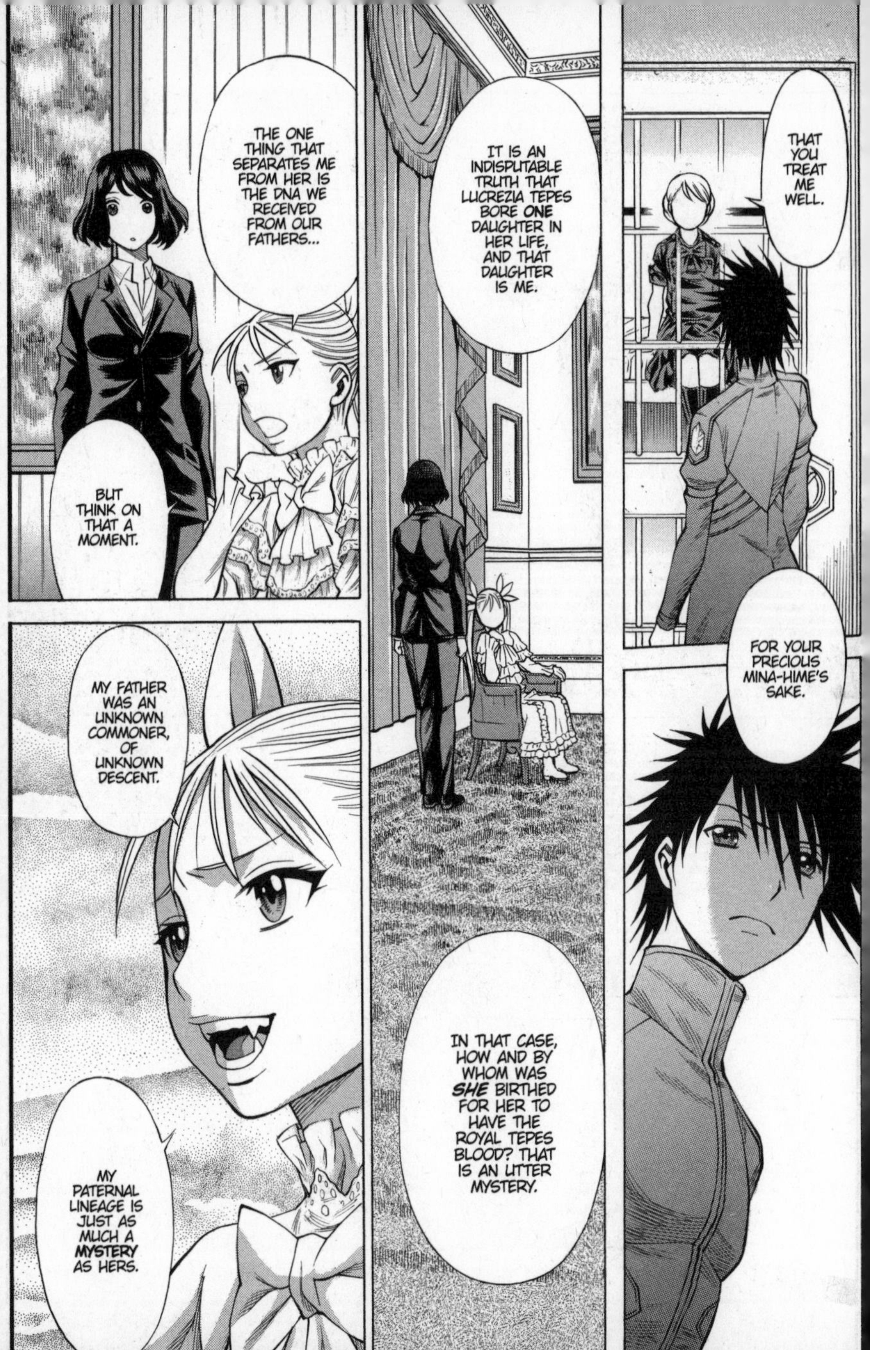
THAT YOU TREAT ME WELL.
FOR YOUR PRECIOUS MINA-HIME'S SAKE.
IT IS AN INDISPUTABLE TRUTH THAT LUCREZIA TEPES BORE **ONE** DAUGHTER IN HER LIFE, AND THAT DAUGHTER IS ME.
IN THAT CASE, HOW AND BY WHOM WAS ***SHE*** BIRTHED FOR HER TO HAVE THE ROYAL TEPES BLOOD? THAT IS AN UTTER MYSTERY.
THE ONE THING THAT SEPARATES ME FROM HER IS THE DNA WE RECEIVED FROM OUR FATHERS...
BUT THINK ON THAT A MOMENT.
MY FATHER WAS AN UNKNOWN COMMONER, OF UNKNOWN DESCENT.
MY PATERNAL LINEAGE IS JUST AS MUCH A **MYSTERY** AS HERS.

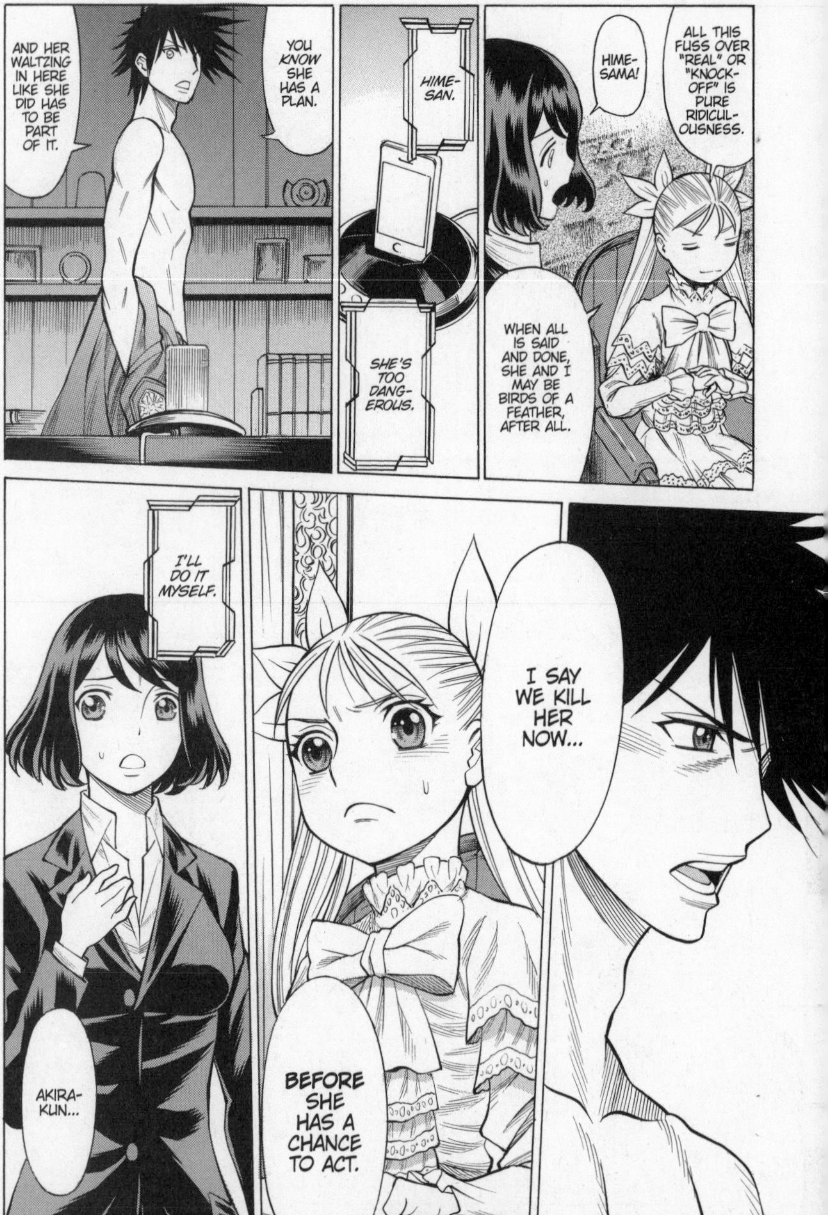
ALL THIS FUSS OVER "REAL" OR "KNOCK-OFF" IS PURE RIDICULOUSNESS.
HIME-SAMA!
WHEN ALL IS SAID AND DONE, SHE AND I MAY BE BIRDS OF A FEATHER, AFTER ALL.
HIME-SAN.
SHE'S TOO DANGEROUS.
YOU KNOW SHE HAS A PLAN.
AND HER WALTZING IN HERE LIKE SHE DID HAS TO BE PART OF IT.
I SAY WE KILL HER NOW...
BEFORE SHE HAS A CHANCE TO ACT.
I'LL DO IT MYSELF.
AKIRA-KUN...

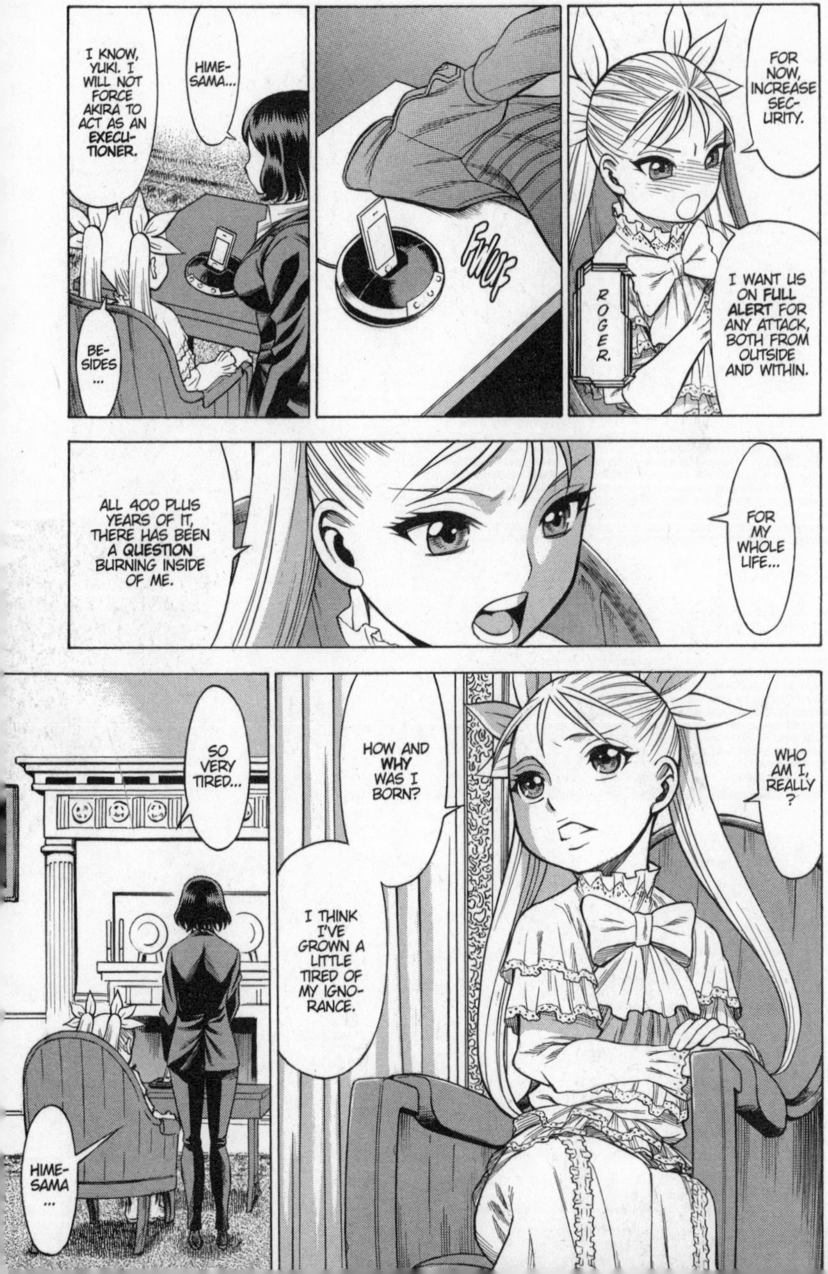
FOR NOW, INCREASE SECURITY.
I WANT US ON FULL ALERT FOR ANY ATTACK, BOTH FROM OUTSIDE AND WITHIN.
ROGER.
FWUP
HIME-SAMA...
I KNOW, YUKI. I WILL NOT FORCE AKIRA TO ACT AS AN EXECUTIONER.
BESIDES...
FOR MY WHOLE LIFE...
ALL 400 PLUS YEARS OF IT, THERE HAS BEEN A QUESTION BURNING INSIDE OF ME.
WHO AM I, REALLY?
HOW AND WHY WAS I BORN?
I THINK I'VE GROWN A LITTLE TIRED OF MY IGNORANCE.
SO VERY TIRED...
HIME-SAMA...

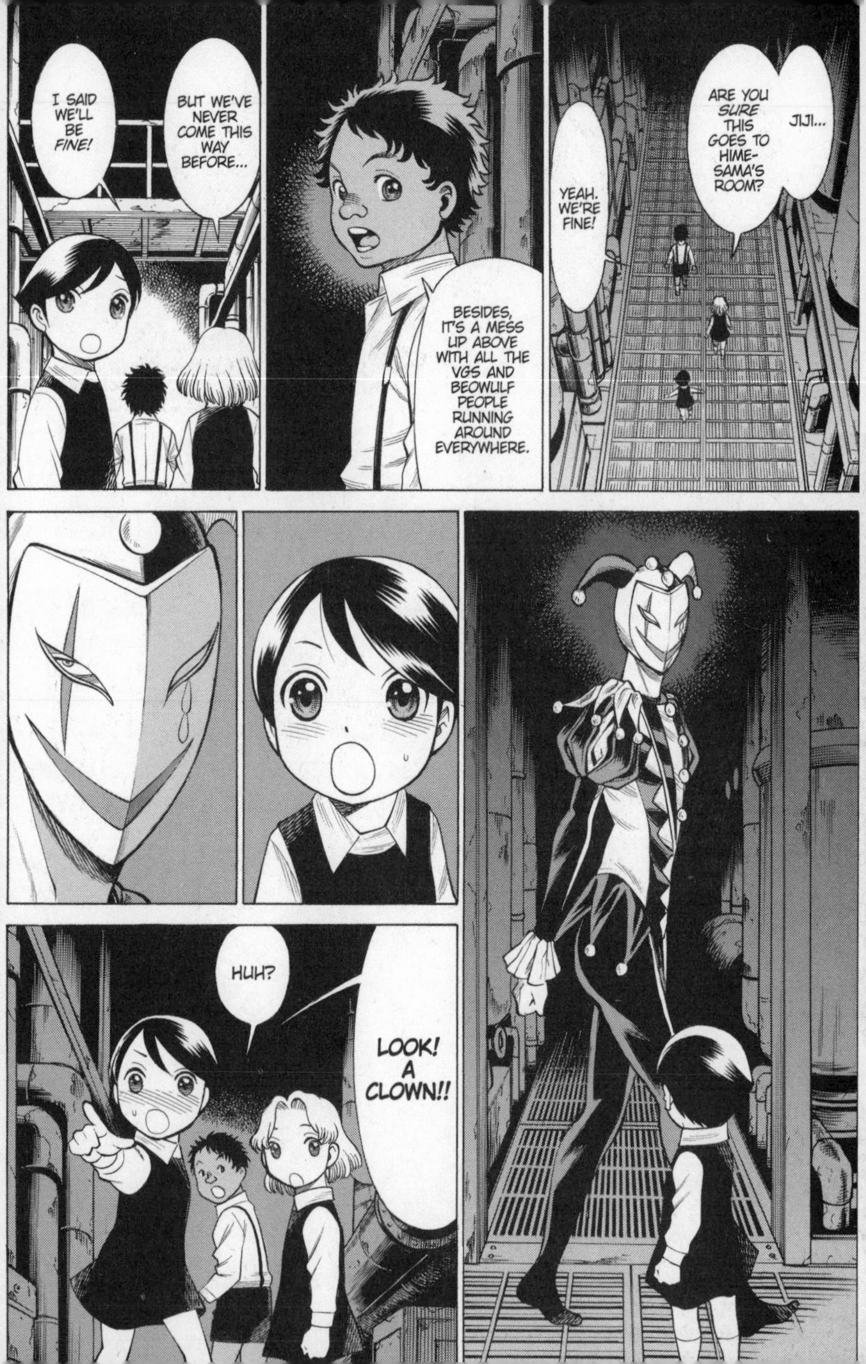
JIJI...
ARE YOU SURE THIS GOES TO HIME-SAMA'S ROOM?
YEAH. WE'RE FINE!
BESIDES, IT'S A MESS UP ABOVE WITH ALL THE VGS AND BEOWULF PEOPLE RUNNING AROUND EVERYWHERE.
BUT WE'VE NEVER COME THIS WAY BEFORE...
I SAID WE'LL BE FINE!
LOOK! A CLOWN!!
HUH?

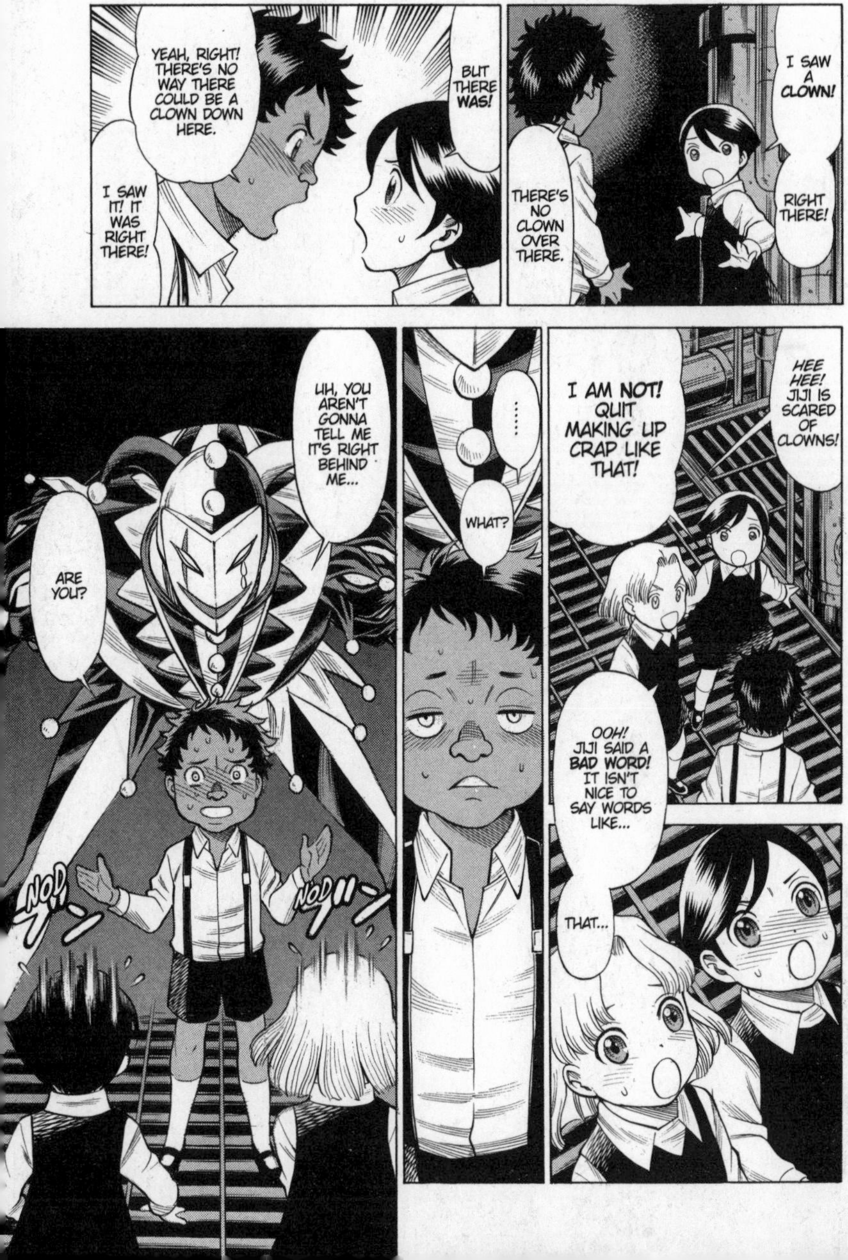
I SAW A CLOWN!
RIGHT THERE!
THERE'S NO CLOWN OVER THERE.
BUT THERE WAS!
YEAH, RIGHT! THERE'S NO WAY THERE COULD BE A CLOWN DOWN HERE.
I SAW IT! IT WAS RIGHT THERE!
HEE HEE! JIJI IS SCARED OF CLOWNS!
I AM NOT! QUIT MAKING UP CRAP LIKE THAT!
OOH! JIJI SAID A BAD WORD! IT ISN'T NICE TO SAY WORDS LIKE...
THAT...
......
WHAT?
UH, YOU AREN'T GONNA TELL ME IT'S RIGHT BEHIND ME...
ARE YOU?
NOD
NOD

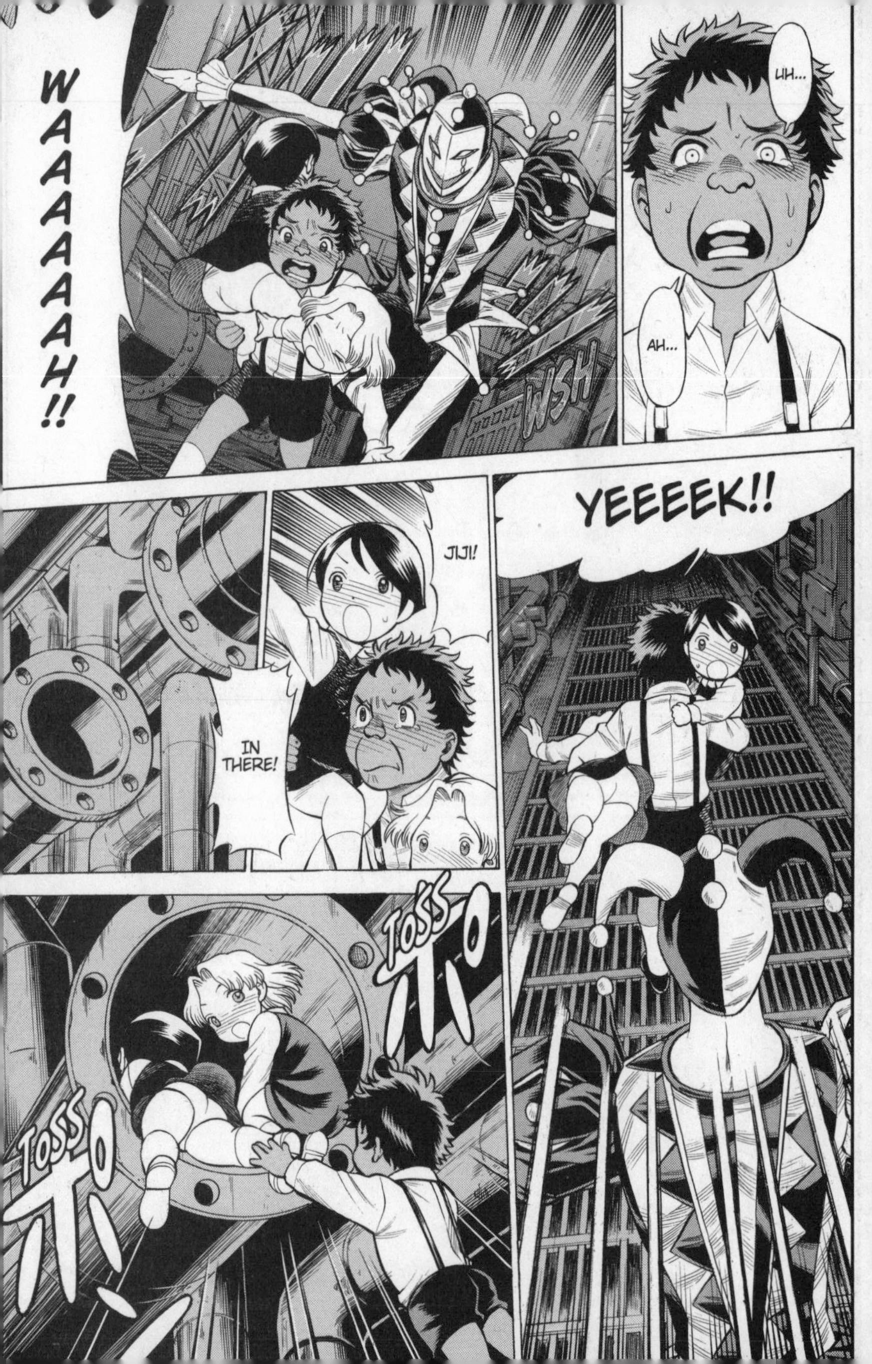
UH...
AH...
WAAAAAAH!!
WSH
YEEEEK!!
JIJI!
IN THERE!
TOSS
TOSS

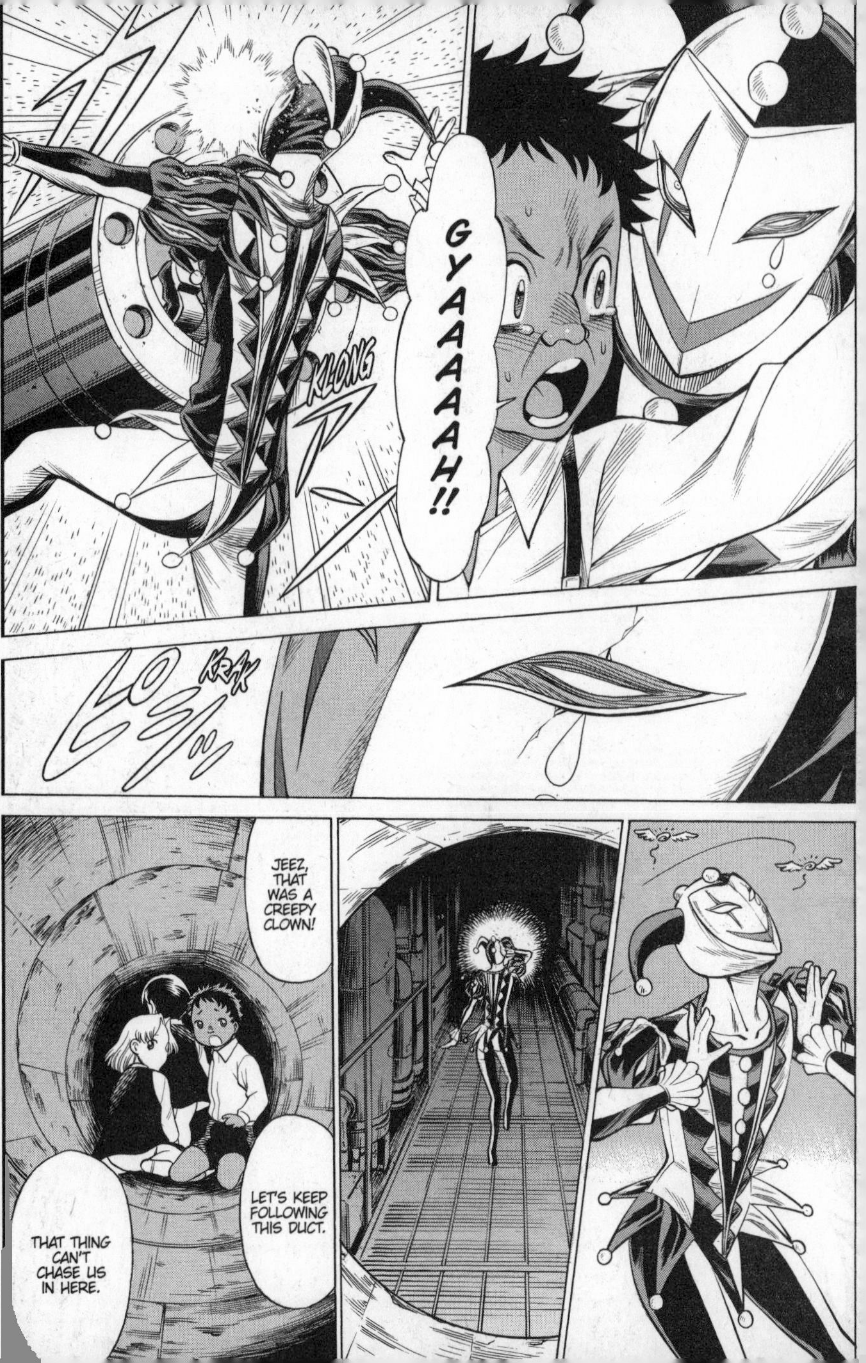
GYAAAAAH!!
KLONG
KRAK
JEEZ, THAT WAS A CREEPY CLOWN!
LET'S KEEP FOLLOWING THIS DUCT.
THAT THING CAN'T CHASE US IN HERE.

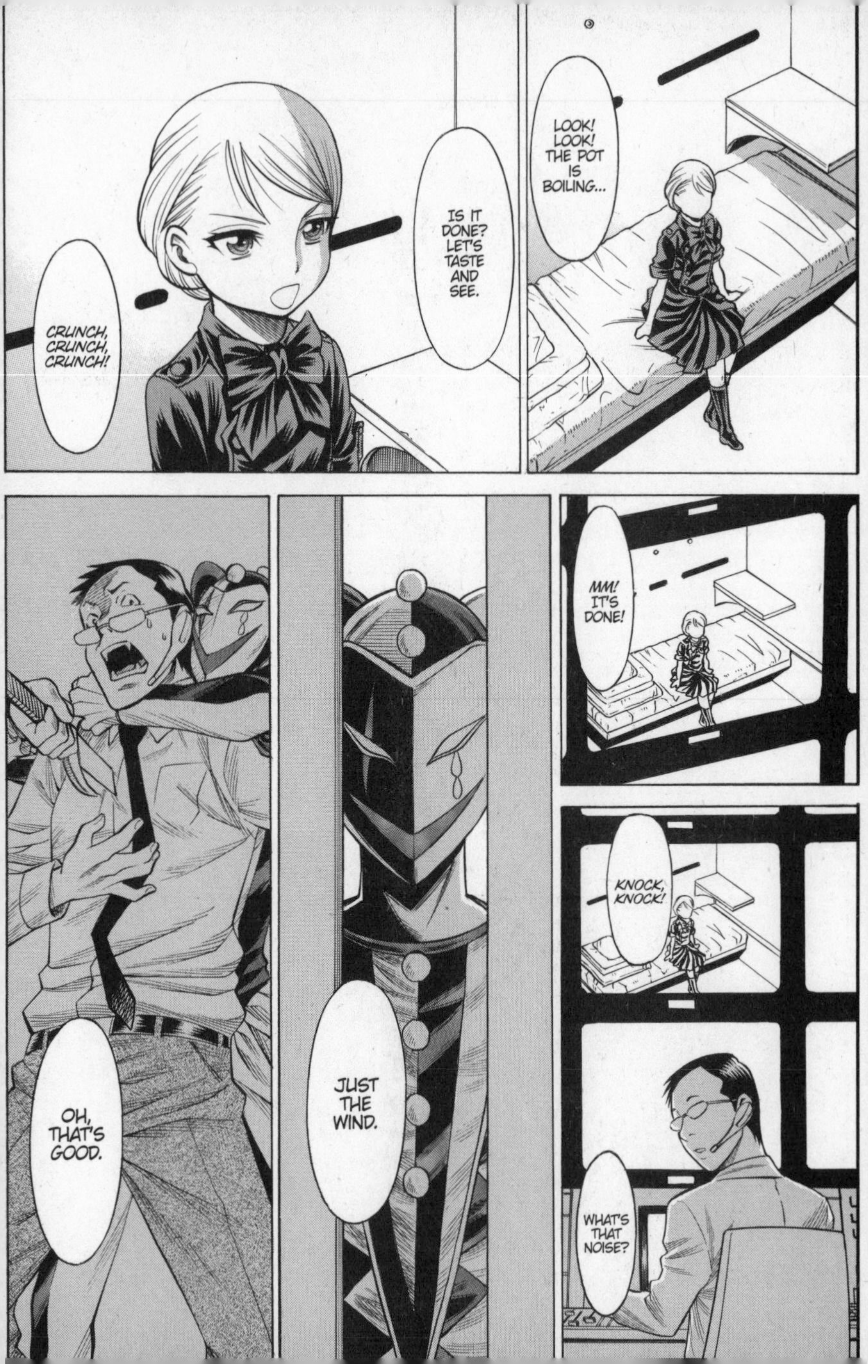
LOOK! LOOK! THE POT IS BOILING...
IS IT DONE? LET'S TASTE AND SEE.
CRUNCH, CRUNCH, CRUNCH!
MM! IT'S DONE!
KNOCK, KNOCK!
WHAT'S THAT NOISE?
JUST THE WIND.
OH, THAT'S GOOD.

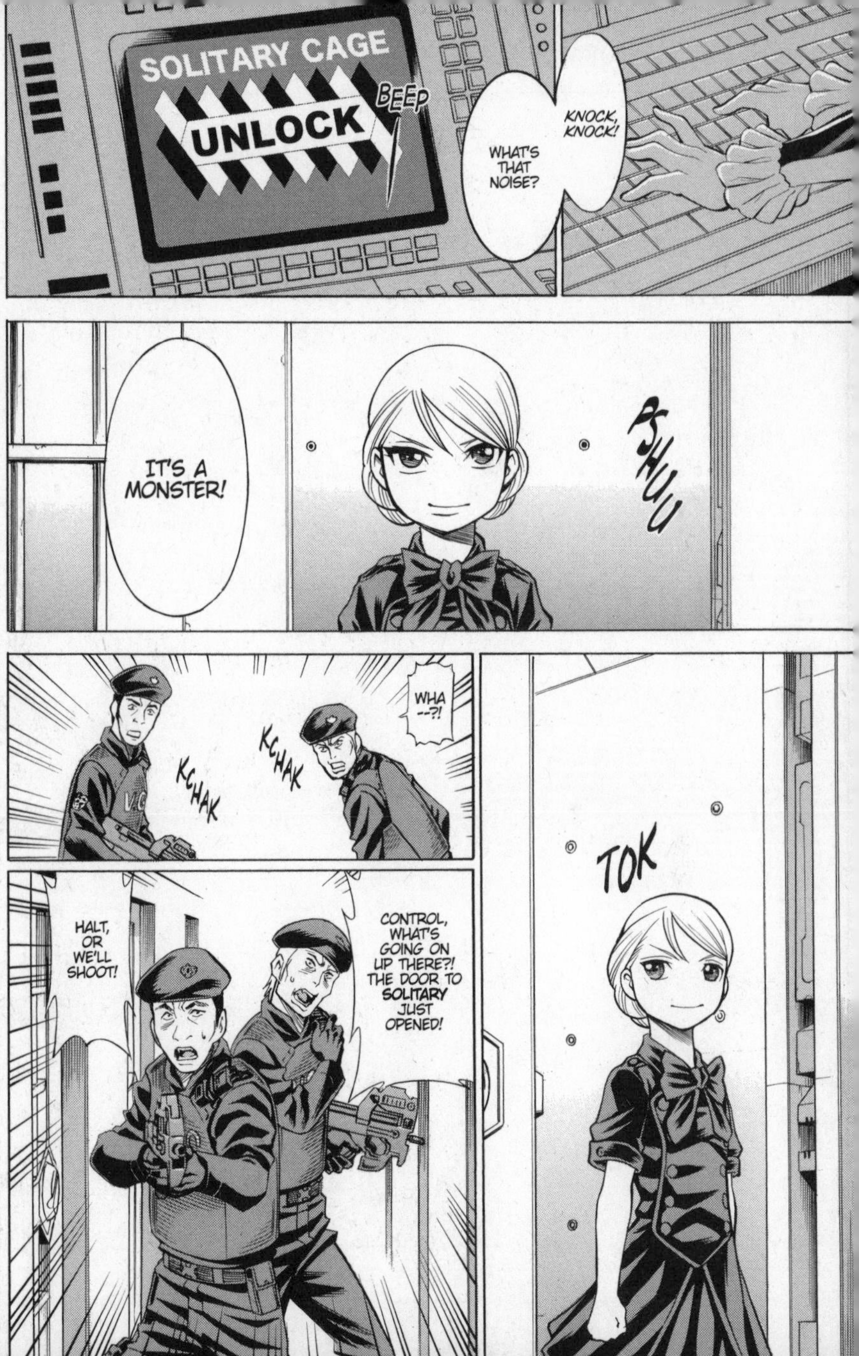
KNOCK, KNOCK!
WHAT'S THAT NOISE?
SOLITARY CAGE
UNLOCK
BEEP
PSHUUU
IT'S A MONSTER!
TOK
WHA --?!
KCHAK
KCHAK
CONTROL, WHAT'S GOING ON UP THERE?! THE DOOR TO **SOLITARY** JUST OPENED!
HALT, OR WE'LL SHOOT!

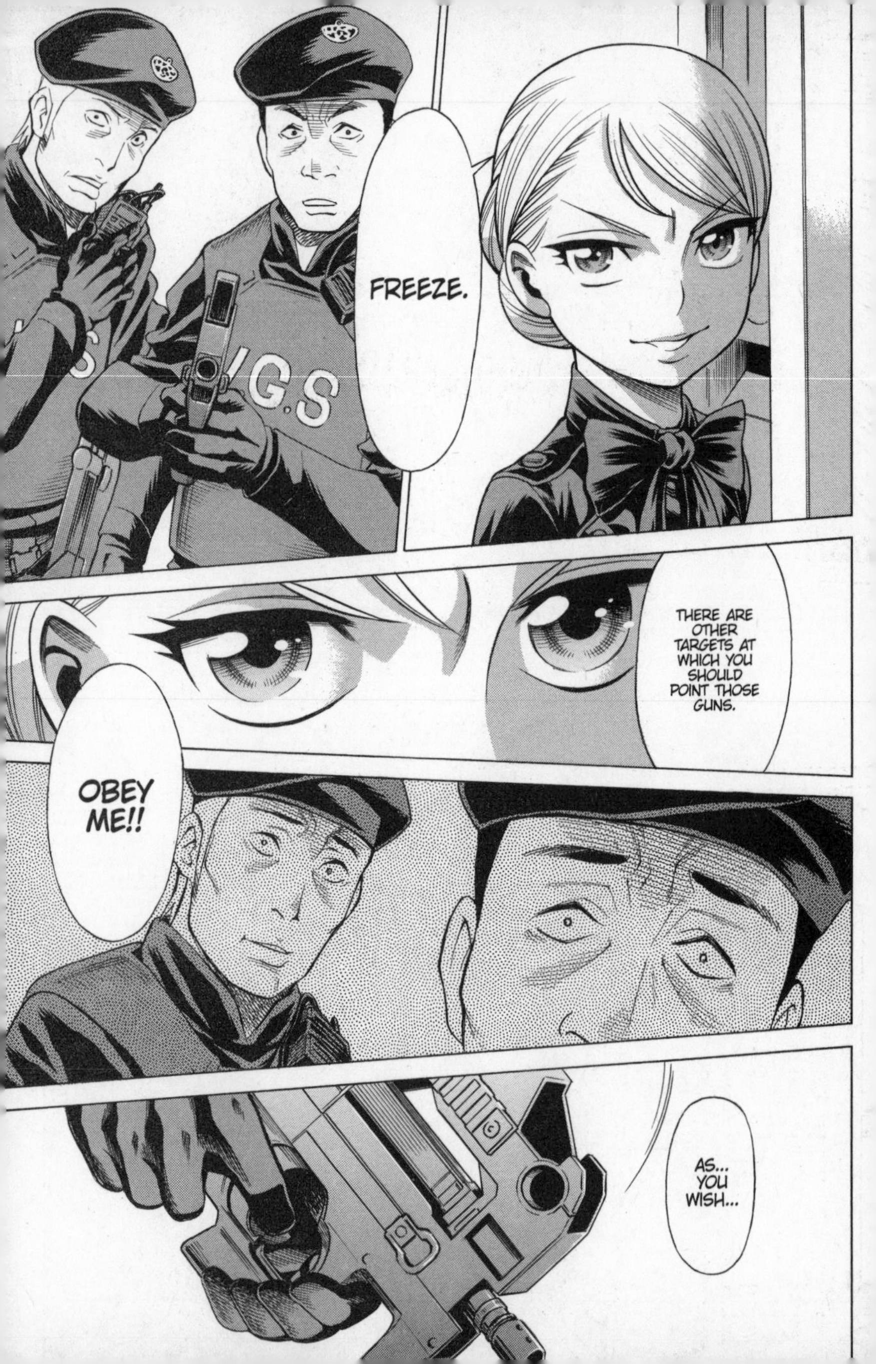
FREEZE.
G.S
THERE ARE OTHER TARGETS AT WHICH YOU SHOULD POINT THOSE GUNS.
OBEY ME!!
AS... YOU WISH...

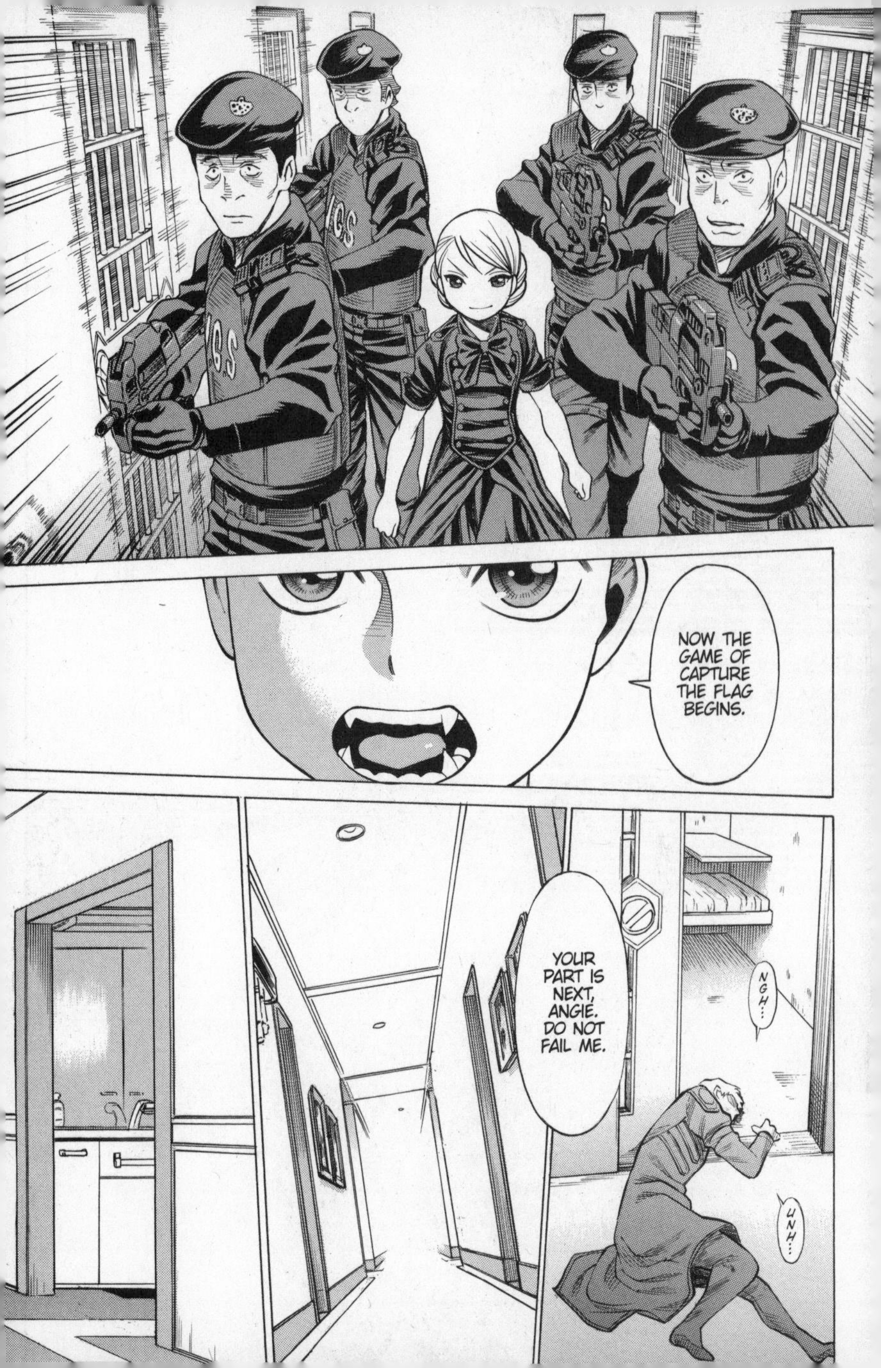
NOW THE GAME OF CAPTURE THE FLAG BEGINS.
NGH...
YOUR PART IS NEXT, ANGIE. DO NOT FAIL ME.
UNH...

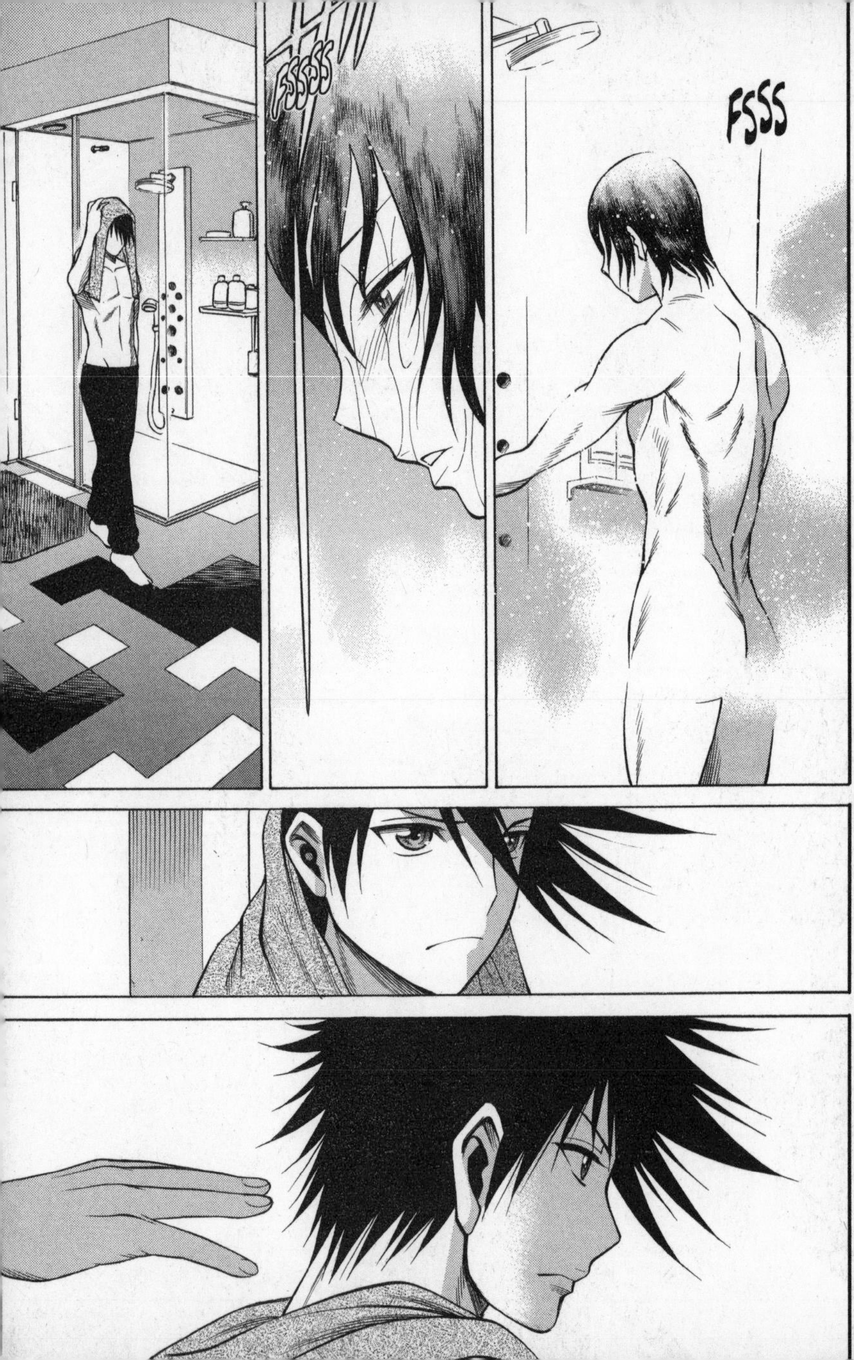
FSSS
FSSSSS

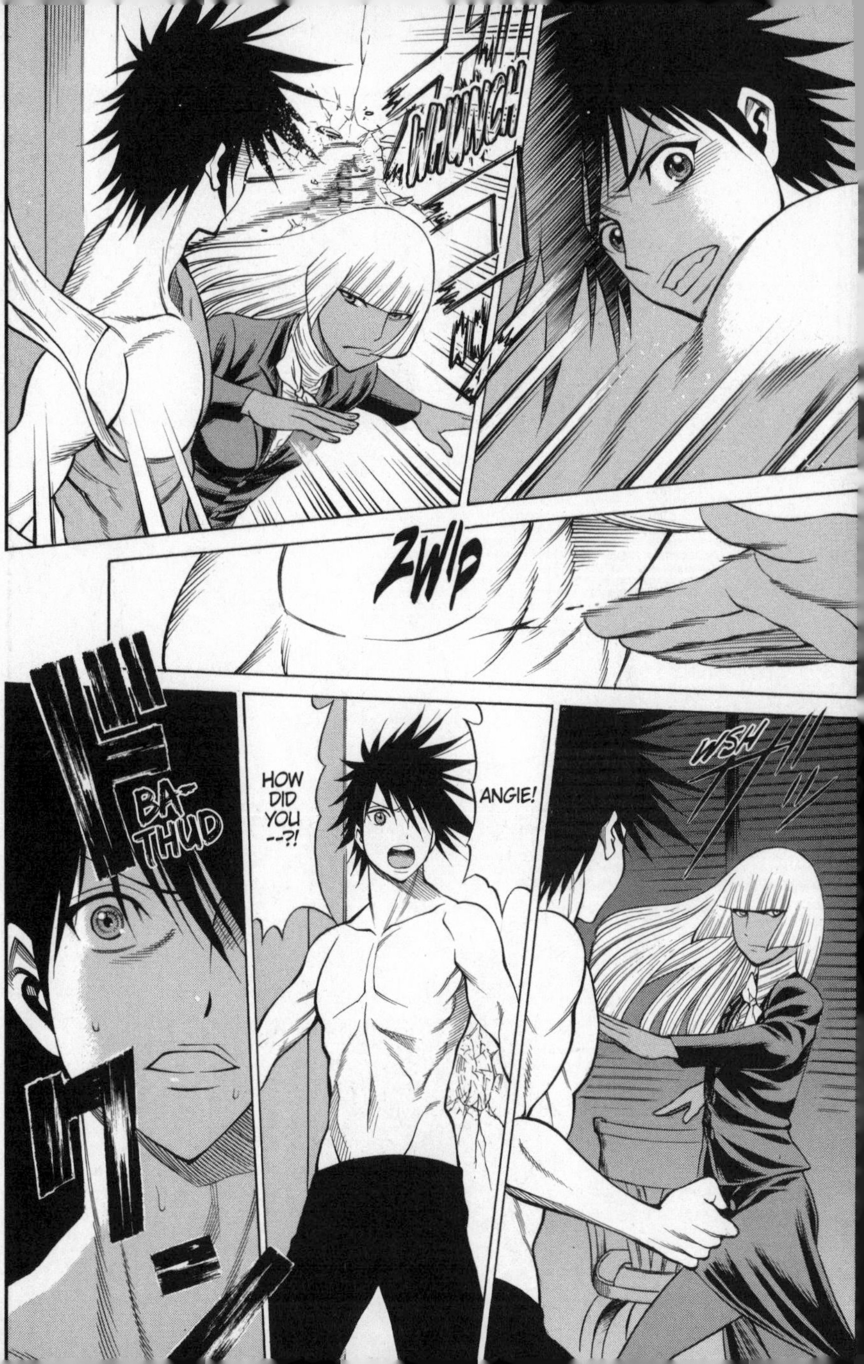
WHUNCH
ZWIP
WSH
ANGIE!
HOW DID YOU --?!
BA-THUD

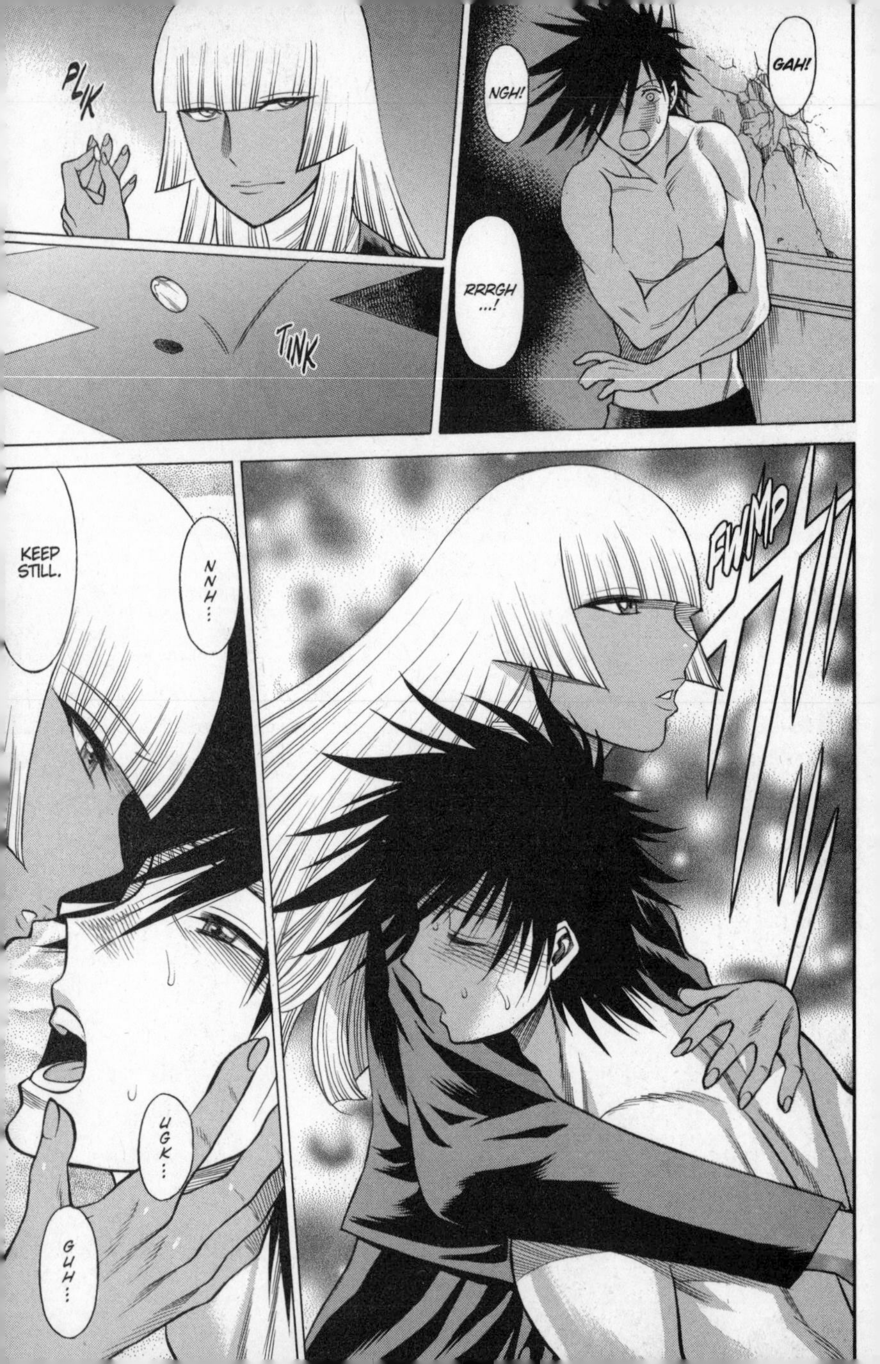
GAH!
NGH!
RRRGH ...!
PLIK
TINK
FWIMP
NNH...
KEEP STILL.
UGK...
GUH...

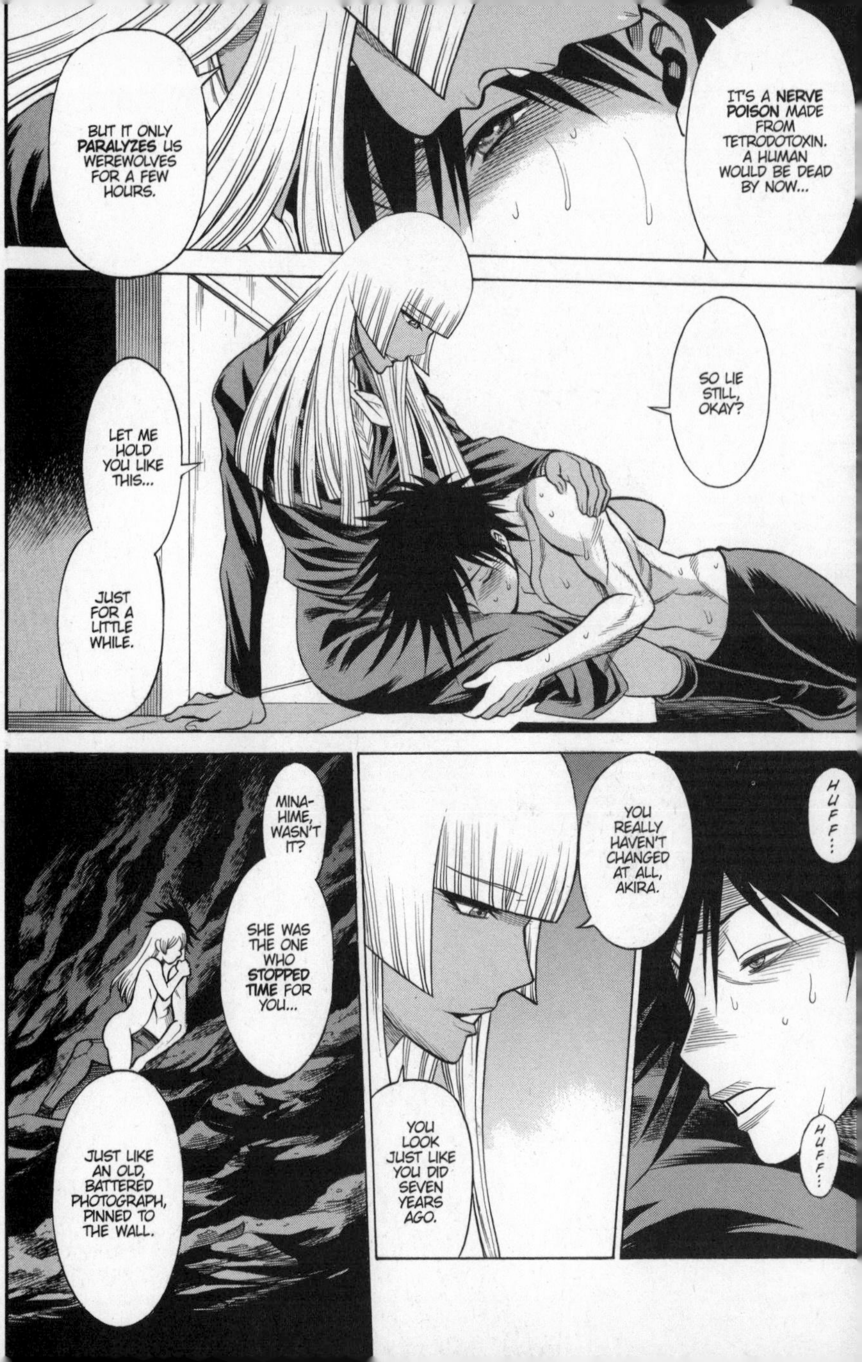
IT'S A **NERVE POISON** MADE FROM TETRODOTOXIN. A HUMAN WOULD BE DEAD BY NOW...
BUT IT ONLY **PARALYZES** US WEREWOLVES FOR A FEW HOURS.
SO LIE STILL, OKAY?
LET ME HOLD YOU LIKE THIS...
JUST FOR A LITTLE WHILE.
HUFF...
HUFF...
YOU REALLY HAVEN'T CHANGED AT ALL, AKIRA.
YOU LOOK JUST LIKE YOU DID SEVEN YEARS AGO.
MINA-HIME, WASN'T IT?
SHE WAS THE ONE WHO **STOPPED TIME** FOR YOU...
JUST LIKE AN OLD, BATTERED PHOTOGRAPH, PINNED TO THE WALL.

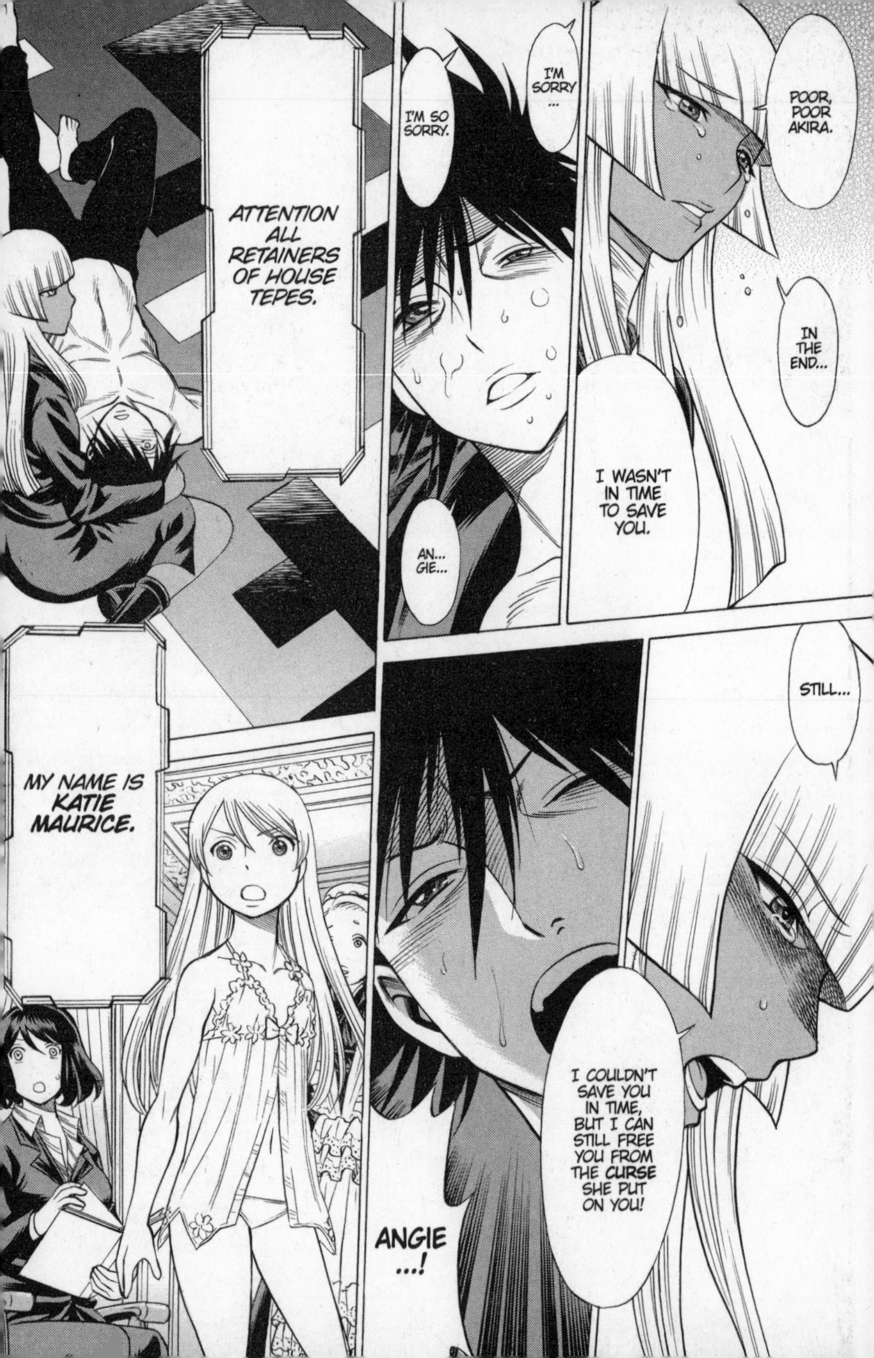
POOR, POOR AKIRA.
IN THE END...
I WASN'T IN TIME TO SAVE YOU.
I'M SORRY...
I'M SO SORRY.
AN... GIE...
STILL...
I COULDN'T SAVE YOU IN TIME, BUT I CAN STILL FREE YOU FROM THE CURSE SHE PUT ON YOU!
ANGIE ...!
ATTENTION ALL RETAINERS OF HOUSE TEPES.
MY NAME IS KATIE MAURICE.

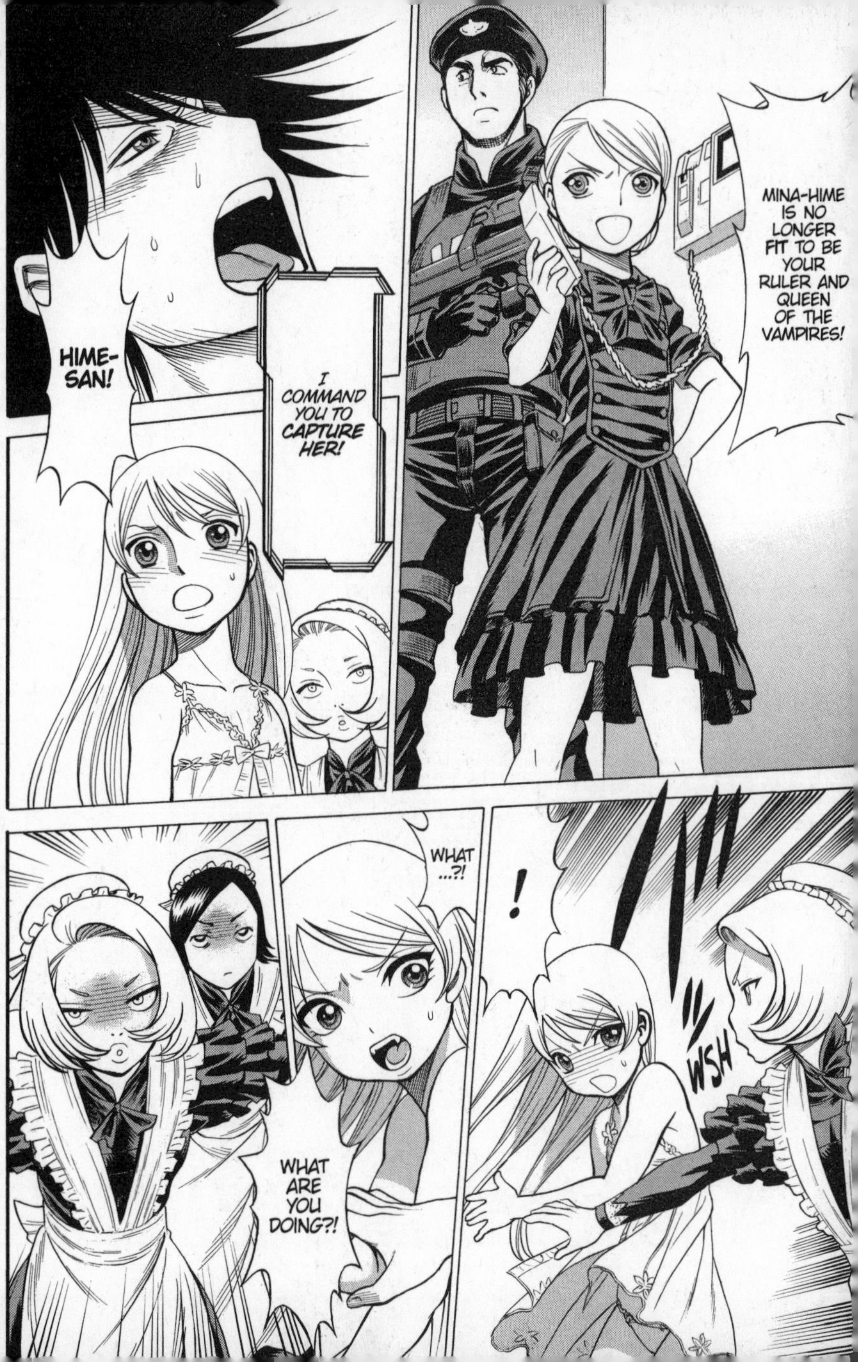
MINA-HIME IS NO LONGER FIT TO BE YOUR RULER AND QUEEN OF THE VAMPIRES!
I COMMAND YOU TO CAPTURE HER!
HIME-SAN!
!
WSH
WHAT ...?!
WHAT ARE YOU DOING?!

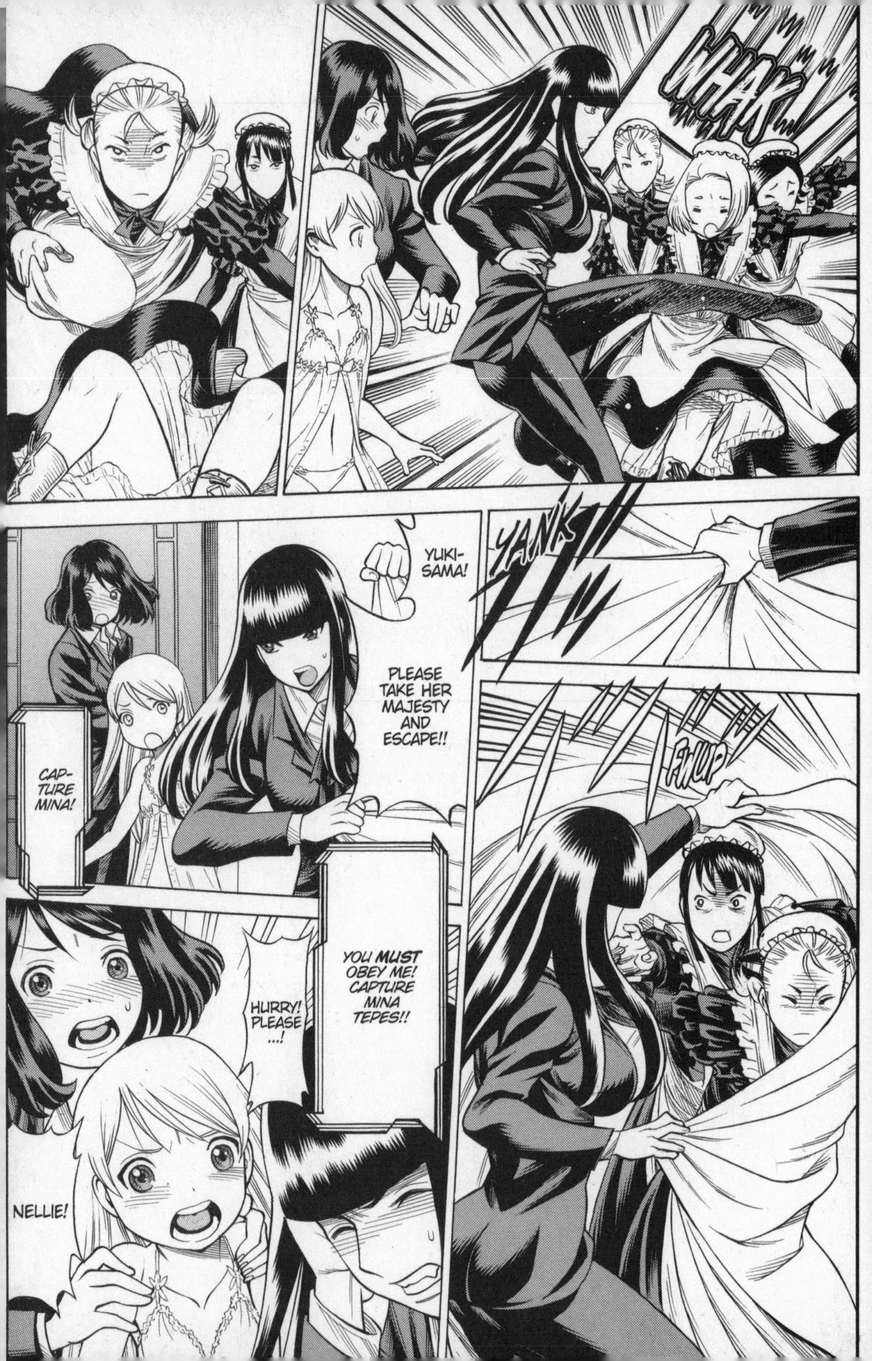
WHAK..!
YANK
FWUP
YUKI-SAMA!
PLEASE TAKE HER MAJESTY AND ESCAPE!!
CAPTURE MINA!
YOU MUST OBEY ME! CAPTURE MINA TEPES!!
HURRY! PLEASE ...!
NELLIE!

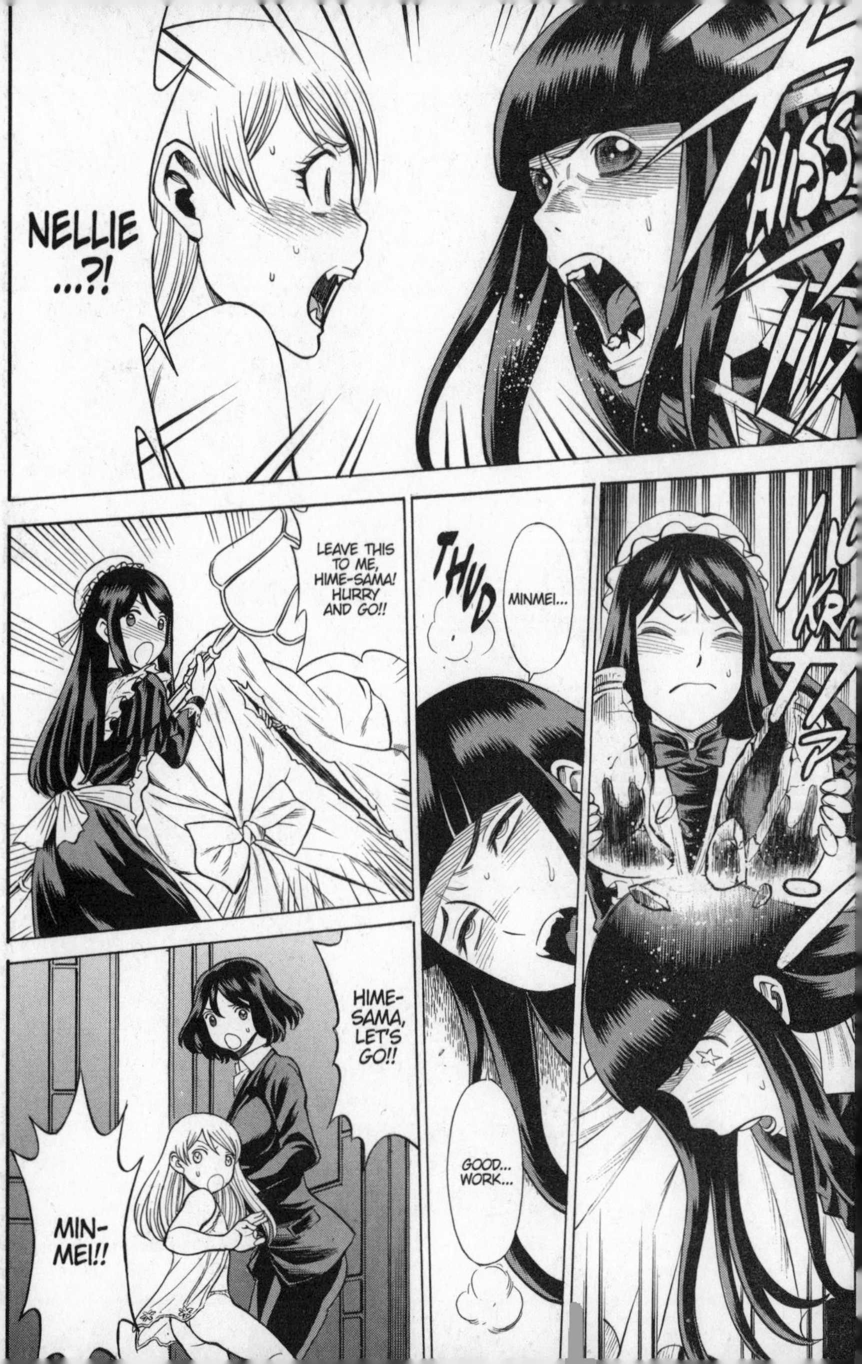

HISS
NELLIE ...?!
THUD
MINMEI...
GOOD... WORK...
LEAVE THIS TO ME, HIME-SAMA! HURRY AND GO!!
HIME-SAMA, LET'S GO!!
MIN-MEI!!

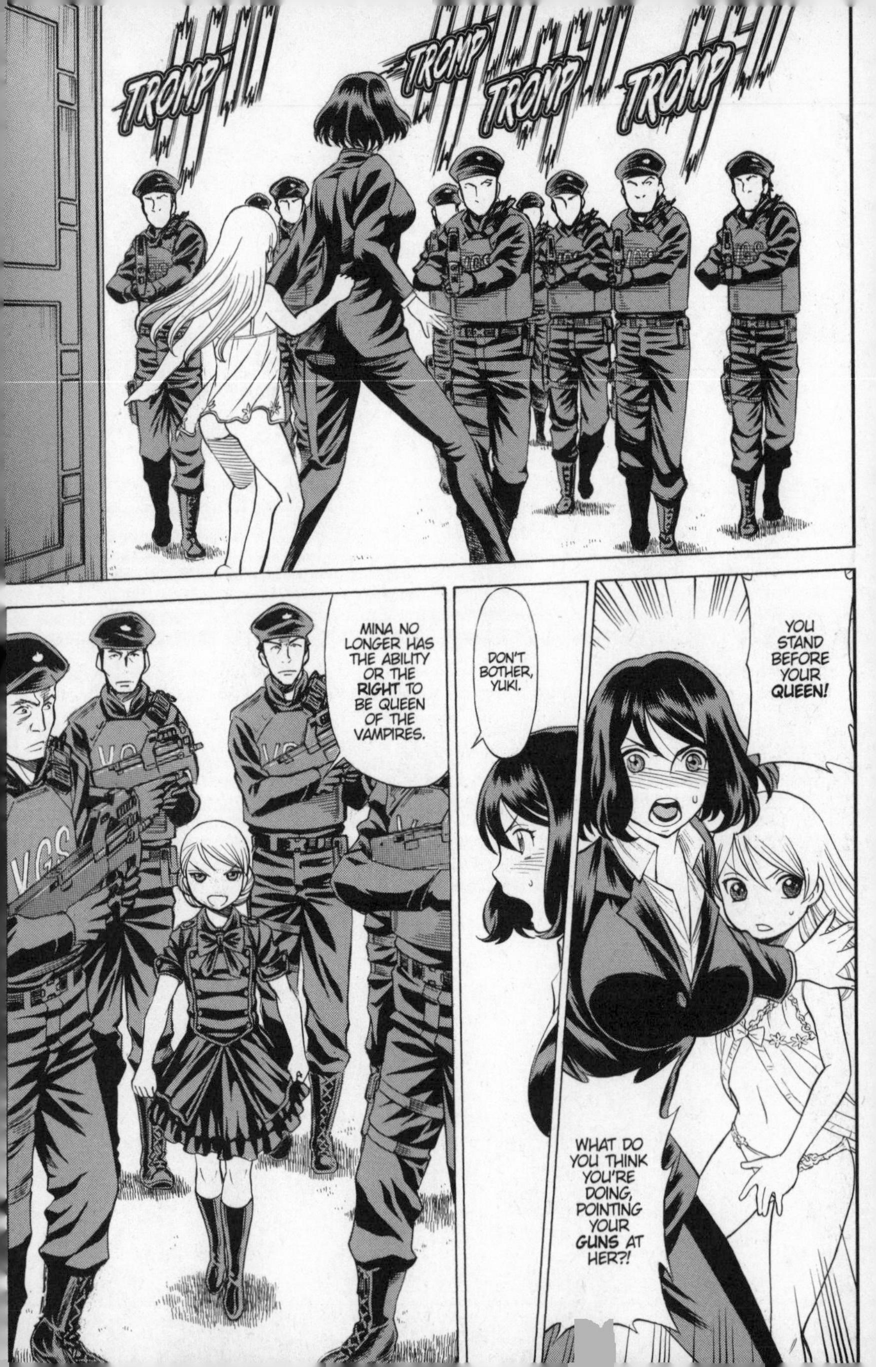
TROMP
TROMP
TROMP
TROMP
YOU STAND BEFORE YOUR QUEEN!
WHAT DO YOU THINK YOU'RE DOING, POINTING YOUR GUNS AT HER?!
DON'T BOTHER, YUKI.
MINA NO LONGER HAS THE ABILITY OR THE RIGHT TO BE QUEEN OF THE VAMPIRES.

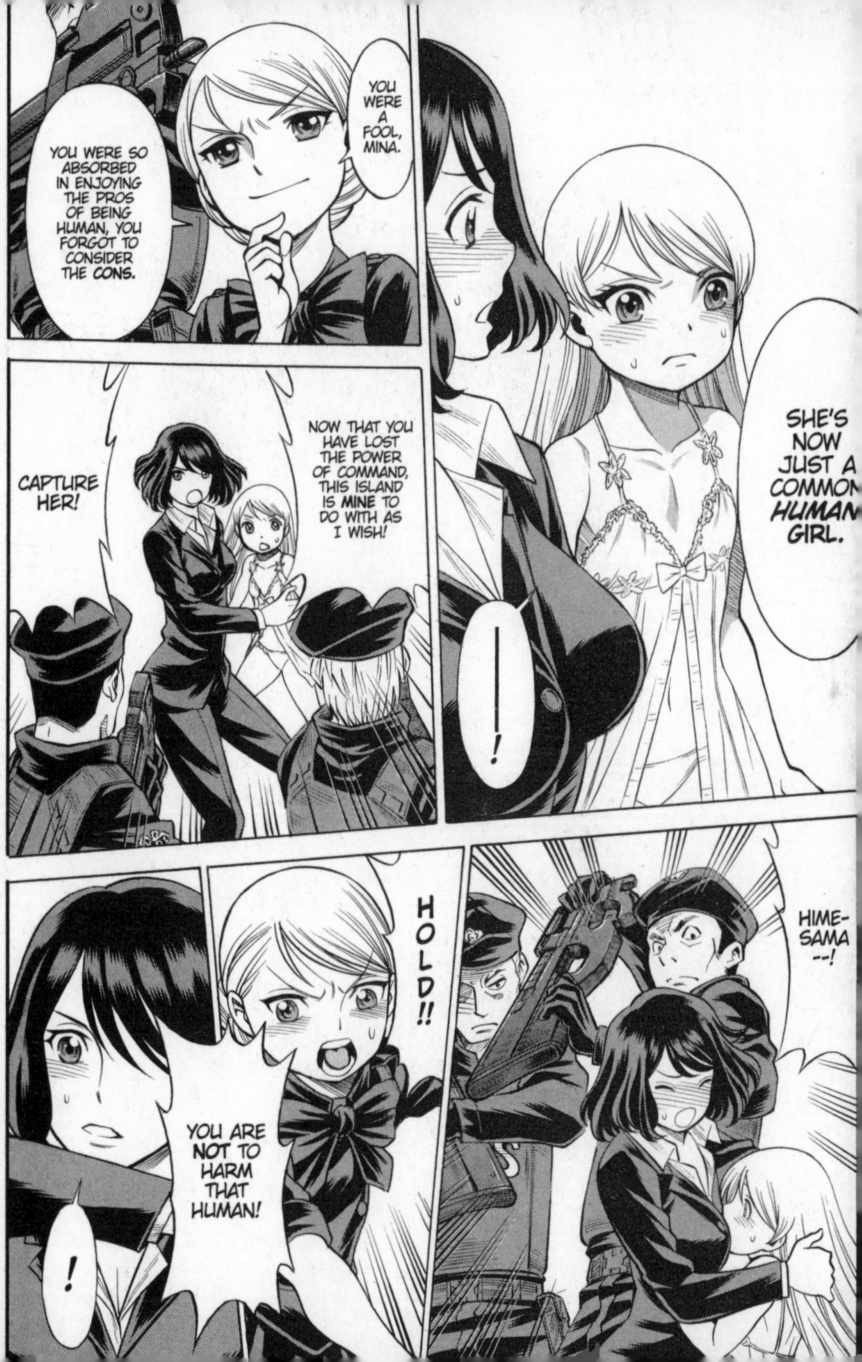
SHE'S NOW JUST A COMMON HUMAN GIRL.
--!
YOU WERE A FOOL, MINA.
YOU WERE SO ABSORBED IN ENJOYING THE PROS OF BEING HUMAN, YOU FORGOT TO CONSIDER THE CONS.
NOW THAT YOU HAVE LOST THE POWER OF COMMAND, THIS ISLAND IS MINE TO DO WITH AS I WISH!
CAPTURE HER!
HIME-SAMA--!
HOLD!!
YOU ARE NOT TO HARM THAT HUMAN!
!

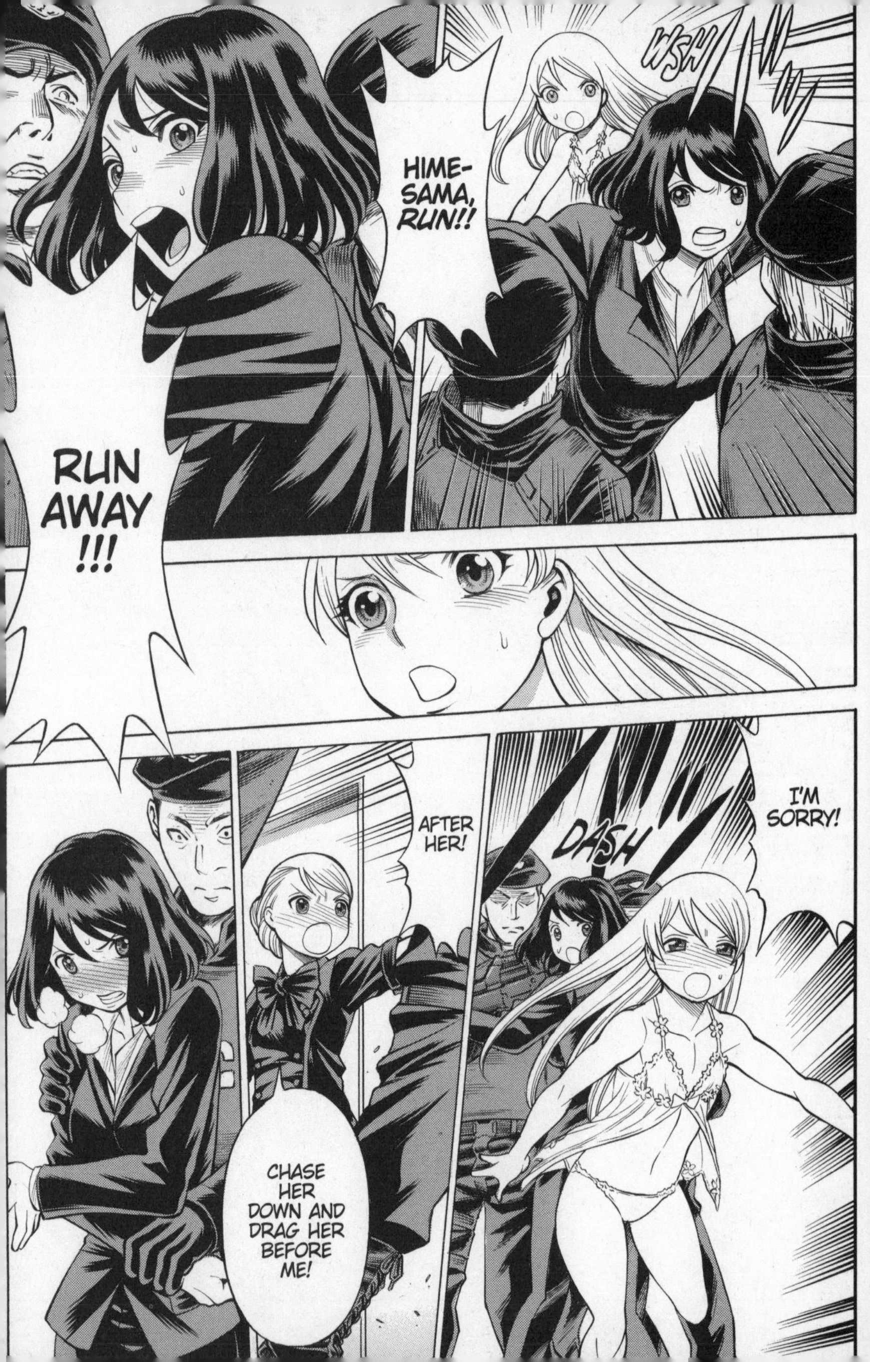
WSH
HIME-SAMA, RUN!!
RUN AWAY !!!
I'M SORRY!
DASH
AFTER HER!
CHASE HER DOWN AND DRAG HER BEFORE ME!

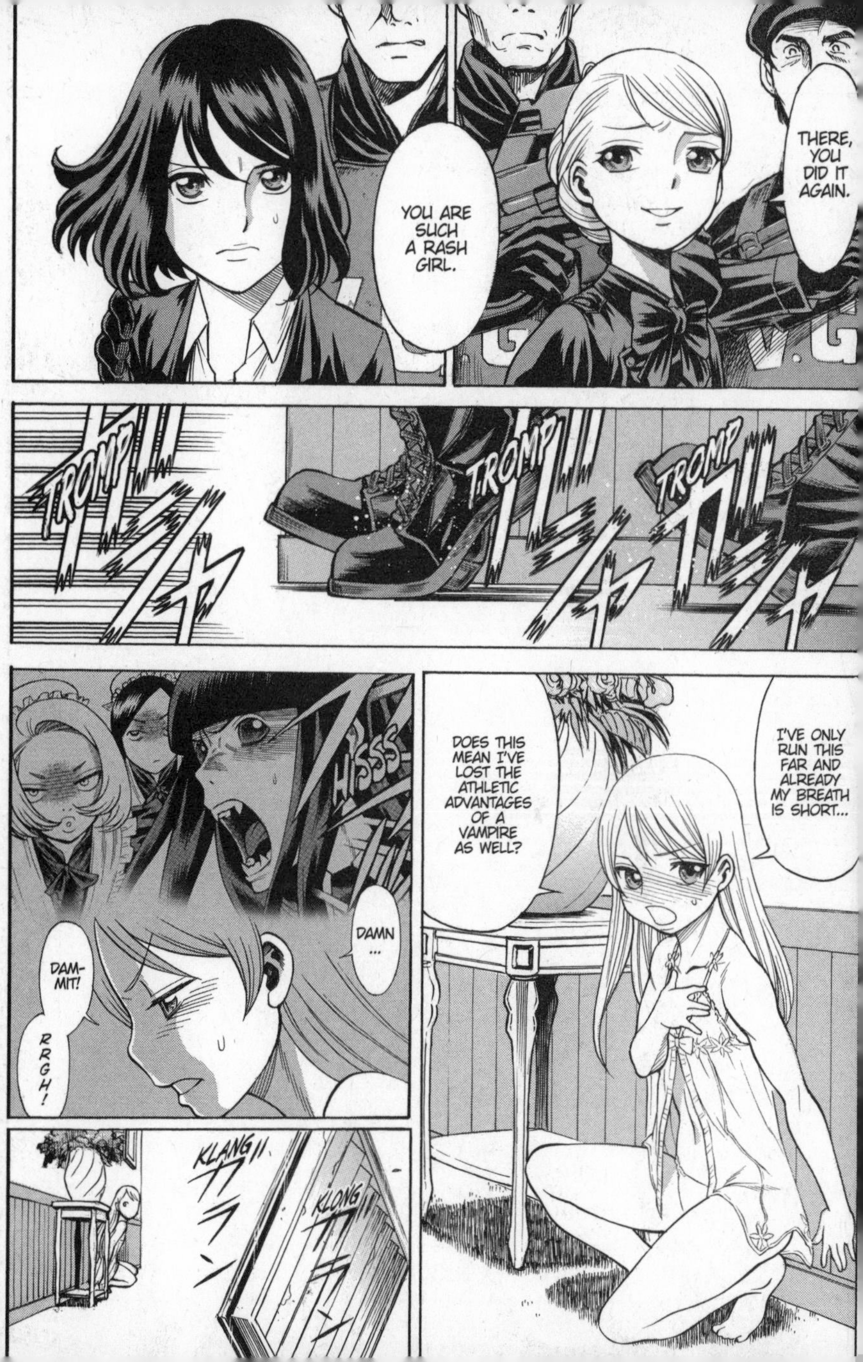
THERE, YOU DID IT AGAIN.
YOU ARE SUCH A RASH GIRL.
TROMP
TROMP!!
TROMP!!
I'VE ONLY RUN THIS FAR AND ALREADY MY BREATH IS SHORT...
DOES THIS MEAN I'VE LOST THE ATHLETIC ADVANTAGES OF A VAMPIRE AS WELL?
HISSS
DAMN...
DAM-MIT!
RRGH!
KLANG!!
KLONG

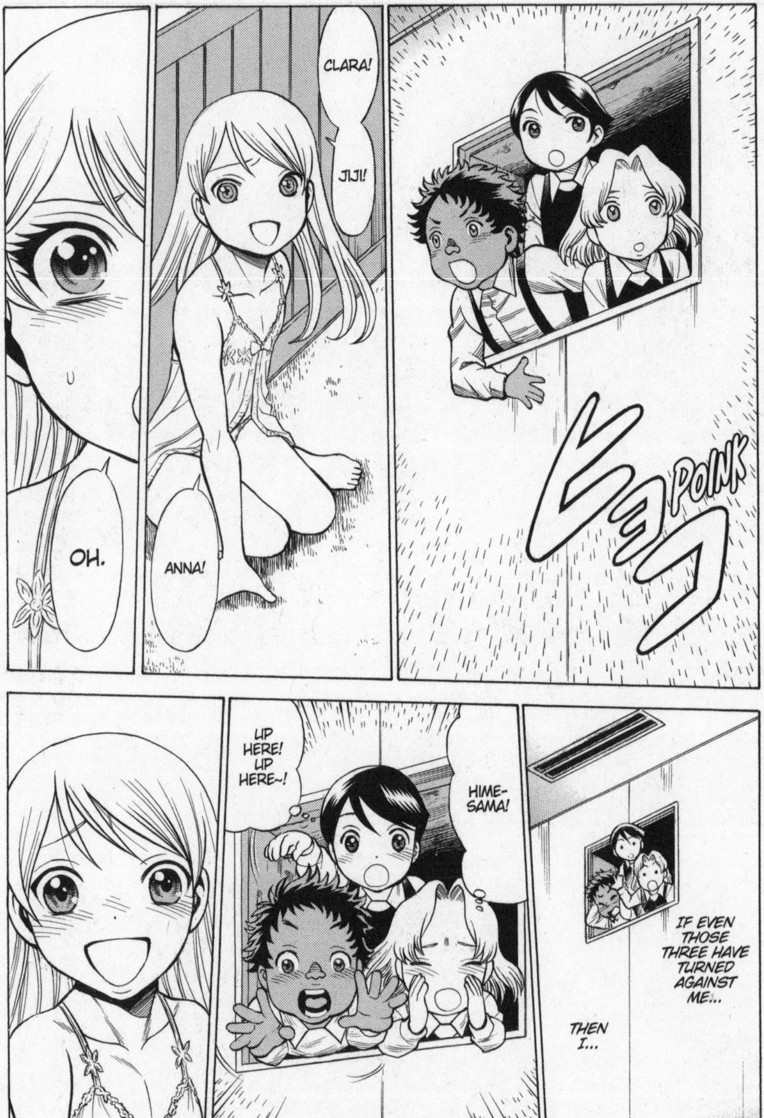
ヒョコ
POINK
CLARA!
JIJI!
ANNA!
OH.
IF EVEN THOSE THREE HAVE TURNED AGAINST ME...
THEN I...
HIME-SAMA!
UP HERE! UP HERE~!

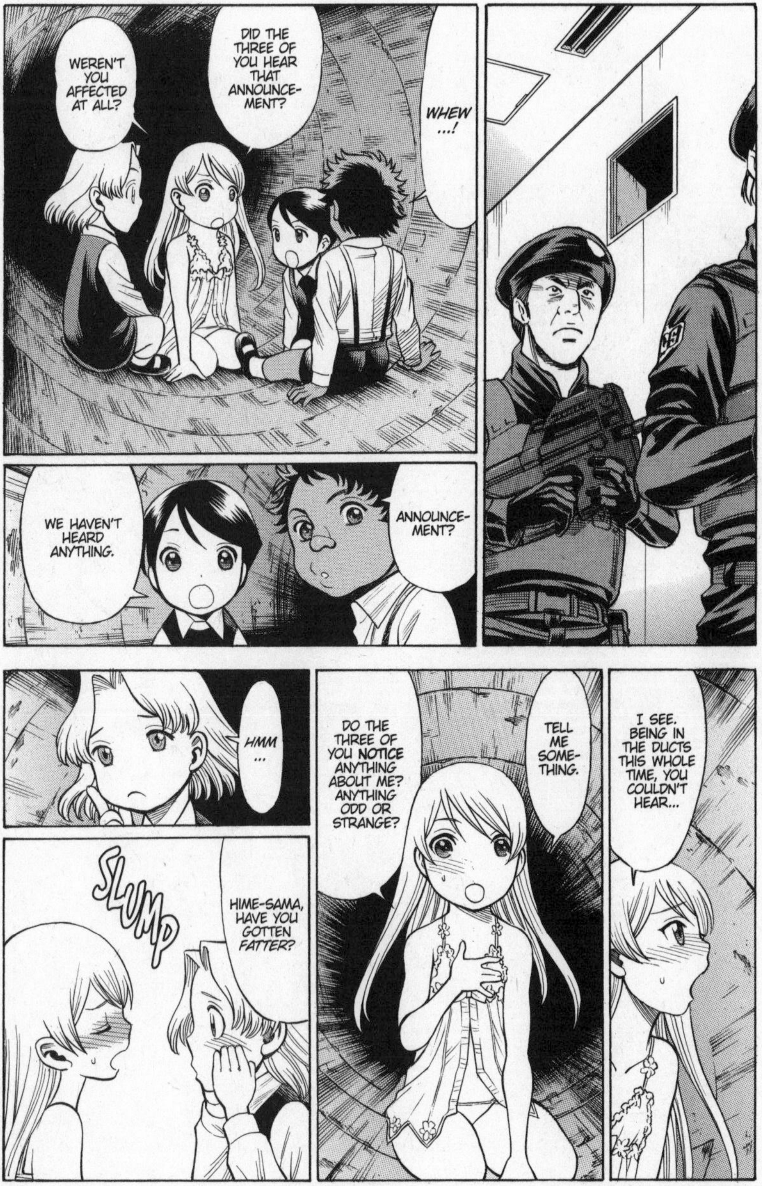
WHEW...!
DID THE THREE OF YOU HEAR THAT ANNOUNCEMENT?
WEREN'T YOU AFFECTED AT ALL?
ANNOUNCEMENT?
WE HAVEN'T HEARD ANYTHING.
I SEE. BEING IN THE DUCTS THIS WHOLE TIME, YOU COULDN'T HEAR...
TELL ME SOMETHING.
DO THE THREE OF YOU NOTICE ANYTHING ABOUT ME? ANYTHING ODD OR STRANGE?
HMM...
HIME-SAMA, HAVE YOU GOTTEN FATTER?
SLUMP

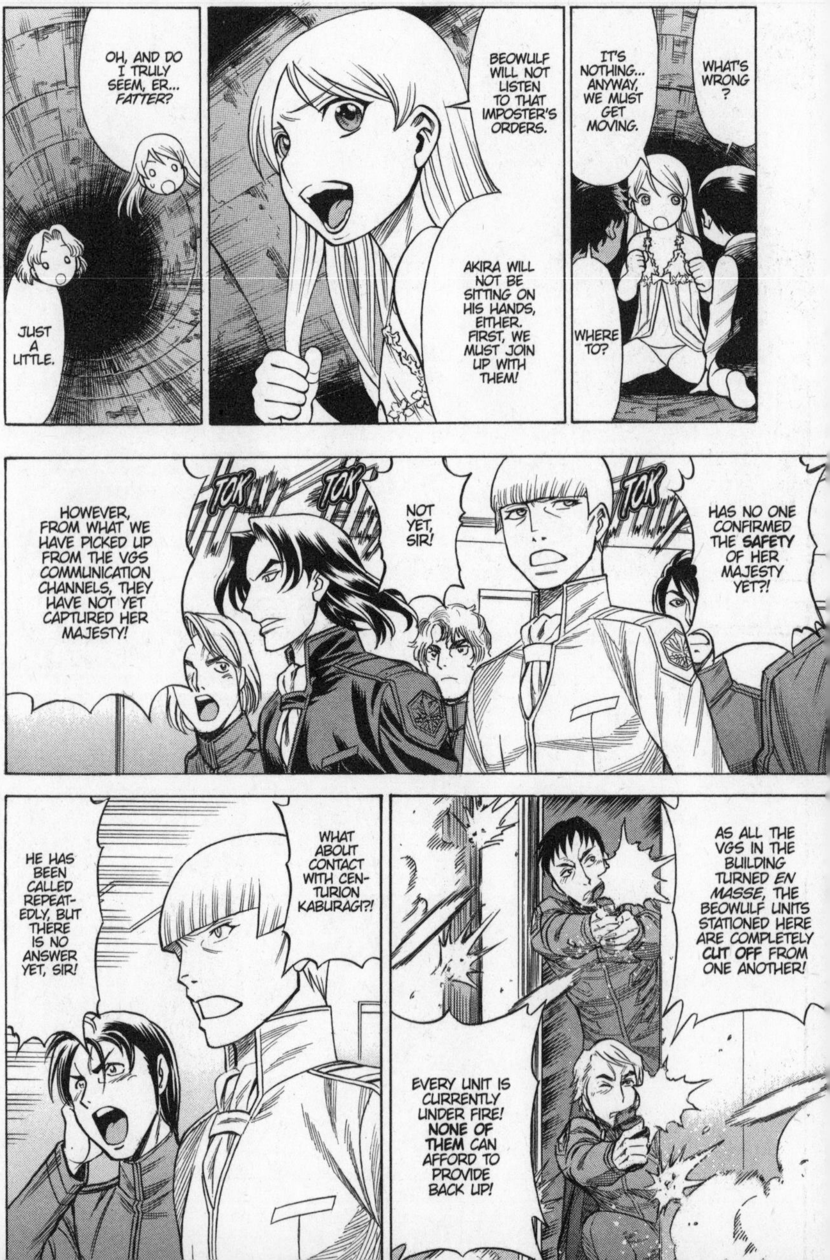
WHAT'S WRONG?
IT'S NOTHING... ANYWAY, WE MUST GET MOVING.
WHERE TO?
BEOWULF WILL NOT LISTEN TO THAT IMPOSTER'S ORDERS.
AKIRA WILL NOT BE SITTING ON HIS HANDS, EITHER. FIRST, WE MUST JOIN UP WITH THEM!
OH, AND DO I TRULY SEEM, ER... *FATTER?*
JUST A LITTLE.
TOK
TOK
TOK
HAS NO ONE CONFIRMED THE **SAFETY** OF HER MAJESTY YET?!
NOT YET, SIR!
HOWEVER, FROM WHAT WE HAVE PICKED UP FROM THE VGS COMMUNICATION CHANNELS, THEY HAVE NOT YET CAPTURED HER MAJESTY!
AS ALL THE VGS IN THE BUILDING TURNED *EN MASSE*, THE BEOWULF UNITS STATIONED HERE ARE COMPLETELY **CUT OFF** FROM ONE ANOTHER!
EVERY UNIT IS CURRENTLY UNDER FIRE! **NONE OF THEM CAN** AFFORD TO PROVIDE BACK UP!
WHAT ABOUT CONTACT WITH CEN-TURION KABURAGI?!
HE HAS BEEN CALLED REPEAT-EDLY, BUT THERE IS NO ANSWER YET, SIR!

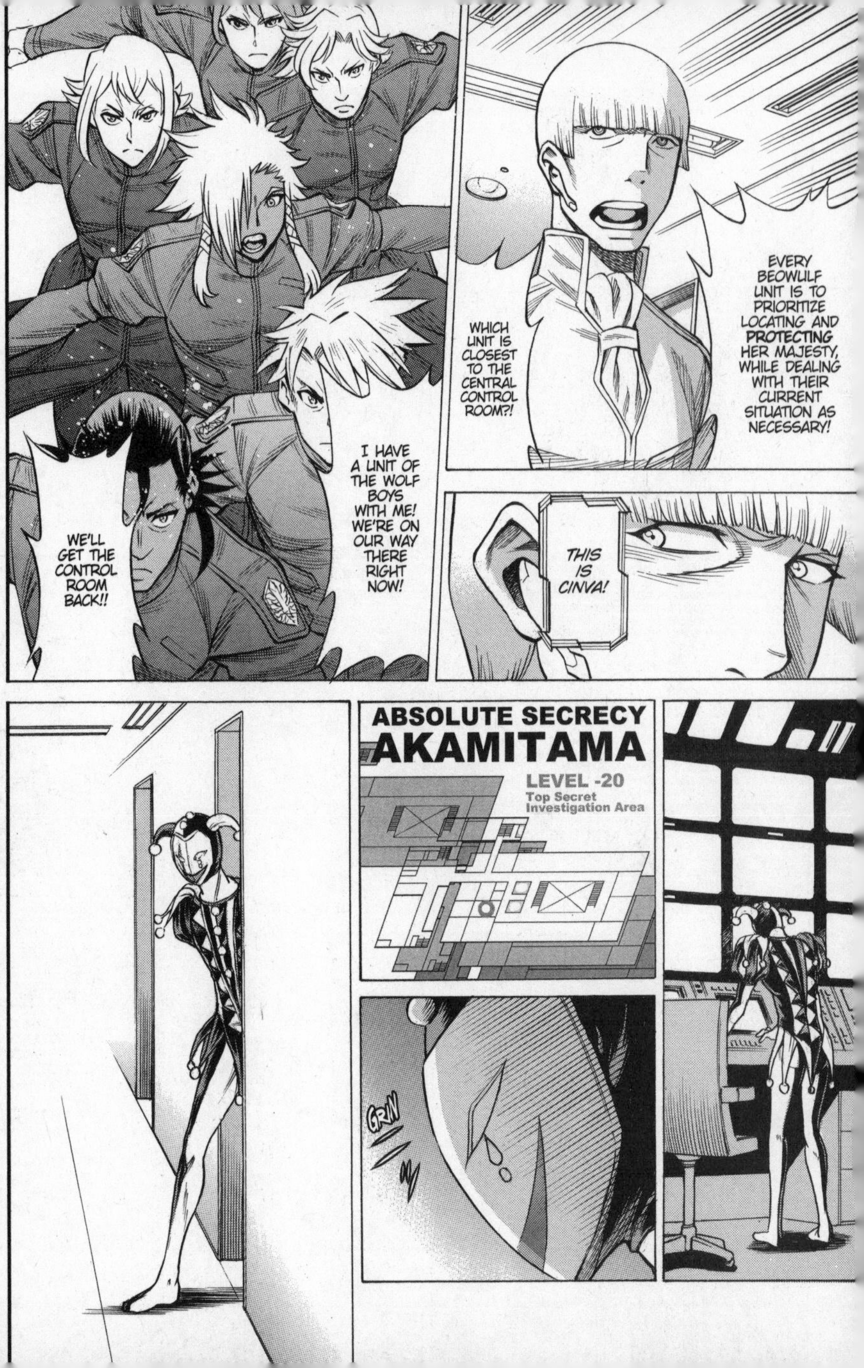
EVERY BEOWULF UNIT IS TO PRIORITIZE LOCATING AND PROTECTING HER MAJESTY, WHILE DEALING WITH THEIR CURRENT SITUATION AS NECESSARY!
WHICH UNIT IS CLOSEST TO THE CENTRAL CONTROL ROOM?!
THIS IS CINVA!
I HAVE A UNIT OF THE WOLF BOYS WITH ME! WE'RE ON OUR WAY THERE RIGHT NOW!
WE'LL GET THE CONTROL ROOM BACK!!
ABSOLUTE SECRECY
AKAMITAMA
LEVEL -20
Top Secret
Investigation Area
GRIN

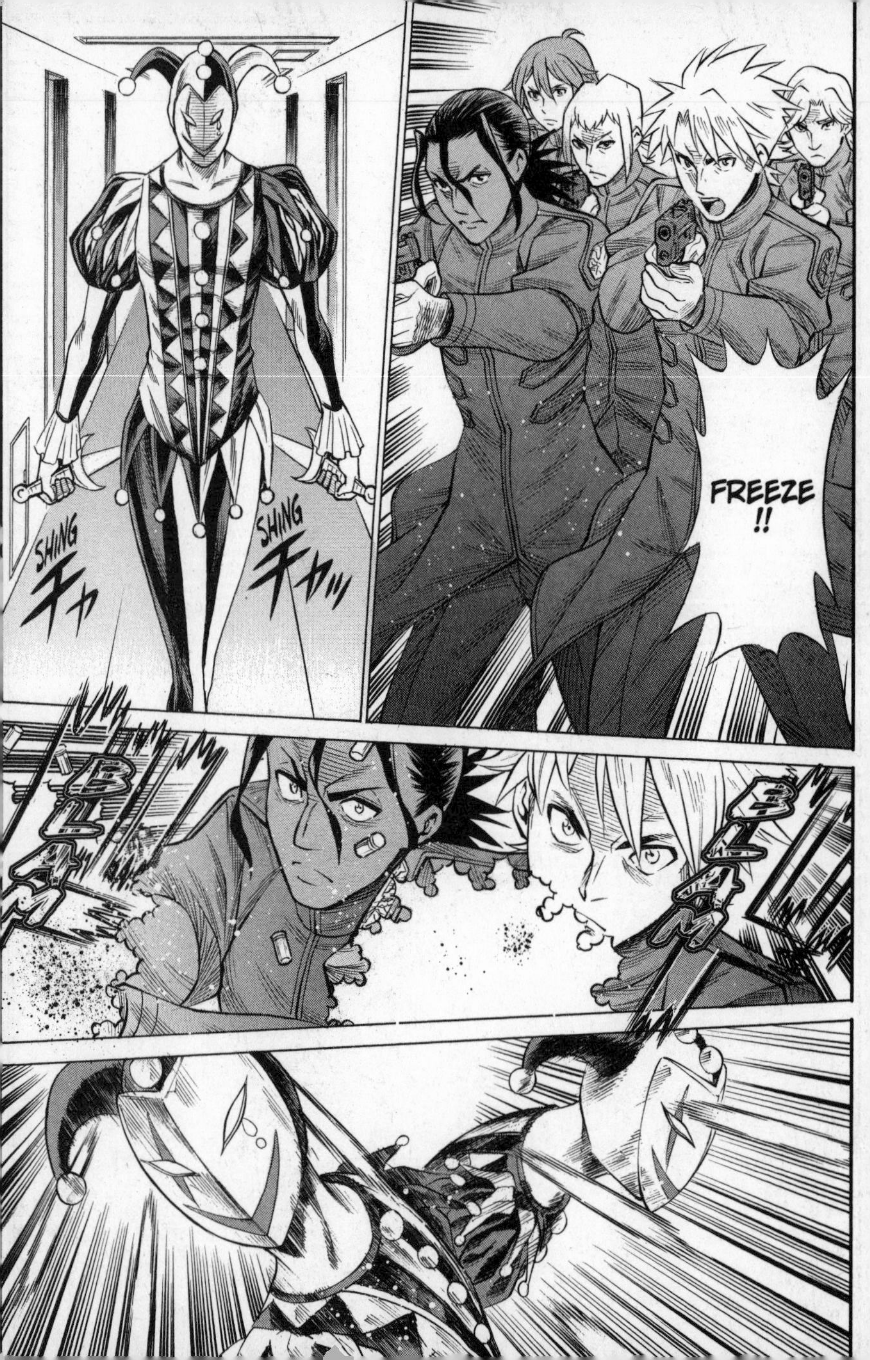
FREEZE!!
SHING チャッ
SHING チャ
BLAM
BLAM

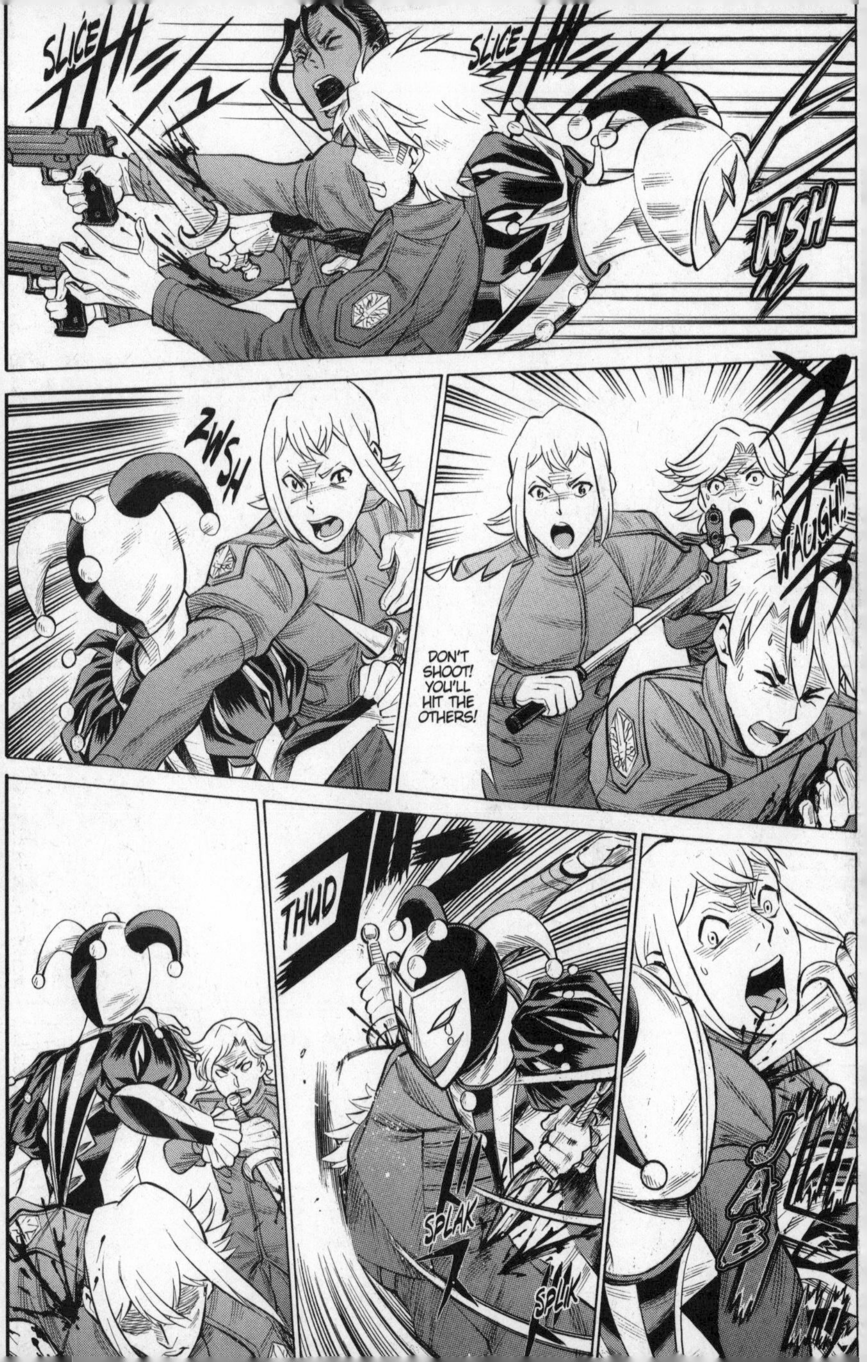
WSH
SLICE
SLICE
WAUGH!!
DON'T SHOOT! YOU'LL HIT THE OTHERS!
ZWSH
JAB
SPLIK
SPLAK
THUD

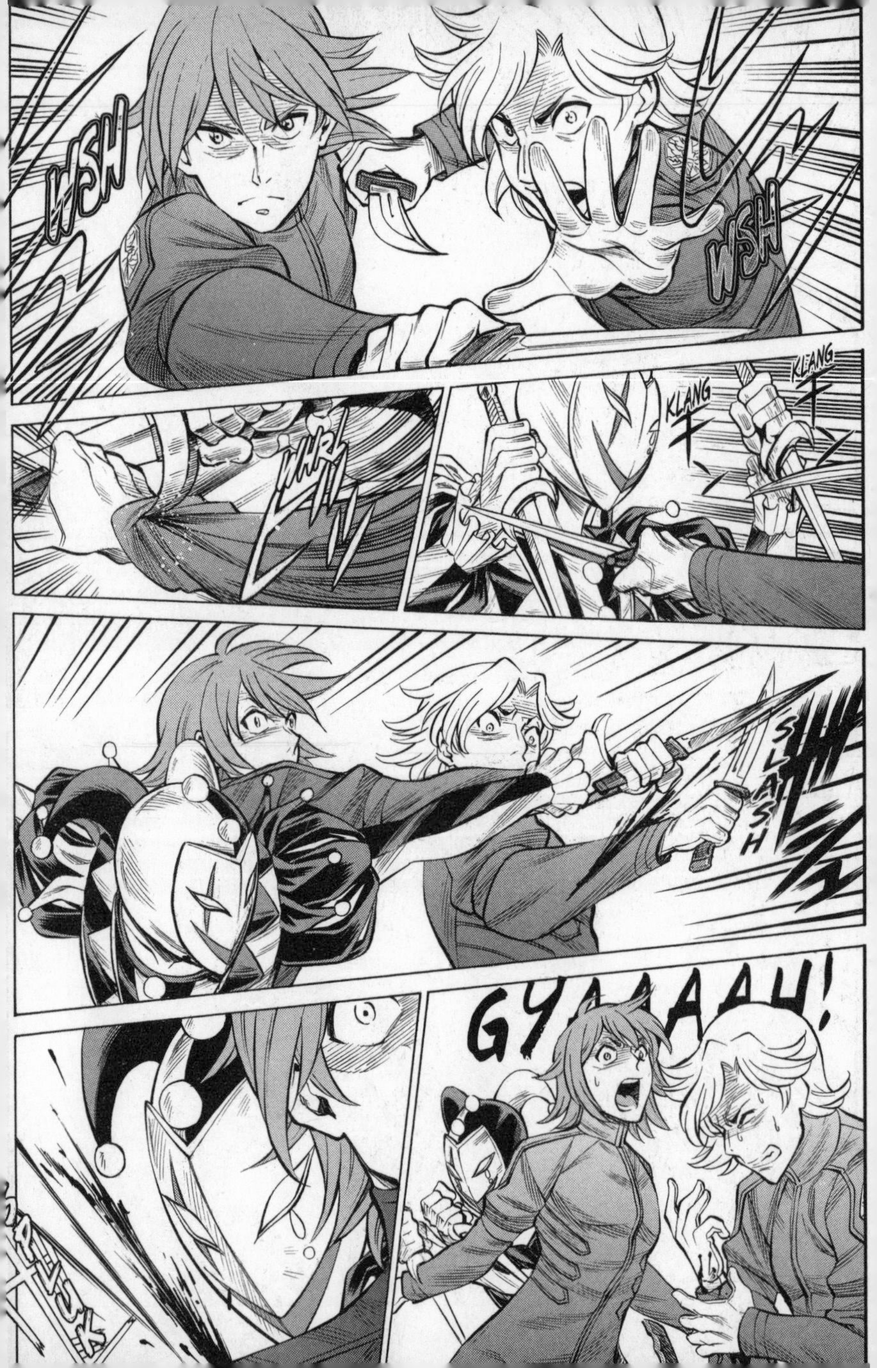
WSH
WSH
KLANG
KLANG
WHRL
SLASH
GYAAAAH!

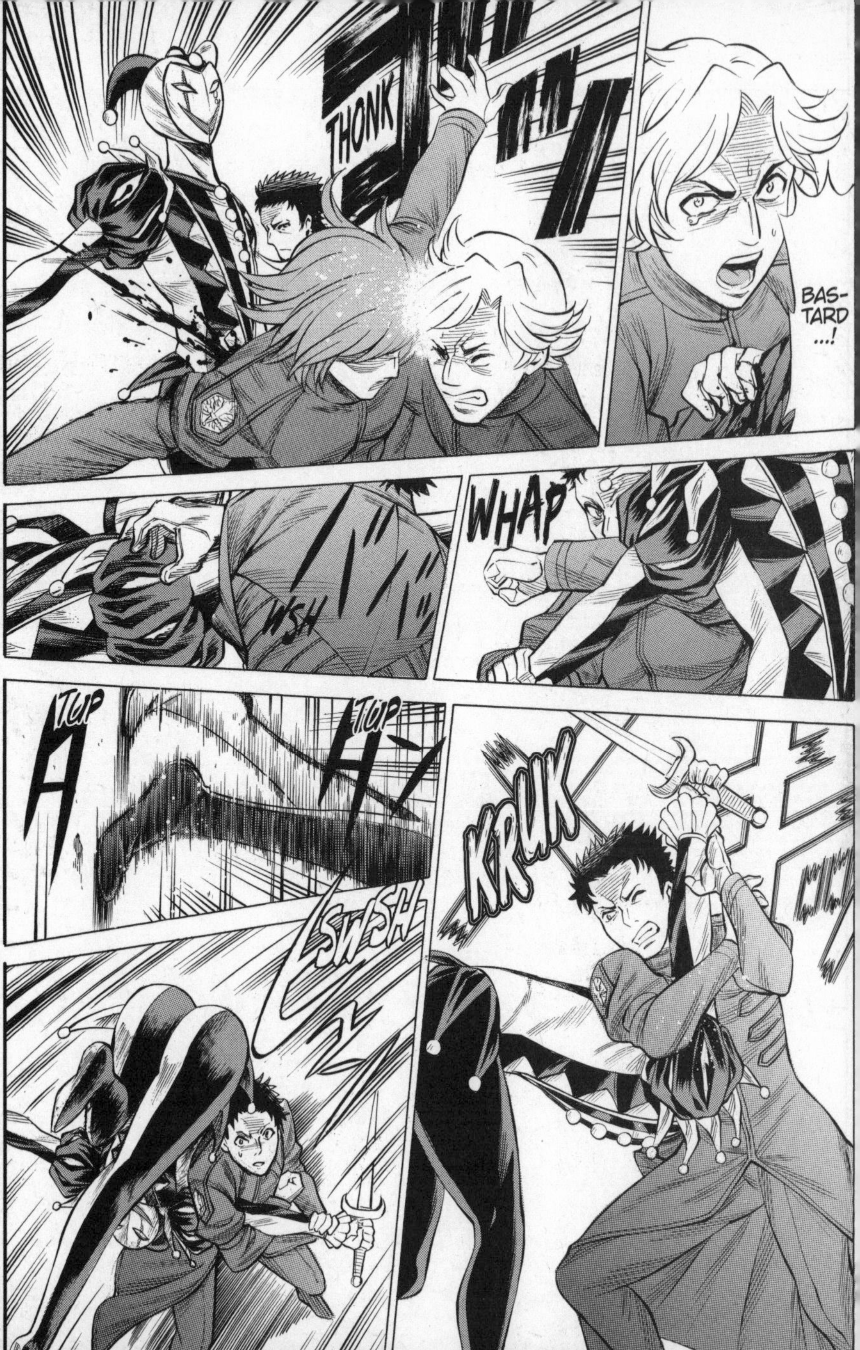
BAS-
TARD
...!
THONK
WHAP
WSH
KRUK
TUP
TUP
SWISH

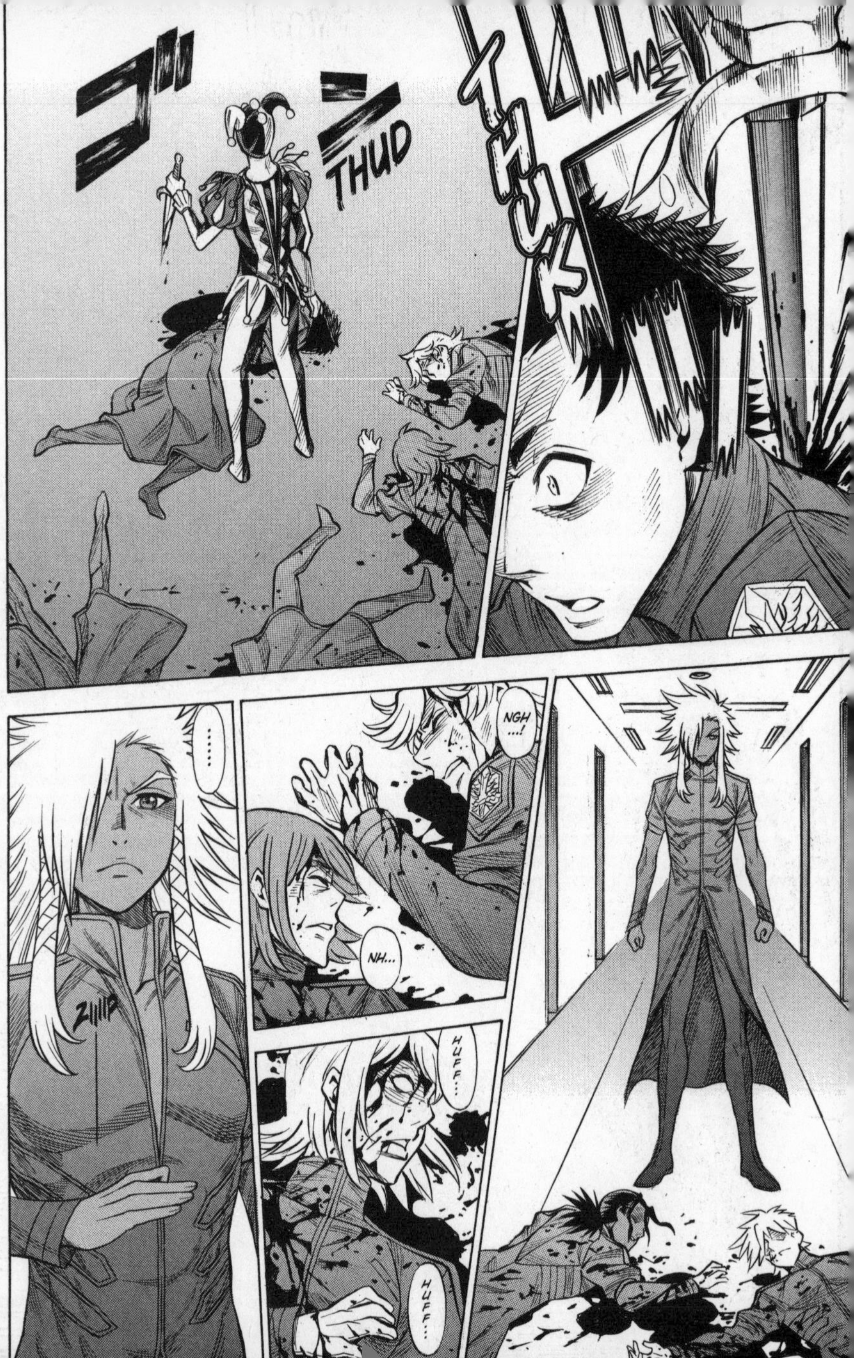
THUK
ゴン
THUD
NGH...!
NH...
HUFF...
HUFF...
......
ZIIIP

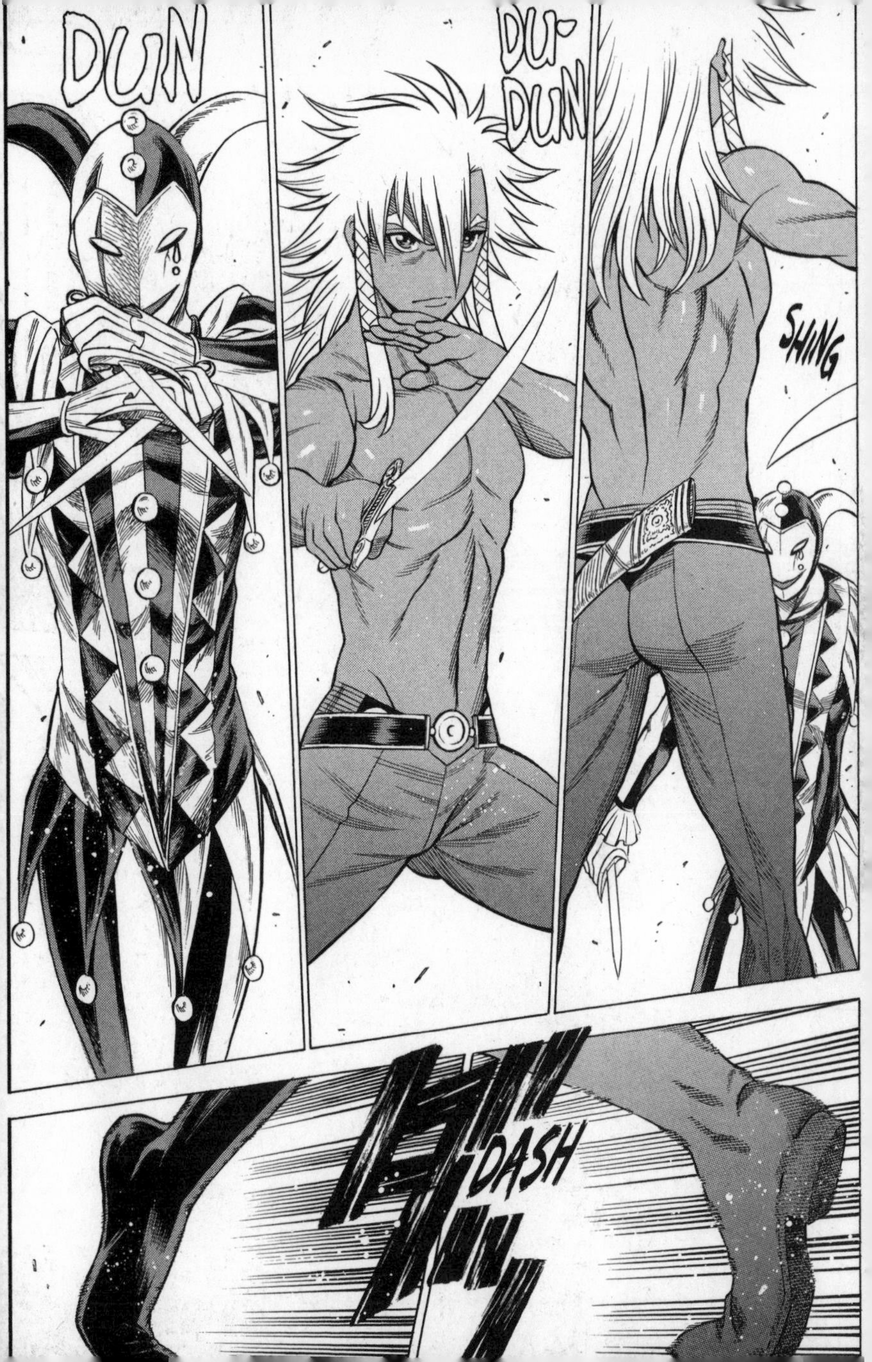
SHING
DU-DUN
DUN
DASH

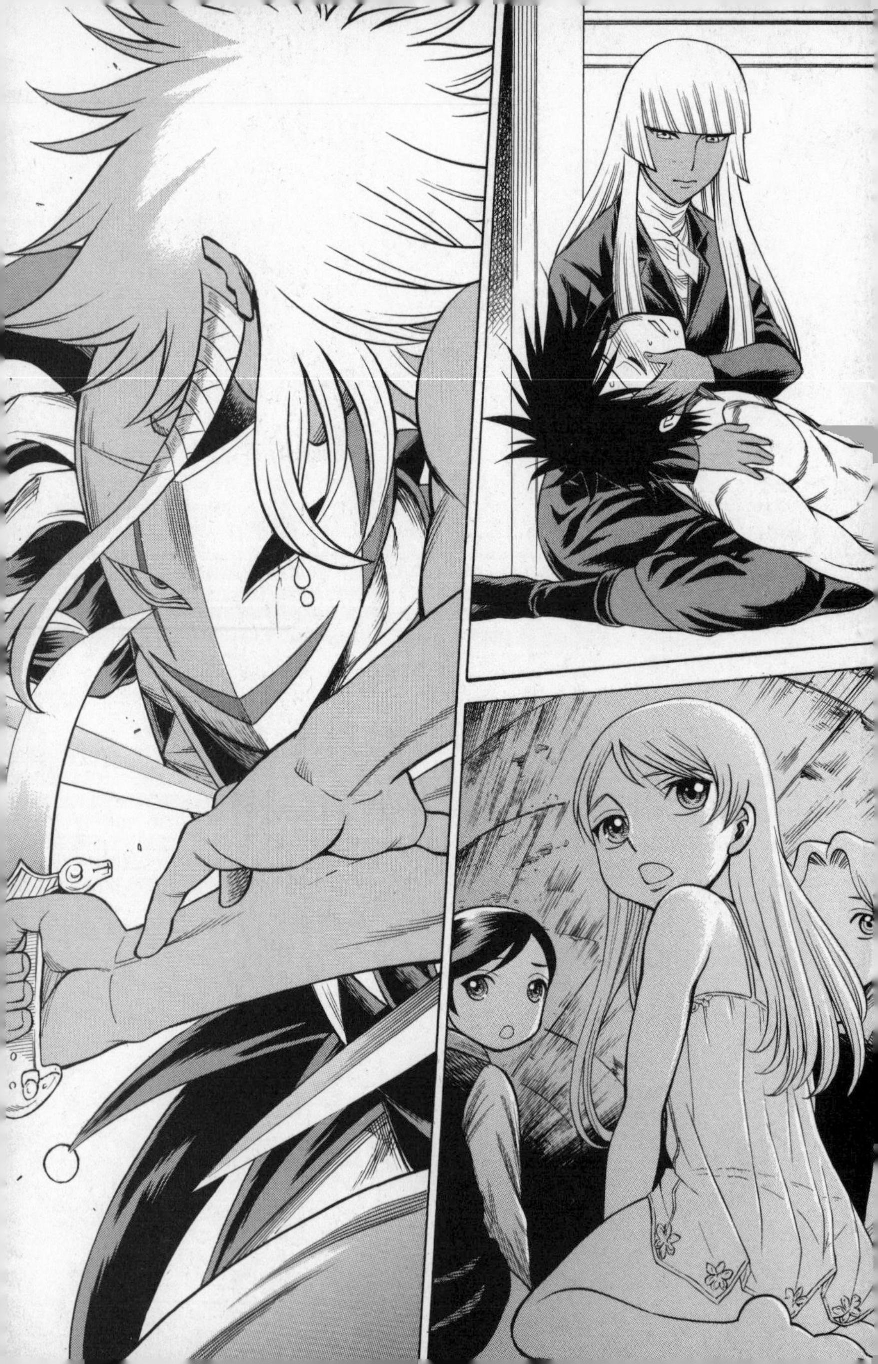

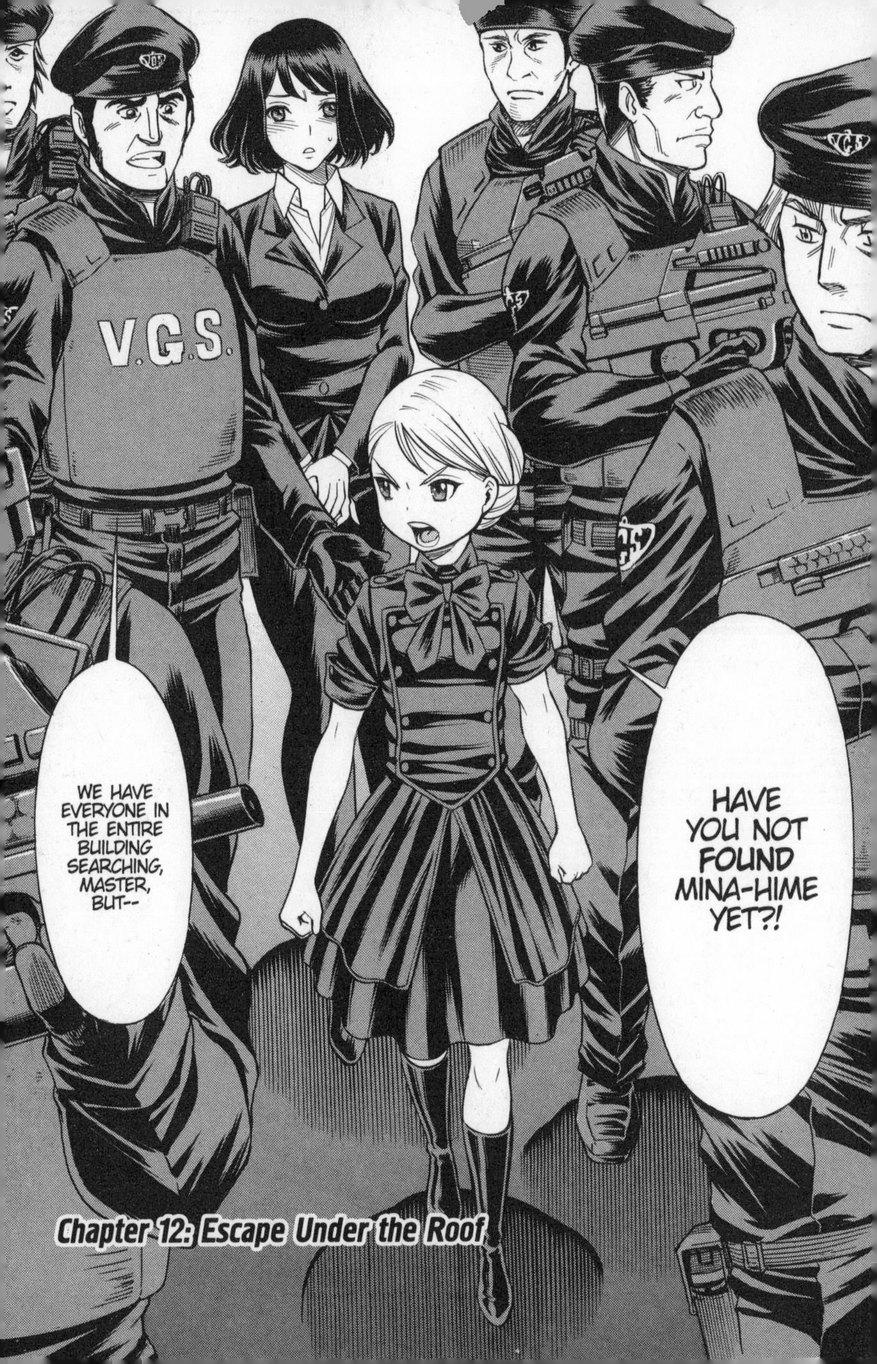
HAVE YOU NOT FOUND MINA-HIME YET?!
WE HAVE EVERYONE IN THE ENTIRE BUILDING SEARCHING, MASTER, BUT--
Chapter 12: Escape Under the Roof

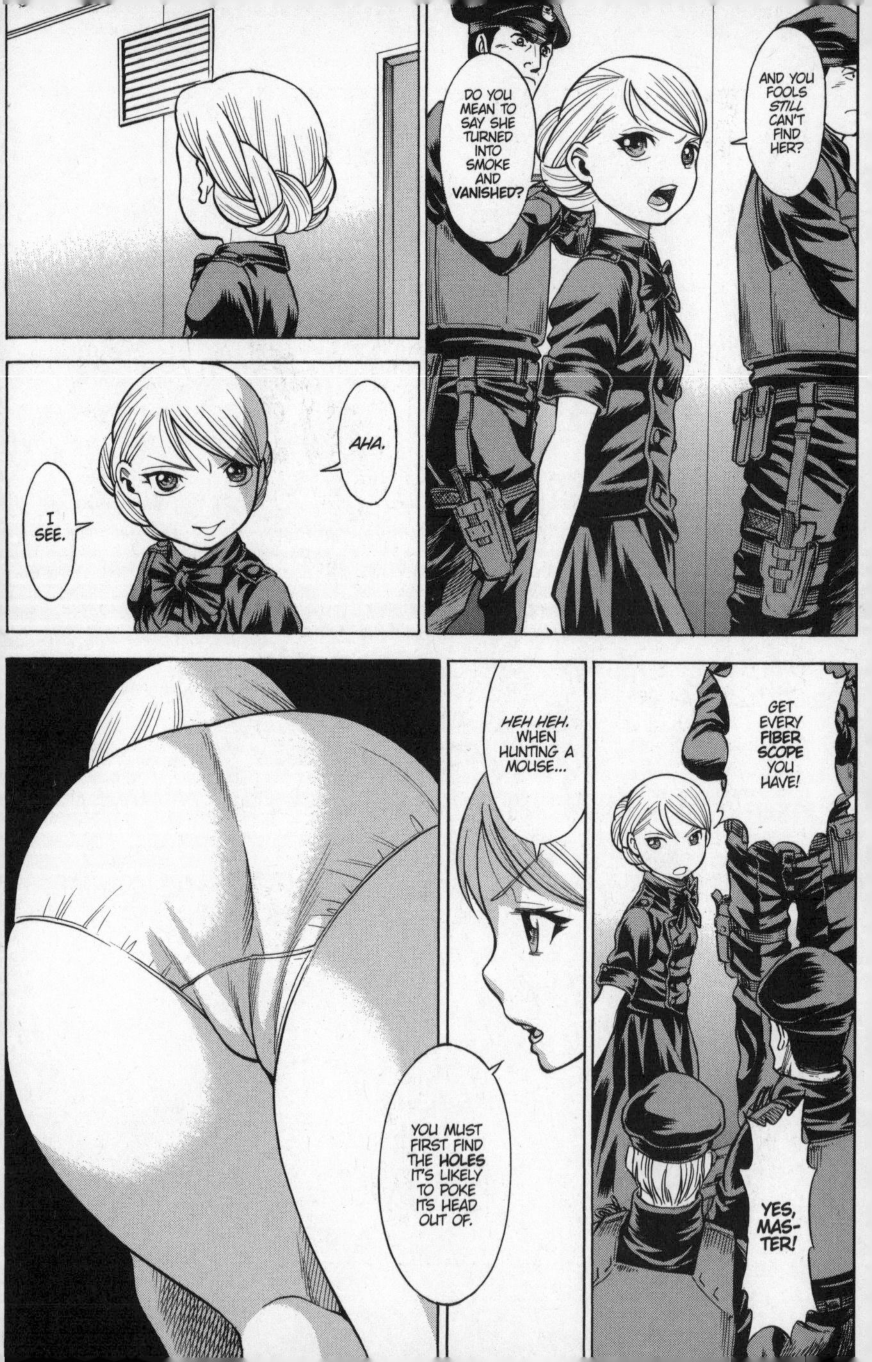
AND YOU FOOLS STILL CAN'T FIND HER?
DO YOU MEAN TO SAY SHE TURNED INTO SMOKE AND VANISHED?
AHA.
I SEE.
GET EVERY FIBER SCOPE YOU HAVE!
YES, MASTER!
HEH HEH. WHEN HUNTING A MOUSE...
YOU MUST FIRST FIND THE HOLES IT'S LIKELY TO POKE ITS HEAD OUT OF.

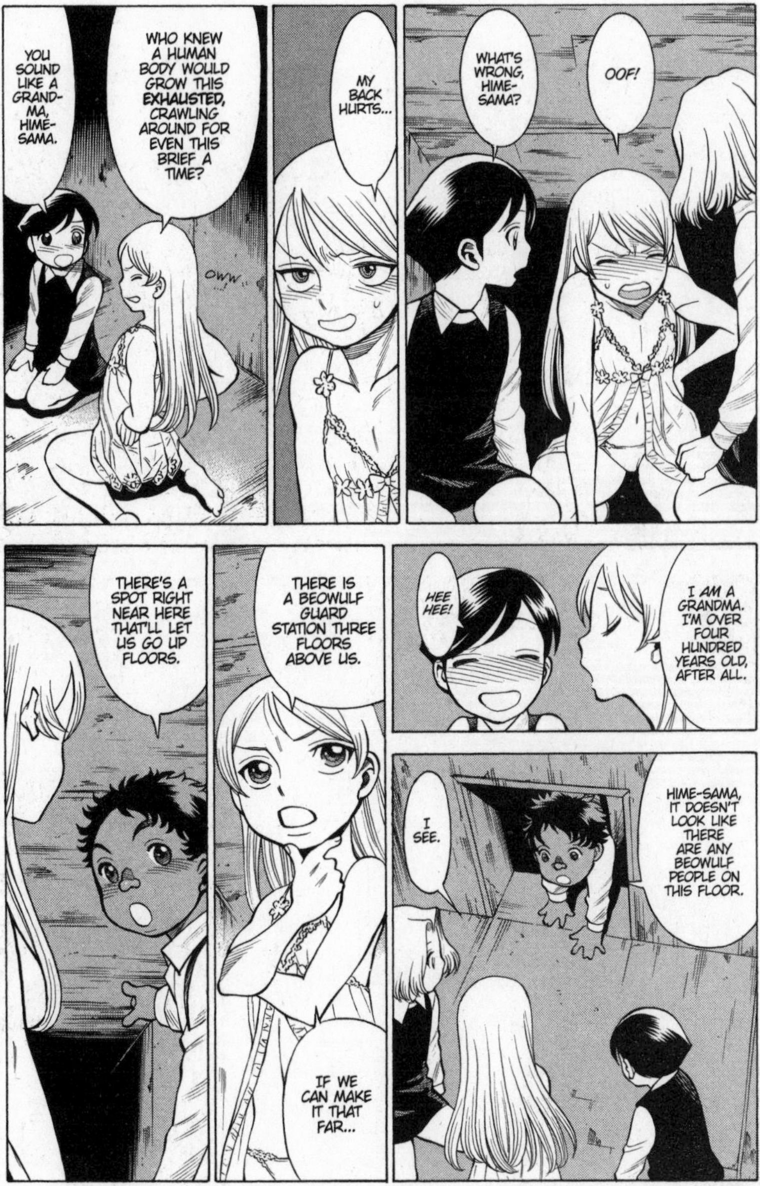
OOF!
WHAT'S WRONG, HIME-SAMA?
MY BACK HURTS...
WHO KNEW A HUMAN BODY WOULD GROW THIS **EXHAUSTED,** CRAWLING AROUND FOR EVEN THIS BRIEF A TIME?
OWW
YOU SOUND LIKE A GRAND-MA, HIME-SAMA.
I AM A GRANDMA. I'M OVER FOUR HUNDRED YEARS OLD, AFTER ALL.
HEE HEE!
HIME-SAMA, IT DOESN'T LOOK LIKE THERE ARE ANY BEOWULF PEOPLE ON THIS FLOOR.
I SEE.
THERE IS A BEOWULF GUARD STATION THREE FLOORS ABOVE US.
IF WE CAN MAKE IT THAT FAR...
THERE'S A SPOT RIGHT NEAR HERE THAT'LL LET US GO UP FLOORS.

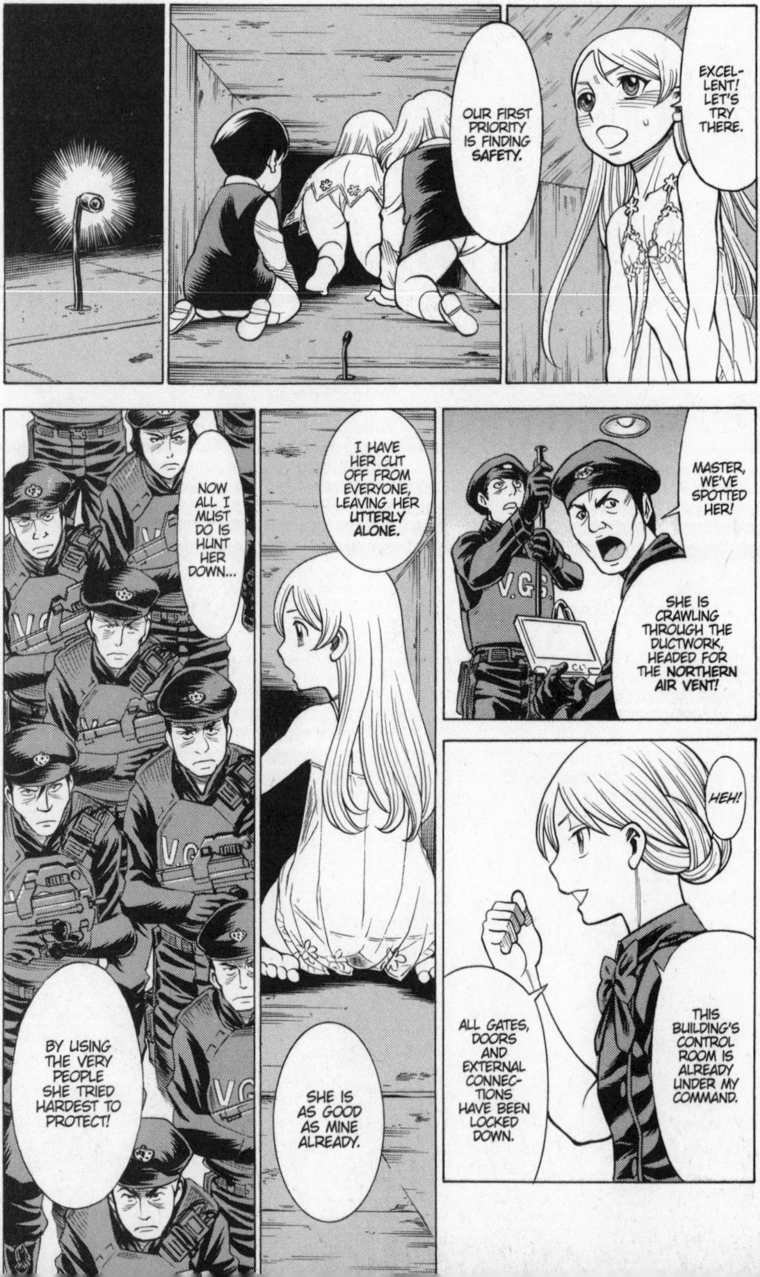
EXCEL-LENT! LET'S TRY THERE.
OUR FIRST PRIORITY IS FINDING SAFETY.
MASTER, WE'VE SPOTTED HER!
SHE IS CRAWLING THROUGH THE DUCTWORK, HEADED FOR THE NORTHERN AIR VENT!
HEH!
THIS BUILDING'S CONTROL ROOM IS ALREADY UNDER MY COMMAND.
ALL GATES, DOORS AND EXTERNAL CONNEC-TIONS HAVE BEEN LOCKED DOWN.
I HAVE HER CUT OFF FROM EVERYONE, LEAVING HER UTTERLY ALONE.
SHE IS AS GOOD AS MINE ALREADY.
NOW ALL I MUST DO IS HUNT HER DOWN...
BY USING THE VERY PEOPLE SHE TRIED HARDEST TO PROTECT!

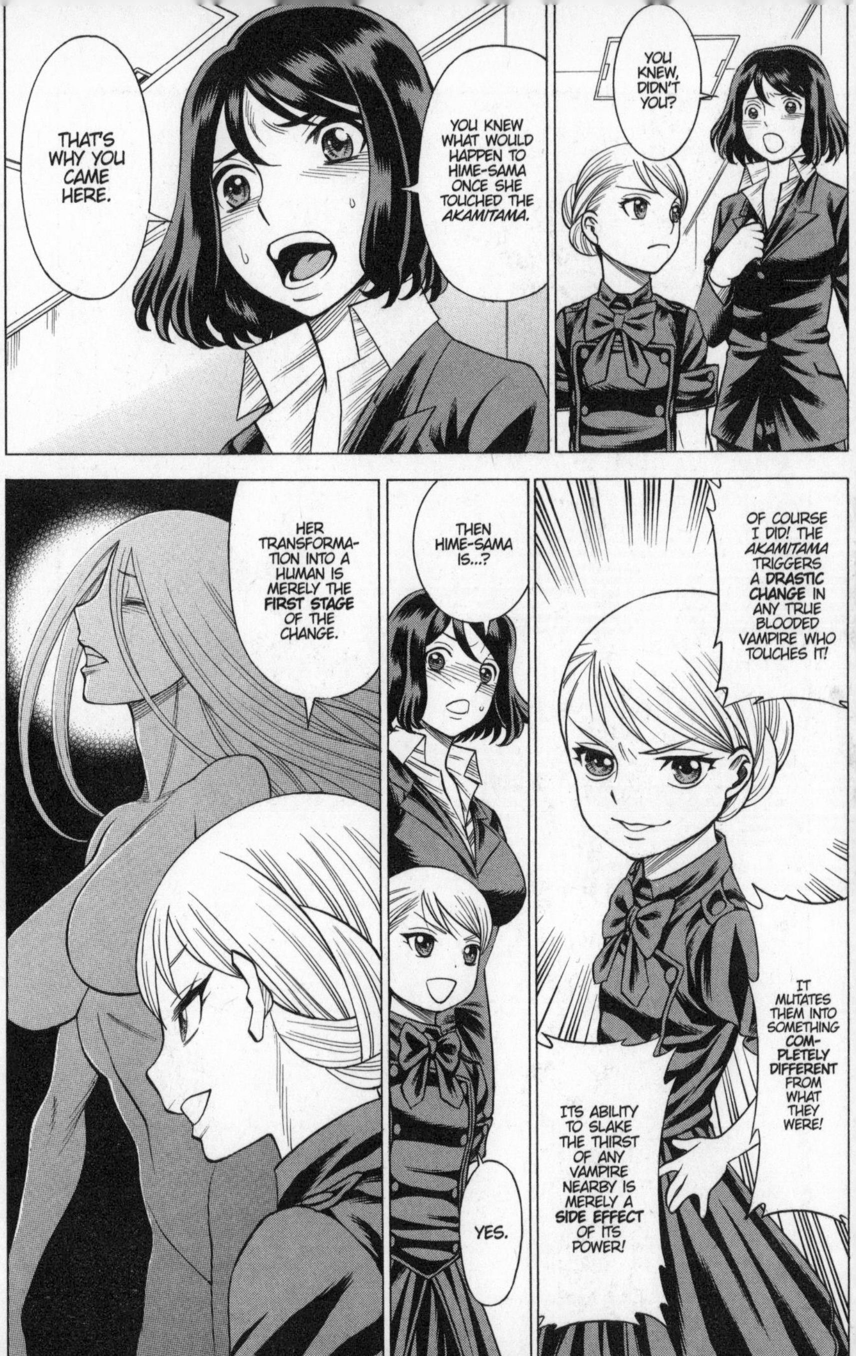
YOU KNEW, DIDN'T YOU?
YOU KNEW WHAT WOULD HAPPEN TO HIME-SAMA ONCE SHE TOUCHED THE *AKAMITAMA.*
THAT'S WHY YOU CAME HERE.
OF COURSE I DID! THE *AKAMITAMA* TRIGGERS A **DRASTIC CHANGE** IN ANY TRUE BLOODED VAMPIRE WHO TOUCHES IT!
IT MUTATES THEM INTO SOMETHING COMPLETELY **DIFFERENT** FROM WHAT THEY WERE!
ITS ABILITY TO SLAKE THE THIRST OF ANY VAMPIRE NEARBY IS MERELY A **SIDE EFFECT** OF ITS POWER!
THEN HIME-SAMA IS...?
YES.
HER TRANSFORMATION INTO A HUMAN IS MERELY THE **FIRST STAGE** OF THE CHANGE.

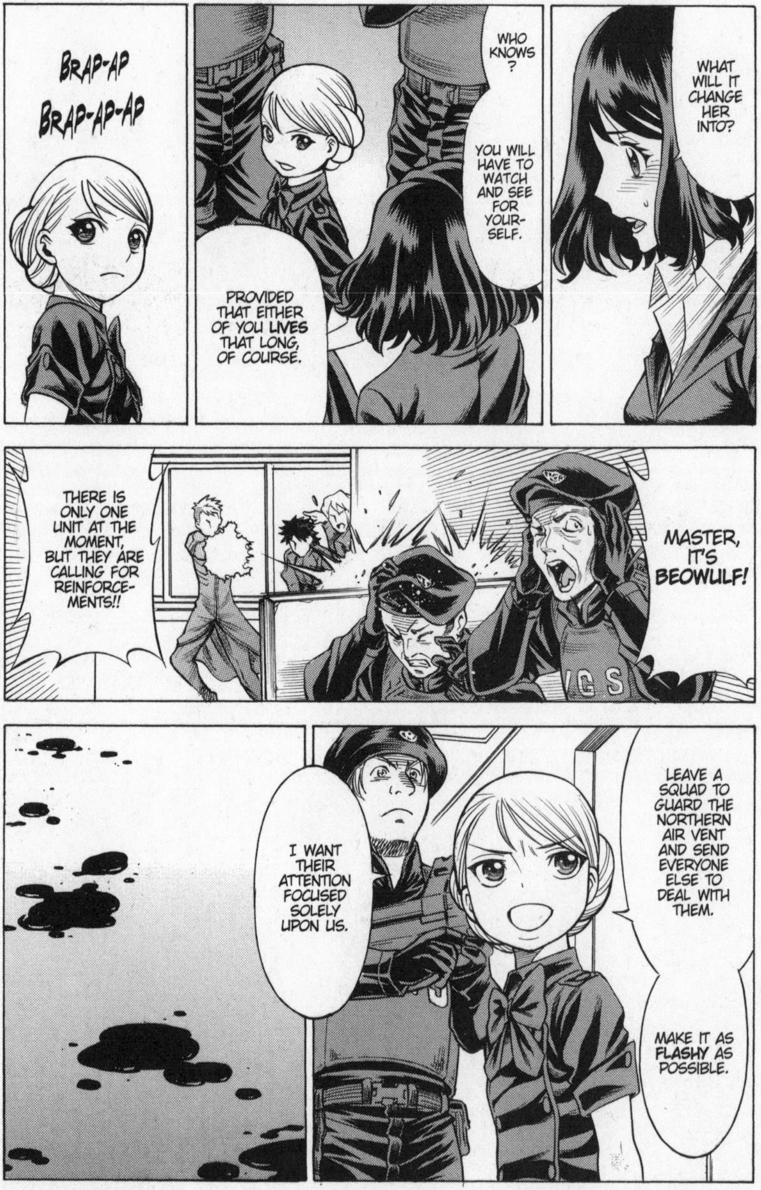
WHAT WILL IT CHANGE HER INTO?
WHO KNOWS?
YOU WILL HAVE TO WATCH AND SEE FOR YOURSELF.
PROVIDED THAT EITHER OF YOU LIVES THAT LONG, OF COURSE.
BRAP-AP BRAP-AP-AP
MASTER, IT'S BEOWULF!
THERE IS ONLY ONE UNIT AT THE MOMENT, BUT THEY ARE CALLING FOR REINFORCEMENTS!!
LEAVE A SQUAD TO GUARD THE NORTHERN AIR VENT AND SEND EVERYONE ELSE TO DEAL WITH THEM.
I WANT THEIR ATTENTION FOCUSED SOLELY UPON US.
MAKE IT AS FLASHY AS POSSIBLE.

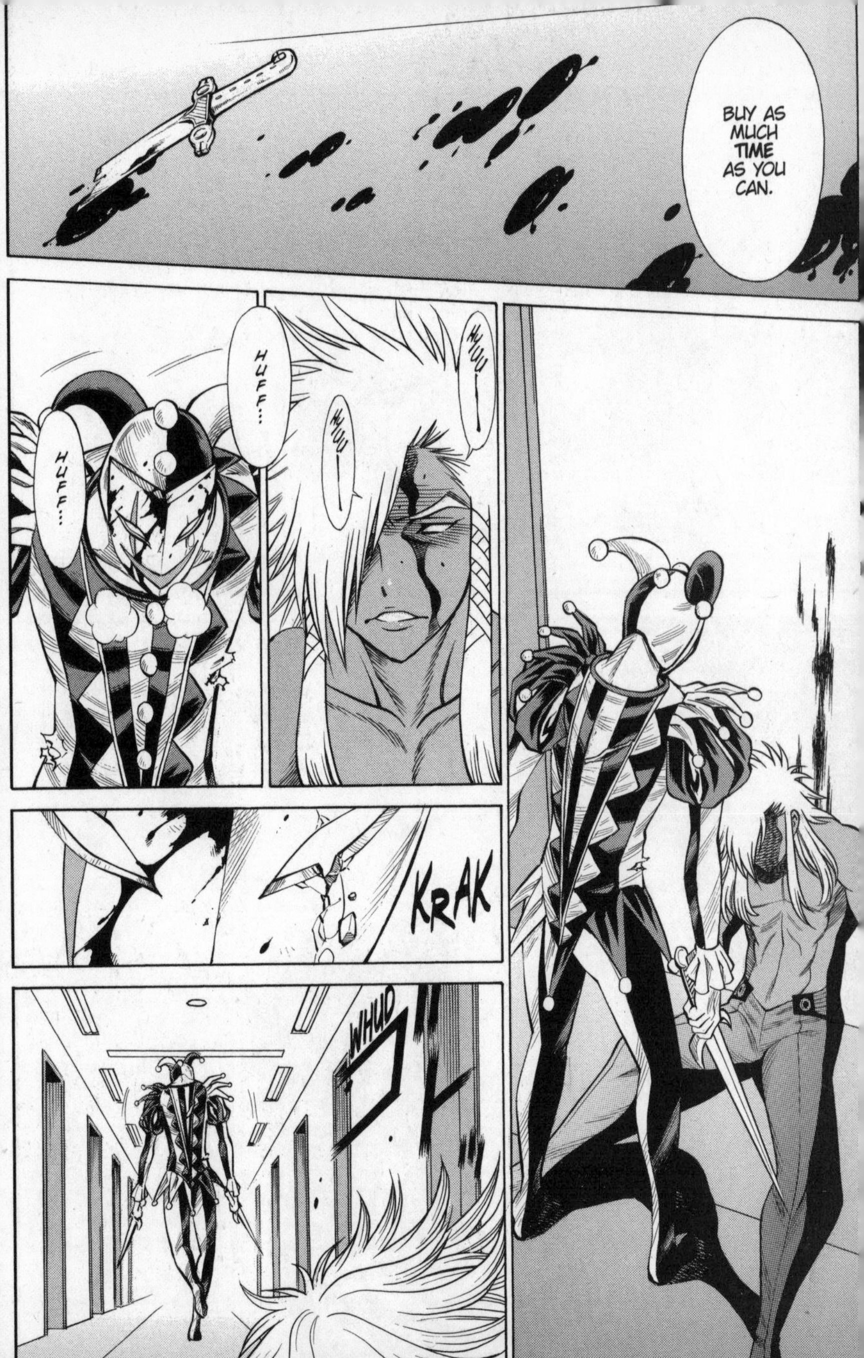
BUY AS MUCH TIME AS YOU CAN.
HYUU...
HYUU...
HUFF...
HUFF...
KRAK
WHUD

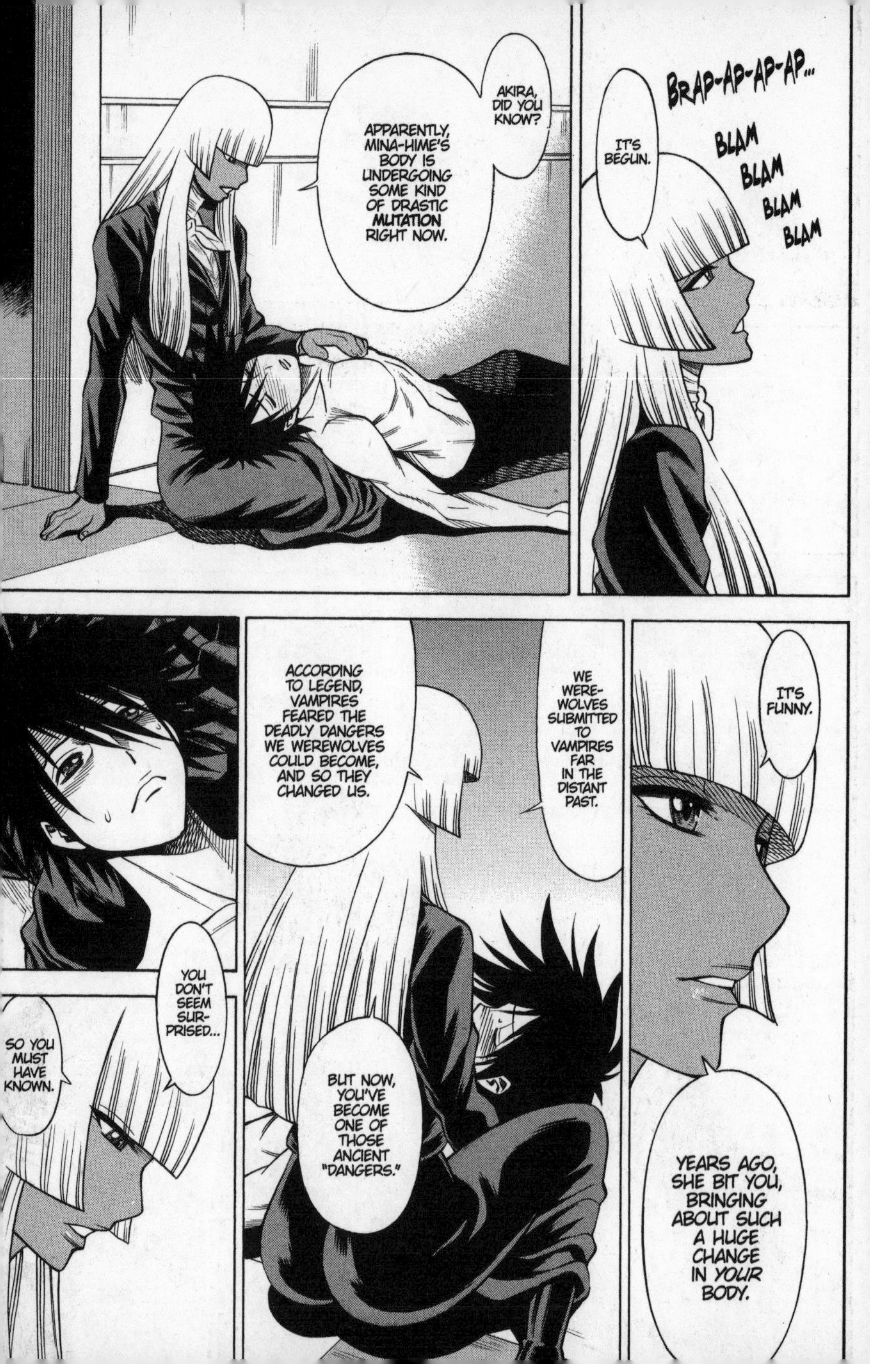
BRAP-AP-AP-AP...
BLAM BLAM BLAM BLAM
IT'S BEGUN.
AKIRA, DID YOU KNOW?
APPARENTLY, MINA-HIME'S BODY IS UNDERGOING SOME KIND OF DRASTIC MUTATION RIGHT NOW.
IT'S FUNNY.
YEARS AGO, SHE BIT YOU, BRINGING ABOUT SUCH A HUGE CHANGE IN *YOUR* BODY.
WE WERE-WOLVES SUBMITTED TO VAMPIRES FAR IN THE DISTANT PAST.
ACCORDING TO LEGEND, VAMPIRES FEARED THE DEADLY DANGERS WE WEREWOLVES COULD BECOME, AND SO THEY CHANGED US.
BUT NOW, YOU'VE BECOME ONE OF THOSE ANCIENT "DANGERS."
YOU DON'T SEEM SUR-PRISED...
SO YOU MUST HAVE KNOWN.

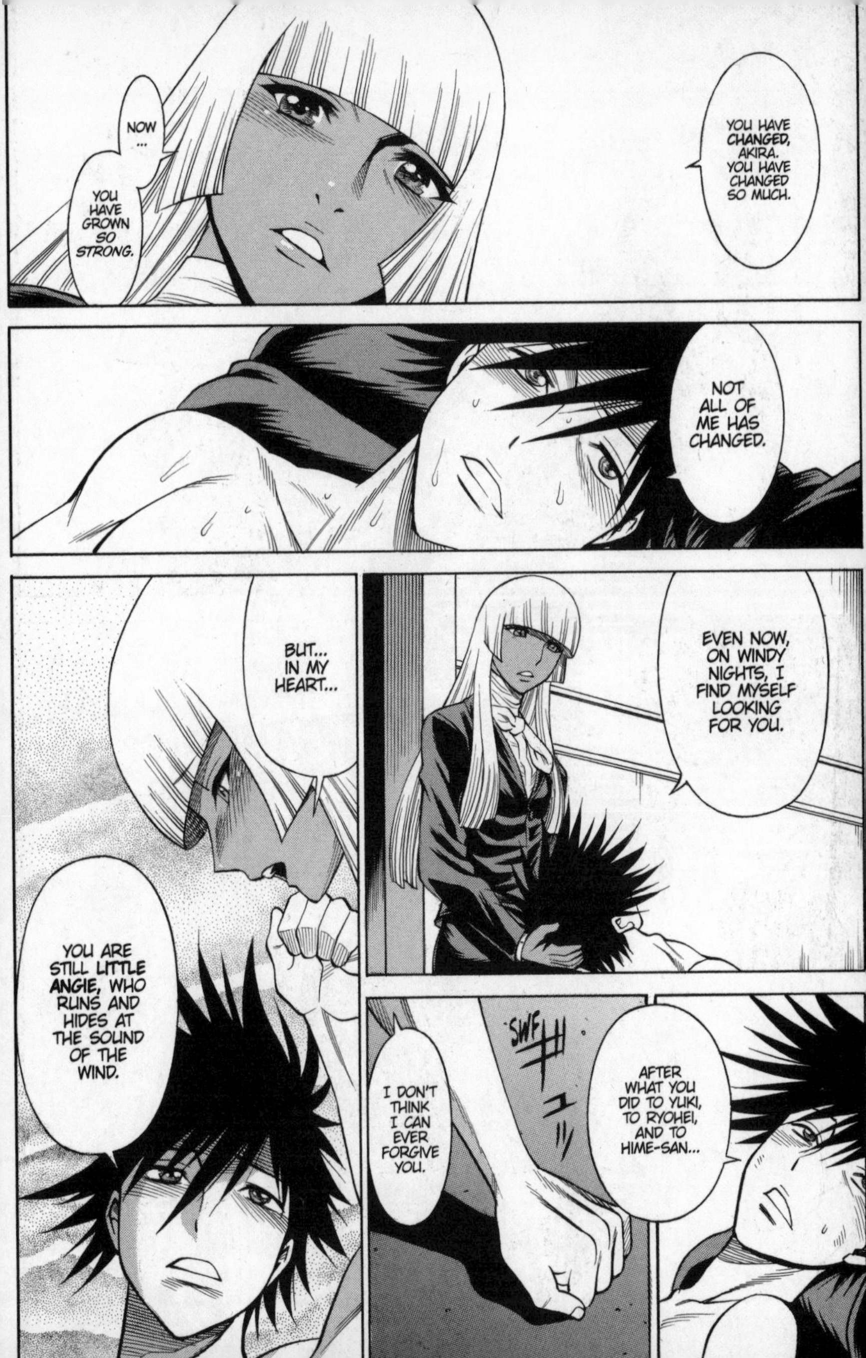
YOU HAVE CHANGED, AKIRA. YOU HAVE CHANGED SO MUCH.
NOW... YOU HAVE GROWN SO STRONG.
NOT ALL OF ME HAS CHANGED.
EVEN NOW, ON WINDY NIGHTS, I FIND MYSELF LOOKING FOR YOU.
AFTER WHAT YOU DID TO YUKI, TO RYOHEI, AND TO HIME-SAN...
SWF
I DON'T THINK I CAN EVER FORGIVE YOU.
BUT... IN MY HEART...
YOU ARE STILL LITTLE ANGIE, WHO RUNS AND HIDES AT THE SOUND OF THE WIND.

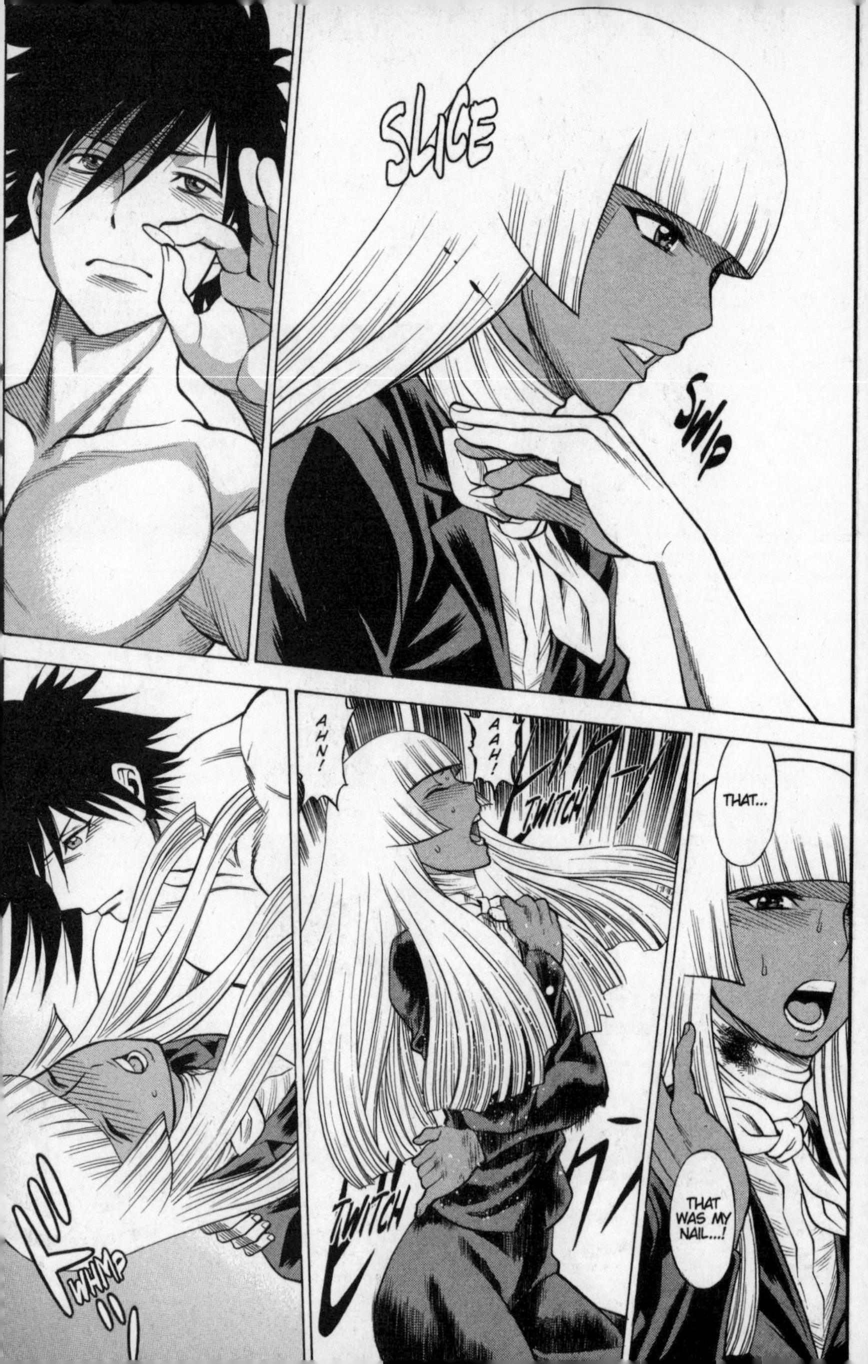
SLICE
SWIP
THAT...
THAT WAS MY NAIL...!
AAH!
TWITCH
AHN!
TWITCH
WHMP

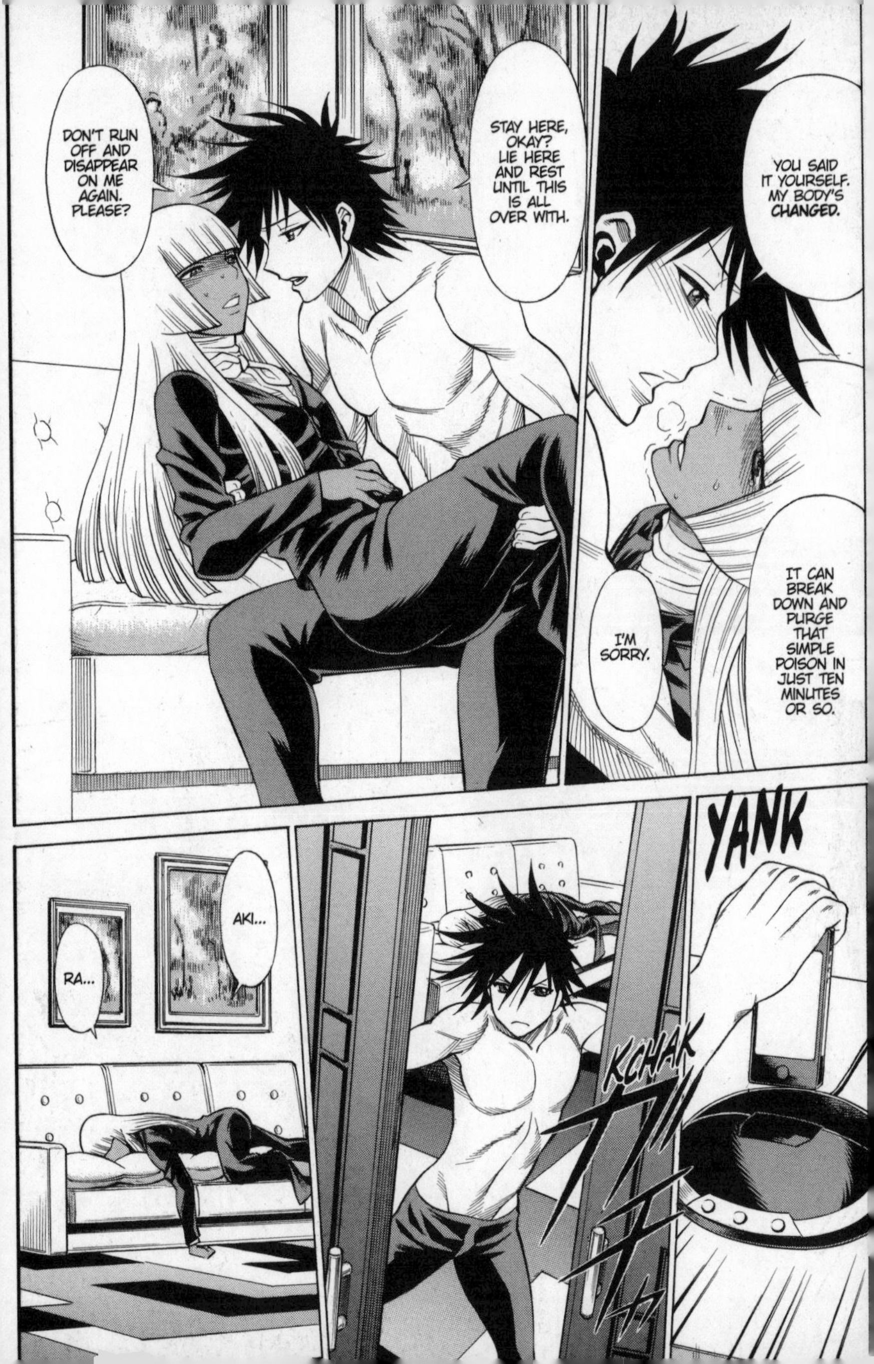
YOU SAID IT YOURSELF. MY BODY'S **CHANGED.**
IT CAN BREAK DOWN AND PURGE THAT SIMPLE POISON IN JUST TEN MINUTES OR SO.
I'M SORRY.
STAY HERE, OKAY? LIE HERE AND REST UNTIL THIS IS ALL OVER WITH.
DON'T RUN OFF AND DISAPPEAR ON ME AGAIN. PLEASE?
YANK
KCHAK
AKI...
RA...

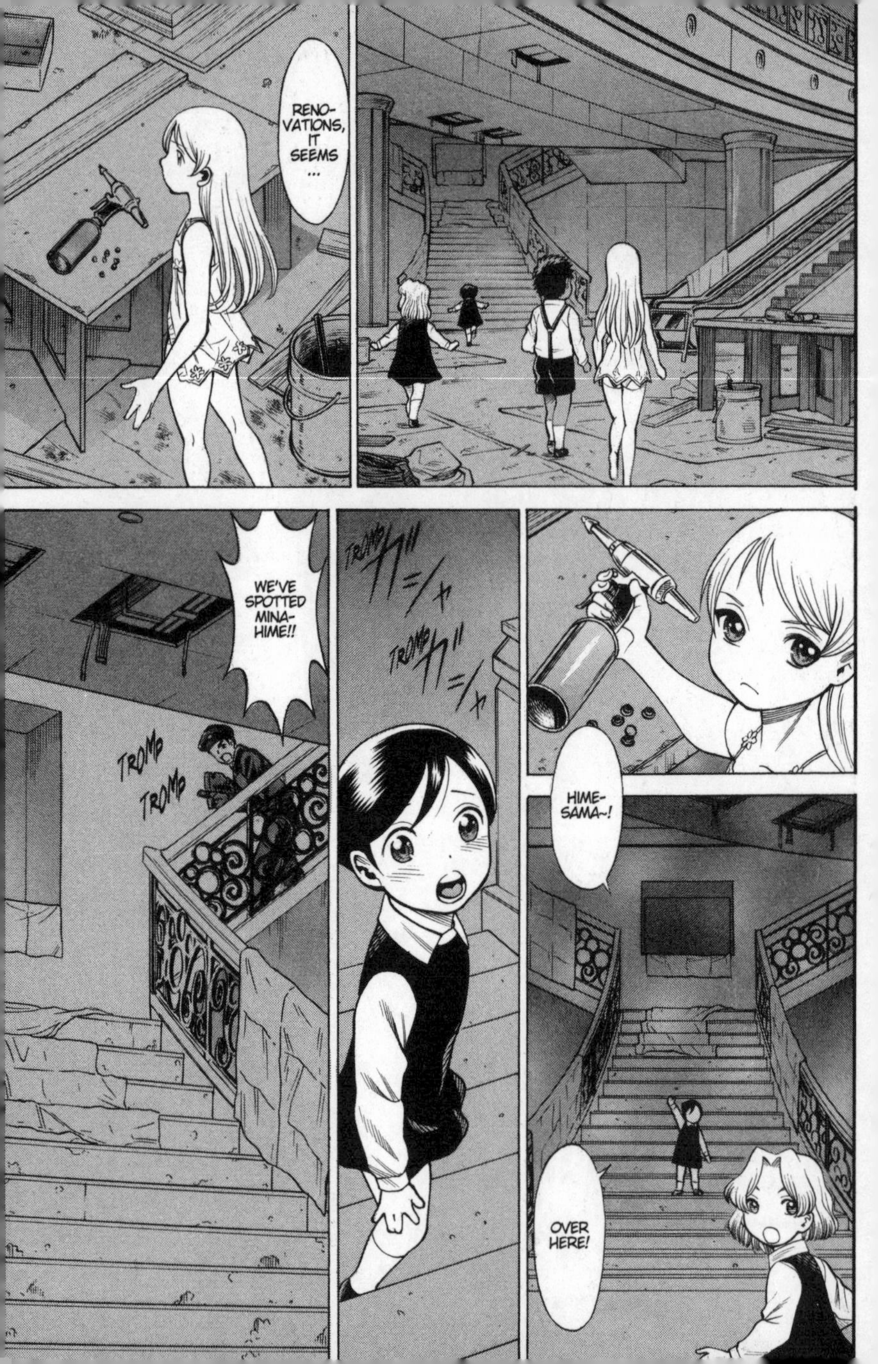
RENO-VATIONS, IT SEEMS ...
HIME-SAMA~!
OVER HERE!
TROMP
TROMP
WE'VE SPOTTED MINA-HIME!!
TROMP
TROMP

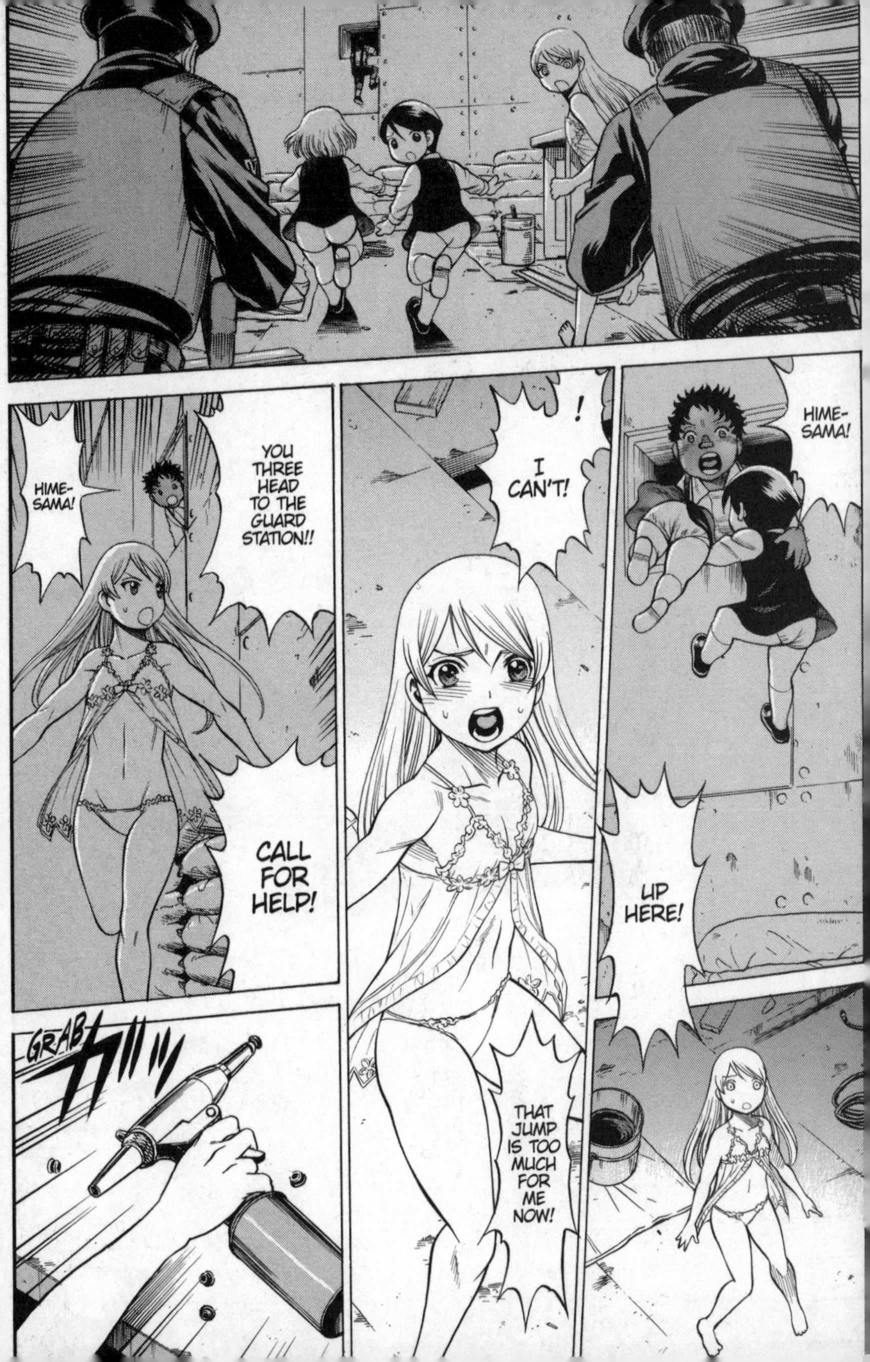
HIME-SAMA!
UP HERE!
!
I CAN'T!
THAT JUMP IS TOO MUCH FOR ME NOW!
YOU THREE HEAD TO THE GUARD STATION!!
HIME-SAMA!
CALL FOR HELP!
GRAB

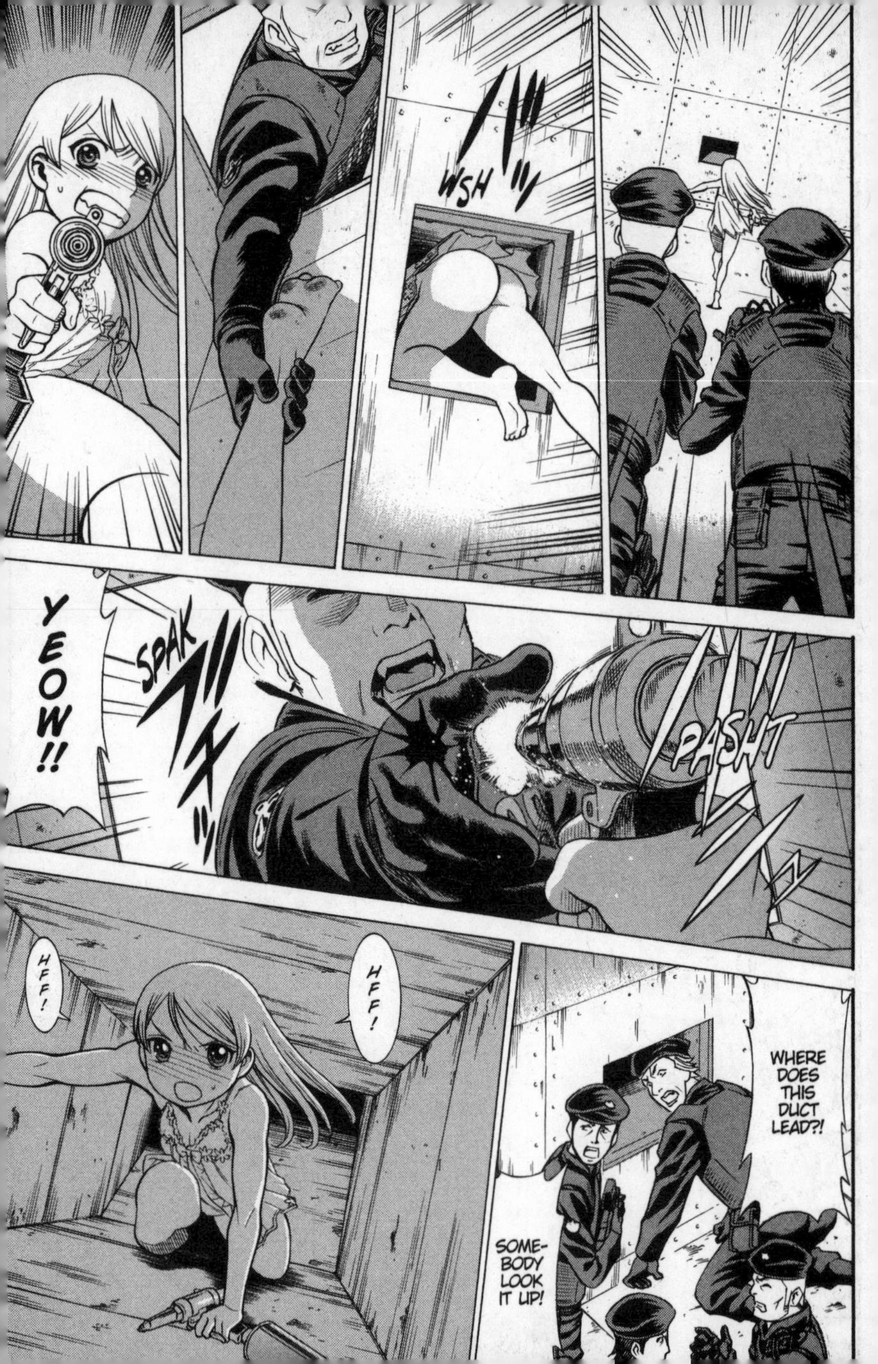
WSH
PASHT
SPAK
YEOW!!
WHERE DOES THIS DUCT LEAD?!
SOME-BODY LOOK IT UP!
HFF!
HFF!

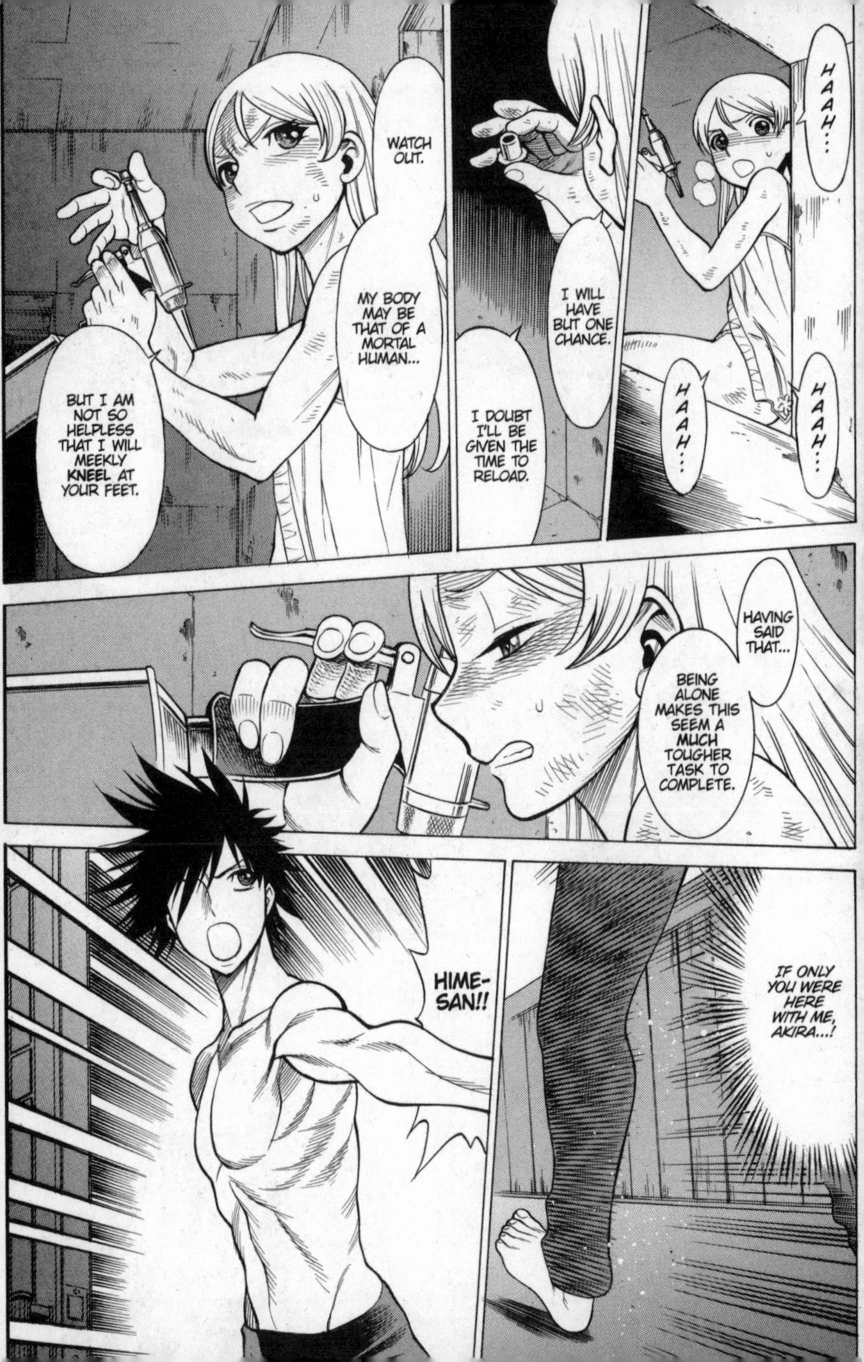
HAAAH...
HAAAH...
HAAAH...
I WILL HAVE BUT ONE CHANCE.
I DOUBT I'LL BE GIVEN THE TIME TO RELOAD.
WATCH OUT.
MY BODY MAY BE THAT OF A MORTAL HUMAN...
BUT I AM NOT SO HELPLESS THAT I WILL MEEKLY KNEEL AT YOUR FEET.
HAVING SAID THAT...
BEING ALONE MAKES THIS SEEM A MUCH TOUGHER TASK TO COMPLETE.
IF ONLY YOU WERE HERE WITH ME, AKIRA...!
HIME-SAN!!

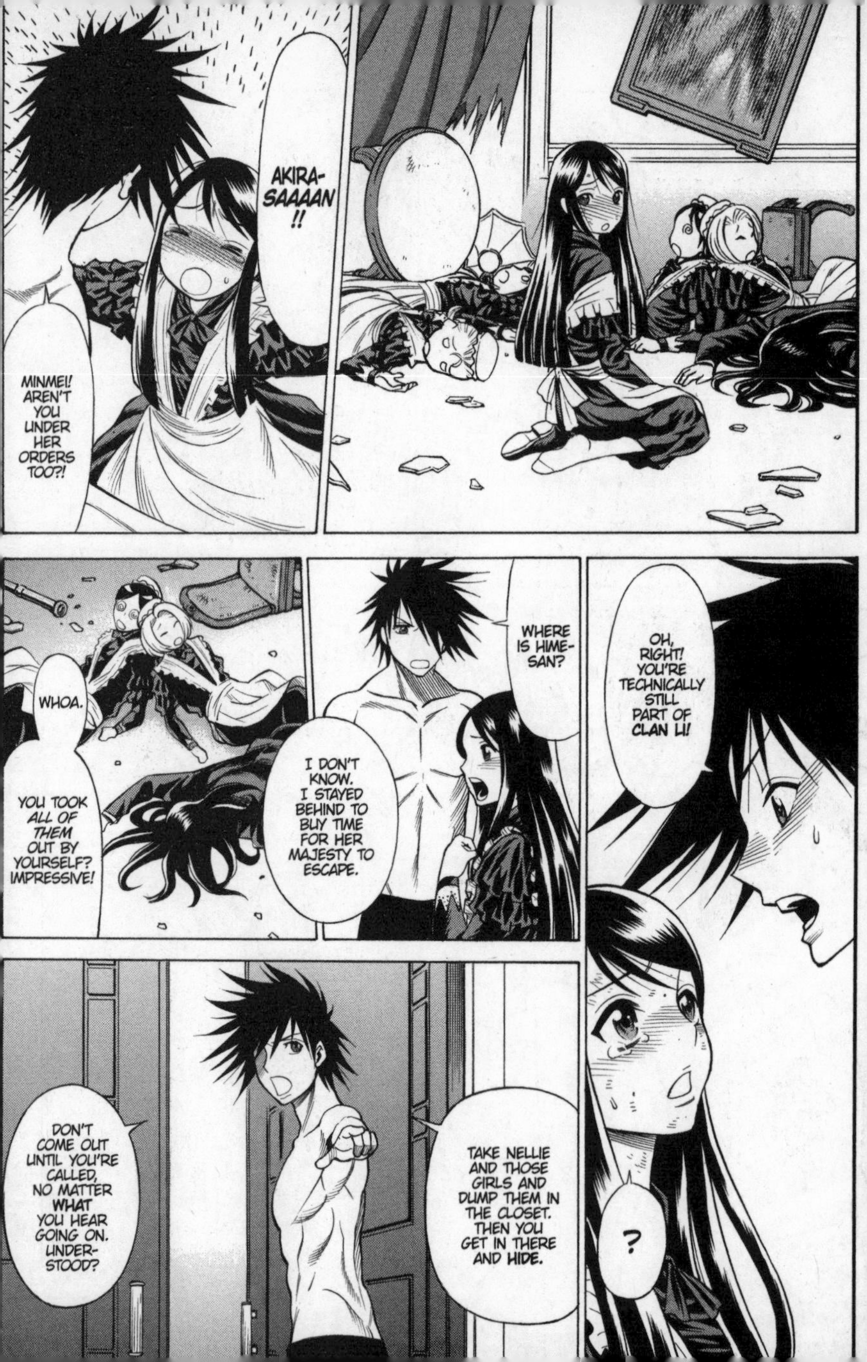
AKIRA-SAAAAN!!
MINMEI! AREN'T YOU UNDER HER ORDERS TOO?!
OH, RIGHT! YOU'RE TECHNICALLY STILL PART OF CLAN LI!
WHERE IS HIME-SAN?
I DON'T KNOW. I STAYED BEHIND TO BUY TIME FOR HER MAJESTY TO ESCAPE.
WHOA.
YOU TOOK ALL OF THEM OUT BY YOURSELF? IMPRESSIVE!
TAKE NELLIE AND THOSE GIRLS AND DUMP THEM IN THE CLOSET. THEN YOU GET IN THERE AND HIDE.
?
DON'T COME OUT UNTIL YOU'RE CALLED, NO MATTER WHAT YOU HEAR GOING ON. UNDER-STOOD?

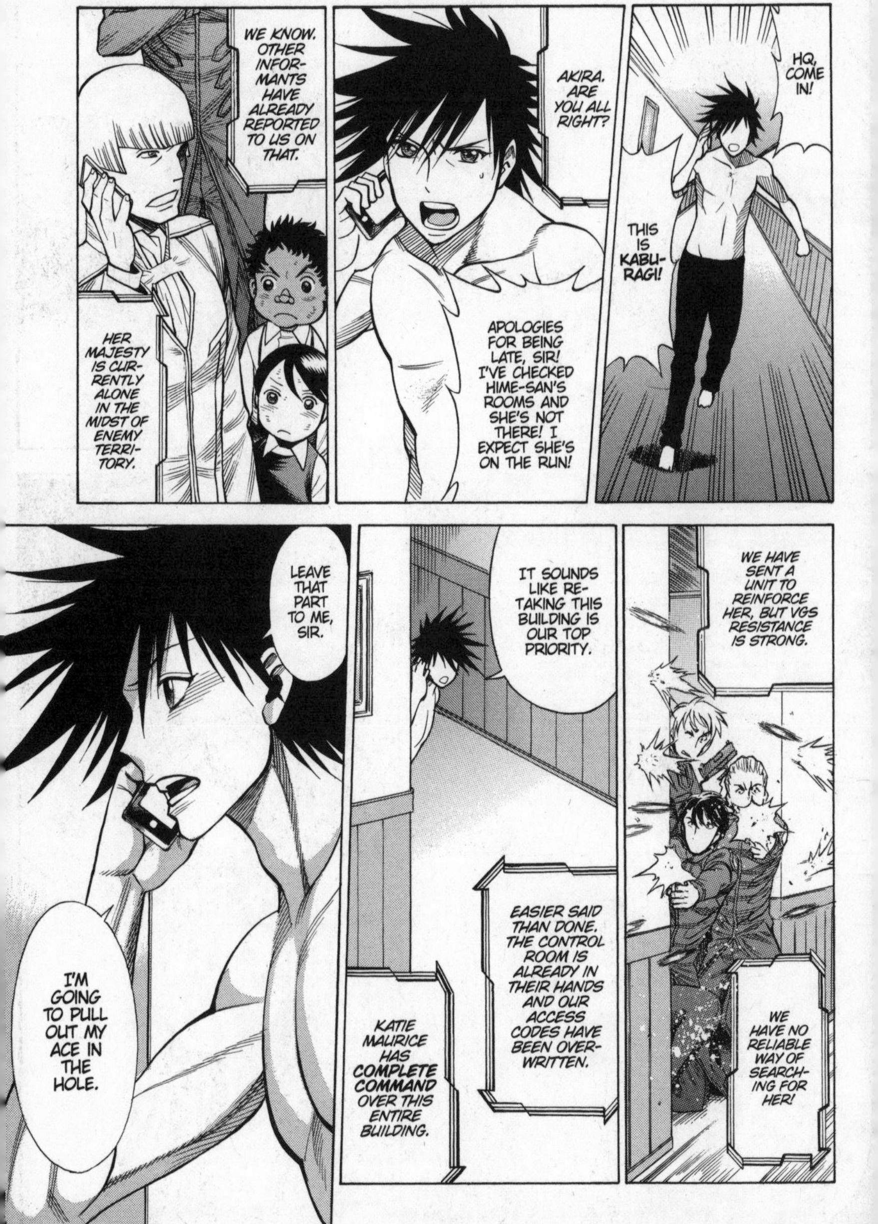
HQ, COME IN!
THIS IS KABURAGI!
AKIRA. ARE YOU ALL RIGHT?
APOLOGIES FOR BEING LATE, SIR! I'VE CHECKED HIME-SAN'S ROOMS AND SHE'S NOT THERE! I EXPECT SHE'S ON THE RUN!
WE KNOW. OTHER INFORMANTS HAVE ALREADY REPORTED TO US ON THAT.
HER MAJESTY IS CURRENTLY ALONE IN THE MIDST OF ENEMY TERRITORY.
WE HAVE SENT A UNIT TO REINFORCE HER, BUT VGS RESISTANCE IS STRONG.
WE HAVE NO RELIABLE WAY OF SEARCHING FOR HER!
IT SOUNDS LIKE RETAKING THIS BUILDING IS OUR TOP PRIORITY.
EASIER SAID THAN DONE. THE CONTROL ROOM IS ALREADY IN THEIR HANDS AND OUR ACCESS CODES HAVE BEEN OVERWRITTEN.
KATIE MAURICE HAS COMPLETE COMMAND OVER THIS ENTIRE BUILDING.
LEAVE THAT PART TO ME, SIR.
I'M GOING TO PULL OUT MY ACE IN THE HOLE.

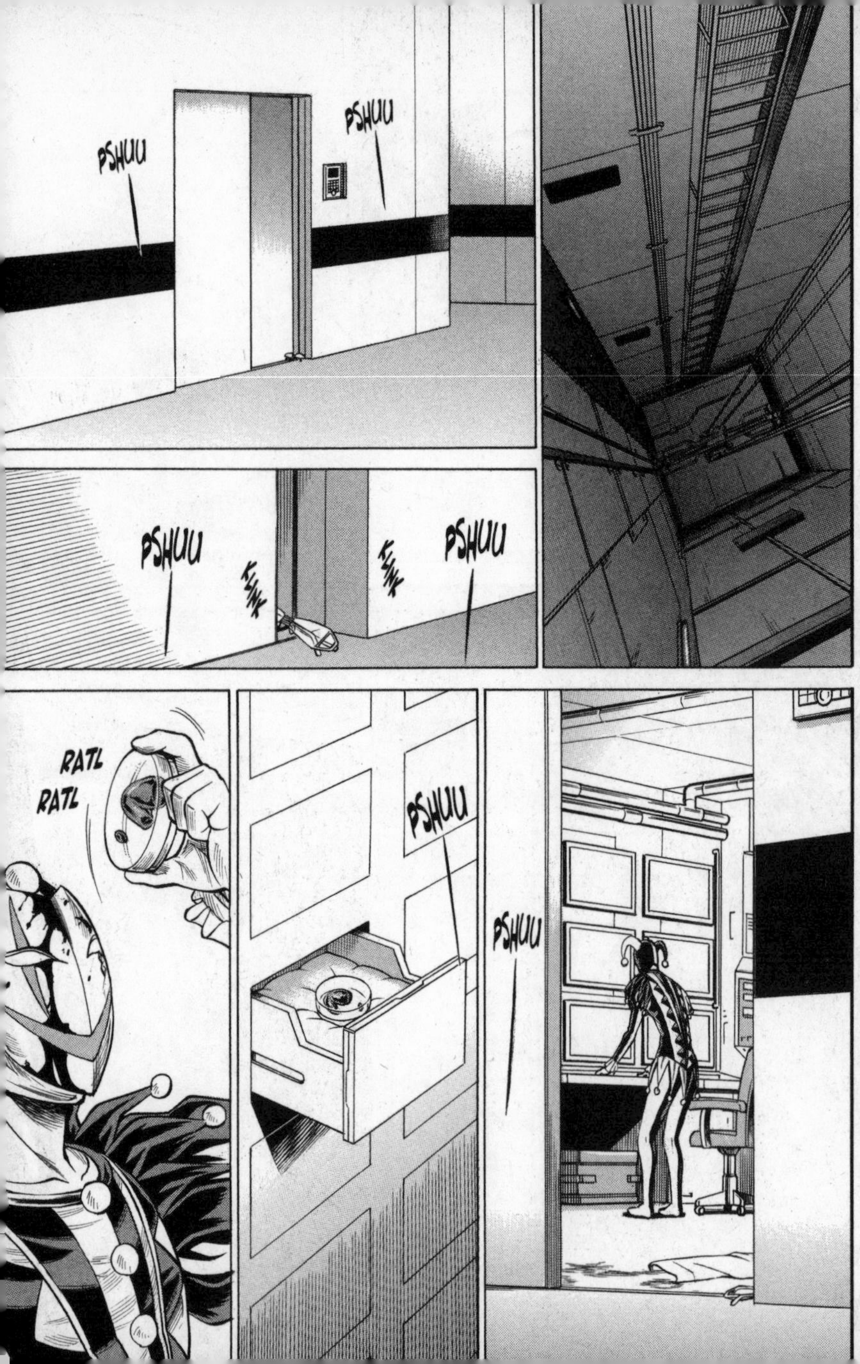
PSHUU
PSHUU
PSHUU
KLINK
KLINK
PSHUU
PSHUU
PSHUU
RATL
RATL

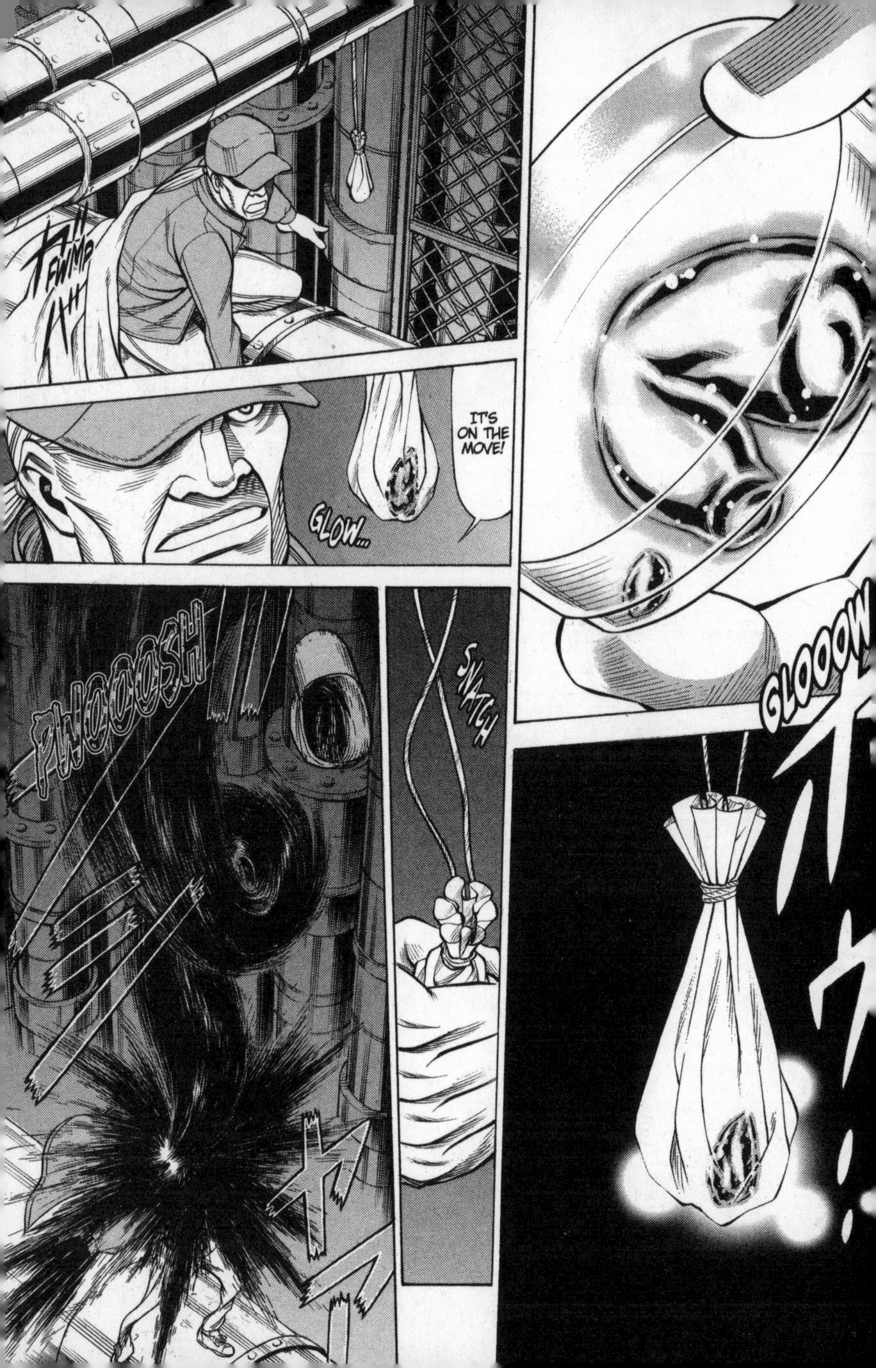
GLOOOW
FWIMP
GLOW...
IT'S ON THE MOVE!
SNATCH
PWOOOSH

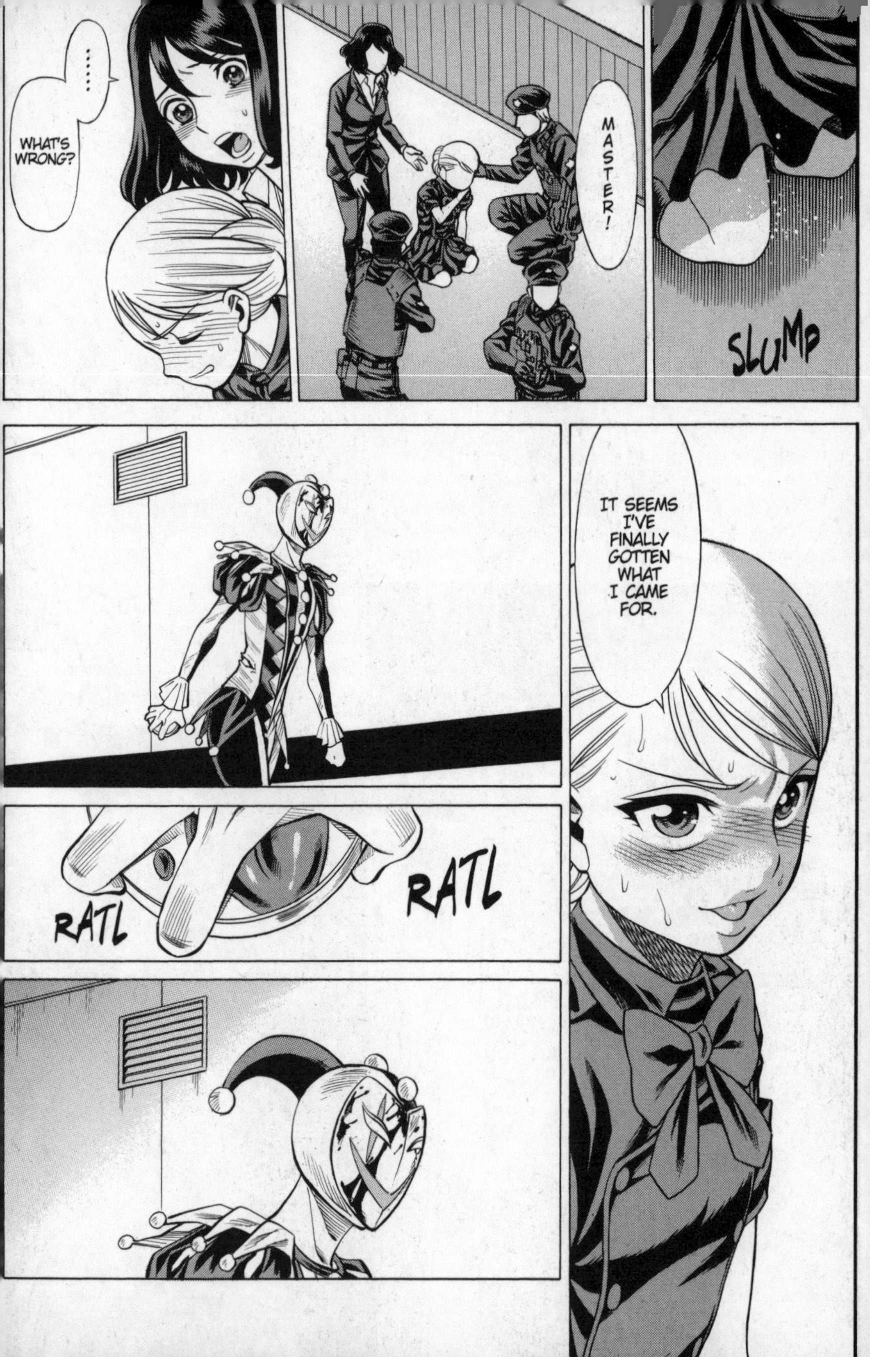
SLUMP
MASTER!
......
WHAT'S WRONG?
IT SEEMS I'VE FINALLY GOTTEN WHAT I CAME FOR.
RATL
RATL

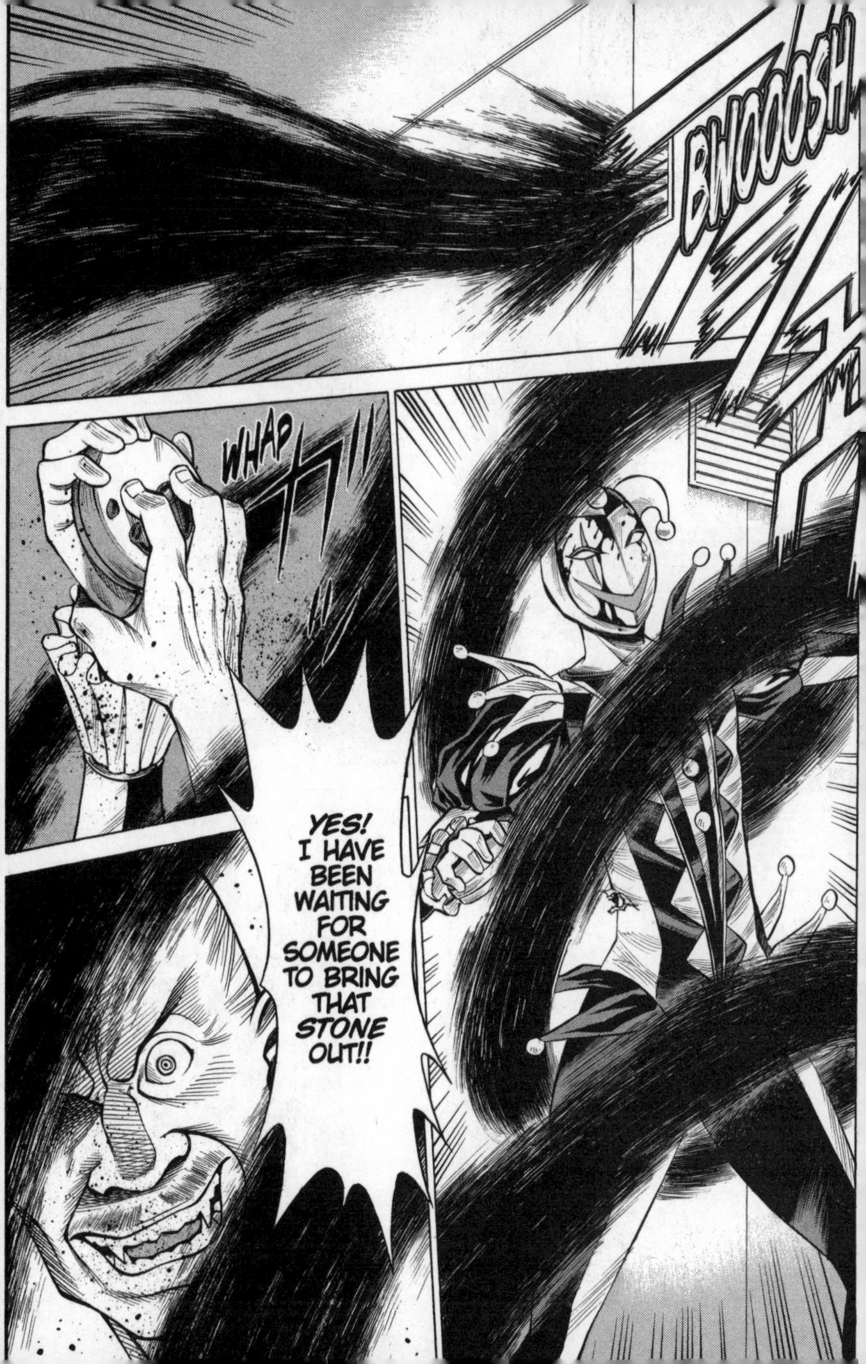
BWOOOSH
WHAP
YES! I HAVE BEEN WAITING FOR SOMEONE TO BRING THAT STONE OUT!!

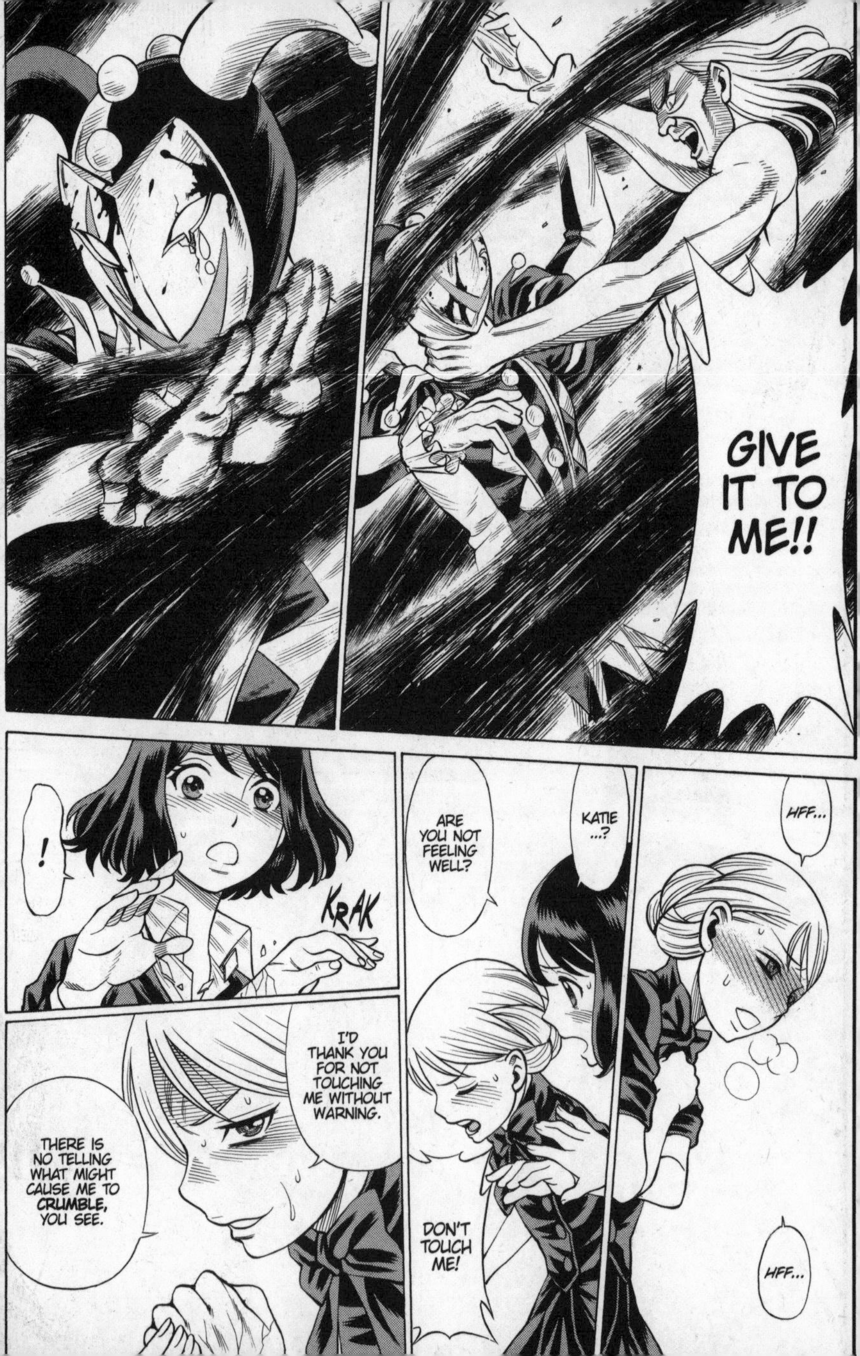
GIVE IT TO ME!!
HFF...
HFF...
KATIE ...?
ARE YOU NOT FEELING WELL?
DON'T TOUCH ME!
!
KRAK
I'D THANK YOU FOR NOT TOUCHING ME WITHOUT WARNING.
THERE IS NO TELLING WHAT MIGHT CAUSE ME TO CRUMBLE, YOU SEE.

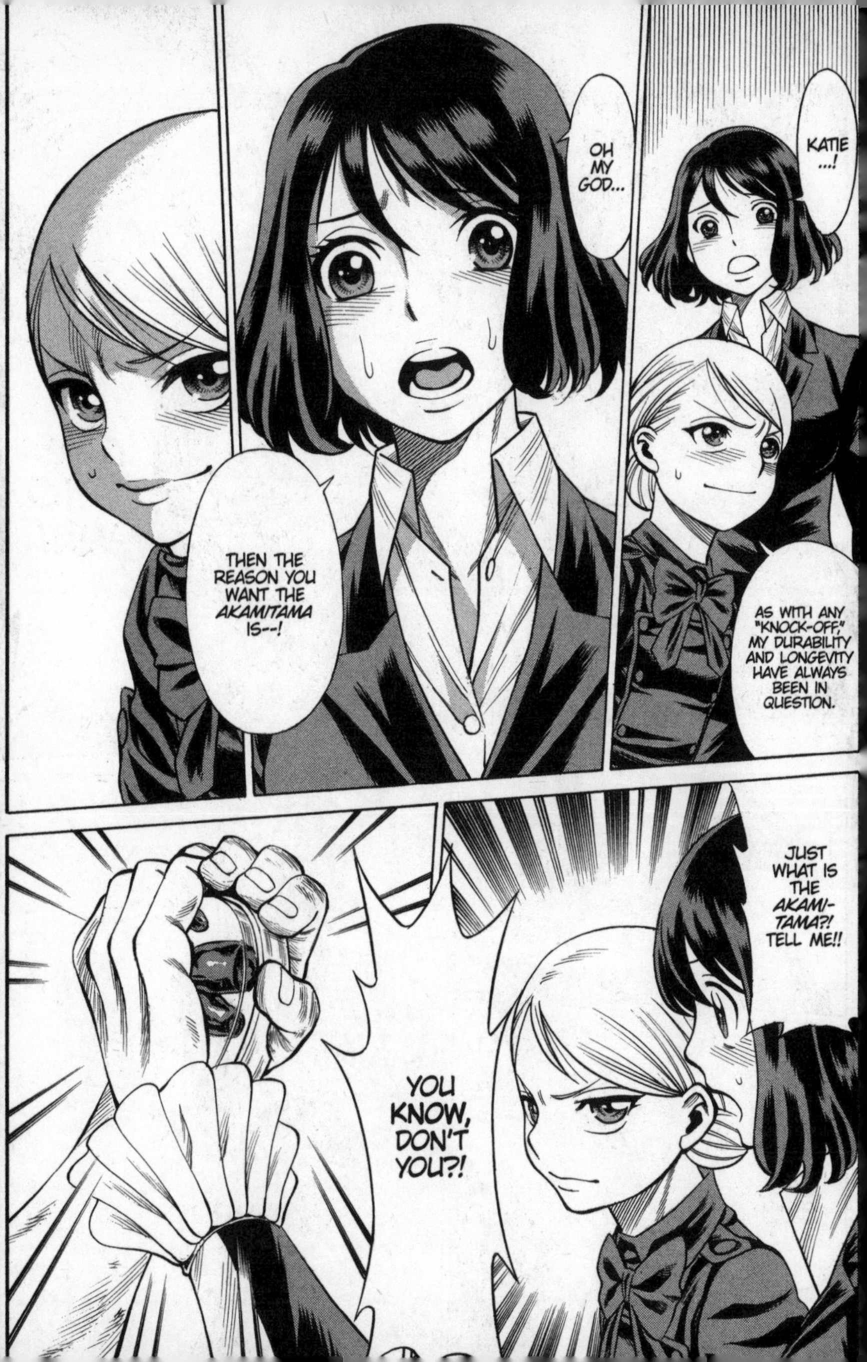
KATIE ...!
AS WITH ANY "KNOCK-OFF," MY DURABILITY AND LONGEVITY HAVE ALWAYS BEEN IN QUESTION.
OH MY GOD...
THEN THE REASON YOU WANT THE *AKAMITAMA* IS--!
JUST WHAT IS THE *AKAMI-TAMA*?! TELL ME!!
YOU KNOW, DON'T YOU?!

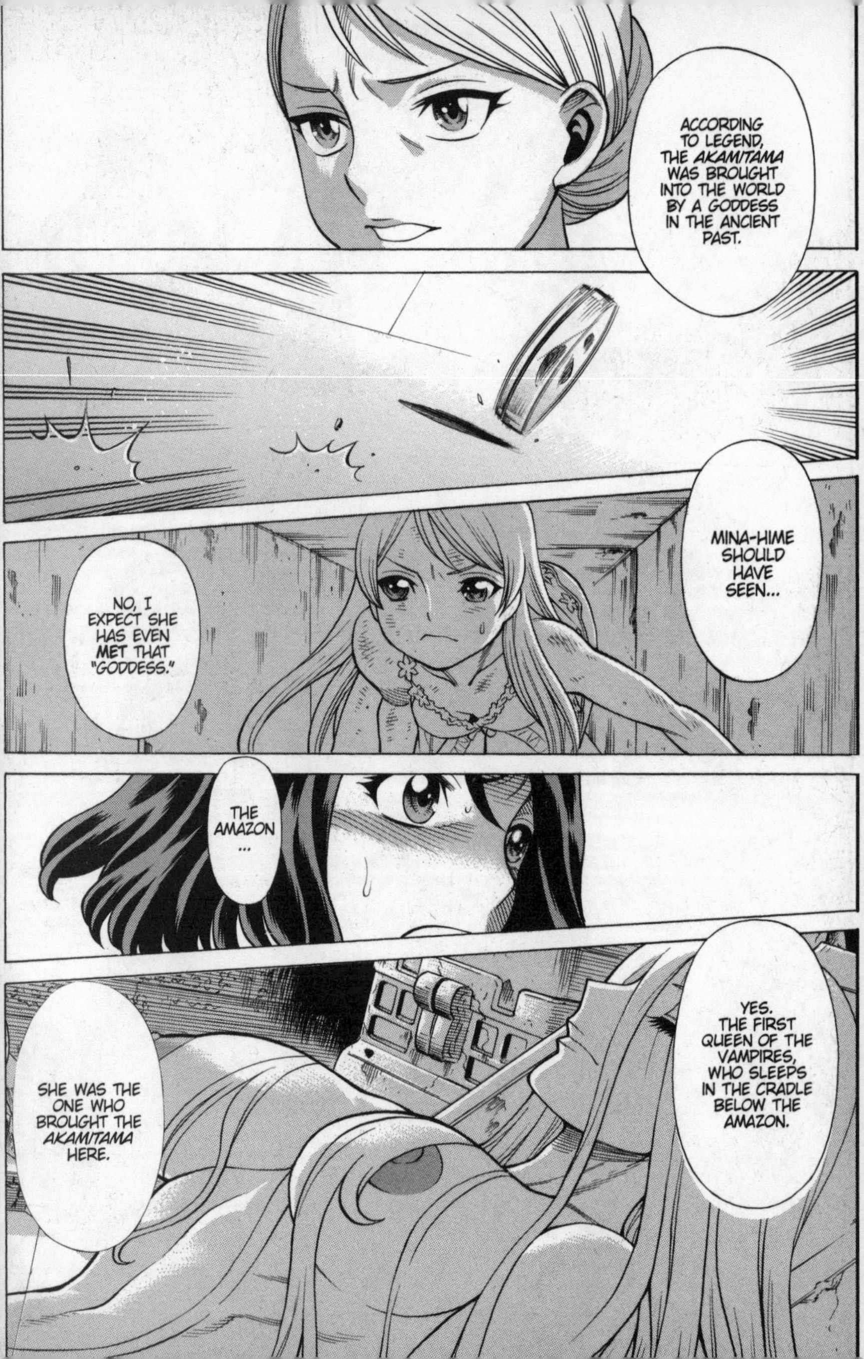
ACCORDING TO LEGEND, THE *AKAMITAMA* WAS BROUGHT INTO THE WORLD BY A GODDESS IN THE ANCIENT PAST.
MINA-HIME SHOULD HAVE SEEN...
NO, I EXPECT SHE HAS EVEN MET THAT "GODDESS."
THE AMAZON ...
YES. THE FIRST QUEEN OF THE VAMPIRES, WHO SLEEPS IN THE CRADLE BELOW THE AMAZON.
SHE WAS THE ONE WHO BROUGHT THE *AKAMITAMA* HERE.

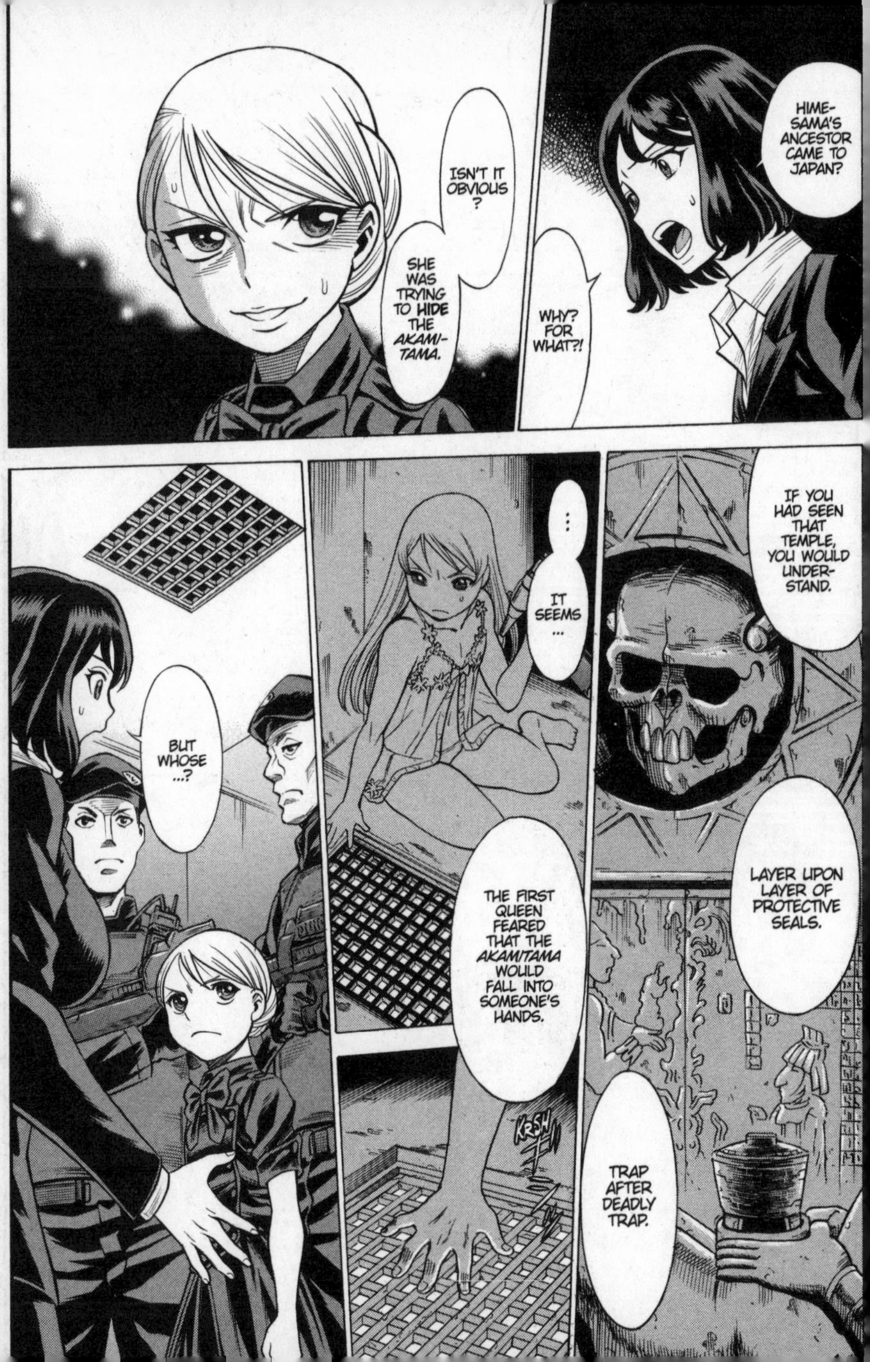
HIME-SAMA'S ANCESTOR CAME TO JAPAN?
WHY? FOR WHAT?!
ISN'T IT OBVIOUS?
SHE WAS TRYING TO HIDE THE AKAMITAMA.
IF YOU HAD SEEN THAT TEMPLE, YOU WOULD UNDERSTAND.
LAYER UPON LAYER OF PROTECTIVE SEALS.
TRAP AFTER DEADLY TRAP.
...
IT SEEMS...
THE FIRST QUEEN FEARED THAT THE AKAMITAMA WOULD FALL INTO SOMEONE'S HANDS.
KRSH
BUT WHOSE...?

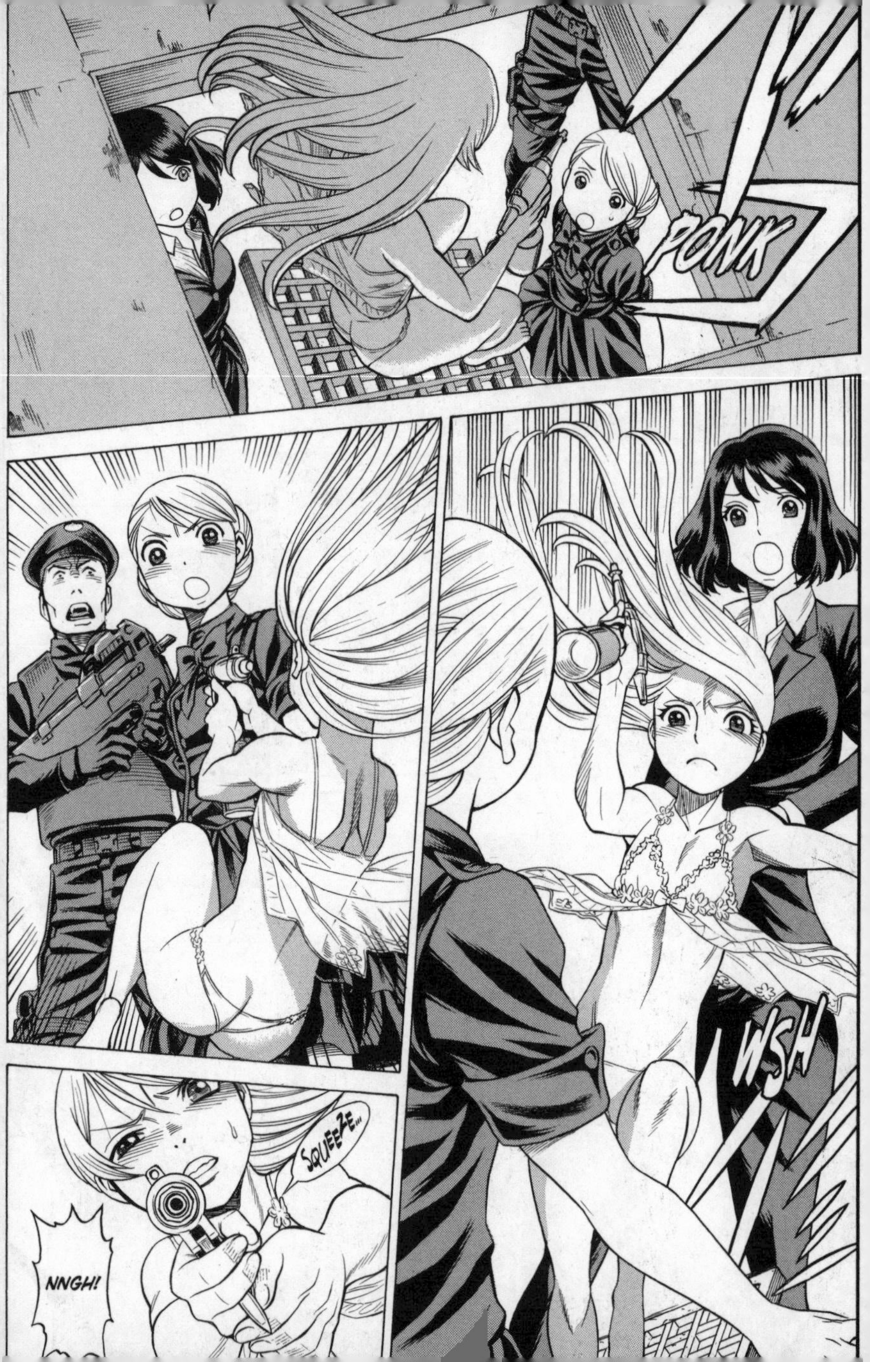
PONK
WSH
SQUEEZE...
NNGH!

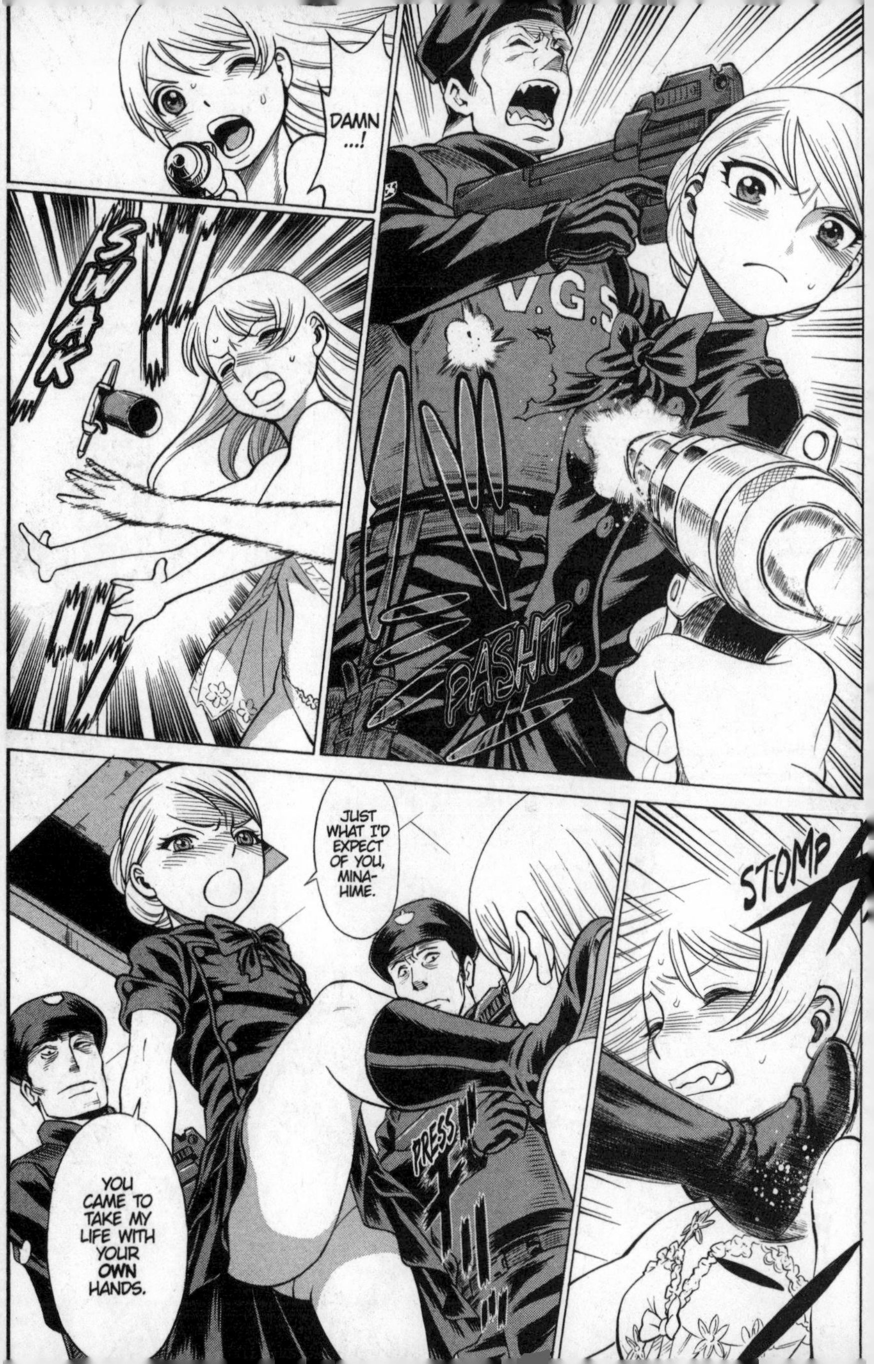
PASHT
DAMN ...!
SWAK
STOMP
JUST WHAT I'D EXPECT OF YOU, MINA-HIME.
PRESS
YOU CAME TO TAKE MY LIFE WITH YOUR OWN HANDS.

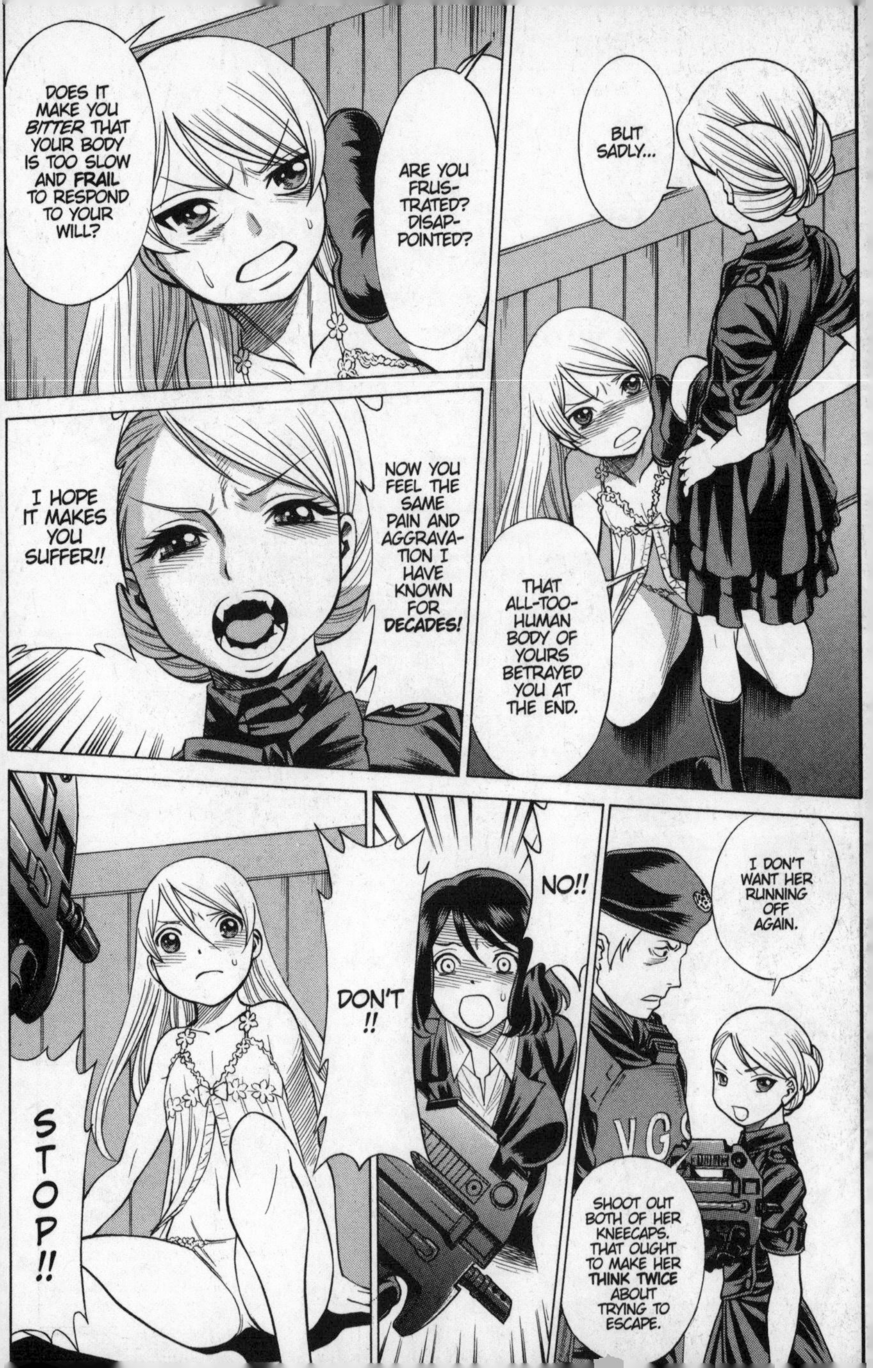
BUT SADLY...
THAT ALL-TOO-HUMAN BODY OF YOURS BETRAYED YOU AT THE END.
ARE YOU FRUS-TRATED? DISAP-POINTED?
DOES IT MAKE YOU *BITTER* THAT YOUR BODY IS TOO SLOW AND **FRAIL** TO RESPOND TO YOUR WILL?
NOW YOU FEEL THE SAME PAIN AND AGGRAVA-TION I HAVE KNOWN FOR **DECADES!**
I HOPE IT MAKES YOU SUFFER!!
I DON'T WANT HER RUNNING OFF AGAIN.
SHOOT OUT BOTH OF HER KNEECAPS. THAT OUGHT TO MAKE HER **THINK TWICE** ABOUT TRYING TO ESCAPE.
NO!!
DON'T !!
STOP!!

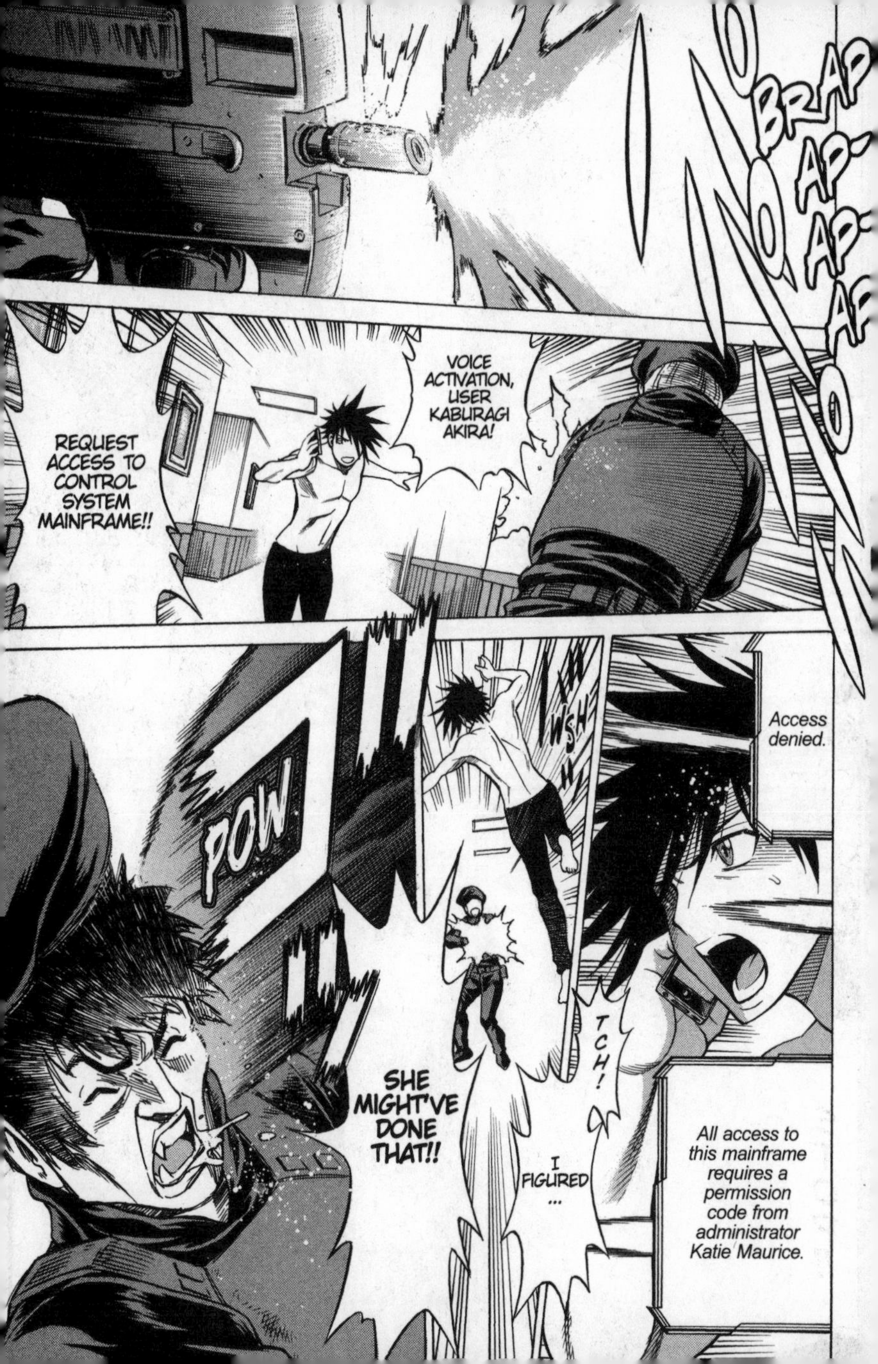
BRAP
AP-
AP-
AP
VOICE ACTIVATION, USER KABURAGI AKIRA!
REQUEST ACCESS TO CONTROL SYSTEM MAINFRAME!!
Access denied.
All access to this mainframe requires a permission code from administrator Katie Maurice.
WSH
TCH!
I FIGURED ...
SHE MIGHT'VE DONE THAT!!
POW

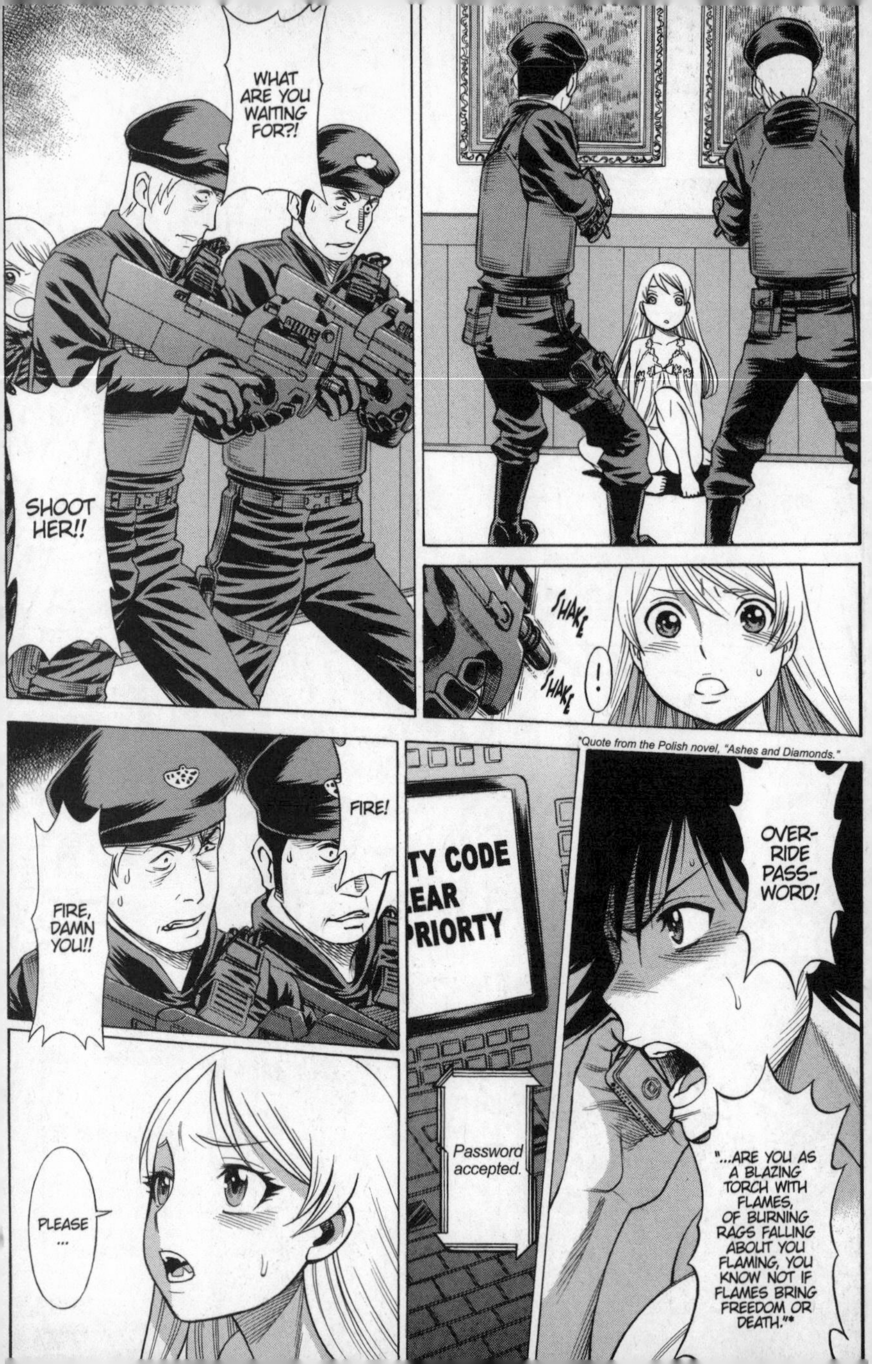
SHAKE
SHAKE
!
WHAT ARE YOU WAITING FOR?!
SHOOT HER!!
OVER-RIDE PASS-WORD!
"...ARE YOU AS A BLAZING TORCH WITH FLAMES, OF BURNING RAGS FALLING ABOUT YOU FLAMING, YOU KNOW NOT IF FLAMES BRING FREEDOM OR DEATH."*
TY CODE
LEAR
PRIORTY
Password accepted.
FIRE!
FIRE, DAMN YOU!!
PLEASE ...

*Quote from the Polish novel, "Ashes and Diamonds."

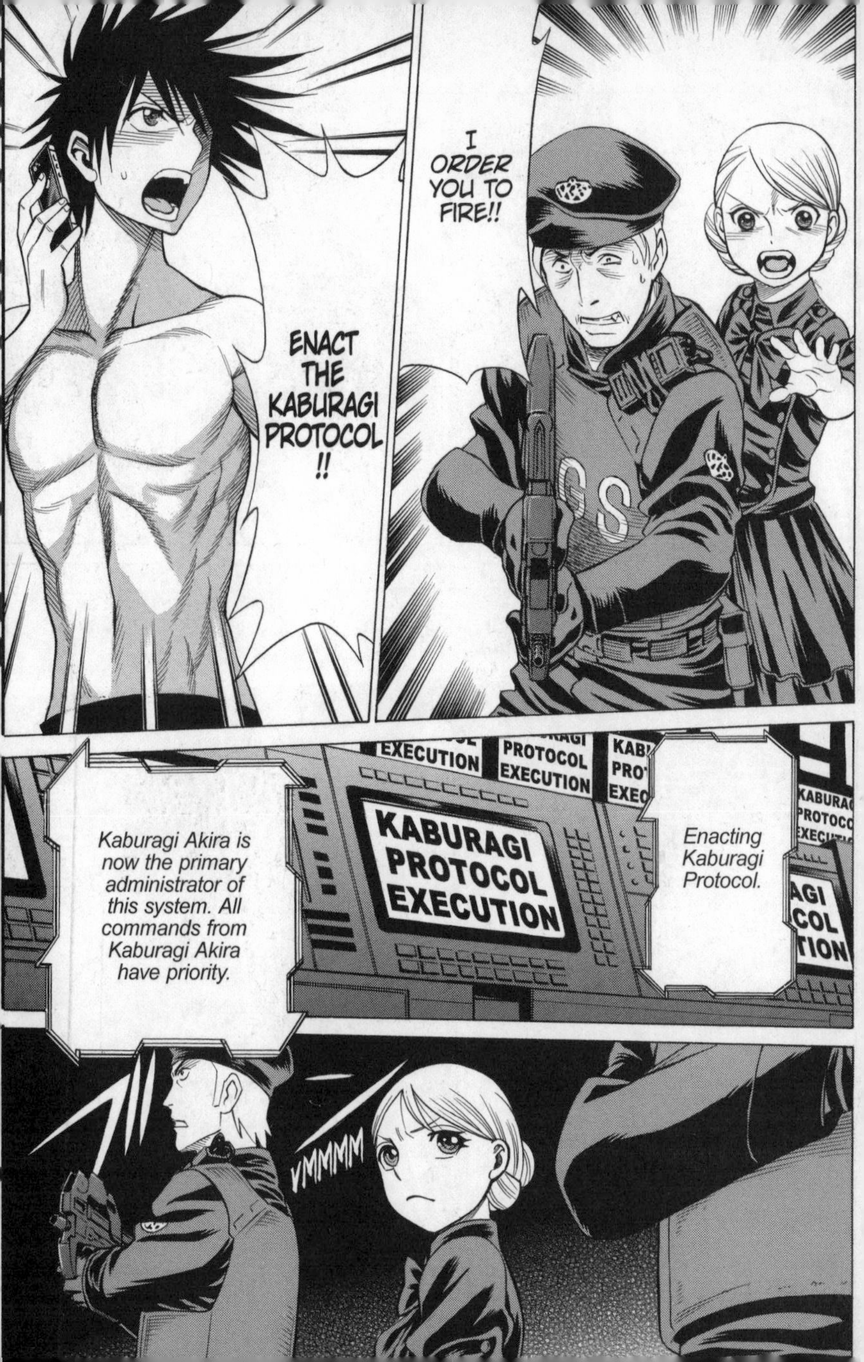
I ORDER YOU TO FIRE!!
ENACT THE KABURAGI PROTOCOL!!
Enacting Kaburagi Protocol.
KABURAGI PROTOCOL EXECUTION
Kaburagi Akira is now the primary administrator of this system. All commands from Kaburagi Akira have priority.
VMMMM

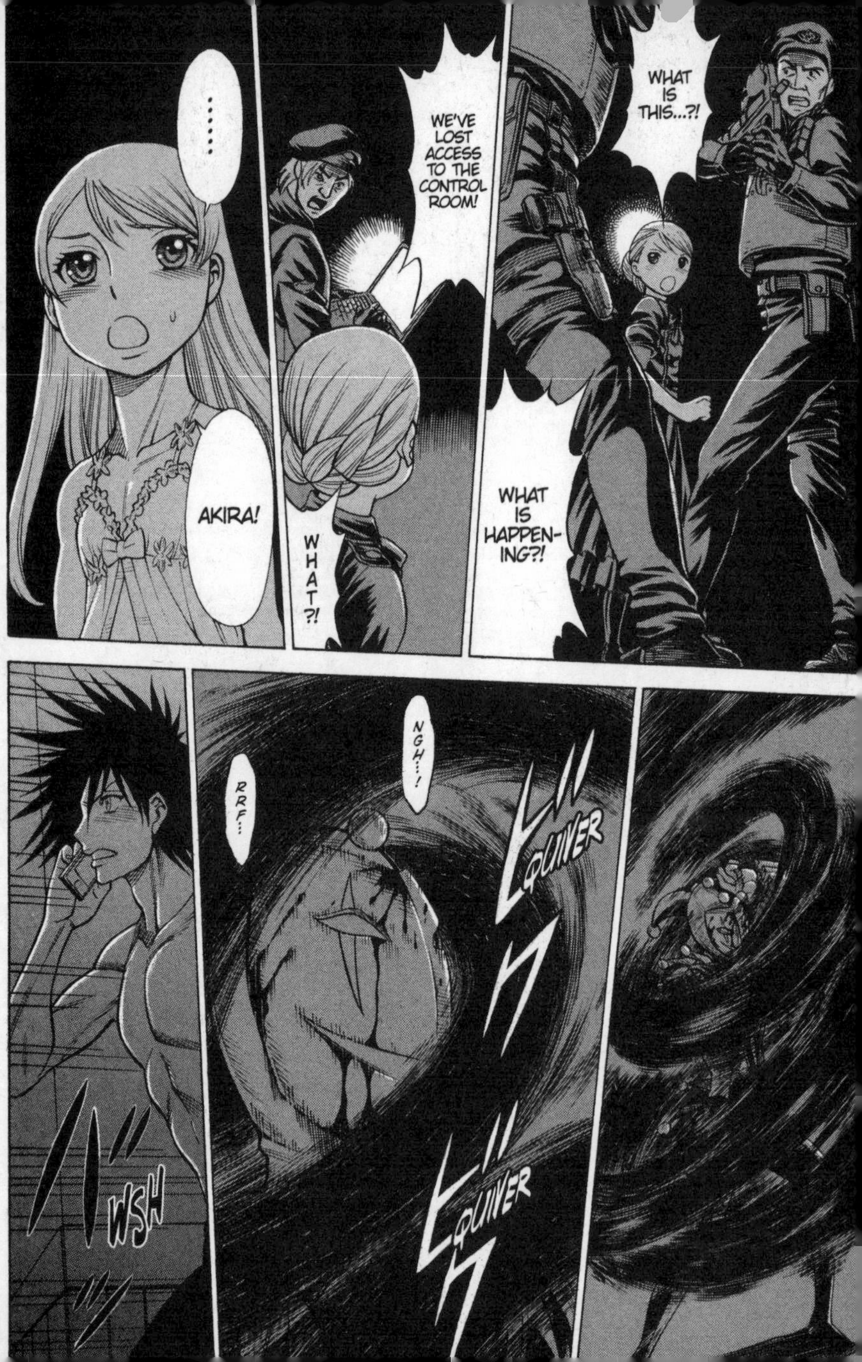
WHAT IS THIS...?!
WHAT IS HAPPENING?!
WE'VE LOST ACCESS TO THE CONTROL ROOM!
WHAT?!
......
AKIRA!
NGH...!
RRF...
QUIVER
QUIVER
WSH

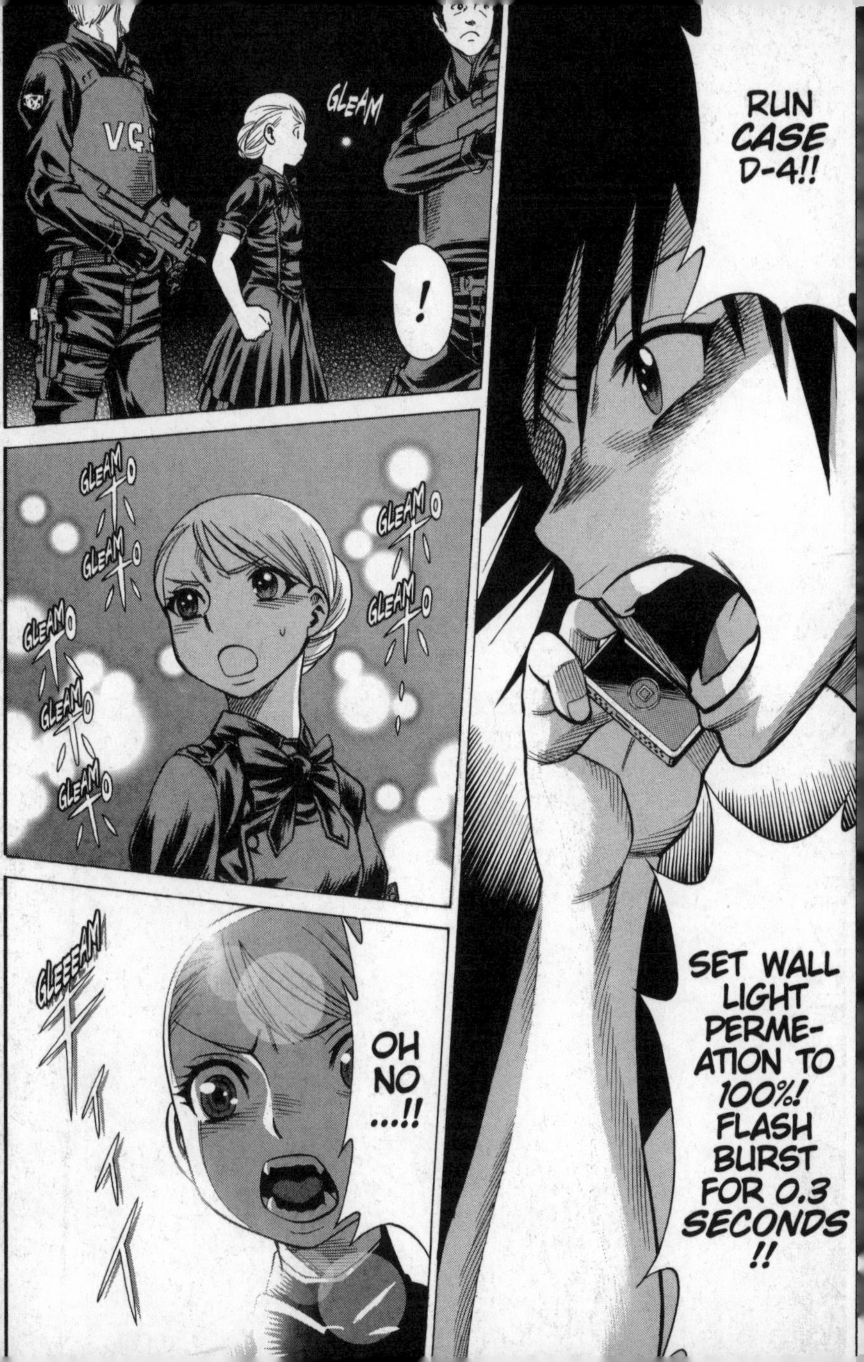
RUN CASE D-4!!
SET WALL LIGHT PERME-ATION TO 100%! FLASH BURST FOR 0.3 SECONDS!!
GLEAM
!
GLEAM
GLEAM
GLEAM
GLEAM
GLEAM
GLEAM
GLEAM
GLEEEEAM
OH NO ...!!

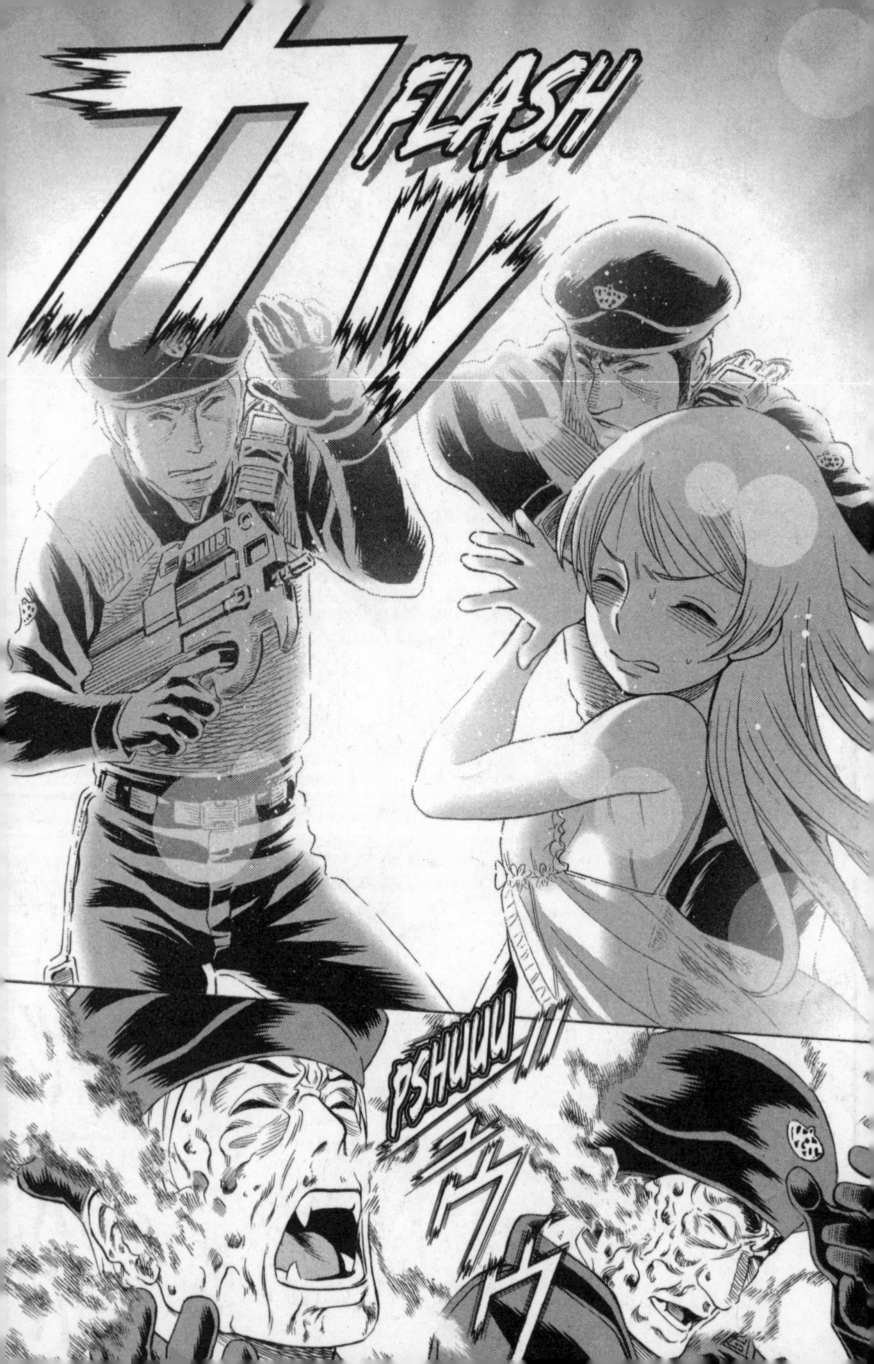
FLASH
PSHUUU

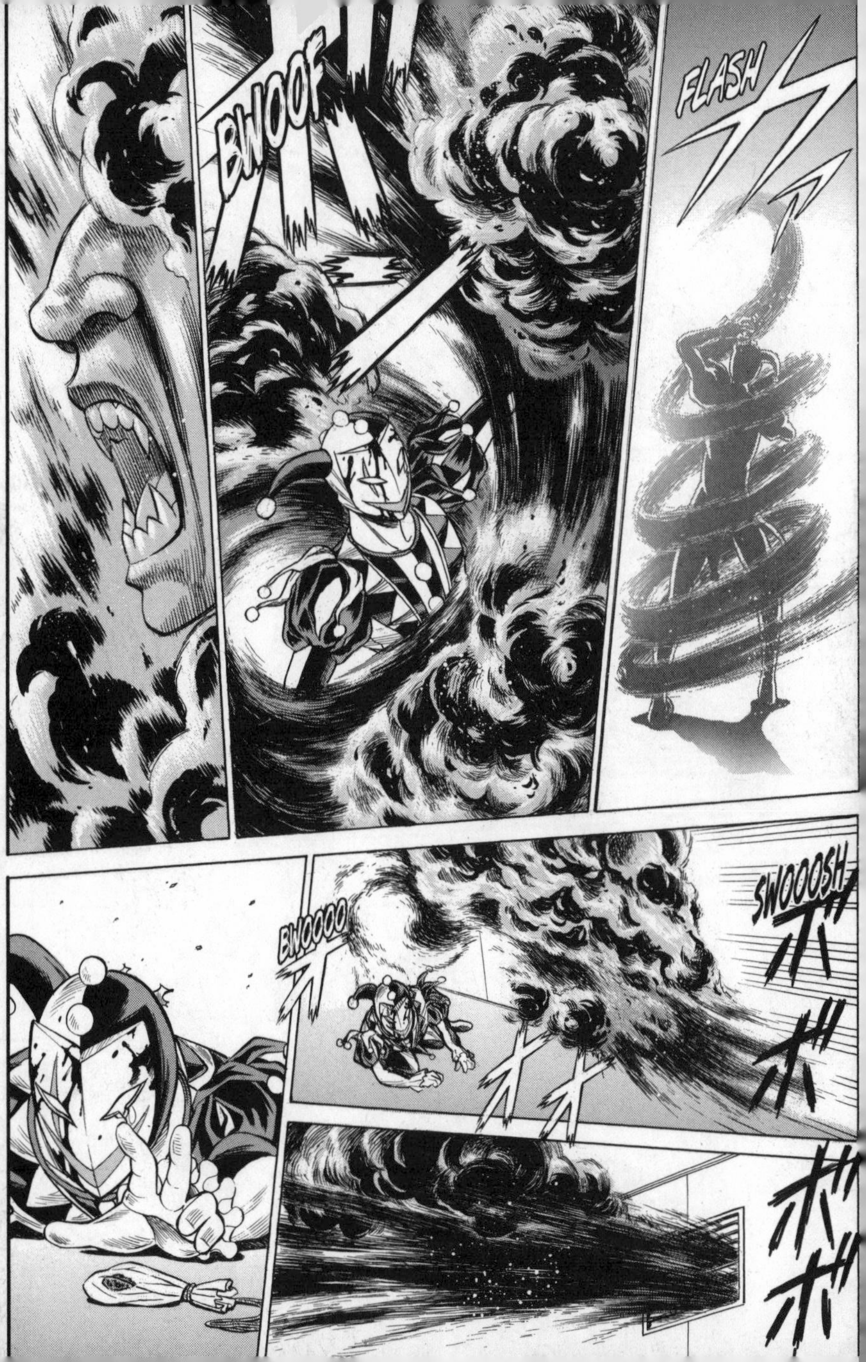
FLASH
BWOOF
SWOOOSH
BWOOOO

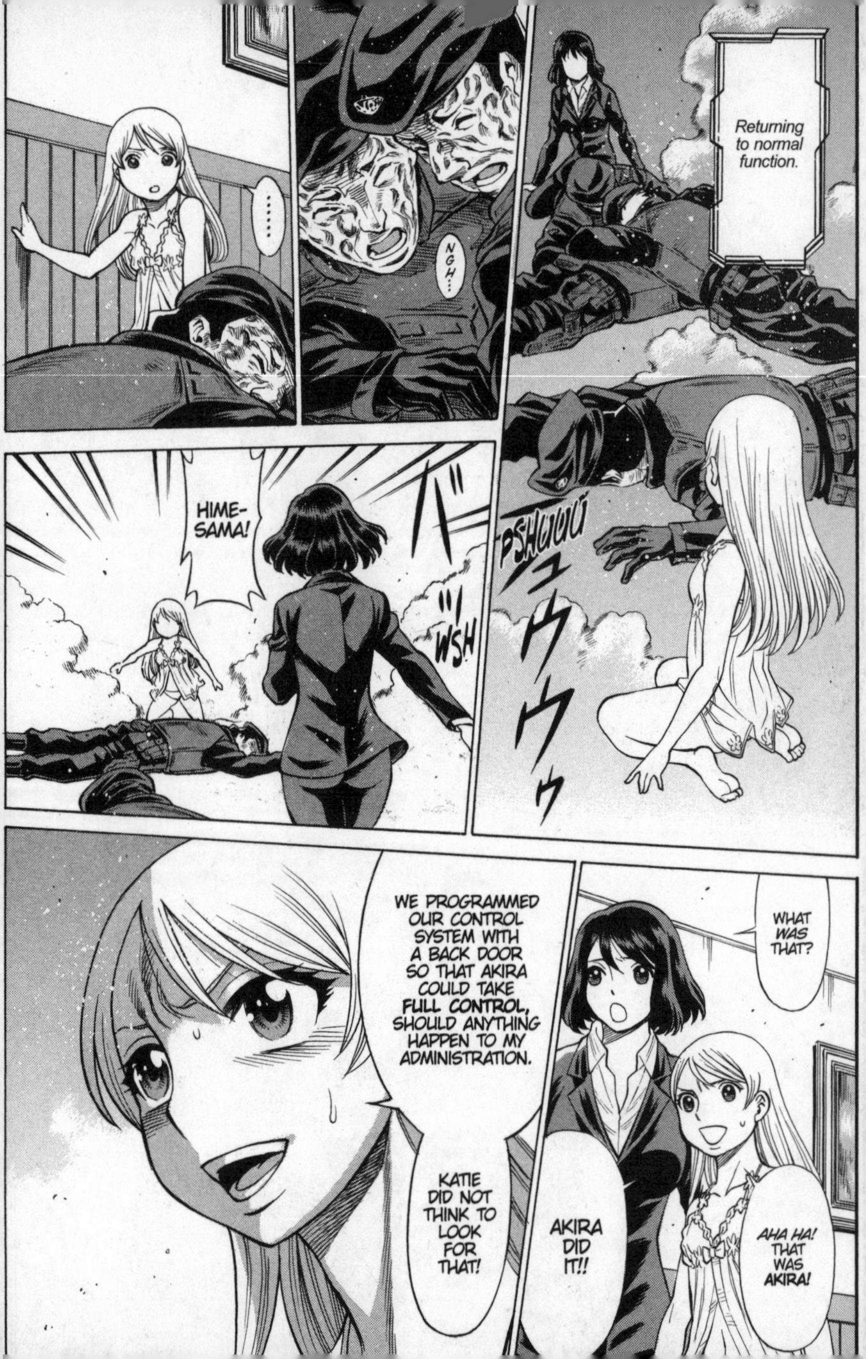
Returning to normal function.
NGH...
......
PSHUUU
HIME-SAMA!
WSH
WHAT WAS THAT?
AHA HA! THAT WAS AKIRA!
AKIRA DID IT!!
WE PROGRAMMED OUR CONTROL SYSTEM WITH A BACK DOOR SO THAT AKIRA COULD TAKE FULL CONTROL, SHOULD ANYTHING HAPPEN TO MY ADMINISTRATION.
KATIE DID NOT THINK TO LOOK FOR THAT!

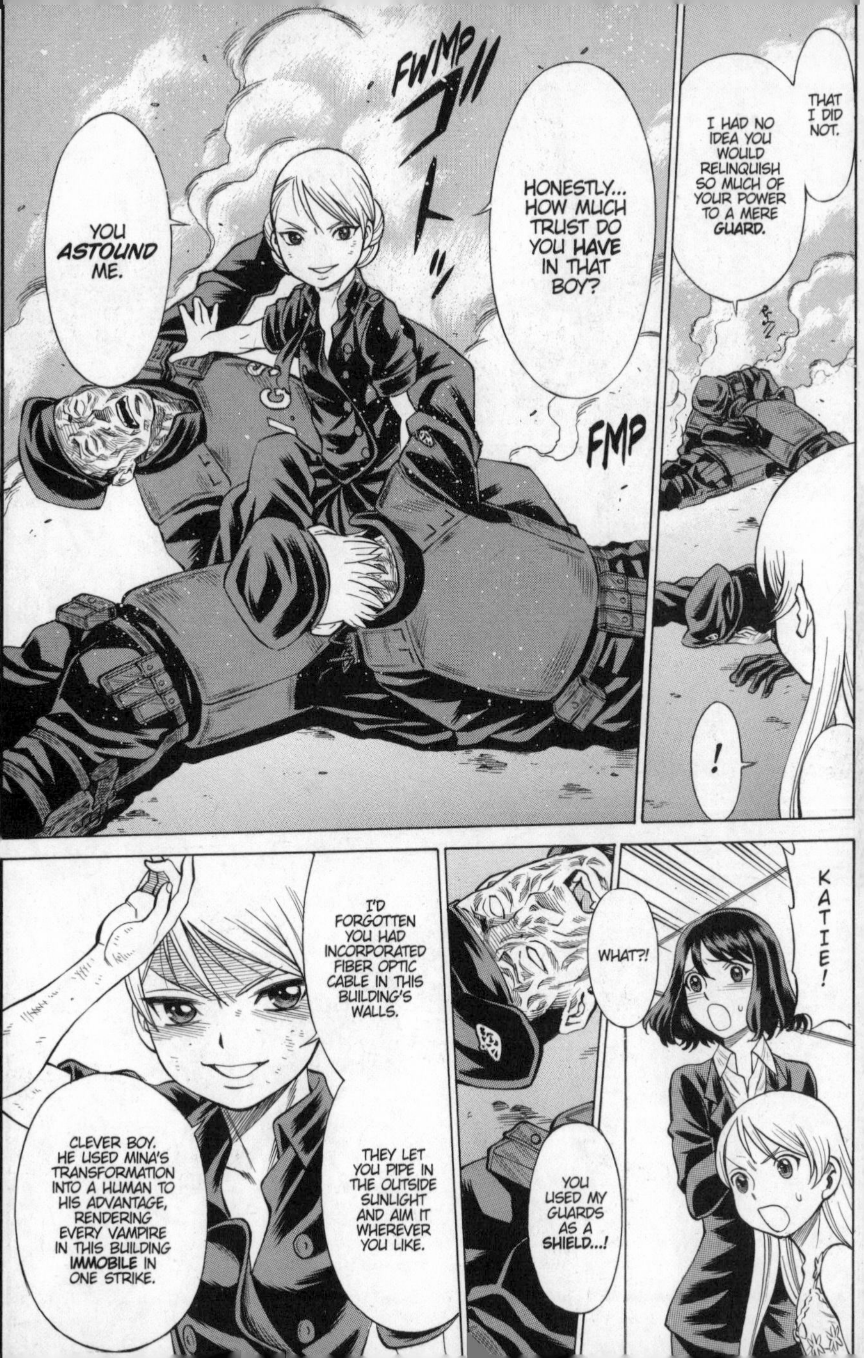
THAT I DID NOT.
I HAD NO IDEA YOU WOULD RELINQUISH SO MUCH OF YOUR POWER TO A MERE GUARD.
!
FWMP
HONESTLY... HOW MUCH TRUST DO YOU HAVE IN THAT BOY?
YOU ASTOUND ME.
FMP
KATIE!
WHAT?!
YOU USED MY GUARDS AS A SHIELD...!
I'D FORGOTTEN YOU HAD INCORPORATED FIBER OPTIC CABLE IN THIS BUILDING'S WALLS.
THEY LET YOU PIPE IN THE OUTSIDE SUNLIGHT AND AIM IT WHEREVER YOU LIKE.
CLEVER BOY. HE USED MINA'S TRANSFORMATION INTO A HUMAN TO HIS ADVANTAGE, RENDERING EVERY VAMPIRE IN THIS BUILDING IMMOBILE IN ONE STRIKE.

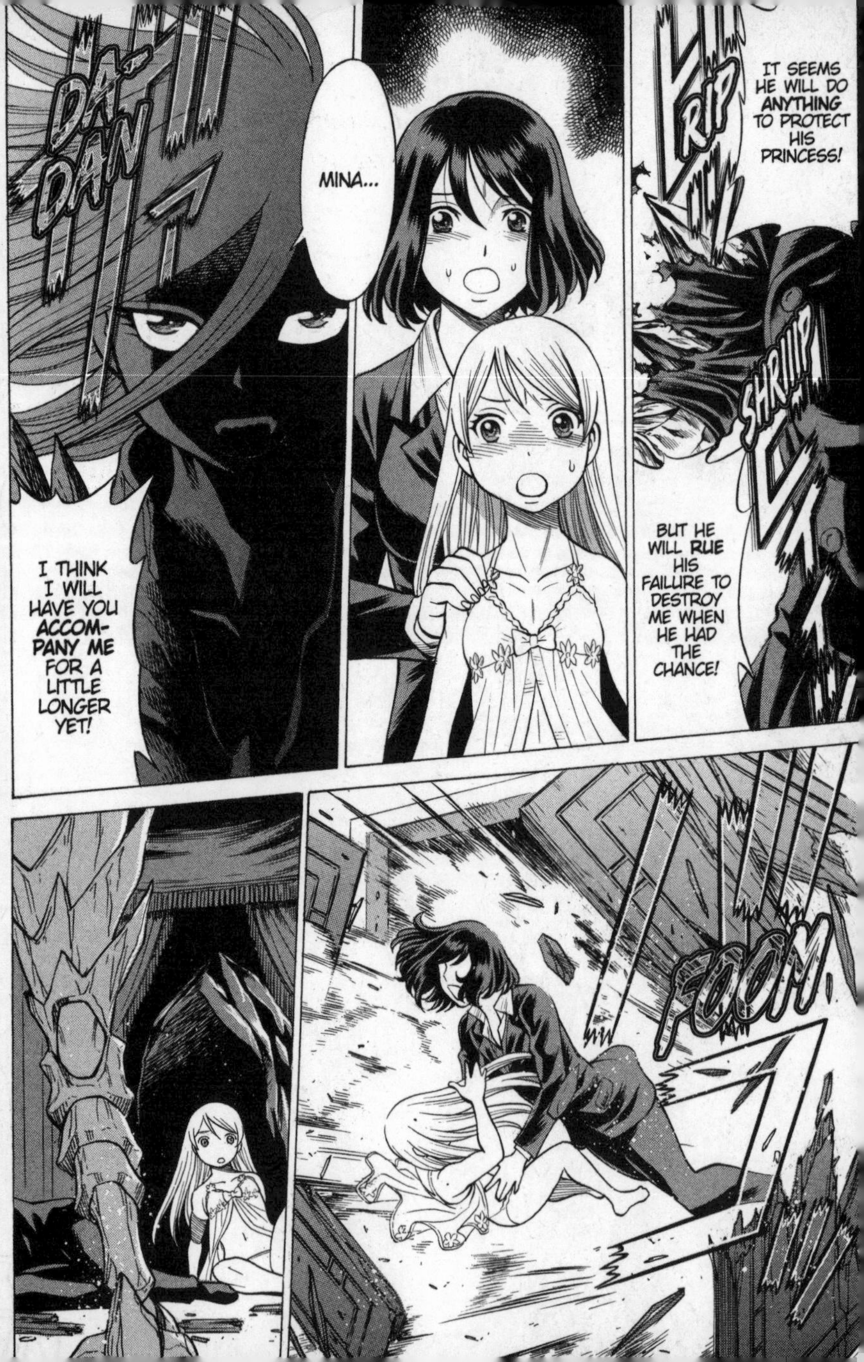
IT SEEMS HE WILL DO ANYTHING TO PROTECT HIS PRINCESS!
RIP
SHRUUP
BUT HE WILL RUE HIS FAILURE TO DESTROY ME WHEN HE HAD THE CHANCE!
MINA...
DA-DAN
I THINK I WILL HAVE YOU ACCOMPANY ME FOR A LITTLE LONGER YET!
FOOM

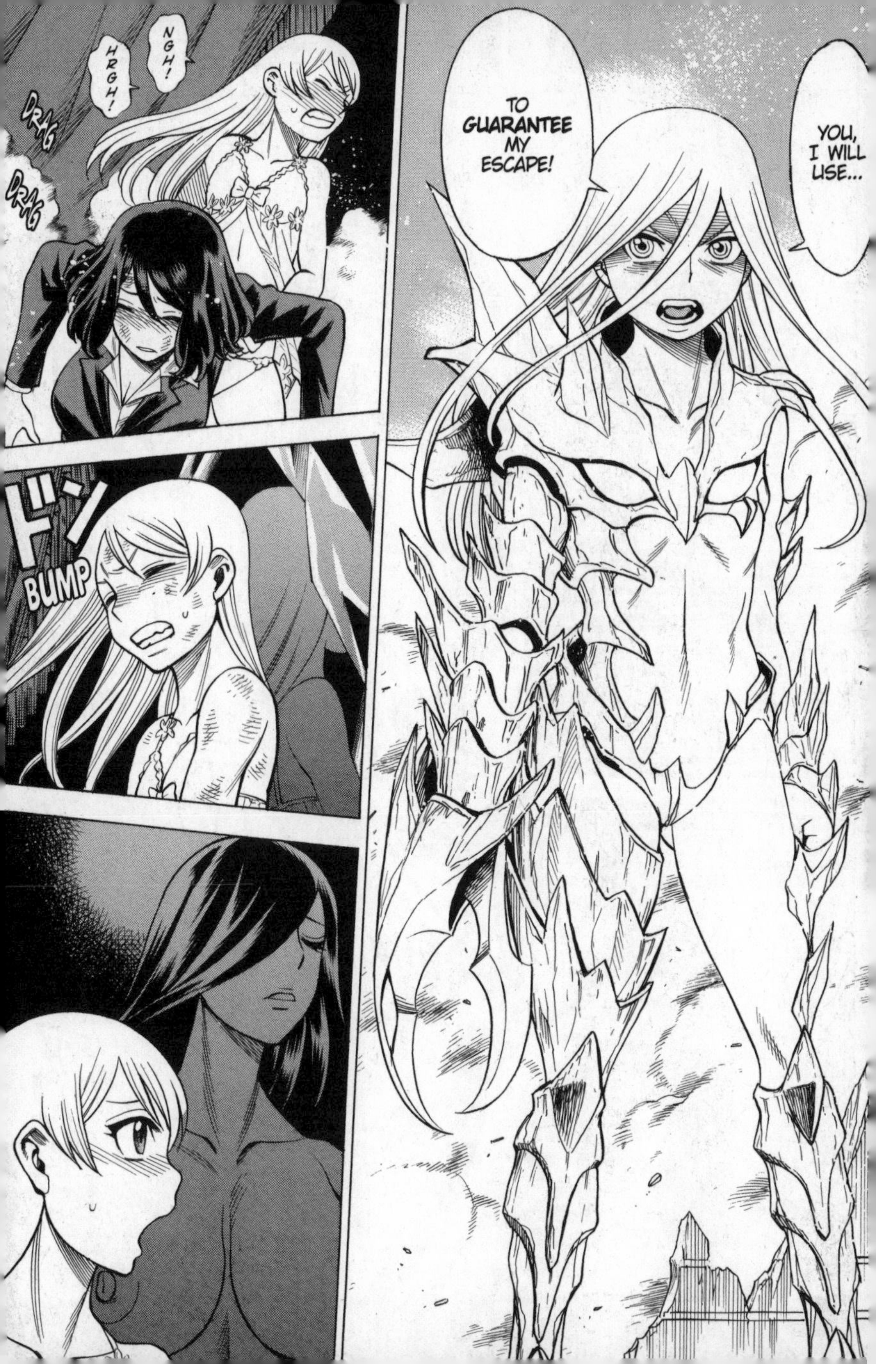
YOU, I WILL USE...
TO GUARANTEE MY ESCAPE!
NGH!
HRGH!
DRAG
DRAG
ドン
BUMP

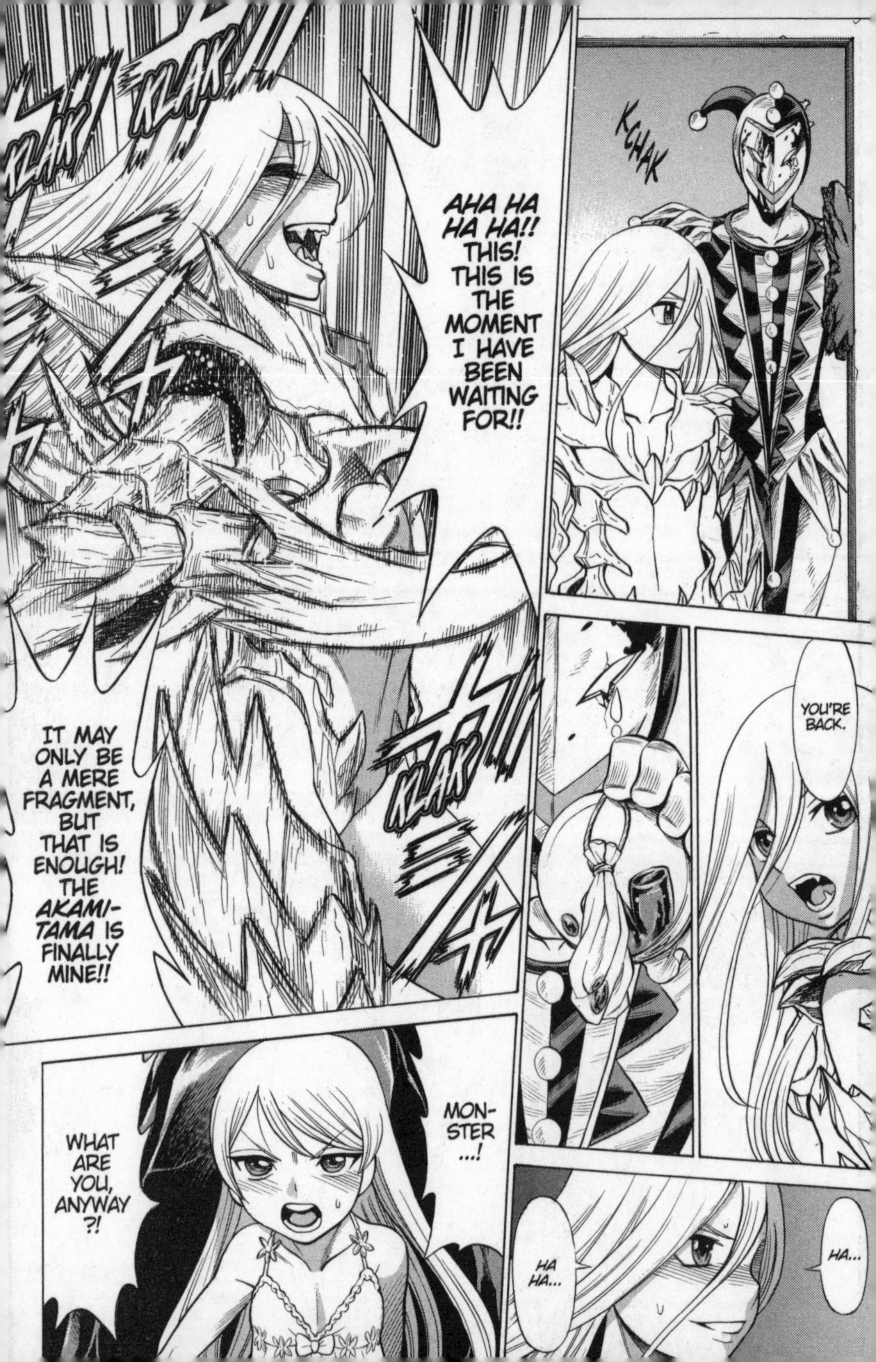
KCHAK
YOU'RE BACK.
KLAK! KLAK!!
AHA HA HA HA!! THIS! THIS IS THE MOMENT I HAVE BEEN WAITING FOR!!
KLAK
IT MAY ONLY BE A MERE FRAGMENT, BUT THAT IS ENOUGH! THE AKAMITAMA IS FINALLY MINE!!
HA...
HA HA...
MON-STER...!
WHAT ARE YOU, ANYWAY?!

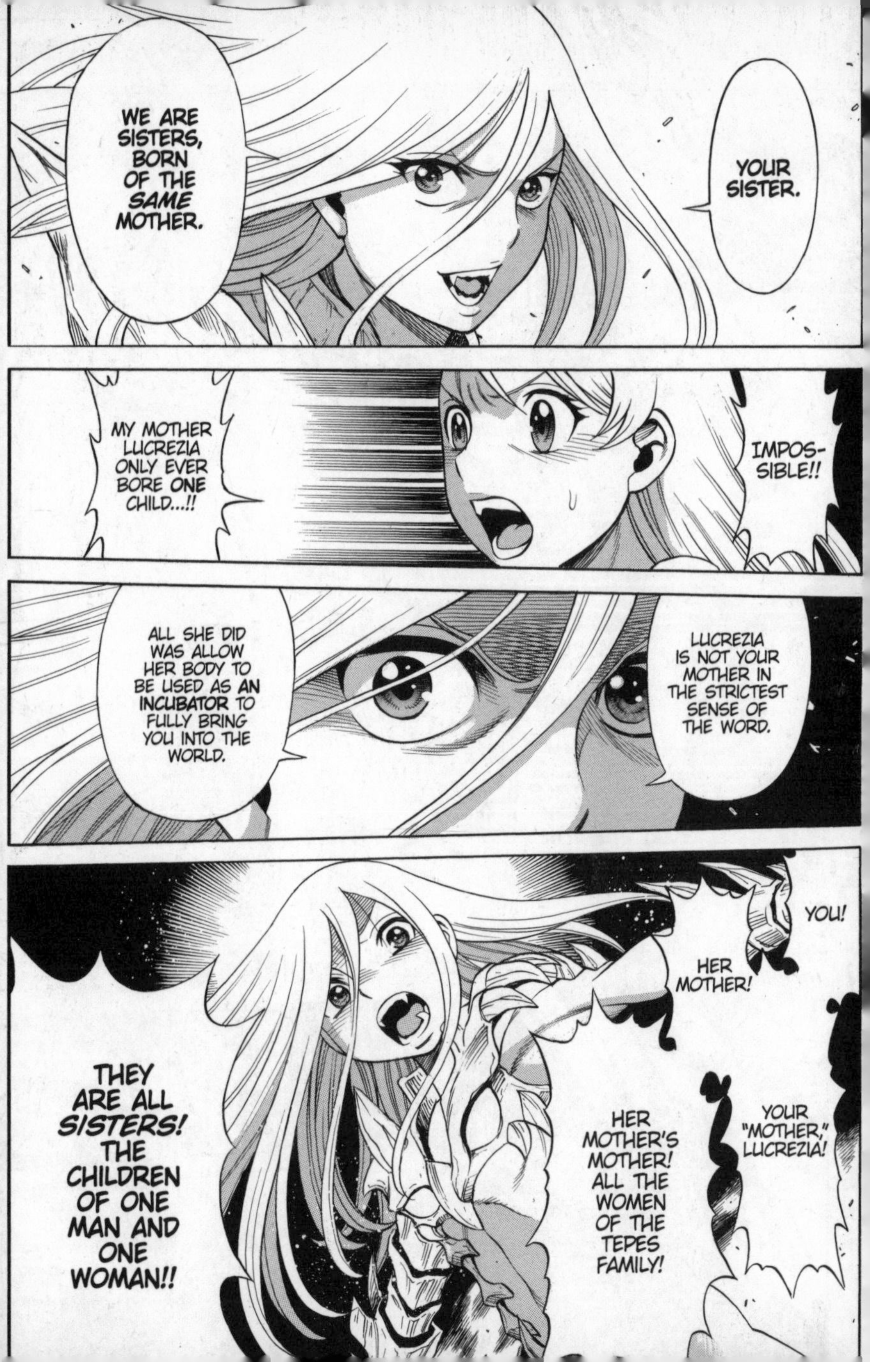
YOUR SISTER.
WE ARE SISTERS, BORN OF THE *SAME* MOTHER.
IMPOS-SIBLE!!
MY MOTHER LUCREZIA ONLY EVER BORE ONE CHILD...!!
LUCREZIA IS NOT YOUR MOTHER IN THE STRICTEST SENSE OF THE WORD.
ALL SHE DID WAS ALLOW HER BODY TO BE USED AS AN **INCUBATOR** TO FULLY BRING YOU INTO THE WORLD.
YOU!
HER MOTHER!
YOUR "MOTHER," LUCREZIA!
HER MOTHER'S MOTHER! ALL THE WOMEN OF THE TEPES FAMILY!
THEY ARE ALL *SISTERS!* THE CHILDREN OF ONE MAN AND ONE WOMAN!!

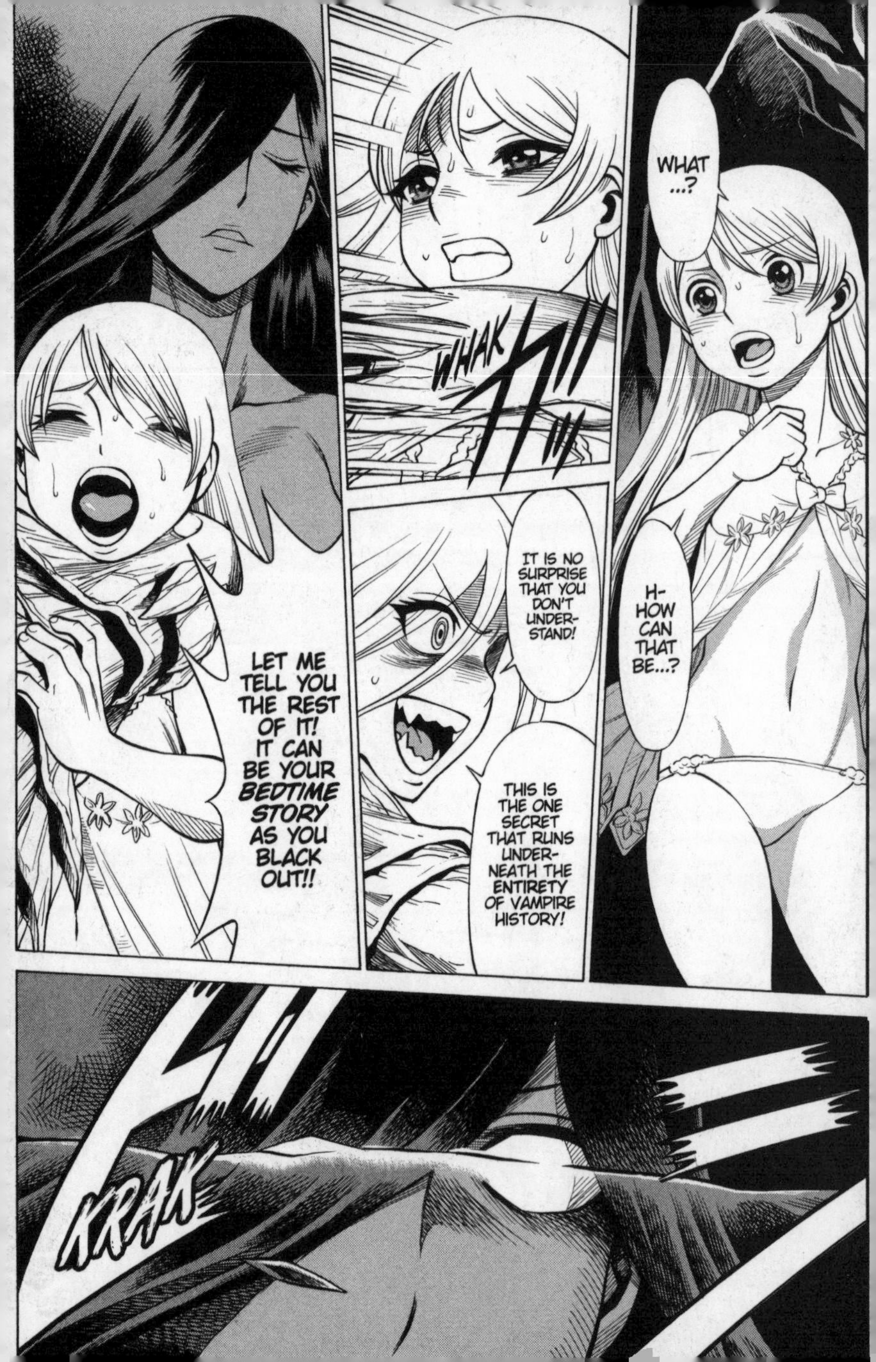
WHAT ...?
H-HOW CAN THAT BE...?
WHAK
IT IS NO SURPRISE THAT YOU DON'T UNDER-STAND!
THIS IS THE ONE SECRET THAT RUNS UNDER-NEATH THE ENTIRETY OF VAMPIRE HISTORY!
LET ME TELL YOU THE REST OF IT! IT CAN BE YOUR *BEDTIME STORY* AS YOU BLACK OUT!!
KRAK

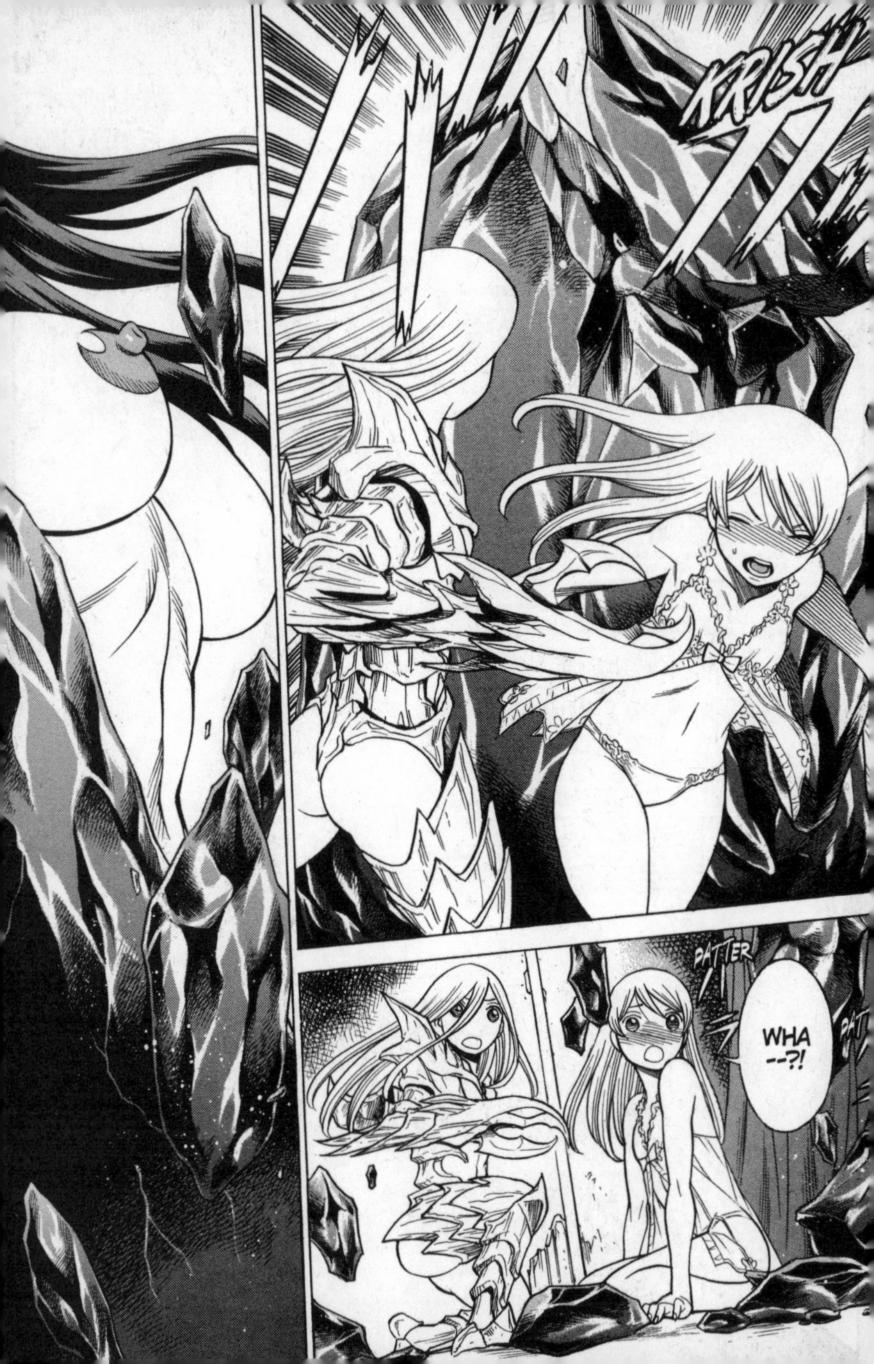
KRISH
PATTER
PAT
WHA --?!

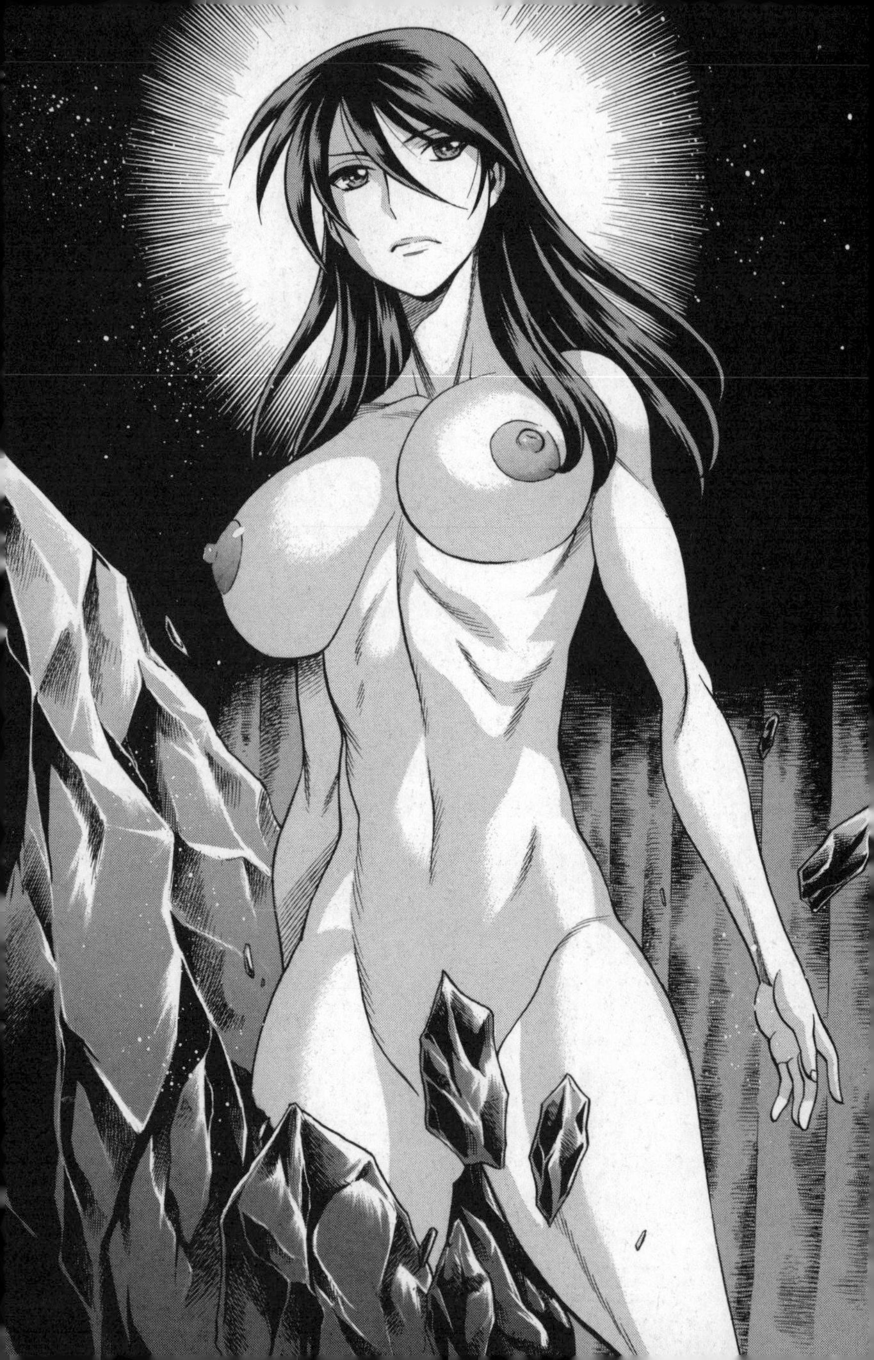

Dance in the
VampireBund III
SCARLET ORDER

TO BE CONTINUED...

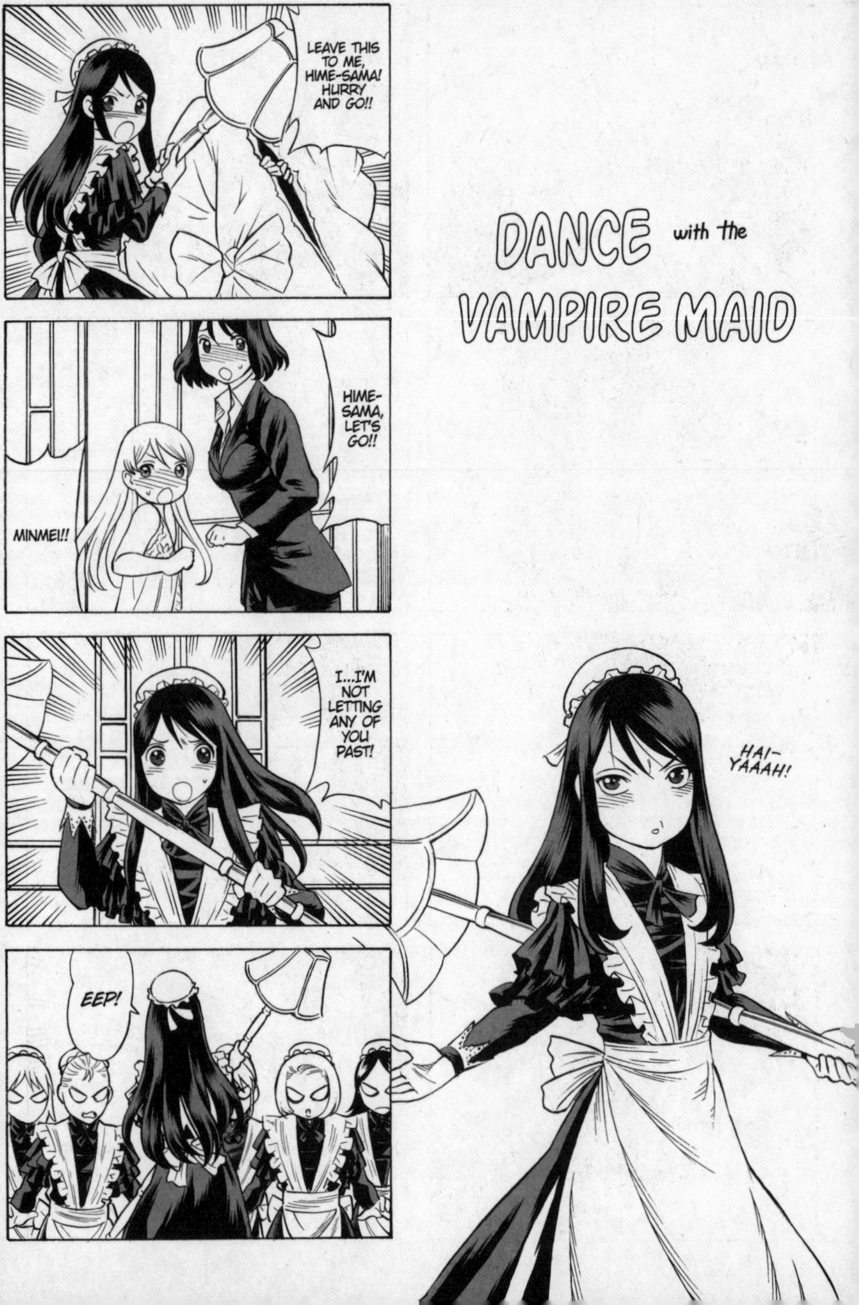
DANCE with the VAMPIRE MAID
HAI-YAAAH!
LEAVE THIS TO ME, HIME-SAMA! HURRY AND GO!!
HIME-SAMA, LET'S GO!!
MINMEI!!
I...I'M NOT LETTING ANY OF YOU PAST!
EEP!

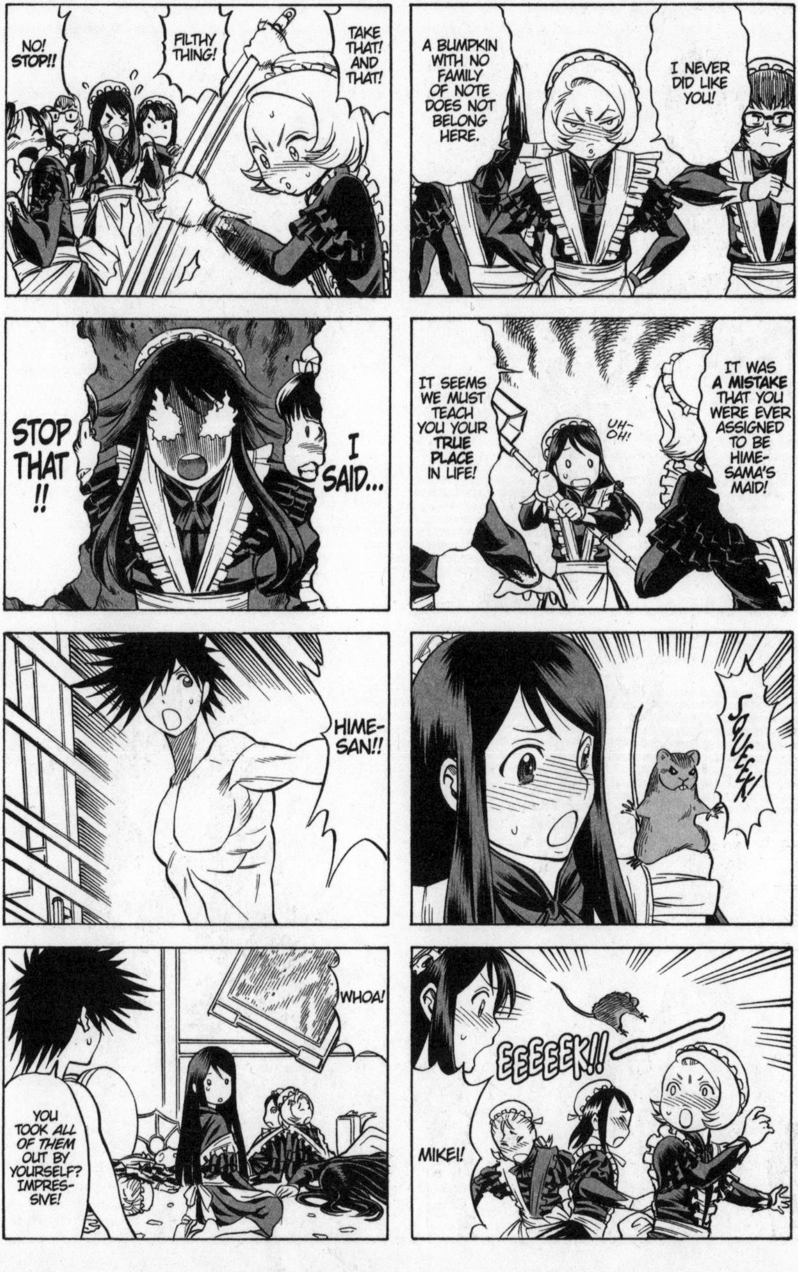
I NEVER DID LIKE YOU!
A BUMPKIN WITH NO FAMILY OF NOTE DOES NOT BELONG HERE.
TAKE THAT! AND THAT!
FILTHY THING!
NO! STOP!!
IT WAS A MISTAKE THAT YOU WERE EVER ASSIGNED TO BE HIME-SAMA'S MAID!
UH-OH!
IT SEEMS WE MUST TEACH YOU YOUR TRUE PLACE IN LIFE!
I SAID...
STOP THAT !!
SQUEEEK!
HIME-SAN!!
EEEEEK!!
MIKE!!
WHOA!
YOU TOOK ALL OF THEM OUT BY YOURSELF? IMPRESSIVE!

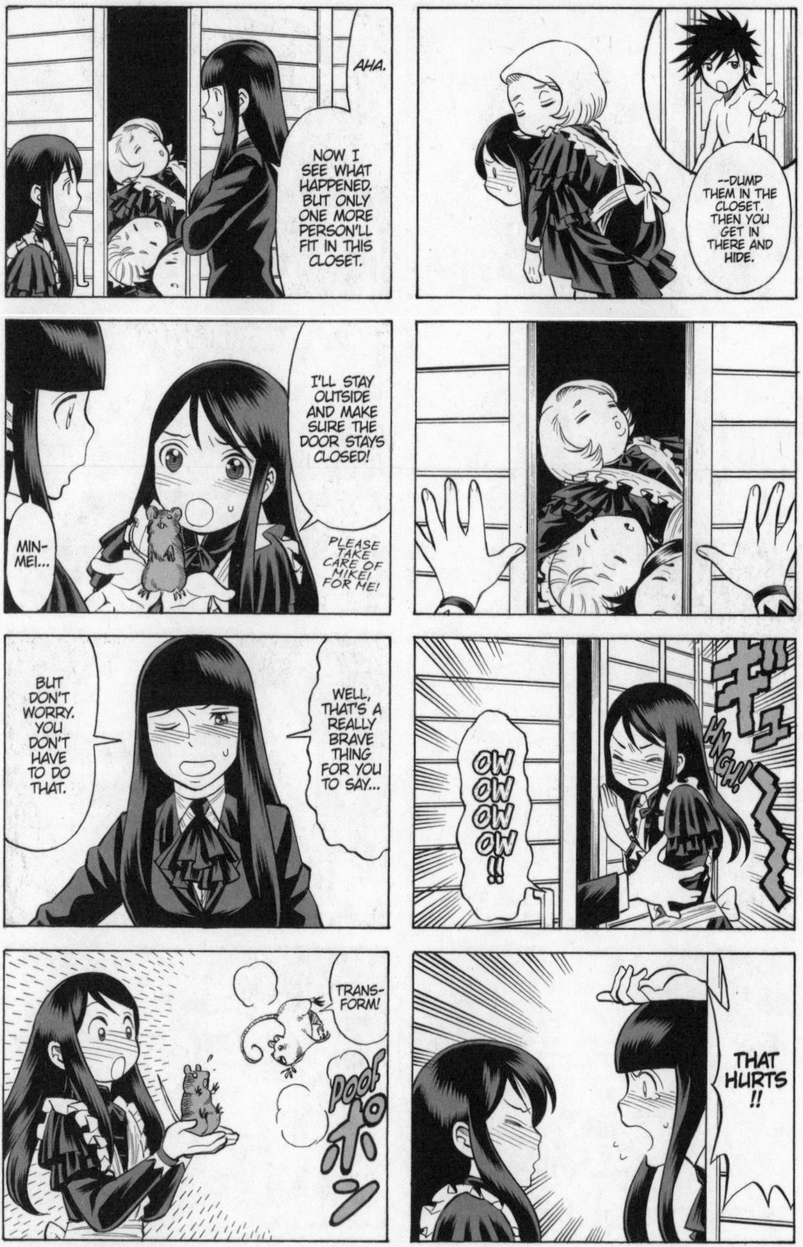

--DUMP THEM IN THE CLOSET. THEN YOU GET IN THERE AND HIDE.
AHA.
NOW I SEE WHAT HAPPENED. BUT ONLY ONE MORE PERSON'LL FIT IN THIS CLOSET.
I'LL STAY OUTSIDE AND MAKE SURE THE DOOR STAYS CLOSED!
PLEASE TAKE CARE OF MIKE! FOR ME!
MIN-MEI...
ギュ
HNGH!
OW OW OW OW!!
WELL, THAT'S A REALLY BRAVE THING FOR YOU TO SAY...
BUT DON'T WORRY. YOU DON'T HAVE TO DO THAT.
THAT HURTS!!
TRANS-FORM!
Poof
ポン

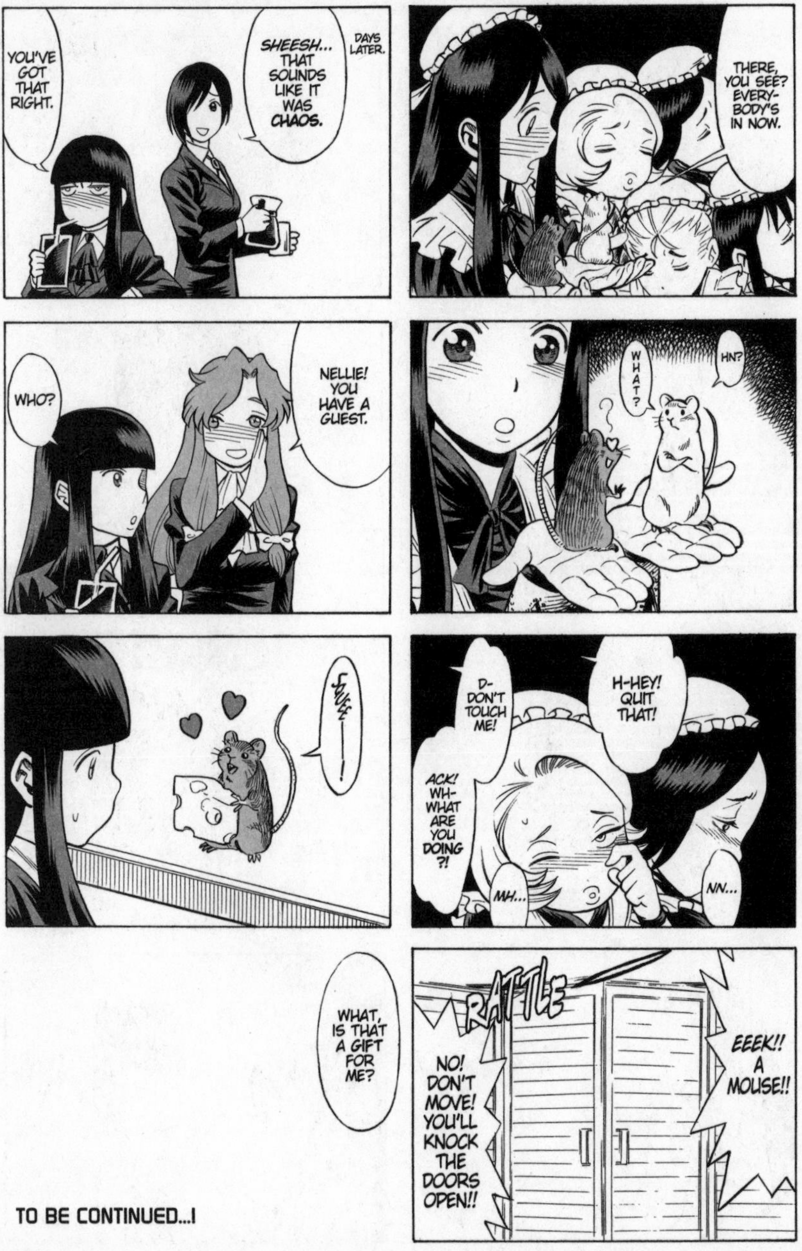
THERE, YOU SEE? EVERYBODY'S IN NOW.
DAYS LATER.
SHEESH... THAT SOUNDS LIKE IT WAS CHAOS.
YOU'VE GOT THAT RIGHT.
HN?
WHAT?
NELLIE! YOU HAVE A GUEST.
WHO?
H-HEY! QUIT THAT!
D-DON'T TOUCH ME!
ACK! WH-WHAT ARE YOU DOING?!
NN...
MH...
SQUEE—!
EEEK!! A MOUSE!!
RATTLE
NO! DON'T MOVE! YOU'LL KNOCK THE DOORS OPEN!!
WHAT, IS THAT A GIFT FOR ME?

TO BE CONTINUED...!

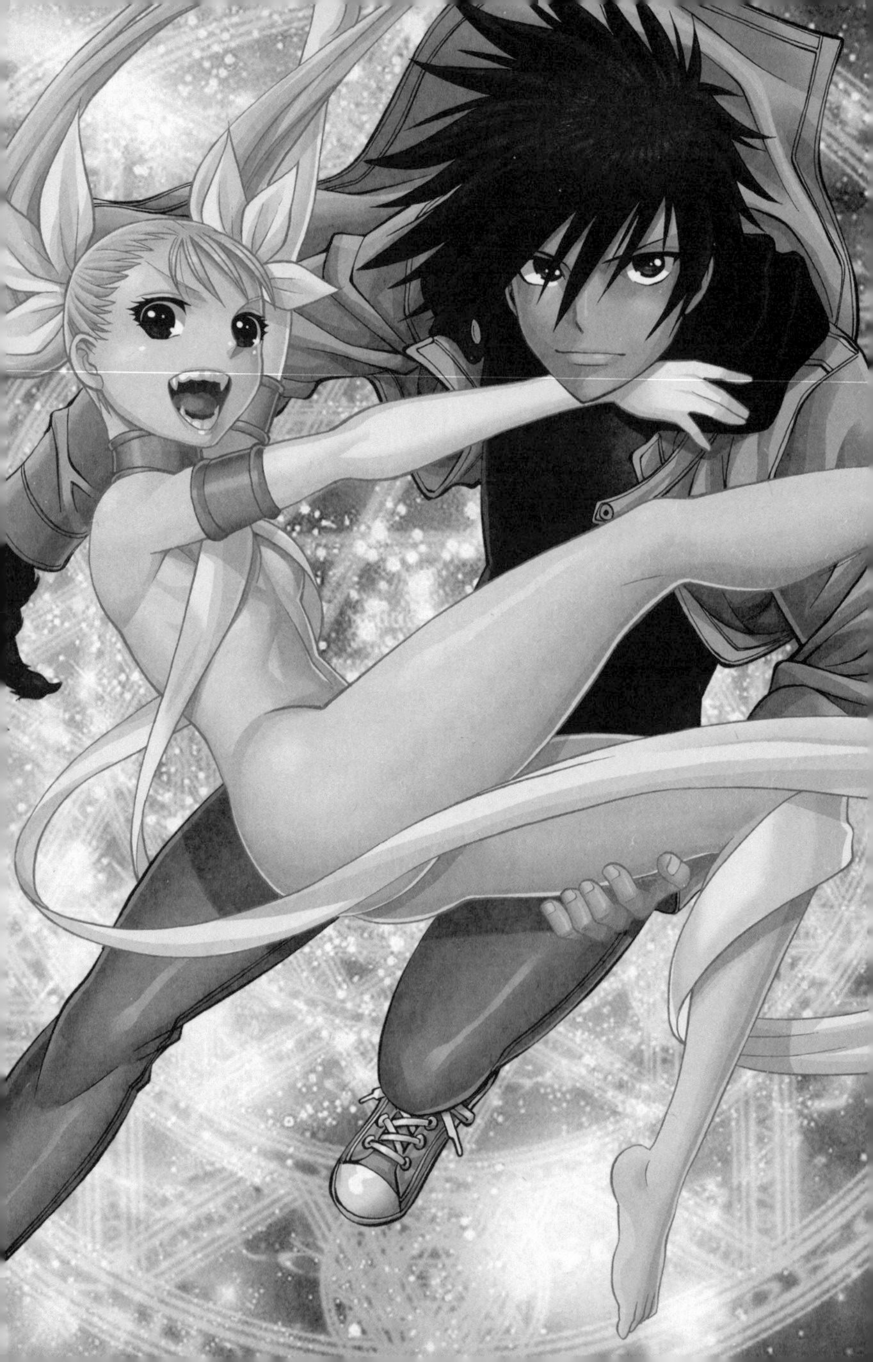

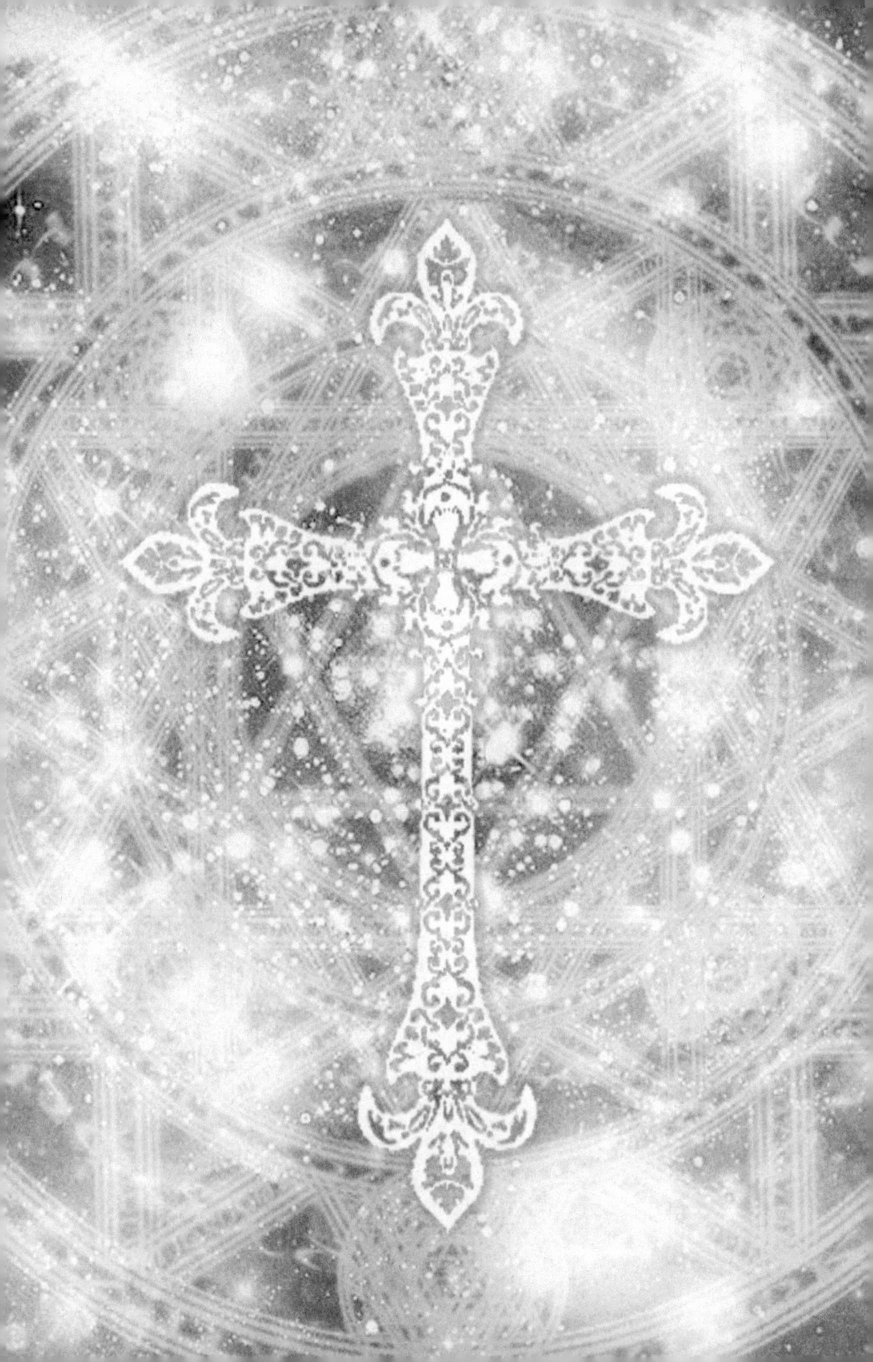

Dance in the Vampire Bund III

Scarlet Order

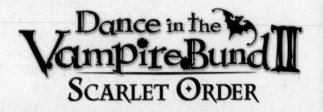